The Mariavites

The Mariavites
Heresy, The Apocalypse, and Poland's Female Savior

Damian Cyrocki

SHEFFIELD UK   BRISTOL CT

Published by Equinox Publishing Ltd.
UK: Office 415, The Workstation, 15 Paternoster Row, Sheffield,
        South Yorkshire S1 2BX
USA: ISD, 70 Enterprise Drive, Bristol, CT 06010

www.equinoxpub.com

First published 2025
© Damian Cyrocki 2025
All rights reserved. No part of this publication may be reproduced or transmitted in any form or by any means, electronic or mechanical, including photocopying, recording or any information storage or retrieval system, without prior permission in writing from the publishers.

British Library Cataloguing-in-Publication Data
A catalogue record for this book is available from the British Library.

ISBN-13   978 1 80050 564 3 (hardback)
          978 1 80050 565 0 (paperback)
          978 1 80050 566 7 (ePDF)
          978 1 80050 666 4 (ePub)

Library of Congress Cataloging-in-Publication Data

Names: Cyrocki, Damian author.
Title: The Mariavites : heresy, the apocalypse, and Poland's female savior / Damian Cyrocki.
Other titles: Implementing God's kingdom on Earth
Description: Bristol, CT : Equinox Publishing Ltd, 2025. | Slight revision of the author's thesis (doctoral)--Liverpool Hope University, 2021, under the title: Implementing God's kingdom on Earth : early Mariavite history. | Includes bibliographical references and index. | Summary: "The Mariavites are an independent Catholic movement who were excommunicated from the Roman Catholic Church in late 1906. This book gives a history of the beginnings of the movement focusing on how the early Mariavites understood the establishment the Kingdom of God on earth (and, more precisely, in Poland). With reference to the original Polish documents, the volume clarifies for the first time the ideology, logic, motives, and theological tradition underpinning of this new religious movement"-- Provided by publisher.
Identifiers: LCCN 2025003255 (print) | LCCN 2025003256 (ebook) | ISBN 9781800505643 hardback | ISBN 9781800505650 paperback | ISBN 9781800505667 pdf | ISBN 9781800506664 epub
Subjects: LCSH: Mariavites--History | KozÅ‚owska, Feliksa, 1862-1921 | Poland--Church history--19th century
Classification: LCC BX4795.M23 C97 2025 (print) | LCC BX4795.M23 (ebook) | DDC 284/.8--dc23/eng/20250505
LC record available at https://lccn.loc.gov/2025003255
LC ebook record available at https://lccn.loc.gov/2025003256

Typeset by S.J.I. Services, New Delhi, India

For my grandparents

Contents

Acknowledgements	ix
List of Abbreviations	xi
Preface	xiii

Chapter 1. Introduction — 1
1. Methodology and Presuppositions — 1
2. Terminology — 3
3. Mariavite Literature — 7
4. Structure of this Study — 19

Chapter 2. Events Leading up to the 1893 Revelations — 21
1. The State of the Catholic Church in Congress Poland in the Nineteenth Century — 21
2. Polish Romantic Messianism — 26
3. Feliksa Kozłowska's Life up to 1893 — 32

Chapter 3. Mariavites in the Roman Catholic Church — 42
1. The Revelations of 1893 — 42
2. The Spread of the Congregation — 50
3. Attempts to Obtain Official Approval in Rome — 56
4. After the Decree Abolishing the Congregation — 63
5. The Termination of Obedience — 68
6. The Final Break with Rome — 75

Chapter 4. From the Schism with Rome to Mateczka's Death — 86
1. The First Years after the Schism and Problems with Self-Identification — 86
2. The Significance of the General Chapter after 1907 — 96
3. Union with the Old Catholics — 100

    4. Maria Czychlarzowa and Wacław Żebrowski   104
    5. The Temple of Mercy and Charity   108
    6. The Cessation of the Eucharist and the Book of Life   111
    7. Mateczka's Death   118

Chapter 5. Reforms in the Church of Mariavites   **122**
    1. Mateczka's Identity   122
    2. Kowalski's Identity   130
    3. Antecedents of Mariavite Marriage   136
    4. The Nature of Mariavite Marriage   141
    5. Reactions and Accusations of Immortality   151
    6. Children Born without Original Sin   156
    7. The Ordination of Women   159
    8. The Priesthood of the Laity   168

Chapter 6. The Aftermath of the Reforms   **175**
    1. The Schism   175
    2. What about the Reforms?   180
    3. The Trinity   184
    4. The Kingdom of God   192

Conclusions   201

Bibliography   204

Index of Names   238

Acknowledgements

This book is a slightly revised version of my doctoral thesis, supervised by James Crossley, then Professor of Bible and Society at St Mary's University, London. It was thanks to him that I decided to write and defend my doctorate in London. Moreover, he convinced me to revisit the subject of the Mariavites, which I first encountered during my studies at the Institute of Religious Studies at the Jagiellonian University in Krakow. Sadly, two people who were instrumental in arousing my interest in this subject passed away too soon. The first was Father Professor Konrad Maria Paweł Rudnicki, who died on 12 November 2013. He was by far one of the most outstanding Mariavite theologians that the church has ever had. The second was Pastor Jarosław Kubacki, who died on 5 January 2025. He was a walking encyclopaedia of the history of Old Catholic currents in Poland and the one who first made me realise that Christianity's great strength is its diversity. I will never forget the contribution they made to my intellectual development.

Initially, when I left for London, I had planned to write a dissertation on Jesus' relationship to his own family in the Gospel of Mark. These plans were soon to change. Inspired by Joan E. Taylor and Helen Bond's reflections on Cerula, who may have been a female bishop in the sixth century, I gave a talk at a conference on Polish female bishops in the Church of Mariavites. When Crossley, who was present at the event and is also one of the academic directors of the Centre for the Critical Study of Apocalyptic and Millenarian Movements, learned that the Mariavites had spent much time exploring the biblical book of Revelation, he suggested I look more deeply into this very subject. This turned out to be a great idea, and all credit goes to James for showing me this path and motivating me to follow it. I wish every student had such a thesis supervisor.

I would like to thank the Centre for the *Social-Scientific Study* of the *Bible at St Mary's University* for partially funding my travels to places related to Mariavitism, during which I was able to collect source material and hold important conversations with members of the movement, as well as researchers on the subject. I am extremely grateful for this.

I would also like to express my warmest thanks to the other people who discussed various issues related to this study with me, in particular, my friend Dr Tomasz Dariusz Maria Daniel Mames, who serves as Bishop of the Old Catholic Mariavite Church in the Province of France. Not only did he offer advice, point out errors, and recommend literature, but he also hosted me at his rectory in Paris and even cooked for me. Such a friend and discussion partner is a treasure. I could not, of course, forget to thank the other Mariavite clergy with whom I spoke and exchanged comments, both from the Old Catholic Mariavite Church and the Catholic Mariavite Church. There are too many to mention by name and not leave someone out in the process. I have therefore decided to thank them collectively for their kindness and hospitality.

I have had the pleasure, albeit mostly only once, of meeting several scholars involved in the history of Mariavitism. When I studied at the Jagiellonian University, one of my lecturers was Dr Rafał Łętocha. In later years, he published, together with Dr Andrzej Dwojnych, *W stronę Królestwa Bożego na ziemi: Myśl społeczno-polityczna mariawitów polskich* (Towards the Kingdom of God on Earth: The Socio-Political Thought of the Polish Mariavites). This book opened my eyes to many issues related to the political orientation of the early Mariavites. Even before its publication, we had the opportunity to exchange a few remarks on, in particular, the priesthood of women and the gender of the Holy Spirit in ancient Christianity, which influenced Archbishop Kowalski when he was drafting his concept of the Trinity. I also had the chance to talk to Dr Sławomir Gołębiowski and Dr Krzysztof Mazur, whose contribution to the rectification of errors related to the history of Mariavitism cannot be overestimated.

Finally, I would like to thank those without whom this work would never have seen the light of day, namely, my parents and my sister. They were the ones who supported me the most both mentally and financially during my academic journey. I could and still can count on their help. I was given the best family I could have dreamed of.

I dedicate this work to my grandparents who passed away too soon. I know they would be proud of me, knowing that the book has finally been published.

List of Abbreviations

Acts	Acts of the Apostles
Col	Colossians
1 Cor	1 Corinthians
2 Cor	2 Corinthians
Dan	Daniel
DMHM	Dzieło Miłosierdzia Historya Maryawitów
DWM	Dzieło Wielkiego Miłosierdzia
Eph	Ephesians
Ex	Exodus
Gal	Galatians
Gen	Genesis
GP	Głos Prawdy
GSK	Głos Staro – Katolicki
Hos	Hosea
Isa	Isaiah
Jb	Job
Jn	John
Jon	Jonah
Josh	Joshua
KBNZ	Królestwo Boże na Ziemi
KKM	Kościół Katolicki Mariawitów
KSM	Kościół Starokatolicki Mariawitów
Lev	Leviticus
Lk	Luke
4 Macc	4 Maccabees
Mal	Malachi
MCPS	Maryawita: Czciciel Przenajświętszego Sakramentu
MD	Mistrzyni Ducha
Mk	Mark
MMN	Mariawicka Myśl Narodowa
MPKSM	Mariawita. Pismo Kościoła Starokatolickiego Mariawitów
Mt	Matthew

NP	Notatki Płockie
NTPP	Nowy Testament po polsku
NTS	New Testament Studies
Num	Numbers
1 Pet	1 Peter
Phil	Philippians
PNS	Praca nad Sobą
Prov	Proverbs
PŚST	Pismo Święte Starego Testamentu
Rev	Book of Revelation
RTChAT	Rocznik Teologiczny Chrześcijańskiej Akademii Teologicznej
Rom	Romans
1 Sam	1 Samuel
Song	Song of Songs
1 Tim	1 Timothy
1 Thess	1 Thessalonians
2 Thess	2 Thessalonians
WDM	Wiadomości. Dodatek do Mariawity
WM	Wiadomości Maryawickie

Preface

This may not be the first attempt to present Mariavitism to the English-speaking audience, but it is the first academic, critical history that presents Mariavitism in a non-polemical way. The lack of such publications in English was one of the main reasons I decided to write this book. Polish publications, which have dominated the subject so far, do not overlap with the area of research undertaken in this work and do not engage in an in-depth analysis of the ideas about the Kingdom of God and Revelation that are central to Mariavite theology. My main aim has been to understand the Mariavite idea of the Kingdom – which they expected to emerge in twentieth-century Poland – with particular attention to the reception history of the book of Revelation, as well as other biblical texts. I argue that, without a proper understanding of their notion of the Kingdom and biblical texts such as Revelation, it is impossible to understand all the seemingly unusual reforms that Archbishop Kowalski introduced after the death of Felicja Maria Franciszka Kozłowska, the founder of Mariavitism. Although it is commonly believed otherwise, I have tried to show that Kowalski created a coherent theology in which all the seemingly minor elements are interconnected and important.

This book employs a standard historical methodology that places the main emphasis on reading the Mariavite primary sources, which have rarely (if ever) been noted in critical scholarship. The first chapter is pro-paedeutic in nature and explains the nature of the relationship between religion and politics in Poland, which took shape particularly during the Partition era (1772–1918). I argue that it was the subjugation to foreign political forces that gave rise to Mariavitism. I also highlight some of the key moments in Kozłowska's life before she received her famous revelations in 1893, which marked the beginning of Mariavitism. The second chapter analyses the fate of Mariavitism in the Roman Catholic Church. The third shows how they shaped their identity after being expelled from the Roman Catholic Church, especially on the basis of their exegesis of biblical texts, in particular the book of Revelation. The fourth chapter is devoted to Archbishop Kowalski's reforms, explaining why he decided to introduce, among other things, marriage between priests and nuns, the priesthood of women, and, finally, the priesthood of lay people. It is argued that all the reforms were interconnected with his and other Mariavites' ideas of the Kingdom. Finally, the last chapter deals with the schism in the Church of Mariavites and shows further nuances in their concept of the Kingdom. There is still much we do not know about the early Mariavites, and this book is a step towards a more comprehensive understanding of this neglected group.

Chapter 1

Introduction

1. Methodology and Presuppositions

The Mariavites are arguably the only indigenous Christian religious group that Poland has ever produced. Their origins can be traced back to 1893, when a certain woman, Feliksa Magdalena Maria Franciszka Kozłowska (1862–1921), a member of a secret religious congregation,[1] claimed to have had revelations in which God asked her to establish a religious congregation called Mariavites. Due to a number of complex factors, they were excommunicated from the Roman Catholic Church in 1906 and founded their own independent church. After the death of Kozłowska in 1921, Archbishop Jan M. Michał Kowalski (1871–1942) introduced a set of reforms in the church, which were considered scandalous in Polish society. Among other things, he instituted marriage between priests and nuns, ordained women, and even planned to abolish the hierarchical priesthood altogether. In fact, all these reforms served the notion of establishing the Kingdom of God on earth and cannot be understood in isolation from such thinking.

This study is the first critical analysis of their core beliefs and use of the Bible. It presents and translates a wide range of primary source material, much of which has not previously been available to a non-Polish-speaking academic or popular audience. In this book, we will focus on how

---

1   There is a subtle difference between religious orders and congregations. An order refers to an institute with an approved rule, while a congregation refers to an institute whose members follow an approved rule, but the institute is not within the structure of an approved order. Furthermore, members of a religious congregation take simple vows, whereas members of religious orders take solemn vows. Changes in canon law, which did not involve the Mariavites after the schism, have made this distinction difficult to grasp, however. Therefore, the terms are used interchangeably in this work. Since the Mariavites were referred to in official documents as a congregation, this nomenclature prevails in the book But the term 'Mariavite Order' can also be found inscholarly literature. See, for example, Brian Porter, *Catholicism, Ethno-Catholics, and the Catholic Church in Modern Poland* (Washington, DC: The National Council for Eurasian and East European Research, 2006), 11.

the Mariavites used, interpreted, and reinterpreted Scripture, most notably the book of Revelation, the writings of the Polish messianists, and closely related ideas about the Kingdom of God. This will involve looking at their use of sources in relevant Polish historical and cultural contexts, and how their exegesis would have been understood. In particular, it will concern the thinking that the end times, mentioned in the 1893 revelations, were interpreted as the fulfilment of the book of Revelation. Only after this fulfilment occurred could the Kingdom of God arrive, beginning in Poland and then spreading worldwide. For some time after her death, Kozłowska was understood to be 'like a son of man' (Rev 1:13), whose mission was to complete Jesus' sacrifice. Her redemptive death ushered in a new epoch in which all things would be made new (Rev 21:5).

I follow a relatively standard historical as well as hermeneutical method, but with reference to data that has largely gone unanalysed or even unremarked by scholars, let alone their understandings of the Bible, the writings of Polish messianists, and the concept of the Kingdom of God.[2] This procedure will include the presentation and analysis of a range of sources (e.g., archival and printed publications), as well as the incorporation of relevant interviews and field research to establish their particular reception of the Bible while telling the largely unknown story of the early Mariavite movement. This is not, obviously, an apologetic work for or against the Mariavites, although such studies do exist, as we shall see below. Rather, I look at their exegesis, ideas, and outputs on the level of historically and culturally located discourse, including how they presented themselves and (to a lesser extent) how they were perceived by others. While the focus will be on how historical and cultural contexts influenced interpretation, this does not of course exclude the importance of the impact of the received interpretations of texts and ideas, and instances will be noted where relevant.[3] Although the main emphasis in this work is on the earliest Mariavites' ideas, their later reinterpretation did not necessarily eradicate the earlier. The interaction between later and earlier interpretations is always fraught with difficulties, as anyone familiar with biblical studies knows. However,

---

[2] An overview of the techniques historians use to reconstruct the past can be found in Martha Howell and Walter Prevenier, *From Reliable Sources: An Introduction to Historical Methods* (Ithaca: Cornell University Press, 2001).

[3] The philosophical or theoretical nuances concerning terms such as 'reception history', *Wirkungsgeschichte*, 'afterlives' of texts, etc., are important but are not directly significant for the aims of this study, which focuses more precisely on establishing the ways in which the texts were understood in the historical context of nineteenth- and twentieth-century Poland. Therefore, the term 'reception' is used in this broad sense.

one advantage the historian of more recent times has is considerably more data which can be explored with much greater certainty.⁴

The reader should bear in mind that, during the period discussed in this book, only what was believed in the Catholic Church during the pontificate of Pope Leo XIII (pontificate 1878–1903) was more or less recognised as doctrine in the Church of Mariavites.⁵ All the other interpretations of the truths of faith were in fact only the views of individual hierarchs or theologians, which had a greater or lesser influence on the faithful. When the Mariavites joined the Union of Utrecht, the statements of the seven ecumenical councils were recognised as doctrine, while other theological statements (such as the Immaculate Conception of the Blessed Virgin Mary) were regarded as certainties of faith.⁶ Only later, and only in one of the churches of the Mariavites, was an institution established that had the authority to teach and introduce new truths of faith.⁷ To avoid complicating matters, however, I often use phrases such as Mariavite beliefs or views, while recognising that these were not necessarily shared by all.

2. Terminology

There are some terms that appear frequently in this work and should be explained at the beginning to avoid misunderstandings arising from their use. Other terms will be explained in the course of the work. The most prominent example of the first category is 'Mariavite' and its derivatives. The term comes from Latin and refers to the imitation of Mary's life (Mariae vita).⁸ Initially, it was applied exclusively to members of Mariavite congregations that were comprised of priests and nuns. The term was later

---

4   But this does not mean that one can work with certainties, omitting distorted memories. Cf. Anthony Le Donne, *Historical Jesus: What Can We Know and How Can We Know It* (Cambridge: Wm. B. Eerdmans, 2011), 106.

5   Technically, it is incorrect to write 'the Mariavite Church'. Kowalski was not ordained as a Mariavite bishop but as an Old Catholic bishop for the Mariavites. Tomasz D. M. Mames, 'Kształtowania się ustroju niezależnego od Rzymu Kościoła mariawitów (1887–1914): Zagadnienia kanoniczno-prawne', *Rocznik Przemyski Historia* 58 (2022): 29–33. But not wishing to complicate matters further for the reader, I will the term 'Mariavite bishop', although it should be emphasized that, in the minds of those about whom this book is written, they were simply Catholic clergy. The same applies to Mariavite parishes, churches (buildings), etc.

6   Tomasz D. M. Mames, *Eucharystia Kościoła Starokatolickiego Mariawitów* (Warsaw: Wyd. Naukowe Chrześcijańskiej Akademii Teologicznej w Warszawie, 2022), 39–40, 73.

7   Ibid., 30–33.

8   Roman M. J. Próchniewski, *Żywot Przeczystej Pani i objawione jej Dzieło Miłosierdzia* (Płock: KSM, unpublished manuscript, 2003), 121.

extended to include members of the Mariavite Union (priests, nuns, tertiaries, and those belonging to the adoration confraternity), and finally it was applied to all members of the churches of the Mariavites. Priests and nuns who joined the congregation were given two monastic names, one of which was Mary, which in this book is denoted by the letter M.[9] The full name is given only on the first occasion when a person is mentioned, and thereafter usually only the surname or title appears. The Mariavites were called to spread the Work of Great Mercy. First, this was understood as a religious programme or initiative to promote certain religious devotions that were transmitted through revelations.[10] It later also became the title of a book, *Dzieło Wielkiego Miłosierdzia*, first published in 1922. The term 'revelations' is used interchangeably with 'visions' in this work. Neither term should be taken as an insult or an endorsement but as purely descriptive. The term 'hallucinations' only appears when it is part of a quotation. It is assumed that historians are not entitled to judge whether revelations are genuine or not.[11] The term Revelation is used interchangeably with Apocalypse to refer to the final book of the Bible.

It is important to note the Mariavites' use of the terms 'church' and 'Catholic'. They were not synonymous. Even after the break with Rome, the Mariavites believed that the churches recognising the supremacy of the pope constituted the Church established by Jesus and were therefore fully Catholic, albeit corrupted. Other Christian churches that, for whatever reason, found themselves outside the Catholic Church were deprived of the fullness of grace that Jesus had provided for his Bride.[12] The Mariavites continued to use the adjective Catholic to describe their own community,

---

9   A rotation of names was possible, especially in the early stages, when someone left the Congregation and the name was given to someone else. They were not given randomly since they were intended to reflect the character of the person. See 'Pismo Święte: Księga Rodzaju Uwagi do Rozdziału IV', *MCPS* 10 (1907): 150. It is worth noting that, in mystical theology, taking someone's name often implies identification with that person. Cf. Tomasz D. M. Mames, 'Charyzmat Eucharystyczny i Maryjny Duchowości Mariawickiej', *PNS* 41 (2006): 8.

10   This multiplicity only underlines the fact that there was a series of revelations given at different times, but which, according to the Mariavites, are fully consistent with each other. As early as 1907, the Mariavites wrote that the prophet receives a new revelation each time because it is not a private privilege but is fully dependent on the will of God. See 'DMHM II', *MCPS* 13 (1907): 208.

11   Ehrman provides a reasonable discussion of the post-resurrection vision of Jesus and the limitations of historians attempting to evaluate these events. Cf. Bart D. Ehrman, *When Jesus became God: The Exaltation of a Jewish Preacher* (New York: Harper Collins, 2014), 95–96.

12   Jan M. M. Kowalski, 'Stanowisko Kapłanów Maryawitów względem hierarchii katolickiej i wyznań chrześcijańskich', *MCPS* 9 (1909): 143.

but the name Catholic Church referred primarily to the ecclesiastical bodies that recognized the authority of the pope.[13] Later, however, the Mariavites modified their opinion and began to view the term Catholic more broadly.[14] For instance, the Mariavite bishop Roman M. Jakub Próchniewski (1872–1954) was able to write in 1938 that the Roman Catholic Church had slowly moved away from the Catholic faith of the Christian Church throughout history.[15] One of the most influential theologians in the history of Mariavitism, Konrad M. Paweł Rudnicki (1926–2013), believed that the term Catholic Church included the Orthodox Churches, the Roman Catholic Church (including the Eastern sui generis Churches, which officially recognise the supremacy of the Roman pontiff) and the Old Catholic churches.[16] His understanding was that the Mariavites were never excommunicated from the Catholic Church but merely expelled from the Roman Catholic Church.[17] Therefore, the Mariavites have always identified themselves as members of the universal (catholic) church but did not necessarily equate the Roman Catholic Church with this body. They never questioned their origins and openly admitted to inheriting some practices

---

13   They decided not to fight about the appellations because they felt that the term *catholic* had been dishonoured, while the term *Mariavite* pointed to the glorious and innocent life of Mary. 'Odpowiedzi Redakcyi', *WDM* 21 (1908): 167.

14   It is difficult to pinpoint the exact moment when this occurred. As early as 1909, they seemed to adhere to the perspective shared by the Old Catholic Churches and epitomised by the famous motto of Vincent of Lerins: 'Quod ubique, quod semper, quod ab omnibus creditum est, id vere catholicum esse'. 'Międzynarodowy Kongres Starokatolicki w Wiedniu', *WDM* 78 (1909): 618. In 1925, Kowalski wrote that the Roman Catholic Church should not be equated with the Catholic Church. Cf. Jan M. M. Kowalski, 'Dary papieży dla Polski. Co rzymski Kościół dał Polsce', *MMN* 11 (1925): 1.

15   Roman M. J. Próchniewski, 'Na marginesie totalizmu katolickiego', *GSK* 1 (1938): 5. After graduating from St Petersburg Academy, Próchniewski became a professor at the Lublin seminary and was ordained a bishop in the Church of Mariavites in 1910. See Zenon M. M. Polkowski, 'Poczet Biskupów Mariawickich', *MPKSM* 8–12 (2010): 31.

16   He most likely included the Oriental Orthodox churches in this category. It is worth noting that this name was only coined at the Addis Ababa Conference to distinguish between Orthodox Churches that accept the decisions of the Council of Chalcedon (451) and those that reject them. Cf. M. B. Ghalli, 'Oriental Orthodox Churches', in *The Coptic Encyclopedia*, vol. 6, ed. Aziz S. Atiya (New York: Macmillan Publishing Company, 2011), 1845. Rudnicki joined the Old Catholic Mariavite Church in the 1950s and was ordained a priest in 1959. He was a well-known professor of astronomy who discovered comet C/1966 T1 and several supernovae. In January 1996, Rudnicki and his mother were recognized by Yad Vashem as belonging to the 'Righteous among the Nations'. His religious journey was described in a short autobiography. See Konrad M. P. Rudnicki, *Moja droga do religii* (Krakow: F. H. U. Elwit, 2008).

17   Jan P. Skupiński, Konrad M. P. Rudnicki, 'Mariawityzm – rzymski katolicyzm: To, co łączy – to, co dzieli', https://www.ekumenizm.pl/publicystyka/mariawityzm-rzymski-katolicyzm-to-co-laczy-to-co-dzieli-rozmowa-z-ks-prof-konradem-m-rudnickim/.

from Rome.[18] To avoid unnecessary confusion, the author of this book has retained conventional terms. The term Catholic Church (used interchangeably with the Roman Catholic Church) refers to all churches that recognise the authority of the Roman pope. The term Orthodox Churches applies to all churches that accept the decisions of the seven Ecumenical Councils as normative and acknowledge the Bishop of Constantinople as first among equals.[19] The Old Catholic Churches constitute the communion of bishops who did not accept the resolutions of the First Vatican Council but did not shun the spiritual and liturgical heritage of Western Christianity. The Protestant Churches are simply those that emerged in the sixteenth century with the protest begun by Martin Luther (1483–1546) and other Reformers. The terms Western or Eastern Churches also appear in this work, but the context usually clarifies their meaning. Such a classification obviously has many disadvantages, but it is convenient for the purposes of analysis, description, and providing context. However, inasmuch as the Mariavites distinguish between the terms Roman Catholic Church and catholic (universal) Church, the reader must constantly bear in mind that the latter category has a broader meaning for them.[20]

Finally, it should be emphasised that various churches use the word 'saint' differently and acknowledge distinct, sometimes opposing individuals as holy.[21] Because of this, we limit the use of this term to proper names, quotations, and brief biographical data in the footnotes. The matter

---

18 Józef M. R. Wojciechowski, 'Wyznanie wiary (1988)', in *Wyznania Wiary i główne zasady doktrynalne. Katolicyzm*, ed. Marcin Karas (Krakow: MEDIA-PRESS, 2000), 196.

19 These seven councils are the First Council of Nicea (325), the First Council of Constantinople (381), the Council of Ephesus (431), the Council of Chalcedon (451), the Second Council of Constantinople (553), the Third Council of Constantinople (680–681), and the Second Council of Nicea (787). These councils were also considered authoritative by the early Mariavites. Cf. 'Dzieło Miłosierdzia. Kronika Maryawicka', *MCPS* 46 (1909): 734–736.

20 It also reflects the position of the Orthodox Churches. The official catechism of the Russian Orthodox Church, compiled in 1822–1823 by Metropolitan Philaret Drozdov (in office 1821–1867), is called Пространный христианский катехизис Православной Кафолической Восточной церкви *(The Longer Catechism of the Orthodox, Catholic, Eastern Church)*. For an Orthodox understanding of the term Catholic, see Laurent Cleenewerck, *His Broken Body: Understanding and Healing the Schism between the Roman Catholic and Eastern Orthodox Churches* (Washington DC: Euclid University Consortium Press, 2007), 61–69.

21 A good example is Photios the Great (810–893). In the West, he is often remembered as the initiator of the so-called 'Photios schism', but to the Orthodox Christians he is a saint. Interestingly, the perspective from which Western Christians viewed him up to the twelfth century is somewhat different from that of today. Cf. Francis Dvornik, *The Photian Schism* (Cambridge: Cambridge University Press, 1948), 308.

of the Kozłowska's being declared a saint is touched upon in several places in this work insofar as it is a significant thread in helping us understand the Mariavite's idea of the Kingdom of God on earth. The names Feliksa (Felicja) Kozłowska, Maria Franciszka, and Mateczka are used interchangeably.[22] The moniker Mateczka is a diminutive of the word mother and can be translated as 'little mother', although 'beloved/dearest mother' seems to better convey the original meaning.[23] It was commonly used in female religious convents to denote the Mother Superior. Later, Maria Franciszka began to be called Mateczka by all members of the Mariavite churches. This name is not related to her status as a saint and is similar to the practice of calling Agnes Gonxha Bojaxhiu 'Mother Theresa', even without acknowledging her sainthood. As far as Jan M. Michał Kowalski is concerned, he is sometimes called Archbishop and sometimes only his surname is used. This has nothing to do with any attempt to depreciate his person or position. The same is true of other people who held certain ecclesiastical positions. The reader must be aware that this is primarily a historical work, so words like sect or heresy (which appears in the title) have no specific theological meaning but are merely descriptive.

3. Mariavite Literature

This book is based primarily, but not exclusively, on the Mariavite sources written before the end of the Second World War. I have made use of all the Mariavite publications known and available to me, although I refer only to those that are related to the subject matter of the book. The literature published by opponents of the Mariavites has been used to a lesser extent since the primary aim of the work is to understand and analyse the Mariavite perspective. Given that it is not possible to discuss all the publications used in this book, this section only contains references to the most important publications. All titles of works that have never been published in English have been translated by me.

It is important to signal some problems with the literature at the outset:

---

22 She was officially given the name Feliksa Magdalena at her baptism but was often called Felicja, which was considered close enough to function as a substitute. See Sławomir Gołębiowski, *Św. Maria Franciszka Feliksa Kozłowska 1862–1921. Życie i Dzieło* (Płock: KSM, 2002), 17.

23 Łukasz Liniewicz, Mariavitism: Mystical, Social, National. A Polish Religious Answer to the Challenges of Modernity (Tilburg: Tilburg University, unpublished Master's thesis, 2013), 10–11.

1. Some important materials have been lost, and we do not know what they contained. This is the case, for example, with the diary that Maria Franciszka kept between 1893 and 1894. The reasons vary widely as to why some sources vanished. For instance, the Mariavite library in Płock was destroyed by the German army during the Second World War.[24] Sometimes, the Mariavites were themselves to blame. After an internal split in 1935, one group was embarrassed by the private memoirs of the sisters, which they felt did not reflect the official position of the Church and could constitute a potential threat.[25] Mateczka herself asked that letters written by her be destroyed after they were read[26] – most likely because she did not want to leave any traces for the Russian authorities.[27] In many cases, however, despite the lack of access to her personal writings, we can reconstruct their contents quite confidently.[28]
2. Some of the literature created by the Mariavites was never intended to be read by outsiders. This may pose potential ethical dilemmas, but there are sound arguments for using these documents. First, they have already been used extensively by non-Mariavites.[29] Second, some of

---

24 On the tragic events that took place at that time, see Władysław S. Ginter, 'Mariawici płoccy w czasie okupacji niemieckiej w latach 1939–1942', *NP* 51 (2006): 36–39.

25 Józef M. R. Wojciechowski, 'Mariawityzm: rys historyczny i odrębność nauki', in *Z dziejów Królestwa*, ed. Józef M. R. Wojciechowski et al. (Felicjanów: KKM, 1972), 71–72. The history of Christianity has witnessed many instances where official (or private) documents were deliberately destroyed after their ideology was challenged. For example, the records of the Council of Constantinople (867), at which Pope Nicholas I (pope 858–867) was condemned, were later destroyed. Cf. Henryk Paprocki, *Focjusz* (Krakow: Wyd. WAM, 2004), 69.

26 Damiana M. B. Szulgowicz and Hanna M. R. Woińska, eds., *Ku Królestwu Bożemu* (Felicjanów: KKM, 2009), 53.

27 There is another reason that Rudnicki pointed out. Mateczka did not want her letters, written to specific people and under specific conditions, to be treated later as models of behaviour and thinking for every occasion. See Konrad M. P. Rudnicki, 'Teksty objawień bł. Marii Franciszki', *RTChAT* 1–2 (1974): 458. Fortunately, some of these letters have survived and have been used in this work.

28 For instance, the manuscript *Pierwotny tekst objawień Mateczki*, i.e., the original text containing Mateczka's revelation written in 1894 is missing. Fortunately, we have copies made by prominent Mariavites while Maria Franciszka was still alive, so we are able to establish its content. Cf. Konrad M. P. Rudnicki, 'Pierwotny tekst objawień Mateczki', *RTChAT* 2 (1979): 196–199.

29 It can be argued that once literature becomes widely known, it should not be ignored, even if it was initially intended to be read only by a few. This is what happened with Origen's *On First Principles*, which was supposedly written for private circulation but was leaked to the public. See Jonathan Hill, *Christianity: The first 400 years* (Oxford: Lion Books, 2013), 167.

the reasons for hiding their contents have long since expired.[30] Third, they are used in this work purely for the purpose of understanding, unaccompanied by any intention to discredit the sources in any way.[31] Potential changes in meaning can only arise from the linguistic limitations that accompany any translation. Furthermore, it should be strongly emphasised that all literature has been obtained legally, in most cases directly from the Mariavites.

3. Finally, it should be noted that some of the ideas contained in these publications were considered sacred by the Mariavites. For many years, the Mariavites faced hostility, the deliberate lack of understanding, and ridicule.[32] Despite having publishing houses and a significant number of believers, they have never possessed sufficient resources to defend their claims against distortions.[33] Even today, they are reluctant to share their knowledge, fearing deliberate manipulation of their positions.[34]

The Bible is at the centre of Mariavite theology.[35] Other publications can only illuminate its importance but do not intend to occupy the same place.

---

30 For instance, some fragments were considered blasphemous, and their dissemination could lead to legal consequences for the Mariavites. Cf. Sławomir Gołębiowski, *W poszukiwaniu prawdy ... Sądowe Procesy Arcybiskupa Jana M. Michała Kowalskiego* (Felicjanów: KKM, 2014), 24–26.

31 The history of Christianity provides many examples in which authors have used the literature of their opponents to denigrate their theology. Many such instances are presented in Bart D. Ehrman, *Forgery and Counterforgery. The Use of Literary Deceit in Early Christian Polemics* (Oxford: Oxford University Press, 2013).

32 As early as 1907, the Mariavites complained that their beliefs were often taken out of context without any desire to understand them. 'DMHM II', *MCPS* 10 (1907): 157–158. Long ago, Clement of Alexandria (150–215) observed that 'revealed knowledge is not for everyone' because some people are either unable to understand it or deliberately twist its meaning. Clement of Alexandria, *Stromateis, Books 1–3*, Fathers of the Church 85, trans. John Ferguson (Washington: The Catholic University of America Press, 1991), 24.

33 In 1906, the newspaper *Kurier Warszawski* (Warsaw Courier) acknowledged that the malice aimed at Maria Franciszka and the Mariavites was unquantifiable due to the number of claims made against them. See Artur Górecki, *Mariawici i mariawityzm – narodziny i pierwsze lata istnienia* (Warsaw: Wyd. DiG, 2011), 35.

34 It is probably in this light that we should understand the words written in a private letter from the current Superior of the Catholic Mariavite Church, Damiana M. Beatrycze Szulgowicz, to Katarzyna Tempczyk that the latter should content herself with the topics that had already been covered in publications. See Katarzyna Tempczyk, *'Nowe przymierze uczynił Pan z nami ...': Teologia Kościoła Katolickiego Mariawitów* (Warsaw: Ex Libris, 2011), 15.

35 As Mames noted, the Mariavites based the construction of their own denominational identity primarily on the Bible. Tomasz M. D. Mames, 'Pismo Święte – Jego autorytet i interpretacja w Kościele (1)', *MPKSM* 4–7 (2008): 15.

The Mariavites, almost immediately after their break with the Roman Catholic Church, decided to produce their own translation for several reasons. First, they needed an authoritative translation to read during religious services since they decided to conduct services in the language of the people.[36] Second, they wanted to educate parishioners and explain their own position, which required knowledge of the Scripture. Third, they felt that the Bible used in the Catholic Church in Poland was not always accurately rendered and contained inaccurate commentary that contradicted the church fathers.[37] The process of creating the Mariavite version was long and complex and was completed between 1921 and 1928.[38] Its origins date back to 1907, when the first excerpts of the translation appeared in the second issue of the newspaper entitled *Maryawita: Czciciel Przenajświętszego Sakramentu* (Mariavite: The Worshipper of the Blessed Sacrament).[39] This Bible was published by Kowalski (1871–1942)[40] with the help of Bishops

---

36 Tomasz M. D. Mames, 'Objawienia świętej Marii Franciszki Kozłowskiej jako instrumentarium egzegetyczne perykop Pisma Świętego', in *Księgi Święte a Słowo Boże*, ed. Łukasz Kamykowski and Zdzisław J. Kijas, (Krakow: Papieska Akademia Teologiczna, 2005), 116.

37 The translation most commonly used by the Catholics in Poland at that time was the version by Jakub (or Jakób) Wujek (1541–1597). It was declared an authoritative translation for the Polish Catholics at the Piotrków synod in 1607. Cf. Robert Auty, 'The Bible in East-Central Europe', in *The Cambridge History of the Bible, vol. 3: The West from the Reformation to the Present Day*, ed. Stanley L. Greenslade (Cambridge: Cambridge University Press, 2008), 134. Kowalski thought that Wujek followed the Clementine Vulgate, published in 1592, uncritically. Nevertheless, he retained passages that he believed had been translated correctly as well as phrases that had become familiar to Polish readers. See Jan M. M. Kowalski, 'Słowo wstępne od Biskupa Mariawitów (17.12.1921)', in *NTPP* (Płock: SKKM 1921), 4.

38 The cover page of the first edition of the New Testament shows the year 1921, but the book also contains the lecture 'Słowo wstępne na Wykład Apokalipsy', which is dated 10 February 1923. The cover page of the first part of the Old Testament shows 1923 and the second 1925, but the last page shows 1927. These dates marked the beginning of the publication of the separate parts. When the Second World War broke out, the New Testament had seen two other editions in 1925 and 1928. A separate edition of the book of Revelation was also published in 1929. Cf. Tomasz M. D. Mames, 'Pismo Święte – Jego autorytet i interpretacja w Kościele (2)', *MPKSM* 11–12 (2008): 15.

39 This was a translation of the first chapter of Genesis with commentaries. See 'Pismo Święte. Księga Rodzaju Rozdział I', *MCPS* 2 (1907): 23–25. The first issue of the newspaper included an introduction to the Bible, encouraging the Mariavites to familiarise themselves with the Scriptures. See 'Pismo Święte', *MCPS* 1 (1907): 6–8.

40 Kowalski graduated from St Petersburg Academy in 1897. In 1903 he was elected the Minister General of the Mariavite Congregation, and in 1909 he was ordained a bishop. After the death of Mateczka, he assumed the title of archbishop. He died at the Nazi Hartheim Euthanasia Centre in Alkoven, Ostmark (Austria) on 26 May 1942 and is considered a saint in the Catholic Mariavite Church. For more information about him, see Damian

Próchniewski and Leon M. Andrzej Gołębiowski (1867–1933), the priests Klemens M. Filip Feldman (1885–1971) and Wacław M. Bartłomiej Przysiecki (1878–1961), as well as other priests and nuns.[41] Kowalski was concerned not only with theological purity but also with maintaining an impeccable literary style. Therefore, the translation was based on the Latin Vulgate and the third edition of the Leopolita Bible published in Krakow in 1577.[42] It is not clear how extensively the Bible of Queen Sophia was consulted.[43] Both Greek and Hebrew texts are mentioned, but we do not know which critical versions were examined.[44] The Mariavite Bible contains several deuterocanonical books. The Prayer of Manasseh, along with the 3rd and 4th Books of Ezra, are included immediately after 1 and 2 Maccabees.[45] The Bible was a product of its time, and thus it contains some words that may be difficult for modern readers to understand, and some theologically loaded terms that could potentially obscure the meaning.[46] The Scripture quotations in this book are from the New International Version,

---

Cyrocki, 'Jan Kowalski', in James Crossley and Alastair Lockhart, eds., *Critical Dictionary of Apocalyptic and Millenarian Movements*, www.cdamm.org/articles/jan-kowalski.

41   Gołębiowski graduated from St Petersburg Academy and worked as a professor at the Płock seminary. He became a bishop in 1910. Feldman was one of six deacons ordained to the priesthood in the newly built Temple of Mercy and Charity. He was consecrated bishop in 1929. After an internal conflict in the Church of Mariavites in 1935, he served as the Prime Bishop of the Old Catholic Mariavite Church until 1942. Przysiecki, like Feldman, became a priest in 1914 and a bishop in 1929. He served as the Prime Bishop from 1955 to 1957. Cf. Zenon M. M. Polkowski, 'Poczet Biskupów Mariawickich', *MPKSM* 8–12 (2010): 31–32.

42   *The Leopolita* Bible was first published in Krakow in 1561 and was based on the Vulgate. We do not possess clear information on authorship, but the Catholic priest Jan 'Leopolita' Nicz (1523–1572), who is credited with corrections before the second publication in 1575, gave the Bible its name. See Auty, 'The Bible', 133. The Mariavite Bible dates to the second rather than the third edition of the Leopolita Bible, to 1577. Apart from the addition of a new title page, however, both versions have the same text. Cf. Kowalski, 'Słowo wstępne od Biskupa Mariawitów (17.12.1921)', 3.

43   This is the oldest attempt to translate the entire Old Testament into Polish. Completed in 1455 and based on an earlier Czech version. Auty, 'The Bible', 133.

44   For instance, a footnote to Mt 28:19 states that the Greek edition has *make disciples* instead of *teach*, but it provides no further information on which Greek text was consulted. 'Ewangelia według św. Mateusza 28:19', *NTPP*, 91.

45   'Porządek Pism Starego Testamentu', in *PŚST* I (Płock: SKKM, 1923), III. The Mariavites were aware that the Western Church did not include them in the canon of sacred writings, but the Eastern Church placed them at the end of the Old Testament. The Mariavites followed the practice of the latter and considered them inspired. See 'Wstęp do Trzeciej i Czwartej Księgi Ezdrasza', in *PŚST* II (Płock: SKKM, 1925), 482.

46   For example, the Jewish Temple is referred to as the Church. Cf. 'Ewangelia według św. Mateusza 21:12', *NTPP*, 65. But this was taken directly from the Jakub (or Jakób) Wujek Bible.

but the Mariavite translation was consulted on every occasion. Where there are significant differences in meaning, additional explanation is provided.

It can be argued that the Bible belongs equally to all Christian denominations. If one wants to see what distinguishes one Christian confession from another, one should examine the catechisms or creeds of individual denominations. *Dzieło Wielkiego Miłosierdzia* (The Work of Great Mercy) takes on the role of a credal book for the Mariavites.[47] There are only two editions of this book that all Mariavites recognise as fully authoritative. The first dates from 1922, and the second from 1927.[48] They contain, among other things, all the revelations Mateczka wrote down,[49] her biography, and other theological and historical treaties.[50] Maria Franciszka claimed to take full responsibility only for those revelations that she personally wrote.[51] This does not mean that the Mariavites do not revere or ignore other revelations of Mateczka transmitted orally, but they are certainly not treated in the same way as the written ones. The edition used in this book is the first one, which dates from 1922.

Early Mariavite publications often contained texts that could be treated independently. In most cases, this was because these publications were printed progressively with additions. Some of the most important works were published as parts of broader compilations. For example, the Mariavite New Testament includes 'Słowo wstępne na Wykład Apokalipsy'

---

47 In such a setting, the Bible can be compared to a monastic rule with the revelations of Mateczka playing the role of a constitution. The role of the latter was to help the Mariavites understand and apply the Bible to their social context. Mames, 'Charyzmat', 7.

48 Other books that included the revelations of Mateczka are, for example, Objawienia Mateczki published in 1967 in Felicjanów; Objawienia Dzieła Miłosierdzia Bożego 1893–1918 published in 1995 in Krakow and Dzieło Wielkiego Miłosierdzia, Wydanie trzecie published in Płock in 2002. The most important editions of Mateczka's revelations are listed in Mames, *Eucharystia*, 13.

49 *Początek Zawiązku Zgromadzenia Kapłanów* (The Beginning of the Congregation of Priests), *Pierwotny tekst Objawień Mateczki* (The Primary Text of Mateczka's Revelations), *Wyjątki z Objawień w roku 1899 i 1900* (The Extracts from the Revelations of 1899 and 1900), *Notatki rekolekcyjne z roku 1911* (The Retreat Notes of 1911) *and Notatki z Objawień Mateczki z Roku Jubileuszowego 1918* (The Notes from Mateczka's Revelations in the Jubilee Year 1918). It is worth noting that Mateczka gave titles to only three of these books; *Pierwotny tekst* and *Notatki z Objawień* were most likely given their titles by Kowalski. Apart from the lost manuscript of *Pierwotny tekst*, all the others are still found today in Felicjanów. Cf. Rudnicki, 'Teksty objawień', 450–463.

50 This work contains the few texts that Mateczka left behind that are not revelations, i.e., *Życie Duchowne* (The Spiritual Life), *Trzydniowe Rekolekcje* (The Three-Day Retreat), and her letters.

51 Jan M. M. Kowalski, 'Krótki Życiorys Mateczki', in *DWM* (Płock: SKKM, 1922), 290.

(Preliminary Notes on the Apocalypse).[52] This is a valuable treatise in which the author attempts to demonstrate the links between the Polish Romantic poets, the book of Revelation, and *Dzieło Wielkiego Miłosierdzia*. Polish Romantic thinkers such as Adam Mickiewicz (1798–1855), Juliusz Słowacki (1809–1849) or Zygmunt Krasiński (1812–1859) are portrayed as heralds of Mariavitism and the Kingdom of God. Their relation to Mateczka and *Dzieło Wielkiego Miłosierdzia* is compared to the relation of the Old Testament prophets to Jesus and His redemptive act. *Wykład na Apokalipsę* (Lecture on the Apocalypse), which was published a little later, develops these ideas even further.[53] As the reader will see, many of the fundamental theological constructs of the Mariavites cannot be understood without becoming familiar with the ideas propounded by the Polish Romantics.

Other invaluable information came from newspapers published by the Mariavites. *Maryawita: Czciciel Przenajświętszego Sakramentu* began to be printed in January 1907 and continued until December 1913.[54] It published articles that explained the basics of Mariavitism and its history. The newspaper contains some of the earliest written interpretations of Mateczka's revelations. *Maryawita* was published together with *Wiadomości* (The News), renamed as *Wiadomości Maryawickie* (Mariavite News) in 1909.[55] Its main purpose was to respond to critics' objections. In addition, readers were informed about current national and international affairs, and the faithful were given help with religious problems. A Lithuanian version of the newspaper titled *Marijavitas: Švečiausiojo Sakramento Garbintojas* first appeared in 1909, together with *Marijavitų Žinios*.[56] *Kalendarz Maryawicki* (The Mariavite Calendar), issued in Łódź

---

52 The text is dated 10 February 1923. See Jan M. M. Kowalski, 'Słowo wstępne na Wykład Apokalipsy', *NTPP*, 785.

53 The text is dated 12 April 1923. Extensive excerpts can be found in Jan M. M. Kowalski, 'Wykład na Apokalipsę', in *MD I*, ed. Damiana M. B. Szulgowicz and Hanna M. R. Woińska (Felicjanów: KKM, 2012), 121–170.

54 Its predecessor was most likely *Maryawita: Dwutygodnik dogmatyczno-ascetyczny ilustrowany* (Mariavite: A Biweekly Dogmatic and Ascetic Illustrated Journal). First published in Kielce in 1903, it changed its name to *Jutrzenka* (Morning Star) after the schism in 1906. See Andrzej Kansy, 'Przegląd prasy mariawitów na ziemiach polskich (1907–2017)', *Studia Medioznawcze* 73 (2018): 41. It is possible that *Maryawita: Czciciel Przenajświętszego Sakramentu* was still being published in 1914. Cf. Andrzej Kansy, *Funkcje prasy wyznaniowej: Studium na przykładzie mariawitów* (Płock: Wyd. Naukowe Mazowieckiej Uczelni Publicznej w Płocku, 2020), 64.

55 Kansy, *Funkcje*, 70–71.

56 In terms of structure and content, it corresponded to the Polish version but also took into account the specifics of the Lithuanian context. Cf. 'Z życia maryawickiego', *WDM* 69 (1909): 550.

between 1908 and 1914, reported on the spread of early Mariavitism, which reached as far as Brazil. The magazine's mission was, among other things, to spread education among the Mariavite community as well as to provide a wealth of useful information on weights and measures, currency, or organised fairs. Works of Polish literature were also published there.[57] *Mariawicka Myśl Narodowa* (Mariavite National Thought) was published for only two years, from 1924 to 1925. Its main editor was Przysiecki, whose interest in the ideas of Polish Messianism was reflected in the newspaper's content. It was also used as a tool to provide reliable information on the marriages between Mariavite priests and nuns. Finally, *Królestwo Boże na ziemi* (The Kingdom of God on Earth) was issued between 1927 and 1939. We can distinguish two main periods in its publication. The first covers the period from 1927 to 1935, i.e., from its foundation to the split in the Church of Mariavites, and the second covers the period from 1935 to 1939, when the magazine was published by those who remained faithful to Archbishop Kowalski, and the publication of *Królestwo* was interrupted by the outbreak of the Second World War.[58] It contained plenty of theological and historical articles on the Mariavite concept of the Kingdom of God, and, from 1930 to 1935, it was published together with *Głos Prawdy* (The Voice of Truth), whose purpose was to respond to criticism coming mainly, but not exclusively, from Roman Catholic circles.[59] Its role can be compared to the earlier *Wiadomości Maryawickie*. This does not, of course, exhaust all the newspapers published by the Mariavites. One could still mention titles such as *Jednodniówka Mariawicka* (The Mariavite One-Day Bulletin),[60] *Templarjusz* (The Templar) or *Światynia Miłosierdzia i Miłości* (The Temple of Mercy and Charity). But the author of this book made limited use of these works since they did not prove to be as useful as those mentioned above.

Books containing rules of faith, breviaries, calendars, and catechisms were also consulted during the writing of this work. The author could mention here, for example, *Główne zasady wiary i ustrój Kościoła Maryawickiego* (The Main Principles of the Faith and Structure of the Mariavite Church) or *Katechizm Życia Zakonnego* (The Catechism of the

---

57 Kansy, *Funkcje*, 86–91.
58 Ibid., 176–177.
59 After 1935, the newspaper, published by those opposed to Kowalski, ceased to be an appendix and gained independence. Initially, the paper was subtitled *Tygodnik Mariawicki* (Mariavite Weekly), but in 1936 it was renamed *Tygodnik Staro-Katolickiego Kościoła Mariawitów* (The Old Catholic Mariavite Church Weekly). See Kansy, 'Przegląd', 46.
60 It was published in 1923, 1924, 1926 and 1935. Its aim was to explain the current political situation in Poland. Cf. Kansy, *Funkcje*, 160–161.

Monastic Life). An important document in the history of Mariavitism is undoubtedly the publication *W obronie zasad Ewangelii* (In Defence of the Principles of the Gospel). The first part was published in 1910, and the second in 1913. The co-authors of this work were Bishops Kowalski and Próchniewski, although the title page does not name them.[61] This publication gained them honorary doctorates in theological studies by the Faculty of Old Catholic Theology in Utrecht.[62]

When discussing the issue of Mariavite marriages between clergy and nuns, reference had to be made to the *Początki Królestwa Bożego na ziemi* (The Beginnings of the Kingdom of God on Earth). The work was included in the second edition of *Dzieło Wielkiego Miłosierdzia*. It contains the memoirs of those personally involved in the marriages of Mariavite priests and nuns. Although it deals with events from 1921 to 1923, most of the recollections were written between 1928 and 1929. They provide insight into the motivations that helped the Mariavites introduce and accept these unions.

The rest of the significant publications from the Mariavites appeared much later and do not constitute the main source for this work. Occasionally, however, they contain information that cannot be found anywhere else. This led to the problem of deciding whether to classify them as sources or literature on the subject. This book simplifies this issue by dividing the publications into those written by the Mariavites and those written by others. Worthy of mention here is the book *Żywot Przeczystej Pani i objawione Jej Dzieło Miłosierdzia* (The Life of the Pristine Lady and the Work of Mercy Revealed to Her), which was written between 1943 and 1952 by Próchniewski but was never officially published. The author knew Mateczka personally and provided first-hand information. Then there is the collective work *Z Dziejów Królestwa* (From the History of the Kingdom), published in Felicjanów in 1972. It presents an interpretation of the reforms and the Kingdom of God from the perspective of of those who remained loyal to Kowalski after 1935. The inclusion of the word Kingdom in the title suggests that the idea of realising the Kingdom of God continued in this environment. Another work in this circle came from the pen of Archbishop Józef M. Rafael Wojciechowski (1917–2005) and was called *Pisma wybrane: Dzieło Bożego Ratunku* (Selected Writings:

---

61 Unfortunately, although the authors of some studies, articles, treatises and books were known, their names did not appear in the works themselves. Sometimes, only initials were given.

62 Sławomir Gołębiowski, *W obronie własnej tożsamości* (Płock: KSM, 2024), 95.

The Work of God's Salvation).[63] Most significantly, it contains information on the understanding of the Trinity from the perspective of the Catholic Mariavite Church. *Ku Królestwu Bożemu* (Towards the Kingdom of God) was published in 2009 and contains letters written by Mateczka that were originally published in the first edition of *Dzieło Wielkiego Miłosierdzia*. Some of the letters included in this work had never been published before. It also includes some of the most momentous pastoral letters and proclamations written by Kowalski. Finally, two volumes of *Mistrzyni Ducha* (The Mistress of Spirit) were released in Felicjanów in 2012 and 2013 to mark the 120th anniversary of Mateczka's revelation and the 150th anniversary of her birth. They comprise several primary sources and many valuable historical essays.

Since 1991, some quite good scholarly works were published on the Mariavites by both members of the church and outsiders. Two publications that came out in 1991 deserve special attention. The first is a book by Krzysztof Mazur, *Mariawityzm w Polsce* (Mariavitism in Poland), and the second is an article by Zbigniew Pasek, 'Geneza Mariawityzmu i przyczyny jego podziału' (The Origins of Mariavitism and Causes of its Division). Both were published by the Institute of Religious Studies at the Jagiellonian University. These are probably the first publications on the Mariavites that meet all academic requirements.[64] Earlier works, although some were written in a balanced way, are characterised by a polemical tone. In the majority of cases, they were written by authors who were not interested in transcending their personal prejudices. In 1992, Stanisław Rybak published *Mariawityzm: Studium historyczne* (Mariavitism: A Historical Study). The author, who was once an advisor to the President of the Supreme Audit Office and Secretary of State at the Ministry of Transportation and Marine Economy, also wrote numerous studies on the history and theology of the Mariavites in later years.[65] In 1996, Rudnicki began publishing *Praca nad sobą* (Working on Yourself). The journal, which appeared at irregular intervals, dealt with various areas of theology and the history of Mariavitism. One of its contributors, Sławomir Gołębiowski, published a biography of

---

63 Wojciechowski was appointed Minister General in 1950. His episcopal ordination took place on 25 November 1956. See Dariusz Bruncz, '100 lat temu urodził się abp M. Rafael Wojciechowski', https://www.ekumenizm.pl/koscioly/katolickie/100-temu-urodzil-sie-abp-m-rafael-wojciechowski/.

64 This does not mean that the authors did not make occasional mistakes. This is demonstrated, for example, by Pasek's uncritical consideration of the document erroneously known as *the Mariavite creed* (in Latin: *Mariavitae credunt*). Cf. Gołębiowski, *W obronie*, 90.

65 For example, see *Mariawityzm: Dzieje i współczesność* (Warsaw: Wyd. Agencja Wydawnicza CB, 2011).

Mateczka in 2002, *Św. Maria Franciszka Feliksa Kozłowska 1862–1921* (Saint Maria Franciszka Feliksa Kozłowska 1862–1921) as well as an important analysis of the trials brought against Kowalski: *W poszukiwaniu prawdy ... Sądowe Procesy Arcybiskupa Jana M. Michała Kowalskiego* (In Search of Truth ... The Judicial Trials of Archbishop Jan M. Michał Kowalski). Another one, Tomasz M. Daniel Mames, now an Old Catholic Mariavite bishop serving in France, has penned many articles and books on various issues related to Mariavitism. His most important publication is a book entitled *Mysteria Mysticorum: Szkice z historii i duchowości mariawitów* (Mysteria Mysticorum: Sketches of Mariavite History and Spirituality), which came out in Krakow in 2009. His most recent work is a book on the meaning of the sacrament of the Eucharist in the Old Catholic Mariavite Church, *Eucharystia Kościoła Starokatolickiego Mariawitów* (The Eucharist of the Old Catholic Mariavite Church). Edward Warchoł (1935–2025), a Catholic priest, authored a vast number of works on various aspects of Mariavitism,[66] including a large number of primary sources. In 2011, Artur Górecki published *Mariawici i mariawityzm: Narodziny i pierwsze lata istnienia* (The Mariavites and Mariavitism: The Birth and First Years of Existence) in which he analyses the issues surrounding the excommunication of the Mariavites from the Roman Catholic Church. Although he chiefly emphasises the Catholic version of events, he does not neglect the Mariavite side. Katarzyna Tempczyk's work, called *Nowe przymierze uczynił Pan z nami ... Teologia Kościoła Katolickiego Mariawitów* (The New Covenant God Made with Us ... Theology of the Catholic Mariavite Church), which was issued in 2011, should also be mentioned. It was generally not well received by the Mariavites, but his effort in bringing together a great deal of material representing conflicting perspectives is certainly laudable. Despite its shortcomings, it remains an important contribution and a helpful partner in the debate. In 2021, the book *W stronę Królestwa Bożego na ziemi: Myśl społeczno-polityczna mariawitów polskich* (Towards the Kingdom of God on Earth. The Sociopolitical Thought of the Polish Mariavites) by Rafał Łętocha and Andrzej Dwojnych was published. The authors rightly point out that the Mariavite ideas about the Kingdom of God did not arise in a vacuum but were based on the views

---

66 For example, *J. M. M. Kowalski Listy i odezwy pasterskie* (Sandomierz: Wyd. Diecezjalne, 2003); *Kontrowersyjna rola arcybiskupa Jana Marii Michała Kowalskiego w Starokatolickim Kościele Mariawitów* (Radom: Wyd. Diecezjalne, 2006); *Prawie wszystko o tak zwanych małżeństwach 'mistycznych' w Starokatolickim Kościele Mariawitów* (Sandomierz: Wyd. Diecezjalne, 2010); *Historia Starokatolickiego Kościoła Mariawitów historią 'Królestwa Bożego na ziemi* (Sandomierz: Wyd. Diecezjalne, 2011).

of the Polish messianists. Lętocha and Dwojnych examined difficult issues with admirable moderation, taking into account a multiplicity of interpretations. Their academic approach should be a standard for future researchers who choose to grapple with complex Mariavite thinking.

Finally, mention should be made of a book written in English by Jerzy Peterkiewicz (Pietrkiewicz)[67] (1916–2007) called *The Third Adam (Trzeci Adam: Opowieść o mariawitach)*. It was published by Oxford University Press in 1975 and was only recently translated into Polish.[68] Although it is an interesting account, it is also highly unreliable. The author admitted in a private conversation that it was mostly a literary fiction.[69] Unfortunately, there has not been any chance to verify the claims it makes.[70] For this reason, the present work is largely a polemic against Peterkiewicz' work.

Following the advice of Papias (c. 60–163), a Christian bishop from the early second century, who stated that nothing 'profit[s] me as much as information from a living and abiding voice',[71] I decided to travel, primarily to Płock, Felicjanów, Warsaw, and Paris, where I had the opportunity to talk to some of the most important people representing Mariavitism. I discussed my ideas with Marek M. Karol Babi, Prime Bishop of the Old Catholic Mariavite Church from 2015 to 2023; Damiana M. Beatrycze Szulgowicz, Superior Bishop of the Catholic Mariavite Church; Bishop Hanna M. Rafaela Woińska; Bishop Tomasz Dariusz M. Daniel Mames; Sławomir Gołębiowski, and Krzysztof Mazur. I also had the pleasure of meeting and talking with Konrad M. Paweł Rudnicki on several occasions before his death in 2013. All of them turned out to be extremely hospitable, kind, and helpful.

---

67 Peterkiewicz' name at birth was Pietrkiewicz, but he changed it when he moved to England, and it was under that name that he published his book *The Third Adam*. See Gołębiowski, *W obronie*, 142.

68 The Polish translation of this book was not published until 2024. For unknown reasons, it was decided to add the subtitle *Opowieść o mariawitach* (The Story of the Mariavites) and to change the author's name. Cf. ibid., 142.

69 Konrad M. P. Rudnicki, 'O Pani Tempczyk i Panu Peterkiewiczu', *PNS* 55 (2009): 19–20.

70 As Mames rightly pointed out, Peterkiewicz' book is first and foremost a literary work, while some of its readers mistakenly saw it as a reliable historical study. Cf. Tomasz D. M. Mames, '*Przyczynek do metaanalizy opowieści o mariawitach Jerzego Pietrkiewicza*', *Studia Teologiczno-Historyczne Śląska Opolskiego* 44 (2025): 112.

71 Papias, 'Fragments 3:4', in *The Apostolic Fathers. Greek Texts and English Translations*, ed. and trans. Michael W. Holmes (Grand Rapids, MI: Baker Academic, 2007), 735.

Introduction 19

4. Structure of this Study

All historical research requires a clear timeframe. This work mainly covers events taking place between 1893 and 1942. Any discussion of affairs outside this timeframe is only intended to shed light on the ideas of the Mariavites associated with the Kingdom or to briefly examine their fate in the following years. The dates have not been chosen arbitrarily. The year 1893 indicates the time when Kozłowska received the revelation of the Work of Great Mercy and 1942 when Kowalski, arguably the most influential thinker in the entire history of the Church of Mariavites was killed. Obviously, this is not a hard and fast delimitation which I follow rigorously; I refer – when necessary – to later literature and interpretations.

Aside from this introductory chapter, there are five additional chapters and a conclusion. The next chapter is propaedeutic in nature. It describes the historical events up 1893 that led to the emergence of Mariavitism and provides a brief biography of Mateczka. The third chapter focuses on the period when the Mariavites operated within the Roman Catholic Church and analyses the content of the revelations given to Kozłowska before the schism in 1906 and their exegesis in relation to the book of Revelation. The fourth chapter deals with the period between 1906 and 1921, when Mateczka died. It attempts to comprehend the self-image of the Mariavites, particularly in relation to the emerging idea of the Kingdom of God. The fifth chapter discusses the reforms of Kowalski that were introduced to hasten the coming of the Kingdom. Great emphasis was then placed on the correct interpretation of the Apocalypse. The sixth chapter examines the schism in the Church of Mariavites and the subsequent fate of the reforms and the idea of the Kingdom.

This book has two main objectives. The first is descriptive and seeks to present the history of the early Mariavites and their theology. The second is analytical and attempts to find the sources of inspiration for Mariavite ideas of the Kingdom and to determine the coherence of the overall concept. I aim to show that the Mariavites sought to anchor all their beliefs either in the Scripture or the Catholic tradition, albeit in a very broad sense. This is not to say that they did not introduce any elements into their theology that they considered entirely new. They certainly did. But they did so only on the condition that the new elements did not contradict any articles of faith, dogmas, or morals recognised in the tradition of the catholic (universal) Church.[72] This is extremely important given the allegations that the

---

72 Jan M. M. Kowalski, 'List pasterski o Nowem Świętych Dziewic Kapłaństwie', *KBNZ* 11 (1929): 83. The Mariavite papers contain ideas coming from the Eastern Churches

Mariavites were inspired by heterodox views from the beginning.[73] They undoubtedly freely discussed unorthodox ideas but did not accept them until they found some kind of legitimacy in authors considered orthodox in the traditional Christian churches.[74] Despite accusations of constant theological changes, it seems that the Mariavites were able to create an intelligible religious system which, however, underwent a long process of evolution and modification.[75] Finally, it should be emphasised that it is not the author's aim to judge the validity of the Mariavites' views. It is irrelevant whether the links to ancient or medieval sources they tried to establish are theologically convincing and justified. It is enough to show that such links existed and that they were aware of them.

---

not in communion with Rome (e.g., Coptic or Syriac). This happened, for example, when the Mariavites tried to affirm the Catholic dogma of the Immaculate Conception. Se 'Niepokalana Marya. Matka Boga', *MCPS* 4 (1907): 61.

73 George Verdin, once a Mariavite from France, attacked his former co-religionists after leaving the church. He claimed that they were inspired by esotericism, the occult, ancient pagan mysteries, and Christian heterodox sects. But no concrete evidence was given to support these claims. Cf. Georges Verdin, *Zza kulis herezji maryjawickiej – na podstawie własnych spostrzeżeń* (Płock: Drukarnia Towarzystwa Wydawniczego 'Dziennik Płocki', 1923), 14. Verdin's credibility is questionable to say the least since he changed his religious affiliation several times and was behind a split in the parish of Nantes. Moreover, the civil authorities arrested him on several criminal charges. Cf. Mames, *Eucharystia*, 248.

74 It is worth mentioning that even Catholic authors use questionable sources. Cf. Luigi Gambero, *Mary and the Fathers of the Church: The Blessed Virgin Mary in the Patristic Thought* (San Francisco: Ignatius Press, 1999), 33–43.

75 For the accusation, see Stefan Gralewski, *Wyznania protestanckie i sekty religijne w Polsce współczesnej* (Lublin: Diecezjalny Zakład Graficzno-Drukarski w Sandomierzu, 1937), 460.

Chapter 2

Events Leading up to the 1893 Revelations

This chapter analyses the political, cultural, and social situation in the nineteenth-century Poland that ultimately led to the emergence of Mariavitism. It will help the reader understand why eschatological ideas were able to develop so easily in Congress Poland and why Mariavitism should not be regarded as a kind of aberration but as something that could be expected to appear in this cultural and historical context. The chapter also briefly discusses the Polish messianists, who were regarded by the early Mariavites as heralds of the coming of the Kingdom of God. Their ideas were widely studied and reinterpreted by the Mariavites, who used them to shape their own theology. Kowalski's 'Lecture on the Apocalypse' has arguably more references to the works of Polish messianists than to the book of Revelation, since the archbishop was convinced that, without their intellectual contribution, the Apocalypse could not be properly understood. Finally, the chapter contains a brief biography of Mateczka up to 1893, when she received the revelation.

1. The State of the Catholic Church in Congress Poland in the Nineteenth Century

The Partition of Poland took place at the end of the eighteenth century and lasted 123 years. In 1815, Congress Poland was established in the regions occupied by Russia. This was an autonomous but not independent kingdom, whose king was the Russian czar. The Sejm, which, together with the Senate, constituted the Polish Parliament, was given prerogatives to conduct legislative activities, and Polish remained the official language. The Russians allowed the Poles to have an autonomous education system and army, making them arguably the most tolerant occupier of Polish lands at the time.[1] Nevertheless, Poles dreamed of full independence, and this sentiment intensified when Nicholas I (1796–1855) became czar in 1825.

1 W. H. Zawadzki, 'Russia and the Reopening of the Polish Question, 1801–1814', *The International History Review* 7 (1985): 20.

His ineffective and ruthless policies led to the outbreak of the November Uprising in 1830.² In the end, the Poles were not strong enough to throw off the yoke of tyranny. After the uprising, the autonomy of the Congress Kingdom was significantly reduced and the Polish army disbanded. As some Polish Catholic bishops supported the insurrection, there was a legitimate fear that the Russians might terminate the relation between the Catholic Church in Poland and Rome. Pope Gregory XVI (pontificate 1831–1846) was compelled to issue an encyclical on civil obedience on 9 June 1832 called *Cum Primum* in which he addressed all archbishops and bishops living in the Kingdom of Poland.³ Assuring them of his prayers, he quoted Rom 13:1, discouraging Poles from opposing the ruling authorities. The encyclical generated diverse reactions.⁴ Although the Poles remained loyal to the pope for the most part, his view did not make them abandon the idea of fighting for the freedom of their homeland.

When Alexander II (1818–1881), son of Nicholas I, came to power after his father's death, another revolution was looming on the horizon. In 1861, Pope Pius IX (pontificate 1846–1878), aware of the mood in the Congress Kingdom, said that the Poles were too preoccupied with national feelings and were neglecting the Kingdom of God. As a consequence, Poland did not have independence.⁵ Like his predecessors, Pius IX was not fond of revolutions,⁶ and that is why he considered the idea of issuing an encyclical in 1862 similar to Gregory XVI's *Cum Primum*, which would condemn

2   Timothy Snyder, 'Ukrainians and Poles', in *The Cambridge History of Russia*, vol. 2: *Imperial Russia 1689–1917*, ed. Dominic Lieven (Cambridge: Cambridge University Press, 2006), 173.

3   Gregory XVI, 'Cum Primum', http://www.papalencyclicals.net/Greg16/g16cumpr.htm. *Cum Primum* contributed to the concept depicting Poland as the Christ of Europe which was subsequently developed by the Polish Romantics and later adopted and modified by the Mariavites. Cf. 'Nasi Mejsaniści' in *MD* II, ed. Damiana M. B. Szulgowicz and Hanna M. R. Woińska (Felicjanów: KKM, 2013), 178.

4   This was shocking to Western liberals and caused hostility among Polish refugees in the West. See Owen Chadwick, *A History of the Popes, 1830–1914* (New York: Oxford University Press, 2002), 410.

5   Zygmunt Zieliński, *Papiestwo i papieże dwóch ostatnich wieków* (Poznań: Wyd. Poznańskie, 2007), 207.

6   The political situation in Italy during his pontificate was unstable. Initially, Pius IX was seen as a progressive, but he later violently opposed Italian unification, accusing Sardinian leaders of radicalism. The union would most likely have led to war with Catholic Austria, which controlled the northern parts of Italy. Moreover, Giuseppe Garibaldi (1807–1882), the Italian general and revolutionary, was known for his antipathy to the papacy and Austria. He supported the emancipation of women and the abolition of church property, but his proposal for social reform was considered moderate even by Karl Marx (1818–1883). Cf. Alister E. McGrath, *Christian History: An Introduction* (West Sussex: Wiley-Blackwell, 2013), 247.

Events Leading up to the 1893 Revelations 23

a potential revolution in Poland before it started.⁷ The Polish Catholics ignored the pope's concerns and the January Uprising broke out in 1863. Sabrina P. Ramet reports that some 300 Catholic priests living in the Kingdom of Poland, about 15 per cent of the total clergy there, strongly supported the initiative and immediately recognised the newly formed Central National Committee, which later became the Polish National Government (1863–1864). It is estimated that they took part in some 1,200 battles, distributing the Eucharist to insurgents, caring for the wounded, and providing food and shelter. Some monasteries were turned into arms depots.⁸ There were also cases where priests actively fought in military campaigns and were subsequently executed.⁹ Jakub Kozłowski (1837–1863), Felicja Kozłowska's father, died on 3 February 1863 fighting for Poland's freedom as an officer at the Battle of Węgrowo.¹⁰

Piotr Wandycz (1923–2017) noted that the insurrection 'accelerated the evolution of the country toward a modern society and reinforced national bonds among the Poles'.¹¹ Moreover, it contributed to the emancipation of the peasantry. All this, however, came at great sacrifice. Thousands died in battle or were forced to emigrate to Siberia.¹² Many Catholic religious orders were shut down, and all property belonging to the Church was confiscated.¹³ Attempts were made to introduce Russian as the liturgical

7   Zieliński, *Papiestwo*, 207.
8   Sabrina P. Ramet, *The Catholic Church in Polish History: From 966 to the Present* (New York: Palgrave Macmillan, 2017), 61.
9   For instance, Antoni Mackiewicz (1828–1863) or Agrypin Konarski (1820–1863); see Marian Banaszak, *Historia Kościoła Katolickiego 3: Czasy nowożytne 1578–1914* (Warsaw: Akademia Teologia Katolickiej, 1991), 305.
10 Opponents of the Mariavites were quite quick to make the accusation that Jakub was executed by the insurgents because of treason. See Antoni J. Nowowiejski, *Płock: monografja historyczna napisana podczas wojny wszechświatowej, poprawiona i uzupełniona w roku 1930* (Płock: B-Cia Detrychowie, 1931), 667. There is no evidence that this ever happened, and no primary sources support this claim. Cf. Gołębiowski, *Św. Maria*, 19.
11 Piotr S. Wandycz, *The Lands of Partitioned Poland, 1795–1918* (London: University of Washington Press, 1974), 179.
12 According to Norman Davies' calculations, this was the largest exile of people in the history of Imperial Russia. See Norman Davies, *Europe: A History* (London: Pimlico, 1997), 827.
13 Russian czars had a long history of diminishing the role of monastics in order to increase secular power. Peter the Great (1672–1725) began the secularisation process by confiscating lands belonging to Orthodox monasteries. Catherine II (1729–1796) continued this process. The tonsure of new female and male monks was banned, and many monasteries were closed because the state felt there was a surplus that needed to be minimised. When the monastic revival took place in the nineteenth century, the number of monasteries, monks and nuns increased significantly. F. Gregory L. Freeze, 'Russian Orthodoxy: Church, People and Politics in Imperial Russia', in *The Cambridge History of Russia: Volume 2*, ed. Lieven, 290–291.

language.¹⁴ The Roman Catholic Theological Academy in St Petersburg (Римско-Католическая духовная академия в Петербурге) became the only academic theological institution that could be attended by clergymen from the Congress Kingdom after the Warsaw Academy was suspended in 1867.¹⁵ Pius IX could not openly sympathise with the national interest of the Poles without undermining his own political position. At one ceremony in April 1864, he declared that the czar had the right to oppose an unjust revolution but no right to discriminate against Polish religious sentiments.¹⁶ Despite his moderate views, conflict soon broke out over the appointment of bishops, leading to the cancellation of the concordat and the severing of ties between the Vatican and Russia. Polish bishops were forbidden to participate in Vatican Council I (1869–1870) and some were exiled, including the bishop of the Płock diocese, Wincenty Teofil Popiel (1825–1912), who later played a significant role in the conflict over Mariavitism.¹⁷ Eventually, Pope Leo XIII resumed contact with Russia, but these were again put to the test after the assassination attempt on Czar Alexander II. The pope took the opportunity to remind the Catholics that political power comes from God and that the idea of a social contract is only a pious illusion.¹⁸ The restoration of official relations did not stop the abuses against the Polish Catholics, although it reduced their intensity.

The state of the Catholic Church in Congress Poland after the January Uprising is often presented as one of the reasons for the rise of Mariavitism.¹⁹ On the one hand, the Polish Catholics were faced with external forms of repression, such as the confiscation of property and the liquidation of monasteries and convents. On the other hand, they also had to cope with an internal crisis in the church. A relatively large number of priests displayed arrogance towards their parishioners, neglecting their pastoral duties. Conflicts over finances were not uncommon and, in some cases, led to open protests. Clergy tended to raise fees for religious services like baptisms,

---

14   Norman Davies, *God's Playground: A History of Poland*, vol. II: *From 1795 to the Present* (New York: Columbia University Press, 2005), 154.

15   Hubert Jedin and John Dolan, eds., *History of the Church: The Church in the Industrial Age* (London: Burns & Oates, 1981), 171.

16   Zieliński, *Papiestwo*, 208.

17   As a result, some dioceses remained without a chief overseer for a long time. In 1870, only one diocese in Congress Poland was staffed. See Neal Pease, *Rome's Most Faithful Daughter: The Catholic Church and Independent Poland, 1914–1939* (Athens: Ohio University Press, 2009), 7.

18   Chadwick, *A History*, 432.

19   Krzysztof Mazur, *Mariawityzm w Polsce* (Krakow: NOMOS, 1991), 9–16.

weddings, and funerals.[20] Disputes between parish priests and their curates over discipline and income distribution intensified.[21] Surprisingly, these abuses did not make Poles less religious. The number of people making annual pilgrimages to Jasna Góra steadily increased, reaching its apogee in 1882, when some half a million pilgrims celebrated the jubilee year of the icon of the Black Madonna of Częstochowa.[22] This was certainly a more mystical and folk form of religiosity that did not place much emphasis on the intellectual side. A significant proportion of the faithful did not know the words of the Lord's Prayer, nor were they familiar with the basic teachings concerning Christ, the sacraments or the Church.[23] This often resulted from the fact that priests were poorly educated due to the restrictions imposed on them by the secular authorities. They began to resemble civil servants, imbued with excessive formalism.[24] Meanwhile, another form of religiosity, namely secret religious congregations, began to gain popularity in the Congress Kingdom. Researchers date their beginnings to 1874 and associate them with the Capuchin friar Honorat Koźmiński (1829–1916).[25] From day one, these secret institutions met with moderate sympathy from the Catholic Church hierarchy. They were not strictly regulated and difficult to supervise. The Russian authorities considered them illegal, and Rome

---

20   A description of the general state of the Catholic Church at the time can be found in Franciszek Stopniak, *Kościół na Lubelszyźnie i Podlasiu na przełomie XIX i XX wieku* (Warsaw: Akademia Teologii Katolickiej, 1975). The book focuses only on certain provinces, but its conclusions can be extended to other areas of Congress Poland.

21   Górecki, *Mariawici*, 29.

22   Ramet, *The Catholic*, 64.

23   Daniel Olszewski, *Przemiany społeczno-religijne w Królestwie Polskim w pierwszej połowie XIX wieku: Analiza środowiska diecezjalnego* (Lublin: Wyd. KUL, 1984), 220. Similar trends could be seen in Imperial Russia, where the average Orthodox parishioner had only a vague understanding of such important Christian concepts as the Trinity and the Eucharist. See Gregory L. Freeze, *The Russian Levites: Parish Clergy in the Eighteenth Century* (Cambridge: Harvard University Press, 1977).

24   Antoni Szech, *W sprawie mankietnictwa* (Kraków 1906), 8. The real author of the book was Izydor Kajetan Wysłouch (1869–1937), a Capuchin friar and social activist who left the monastery in 1908 after the publication of Pope Pius X's encyclical *Pascendi Dominici gregis*, condemning Modernist thought. Information about him can be found in Stanisław Gajewski, *Izydor Kajetan Wysłouch 1867–1937* (Lublin: Wyd. KUL, 1995). *W sprawie mankietnictwa*, directed against the Mariavites, was published in 1906, when Wysłouch was still a member of the Capuchin order.

25   His lay name was Florentyn Wacław Jan Stefan Koźmiński. He entered the Capuchin order in 1848 and was ordained a priest in 1852. He founded more than 20 secret religious congregations and was the spiritual guardian of many communities and people, including Maria Franciszka. He was beatified in 1988 by Pope John Paul II (pontificate 1978–2005). Details of his life are contained in Maria Werner, *O. Honorat Koźmiński, Kapucyn 1829–1916* (Warsaw and Poznań: Wyd. Pallottinum, 1972).

could tolerate their activities only as informal associations.[26] Genetically, Mariavitism emerged from the hidden congregational movement aimed at repairing the miserable religious state of the Polish church. It could be said that it has always been predisposed to encounter serious obstacles.

2. Polish Romantic Messianism

The Mariavites were strongly influenced by Polish Romantic thinkers.[27] References to Polish messianic thought were common in Mariavite literature, and Polish messianists were treated as prophets who had succeeded in understanding the Divine Plan and were supposed to prepare people for the emergence of Mariavitism.[28] It is not surprising, then, that their ideas were used to legitimise certain Mariavite ideas about the Kingdom of God. Not all people were able to perceive these connections, since, in the opinion of the Mariavites, the legacy of the Polish messianists was often misunderstood.[29] A few remarks should therefore be made on this subject. By convention, the terms 'Romantic' and 'messianist' are used interchangeably when referring to this group of Polish writers.

Andrzej Walicki (1930–2020) stated that Poland was the country of nineteenth-century messianism in the same way that France was the country of the Enlightenment and Germany the country of Romantic conservatism.[30] Polish messianic ideas were an integral part of the pan-European tendencies prevalent in the first half of the nineteenth century, but they were simultaneously qualitatively different. According to the dominant continental philosophy of the time, intellectual inquiry into the nature of reality was not enough. Rather, creative ideas were needed that could

---

26 Sacrae Congregatio pro consultationibus Episcoporum, Regularium et aliorum Praelatorum, the Roman Congregation dealing with bishops and the religious, issued the decree *Ecclesia Catholica* on 11 August 1889 approving the activities of secret religious congregations but recognising them only as associations whose members took private vows. Even after the decree was published, most Polish bishops were reluctant to get involved, limiting themselves to giving their formal blessing. The situation changed only after Czar Nicholas II (1868–1918) signed the decree on religious tolerance in 1905. Artur Górecki, *Próby odnowienia życia religijnego w Królestwie Polskim po powstaniu styczniowym – wybrane aspekty* (Toruń: Europejskie Centrum Edukacyjne, 2010), 123–124.

27 Krystyna Darczewska, 'Elementy mesjanistyczne w polskich. Kościołach narodowych', *Studia Religioznawcze* 19 (1984): 75–105.

28 Andrzej Dwojnych and Rafał Łętocha, *W stronę Królestwa Bożego na ziemi: Myśl społeczno-polityczna mariawitów polskich* (Krakow: Wyd. Uniwersytetu Jagiellońskiego, 2021), 51.

29 Wacław M. B. Przysiecki, 'Misja Polski', *GSK* 27 (1939): 417.

30 Andrzej Walicki, *Między filozofią, religią i polityką: Studia o myśli polskiej epoki romantyzmu* (Warsaw: Wyd. Państwowy Instytut Wydawniczy, 1983), 34.

transform societies and save nations.³¹ Many intellectuals from various European countries developed theories on the historical mission of their nations.³² Poland had already had a long tradition of cultivating an historical messianism, particularly embedded in the idea of Antemurale Christianitatis, which can be translated as 'the Bulwark of Christendom'.³³ Polish Romantic thinkers added some distinctive and previously unknown elements to this philosophical orientation. Their ideas not only revolved around historiosophical concepts but also had a distinct millenarian structure with soterio-eschatological goals.³⁴

The Polish messianists never created one coherent system of thought, but some common threads can be found in their writings.³⁵ They devoted a great deal of attention to the failed November Uprising. The tragic events forced many representatives of the Polish intelligentsia to seek refuge in Western European countries, especially France. It was there that they found fertile ground that allowed them to comprehend Poland's role in relation to not only the immediate course of events but also to the eternal divine plan. An extremely important figure in this process turned out to be the French conservative philosopher Joseph de Maistre (1753–1821) and his

---

31 Władysław Tatarkiewicz, *Historia filozofii tom 2: Filozofia nowożytna do roku 1830* (Warsaw: Wyd. Naukowe PWN, 2007), 221.

32 For example, the Russian messianists held different concepts, sometimes radically contradictory. Pyotr Chaadayev (1794–1856), a forerunner of the Westernisers, thought that the Russian people had not achieved anything groundbreaking in human history until the nineteenth century. He believed that Russia was finally called to unleash its immense potential by uniting with Catholicism. On the other hand, the Russian Slavophiles focused on preserving the purity of the Orthodox faith, which they believed was kept alive by the peasantry. Николай А. Бердяев, *Истоки и смысл русского коммунизма* (Paris: YMCA Press, 1955), 20–23.

33 Janusz Tazbir, *Polskie przedmurze chrześcijańskiej Europy: Mity a rzeczywistość historyczna* (Warsaw: Wyd. Książkowe Twój Styl, 2004), 21.

34 Andrzej Walicki, 'Mesjanistyczne koncepcje narodu i późniejsze losy tej tradycji', in *Idee i koncepcje narodu w polskiej myśli politycznej czasów porozbiorowych*, ed. Janusz Goćkowski and Andrzej Walicki (Warsaw: Państwowe Wydawnictwo Naukowe, 1977), 84.

35 Dwojnych, Łętocha, *W stronę Królestwa Bożego*, 41. For the Mariavites, this was not a serious problem. According to them, the Polish messianists took the same position towards the Work of Great Mercy as the Hebrew prophets did towards Jesus and the redemptive act. Both groups occasionally took slightly different positions on certain issues. Therefore, Kowalski could lump Mickiewicz, Słowacki, Krasiński, Cieszkowski, Hoene-Wroński, and Konopnicka together. Kowalski, 'Słowo wstępne na Wykład Apokalipsy', 705. Krystyna Darczewska called this a folk perception of messianism that does not take into account the deep differences between the Polish messianists. Darczewska, 'Elementy mesjanistyczne', 97.

theory of expiation.[36] Attempting to link the French Revolution to the idea of Providence pervading all historical events, de Maistre concluded that social and political upheavals could best be understood in terms of 'a mystical blood sacrifice, of purification and salvation through the shedding of blood'.[37] This was organically linked to his theory of the new revelation, which was quickly picked up by French utopian socialists. It was believed that the French Revolution would bring a new divine intervention epitomised by the reign of the Spirit, access to whom would be available to all, making the agency of an earthly king superfluous.[38] For Jean Fourier (1768–1830) and Henri de Saint-Simon (1760–1825), this meant a new liberation in which the dualism of physicality and spirituality would finally be overcome.[39] On many levels, this corresponded with the ideas represented by Joachim de Fiore (1135–1202), who was convinced of the coming of the third epoch in which the Spirit would communicate with all humanity, making it a universal charismatic community.[40] These ideas, in a slightly modified form, were taken up by the Polish Romantic thinkers, who came to the conclusion that the private sacrifice of Jesus brought salvation to individual souls, while the collective sacrifice of Poland would socially and politically repair entire nations.[41] It is also worth mentioning the influence of Hugues Felicité Robert de Lamennais (1782–1854), a French Catholic priest, philosopher, and political theorist who became dissatisfied with the stance of Pope Gregory XVI towards the November Uprising.[42] Lamennais

---

36   De Maistre was the first European to develop a sociologically oriented theory of sacrifice based on a comparative study of global religious practices. Although he was a conservative Catholic, his theory contained some heterodox elements, which were subsequently adapted by the Polish poets and through them found their way into the theology of the Mariavites. Cf. Owen Bradley, 'Maistre's Theory of Sacrifice', in *Joseph de Maistre's Life, Thought, and Influence*, ed. Richard A. Lebrun (Montreal: McGill-Queen's University Press, 2001), 66–67. The Mariavites were aware of his theories. See 'Przenajświętsza Eucharystya', *MCPS* 46 (1908): 729.

37   Andrzej Walicki, 'Polish Romantic Messianism in Comparative Perspective', *Slavic Studies* 22 (1978): 4.

38   Ceri Crossley, *French Historians and Romanticism: Thierry, Guizot, the Saint-Simonians, Quinet, Michelet* (London: Routledge, 1993), 238.

39   Ewa Starzyńska – Kościuszko, 'Polish Romantic Messianism', *Organon* 48 (2016): 54.

40   Matthias Riedl, 'Longing for the Third Age: Revolutionary Joachism, Communism, and National Socialism', in *A Companion to Joachim of Fiore*, ed. Matthias Riedl (Leiden: Brill, 2018), 293.

41   Walicki, 'Polish', 4–5.

42   Lamennais was a staunch Ultramontane who underwent a surprising intellectual and political change, ending his life outside the Catholic Church. James McMillan, 'Catholic Christianity in France from the Restoration to the Separation of Church and State, 1815–1905'

believed that the pope favoured the royalist cause in France supported by Czar Nicholas I over the Poles' freedom of conscience.[43] Polish messianists shared his views, distancing themselves from international relations built on cold, rational calculations. They stressed that higher values, such as freedom of conscience, should never be betrayed. Despite all these philosophical borrowings, the systems of thought created by the Polish Romantic thinkers were largely unique.

The term Polish messianism was coined by Józef Maria Hoene-Wroński (1776–1853) in the aftermath of the November Uprising.[44] Far from a mystical vision, he foresaw the coming of a new era in which the Slavic peoples would play a providential role. This was to happen only on the condition that the Russians were willing to make reparation for all the wrongs they had inflicted on the Polish nation.[45] Hoene-Wroński represented a rational messianism, a philosophical system that owed much to German idealism. In his theory, the role of Messiah was attributed to philosophy, not to the nation. Only the former had the potential to lead the people to a better tomorrow by uniting goodness, truth, science, and religion.[46] The most sophisticated form of Polish messianism probably developed in the 1840s and was closely associated with the figures of Andrzej Towiański (1799–1878), Adam Mickiewicz, Juliusz Słowacki, Zygmunt Krasiński and August Cieszkowski (1814–1894).

Mickiewicz arrived in Paris in 1832 and became a professor of Slavic literature at the Collège de France in 1840.[47] In 1841 he became involved with

---

in *The Cambridge History of Christianity*, vol. 8: *World Christianities c. 1815–1914*, ed. Sheridan Gilley and Brian Stanley (Cambridge: Cambridge University Press, 2006), 222.

43   The publication of the encyclical *Mirari vos* in 1832 only strengthened his views. See Gregory XVI, 'Mirari Vos', https://www.papalencyclicals.net/greg16/g16mirar.htm.

44   He came from a Czech family and fought in the Kościuszko Uprising as a second lieutenant of artillery on the Polish side. After being taken prisoner, he joined the Russian army. In 1897, Hoene-Wroński resigned from military service and devoted himself entirely to scientific and philosophical work, aiming to revolutionise mathematics, philosophy, astronomy, and technology. Dying at the age of 75, he was not content with the fact that he had failed to achieve everything he had planned. Tatarkiewicz, *Historia*, 260.

45   Of course, Russian intellectuals saw it differently. From their perspective, it was the stubborn Polish people who did not accept the leading role of their superior neighbour. This view was most strongly represented by Alexander Pushkin (1799–1837). Some scholars accused him of writing at the request of Nicholas I, but others emphasised his intellectual independence. Megan Dixon, 'Repositioning Pushkin and the Poems of the Polish Uprising', in *Polish Encounters, Russian Identity*, ed. David L. Ransel and Bozena Shallcross (Indianapolis: Indiana University Press, 2005), 50–51.

46   Tatarkiewicz, *Historia*, 259.

47   There are many publications on the life of Adam Mickiewicz. One of the most recent, written in English, is Roman R. Koropeckyj, *Adam Mickiewicz: The Life of a Romantic*

the religious thinker Towiański who, influenced by certain mystical experiences, founded a religious group known as Koło Sprawy Bożej (Circle of God's Cause). Known to his followers as the Master, Towiański believed in an imminent transformation of the world. This would only occur, however, if the European elites adopted moral principles in international affairs. Towiański's mission was closely intertwined with the idea of a resurrected Poland that would bring salvation to the whole world and establish a new era of Christianity.[48] After a time, the Master's passivity led to Mickiewicz's dissatisfaction.[49] Arguably Poland's most famous seer decidedly criticised Towiański's philosophy for its inactivity but nevertheless retained the idea of messianism.[50] He also fiercely opposed the Enlightenment for its intellectual reductionism and inability to change political reality. His criticism of the Enlightenment placed him with other Polish messianists, as well as with Russian Slavophiles.[51] The only German philosopher who deserved their attention was Fredrich Schelling (1775–1854).[52]

Słowacki was another member of Towiański's circle. He began to travel extensively in 1831, visiting Rome, Naples, Florence, Dresden, Geneva, and Middle Eastern countries, but spent most of his time in Paris. Like Mickiewicz, he was an eclectic thinker, finding inspiration in theosophy, German idealism, and Catholic thought.[53] He also shared with Mickiewicz the notion of revolutionary messianism. According to him, the laws

---

(New York: Cornell University Press, 2008). The reader can also consult Damian Cyrocki, 'Adam Mickiewicz', in James Crossley and Alastair Lockhart, eds., *Critical Dictionary of Apocalyptic and Millenarian Movements*, www.cdamm.org/articles/adam-mickiewicz.

48 Towiański was not overly concerned with Catholic orthodoxy. Jaroszyński detected Gnosticism (the denial of the divinity of Christ), Manichaeism (the world controlled by the evil spirits), Pelagianism (the denial of the original sin), and Protestantism (denial of the institution of the Church) in his works. Cf. Piotr Jaroszyński, 'Mickiewicz Adam', http://www.ptta.pl/pef/pdf/m/mickiewicza.pdf. All these claims, however, must be approached with caution. The Mariavites were later accused of similar beliefs, but this was neither precise nor accurate.

49 Starzyńska – Kościuszko, 'Polish', 56.

50 Adam Mickiewicz, *L'église et le messie I* (Paris: Comptoir des Imprimeurs-Unis, 1845), 21–22. Ewa Starzyńska – Kościuszko classified Mickiewicz as a representative of revolutionary messianism. See Starzyńska – Kościuszko, 'Polish', 58.

51 The latter, however, based his criticism on somewhat different grounds. Cf. Andrzej Walicki, 'The Paris Lectures of Mickiewicz and Russian Slavophilism', *The Slavonic and East European Review* 46 (1968): 156.

52 His understanding of the Trinity and his visions regarding the coming of the Church of St John and the earthly Kingdom of the Holy Spirit had a profound influence on Krasiński and were most likely taken over by the Mariavites. Walicki, 'Polish', 10.

53 As with Mickiewicz, there are a number of monographs devoted to Juliusz Słowacki. One of these is Alina Kowalczykowa, *Słowacki* (Warszawa: Wyd. Naukowe PWN, 1994). The reader may also wish to consult Damian Cyrocki, 'Juliusz Słowacki', in James Crossley

governing spiritual progress were cruel and required a combination of voluntary suffering and heroism. He portrayed Poland as a new Israel, purified by oppression, which could establish a new Jerusalem through revolutionary heroism.[54] The idea of reincarnation, known as social palingenesis, played an important role in his theory. Opposing elitism, Słowacki did not associate more advanced spirits with socially or economically privileged people and opposed established forms of hierarchy. He believed that the spiritual potential of the masses had to be ultimately unleashed if the Kingdom of God was to be established on earth.[55]

Krasiński wrote that the final goal of history is the establishment of the Kingdom of God on earth and the transformation of earth into one great living temple of the Holy Spirit.[56] Although he was the only one of all the major Polish messianists to be careful not to go beyond the framework of Catholic orthodoxy, he was able to criticise certain tendencies in the Church, especially moral hypocrisy.[57] Krasiński also believed in palingenesis, although he had a different perspective on it than the others. He claimed that he could explain social inequality through the theory of reincarnation. In his system, the aristocracy represented the more advanced spiritual beings. Their social position corresponded to the progress they had made in previous incarnations.[58] Unlike Mickiewicz and Słowacki, there was no room for revolution in his theory. Krasiński held a very high opinion of past Poland, which he believed was characterised by tolerance and freedom. He argued that it had to be sacrificed for other nations because it represented the most morally pure European country and the least tainted by crime.[59] The analogy to Jesus, symbolising atonement at its most pure, could not be clearer. The early Mariavites seemed to follow Słowacki in re-evaluating authority and emancipating the people, but they were certainly influenced by Krasiński regarding the nature of Poland.

Krasiński's friend and spiritual father, Cieszkowski, was a great proponent of evolutionary messianism. In his view, spiritual progress could

---

and Alastair Lockhart, eds., *Critical Dictionary of Apocalyptic and Millenarian Movements*, www.cdamm.org/articles/juliusz-słowacki.

54   Walicki, 'Polish', 8–9.
55   Brian Porter, *When Nationalism Began to Hate: Imagining Modern Politics in Nineteenth-Century Poland* (Oxford: Oxford University Press, 2000), 35.
56   Zygmunt Krasiński, *Pisma filozoficzne i polityczne* (Warsaw: Wyd. Spółdzielnia wydawnicza Czytelnik, 1999), 29.
57   Dwojnych, Łętocha, *W stronę Królestwa Bożego*, 49.
58   Walicki, 'Mesjanistyczne', 95.
59   Ibid., 97.

only be achieved through systematic and long-term change.[60] Cieszkowski opposed the view that Jesus' earthly mission had been completed and was now confined exclusively to the heavenly realm. Referring to the Lord's Prayer, which was also interpreted in a prophetic way, he emphasised that the Kingdom was also to be manifested on earth.[61] The messianist philosopher distinguished three stages in human history. The first took place before the coming of Jesus and focused on nature and the body. The second, inaugurated by the coming of the Messiah, brought the spirit to the fore but at the same time placed it in clear opposition to the body. Everything was soon to change. Using the Hegelian categories of thesis, antithesis, and synthesis, Cieszkowski believed that this opposition between body and soul would cease to exist in the third stage. The coming epoch would be known as the Age of the Holy Spirit.[62] It would not appear on its own, however. The new era, also known as the Kingdom of God, had to be introduced by the activity of believers. The era of grace was ending, and the era of merit and action was beginning.[63] This way of thinking, as the reader will soon see, was certainly close to Archbishop Kowalski's thinking. Some Mariavites even believed that Cieszkowski's philosophy was closer to the Work of Great Mercy than to Thomism.[64]

Finally, it should be stated that the Marian cult occupied an important place in the thought of Polish messianists. According to some researchers, it was primarily associated with the vision of women transmitting patriotic and religious traditions in the privacy of the home.[65] By equipping women with rights previously unknown in Polish history, the Mariavites showed that the role of women presented in this vision need not be final.

3. Feliksa Kozłowska's Life up to 1893

William James (1842–1910) published his work on the varieties of religious experience in 1902,[66] and sixteen years later it was translated into

[60] Andrzej Wojnicz, 'Istota Chrześcijaństwa w światopoglądzie Augusta Cieszkowskiego', *PNS* 2 (1997): 8.
[61] Andrzej Walicki, 'Millenaryzm i mesjanizm religijny a romantyczny mesjanizm polski: zarys problematyki', *Pamiętnik Literacki: czasopismo kwartalne poświęcone historii i krytyce literatury polskiej* 62 (1971): 34.
[62] Wojnicz, 'Istota', 7.
[63] August Cieszkowski, *Ojcze Nasz* (Poznań: Fiszer i Majewski, 1922), 138.
[64] Konrad M. P. Rudnicki, 'Od Redakcji'. *PNS* 2 (1997): 12.
[65] Waldemar Chrostowski, 'The Suffering, Chosenness and Mission of the Polish Nation', *Occasional Papers on Religion in Eastern Europe 11* (1991): 6.
[66] William James, *The Varieties of Religious Experience: A Study in Human Nature* (London: Longman, 1902).

Polish by Jan Hempel (1877–1937). The ideas in the book did not strictly conform to the understanding of religion prevalent in Eastern Europe at the time. Some of James' ideas could only be accepted in the religiously atomised societies of the United States or Western Europe. In Germany, for example, Adolf Harnack (1851–1930), building on the theories of Max Weber (1864–1920), emphasised the role of individual charisma in the construction of religious systems, and biographies of Jesus were written in such a way as to reinforce the concept of great men in history.[67] For most Slavs, however, religion was still understood primarily as a corporate affair.[68] Kozłowska's religiosity fit such corporate perspectives, which were only strengthened after the publications of the Polish messianists. Leaving aside periods in her life when she actively sought seclusion and contemplation, she firmly established herself within the boundaries set by the Catholic Church and linked the idea of religion to community.[69] If she had lived a little further west, memories of her might have been shaped much more positively. For this reason, proper attention should be paid to the historical context when analysing this complex figure. James Crossley has convincingly shown what causal factors are overlooked when scholars focus too obsessively on biographical details about key individuals in history.[70] Although the whole Mariavite concept of the Kingdom of God on earth would never have existed without Mateczka, it would be a mistake to overlook other factors leading to the emergence of this religious movement. Finding a balance between social conditions and the role of the individual is therefore a serious challenge for any historian.

The existence of some minor inaccuracies and embellishments in Kozłowska's biography is quite typical, given their presence in the biographies of other religious figures, including Jesus.[71] Undoubtedly, the life of Mateczka was theologised by the Mariavites, who read the events of her life in the light of certain passages in the Bible. But this is not something

---

67 Halvor Moxnes, *Jesus and the Rise of Nationalism: A New Quest for the Nineteenth-Century Quest for Historical Jesus* (London: I. B. Tauris, 2012), 62–69.

68 It is correct to say that James's book found an audience in some circles in Russia, but they were already heavily influenced by Western ideas, especially those about individualisation. See James D. Grossman, 'Philosophers, Decadents, and Mystics: James's Russian Readers in the 1890s', in *William James in Russian Culture*, ed. Joan D. Grossman and Ruth Rischin (Oxford: Lexington Books, 2003), 93–94.

69 Kowalski, 'Krótki', 101.

70 James G. Crossley, *Jesus and the Chaos of History: Redirecting the Life of the Historical Jesus* (Oxford: Oxford University Press, 2015), 13–21.

71 They generally relate to irrelevant issues and potentially stem from different sources of information. Cf. Gołębiowski, *Św. Maria*, 32.

entirely new in the history. The boundary between reality and legend has also been blurred in the lives of other persons considered saints by various Christians.[72] One might even venture to say that theologisation is an integral part of the process of remembering, something that applies equally to all historical figures.[73] This does not mean that Kozłowska's biography should not be read with a certain amount of caution and healthy scepticism. Ultimately, however, the main purpose of this book is to reconstruct the perspective of the early Mariavites without necessarily judging its theological or, even in some cases historical, accuracy.

Feliksa Kozłowska was born on 27 May 1862.[74] Her mother, Anna (1839–1921), considered taking the veil, but Koźmiński allegedly told her that her daughter would follow this path.[75] Fearing repercussions from the Russian authorities after Jakub's death, Anna changed her noble genealogy to a peasant one in official documents.[76] From this point on, Anna and Feliksa were forced to rely on family support. This certainly had an impact on the young girl's mental and spiritual development. Her upbringing instilled in her a strong desire to serve God.[77] Given the context of Polish society after the January Uprising (1863–1864), it is not surprising that her religious life abounded in supernatural phenomena.[78] As a child, she began to communicate with Jesus through private revelations, believing that others had similar experiences.[79] In fact, she was not the

---

72 For example, the family of Francis of Assisi (1182–1226) was reshaped by hagiographers to fit the model of the family of John the Baptist, with Francis' mother, Pica, taking on the characteristics of Elizabeth and his father, Pietro, taking on the characteristics of Zechariah. See Augustine Thompson, *Francis of Assisi: A New Biography* (Ithaca, NY: Cornell University Press, 2012), 7.

73 As Dale C. Allison noticed 'interpretation may always distort, but without interpretation there is no memory and so no past, no possibility of doing history at all'. Cf. Donne, *Historical*, X.

74 Information on her life from the Mariavite perspective can be found in the aforementioned Kowalski, 'Krótki'; Próchniewski, *Żywot*; and Gołębiowski, *Św. Maria*.

75 Anna M. H. Kozłowska, 'Mariae-Vita: Z opowiadań Babci i innych Sióstr Zakonnych', in *Święta Maria Franciszka Kozłowska i Jej Zgromadzenie zakonne we wspomnieniach i pamiętnikach*, ed. Damiana M. B. Szulgowicz and Hanna M. R. Woińska (Felicjanów: KKM, 2007), 61.

76 Kowalski, 'Krótki', 102–103.

77 Władysław S. Ginter, 'Błogosławiona 'Maria Franciszka Kozłowska: (szkic do portretu psychologicznego postaci) cz. I', *NP* 182 (2000): 9.

78 She is said to have seen her late father as a ghost when she was not even a year old. Similarly, she felt the presence of her deceased grandmother. Cf. Kozłowska, 'Mariae-Vita', 37.

79 It is difficult to determine when these mystical conversations (*locutio interna*) began, but Próchniewski claimed that they originated as far back as memory goes, so it must have been very early. See Próchniewski, *Żywot*, 33.

only person to experience such in the history of the Western Church. For instance, Catherine of Siena (1347–1380) was said to have had a vision of Jesus seated on a magnificent throne, dressed in pontifical ornaments and assisted by Peter, Paul, and John, when she was only six years old.[80] These supernatural events helped some Mariavites establish another link between Kozłowska and Mary, the mother of Jesus.[81] In addition to her folkloric religiosity, Feliksa did not neglect the intellectual side of the faith. Her religious education was based mainly on private study and mystical experiences.[82] Around the time of her First Communion, she vowed chastity to Jesus after hearing an inner voice.[83] It is worth noting that mystical experiences accompanying the reception of the Eucharist have quite a rich history in Poland.[84] From that day on, she wanted to receive the Eucharist as often as possible, although always with the permission of her confessor.[85] Quite quickly, she developed a particular devotion to the Blessed Sacrament, beginning to participate in its adoration from the age of twelve.[86] It was not long before ascetic practices began. Kozłowska began fasting as early as the age of seven, which particularly intensified around religious festivals.[87] Together with her mother, she belonged to numerous Catholic confraternities and prayer groups. In 1872, they moved to Warsaw and settled near the Carmelite church in Krakowskie Przedmieście. Feliksa initially studied with private tutors, then attended Countess Skarbek's boarding school, and finally graduated from the female secondary school in Warsaw. Although girls' schools were at a lower level of education than their male counterparts, she received a good formal education,[88] mastering several

---

80 Raymond of Capua, *Life of Saint Catharine of Siena*, trans. Ladies of the Sacred Heart (New York, NY: P. J. Kenedy & Sons, 1862), 26–27.

81 According to Francisco Suárez (1548–1617), a Spanish Jesuit and philosopher, Mary had spiritual visions from early childhood, long before the angel Gabriel's annunciation. Cf. 'Niepokalana Marya. Matka Boga', *MCPS* 50 (1907): 793.

82 The mystery of the Immaculate Conception was to be revealed to her through inner voices from God. She learned that Mary was not only born without original sin but was also elevated above all the angels. See Próchniewski, *Żywot*, 35.

83 Felicja M. F. Kozłowska, 'Protokół przesłuchania Matki Marii Franciszki Kozłowskiej dnia 28 V 1903 roku', in *MDI*, 16.

84 For example, Piotr Skarga (1536–1612) was said to have heard the voice of Jesus while receiving Holy Communion. Marcin Sanak, 'Kult eucharystyczny w Polsce XVII i XVIII wieku', https://www.liturgia.pl/Kult-eucharystyczny-w-Polsce-XVII-i-XVIII-wieku/.

85 Kozłowska, 'Protokół', 15.

86 Kowalski, 'Krótki', 97.

87 When they moved to Warsaw, she gave up eating breakfast, giving away the money she saved to the poor. Kozłowska, 'Mariae-Vita', 49.

88 Girls did not receive a matura/baccalaureate (certificate of passing the high school final exams). They were not taught Greek or Latin and could not study at universities in

foreign languages.[89] Her relationship with her mother was decent, but, as Anna later admitted, she was sometimes too strict with her daughter.[90] In her teenage years, future Mateczka began to engage in various kinds of bodily mortification.[91] Moreover, she tried to avoid all kinds of secular entertainment, including dances, parties, and visits to theatres.[92] Instead, she devoted herself to studying hagiographic literature.[93] This lifestyle may have taken a toll on her health. She struggled with a blood circulation disorder and anaemia, which hampered her studies for some time.[94]

From early childhood, Feliksa was remembered for making a good impression on representatives of the Catholic clergy.[95] When she turned sixteen, a monk was said to have told her that she would become a saint. He also confessed his sins to her.[96] At the age of eighteen, she found a job as a private tutor at the house of General Ulrich, where she taught his children for almost two years.[97] Around the age of twenty, Kozłowska lost sight in her right eye.[98] She wished to enter a religious order, especially

---

Congress Poland. If they had the financial means and passed the necessary examinations, they could have tried to study abroad. See Edmund Staszyński, *Polityka oświatowa caratu w Królestwie Polskim* (Warsaw: Państwowe Zakłady Wydawnictw Szkolnych, 1968).

89   Russian, French, English and German, but with varying degrees of fluency. Cf. Gołębiowski, *Św. Maria*, 21–22.

90   She was relieved to read that her namesake Anna, mother of Mary and grandmother of Jesus, had been told by an angel to bring up her daughter like any other child, despite her privileged status. Kozłowska, 'Mariae-Vita', 72.

91   She kept slats [beams is not the right word here, but I'm not sure slats is either] of wood in her sleeping mattress, wore a cilice and a barbed belt, and limited her time for sleep. When she was 16, she almost completely stopped eating meat. Ibid., 50–51.

92   When she occasionally sang or attended dance classes, she tried to minimise the joy that came from it by, for example, wearing a spiked belt. An unknown woman called allegedly her a saint when she was still a teenager but also added that Satan danced behind her. She took this as a hint to avoid unnecessary pleasures. Ibid., 95.

93   One of the first hagiographic books she read at the age of 15 was the biography of Veronica Giuliani (1660–1727), who had been canonised by Pope Gregory XVI in 1839. Kozłowska, 'Protokół', 16.

94   Stanisław Rybak, *Mariawityzm, studium historyczne* (Warsaw: Wyd. Lege, 1992), 7.

95   When she was six years old, the Bishop of Siedlce, Piotr Szymański (in office 1856–1867), reportedly said that she would become an extraordinary person in the future. Kozłowska, 'Mariae-Vita', 70.

96   But this was not a formal confession. The monk shared his spiritual struggles with her and discussed his religious state. He must surely have considered her worthy of hearing his secrets. Something similar happened when she was 21. Górecki, *Mariawici*, 40.

97   The whole house was Protestant, but this situation was later used to show her apparent Orthodox and Russian sympathies. Gołębiowski, *Św. Maria*, 25.

98   It was later interpreted theologically, referring to the passage in Song 4:9: 'You have stolen my heart, my sister, my bride; you have stolen my heart with one glance of your eyes …'. Another explanation was found in the monastic rule (section 72) of Basil of

the Benedictine Nuns of Perpetual Adoration of the Blessed Sacrament or the Order of the Visitation of Holy Mary, but this was not possible due to the political situation. During a retreat in Zakroczym in 1883, Felicja was received to the Third Order of Saint Francis by the Capuchin Leopold Łukasz Zaczyński (1840–1918) under the name Franciszka (Francesca).[99] At that time, she also experienced an internal revelation recommending that she live according to the Rule of Saint Clare, which she had reportedly not previously known.[100] Seeing religious potential in the young woman, Zaczyński introduced Franciszka to Koźmiński. Upon the latter's urging, she entered one of the secret Warsaw religious convents, the Congregatio Sororum Franciscalium ab Afflictis (the Congregation of Franciscan Sisters of the Suffering).[101] However, it soon became apparent that Przytulisko (The Shelter), as the Congregation was commonly called, was not the right place for Feliksa's spiritual needs. The nuns cared mainly for the sick, often from the upper classes, and some of the sick had negative attitudes towards religion.[102] Kozłowska regarded her ministry in Przytulisko as a prelude to a more contemplative lifestyle. There were moments when she toyed with the possibility of leaving the convent, but she remained there both for reasons of obedience and visions.[103] According to Mariavite sources, her supervisor Gruszczyńska tried to encourage Franciszka to marry a certain nobleman in exchange for financial benefits for the Congregation. When Koźmiński found out about this situation, he allowed Feliksa to leave Przytulisko in 1886.[104] That same year she was sent to Płock, where

---

Caesarea (330–379), where the right eye signified false teachers in the Church who were to be abandoned. See Kowalski, 'Krótki', 106.

99   Kazimierz M. J. Przyjemski, 'Mariae-Vita: Z Pamiętników Ojca Jana, Pierwszego Kapłana Mariawity', in *Święta Maria Franciszka Kozłowska i Jej Zgromadzenie*, 214.

100   Kowalski, 'Krótki', 99.

101   It was founded in 1882 by Kazimiera Gruszczyńska with the help of Koźmiński. It is significant that their patroness was Our Lady of Perpetual Help, who later became the patroness of the Mariavite Congregations. The history of the Congregation can be found in Kazimiera Gruszczyńska, *Historia Zgromadzenia Sióstr Franciszkanek od Cierpiących* (Krakow: Wyd. Avalon, 2019).

102   One of the men turned out to be a former monk who was unable to reconcile himself with the Church. Moved by Kozłowska's prayer, he decided to reconcile with God on the condition that she listen to his confession. Próchniewski, *Żywot*, 49–50.

103   She apparently saw Jesus and Francis of Assisi, who assured her that she should stay. Cf. ibid., 48. This was not the first time she had had a vision of a saint other than Jesus. She had previously seen Felix of Cantalice (1515–1587) in a dream who declared himself her religious patron saint. See Kozłowska, 'Mariae-Vita', 71.

104   Kowalski, 'Krótki', 109. Próchniewski wrote that Koźmiński was not fully convinced by the allegations against Gruszczyńska, but neither did he dismiss them as unfounded. Cf. Próchniewski, *Żywot*, 59. Later, it was believed that Kozłowska was

she managed the Zgromadzenie Sióstr Służek Najświętszej Maryi Panny Niepokalanej (the Congregation of the Servant Sisters of the Blessed Virgin Mary Immaculate)[105] and the Płock Tertiary Sisters, who worked mainly in factories.[106] There are divergent views on her prerogatives, but she undoubtedly acted on Koźmiński's behalf.[107] Soon after, on 8 September 1887, Franciszka established her own Congregation called Zgromadzenie Sióstr Ubogich św. Matki Klary (Poor Clares, officially the Order of Saint Clare, originally referred to as the Order of Poor Ladies) with the consent of her spiritual supervisor.[108] It was also known as Zgromadzenie Sióstr Adoratorek (Congregation of the Sisters of Adoration). There are various explanations as to why the Congregation had two separate names. One is that the name Poor Clares was only used between 1887 and 1888 and was then replaced by the name Congregation of the Sisters of Propitiative Adoration.[109] Despite the formation of her own Congregation, Maria Franciszka continued to visit other congregations to learn about their lives and to hold spiritual conferences with nuns. She also assisted Koźmiński in drafting the religious constitutions for them.[110]

---

expelled from Przytulisko because she showed little religious and monastic spirit. See Ewa K. Czaczkowska, *Mistyczki: Historie kobiet wybranych* (Krakow: Wyd. Znak, 2019), 280, but this does not agree with the earliest available sources and seems to be aimed solely at weakening the relationship between Kozłowska and Koźmiński.

105 The Congregation was created in 1878 by Koźmiński mainly to promote Christian values among rural people. The first superior was Rozalia Szumska (1856–1916). The Congregation was fully recognised by Rome in 1949. A brief history can be found in 'Historia Zgromadzenia', https://sluzki.pl/historia-zgromadzenia/.

106 Borys Przedpełski, 'Powstanie i rozwój Zgromadzenia Sióstr Mariawitek Nieustającej Adoracji Ubłagania w latach 1887–1921', in *MD II*, 22.

107 Perhaps she was sent to various congregations to observe their lives only for her own spiritual benefit, not to supervise them. Cf. Górecki, *Mariawici*, 41–42. On the other hand, she felt entitled to voice her opinions, which sometimes met with the displeasure of the nuns who did not want to listen to the young 'inspector'. See Próchniewski, *Żywot*, 59.

108 Koźmiński did not immediately agree since he thought it would be difficult to lead a life according to the Rule of Clare in a secret congregation, but he eventually gave his blessing to the initiative after Mateczka threatened to go abroad and join a regular convent. See ibid., 60. The problem of combining the contemplative life with the idea of hidden congregations recurred in later years. Cf. Elżbieta M. T. Dębowska, 'Mariae-Vita: Wspomnienia Siostry Elżbiety', in *Święta Maria Franciszka Kozłowska i Jej Zgromadzenie*, 164.

109 They were also known as Zgromadzenie Sióstr Ubogich św. Klary od Nieustającej Adoracji Ubłagania (Poor Clares of Propitiation Adoration). See Tomasz M. D. Mames, *Mysteria Mysticorum: Szkice z duchowości i historii Mariawitów* (Kraków: NOMOS, 2009), 84. For convenience, the name Poor Clares is retained below in this work.

110 Mames, *Eucharystia*, 14.

From the beginning, the Poor Clares lived in very poor conditions and were forced to change their place of residence seven times.[111] In addition to the Rule, they were also guided by their own constitutions, which have unfortunately been lost.[112] Fortunately, it is possible to reconstruct their life from other documents. Initially, they took the three traditional monastic vows – obedience, poverty and chastity – but soon added to these the obligatory adoration of the Blessed Sacrament.[113] Each day they got up at 5 am. After prayers and meditation, they went to Mass at 6. Their ordinary day was filled with work, spiritual readings, the recitation of the rosary and vespers. At half past eight they usually went to bed.[114] The Poor Clares wore ash-coloured dresses with hoods and white collars, slept on straw-filled mattresses and flagellated themselves three times a week.[115] Moreover, they eliminated meat from their diet and severely limited dairy products.[116] They did not solicit alms, working for their own livelihood and sharing their surpluses with the poor.[117] The sisters were mainly involved in sewing, embroidery, and manufacturing church items such In as liturgical vestments.[118] To disguise their religious identity they referred to themselves as employees of Pracownia robót kościelnych Pani Kozłowskiej (Ms. Kozłowska's Church Items Workshop).[119] Some local priests were informed about their true purposes. For example, Kazimierz Weloński (1831–1915), later an opponent of Maria Franciszka, listened to the sisters' confessions, supported them financially, consecrated their flat, and admitted some to the novitiate.[120] Kozłowska's mother did not support her daughter's wish initially to join the secret congregation.[121] After some time, however, she sold

111 It was later given a biblical explanation referring to 6 days of work and the 7th day of rest. See Kozłowska, 'Mariae-Vita', 100–102.

112 Przedpełski, 'Powstanie', 23.

113 It is said to have been added after a thief stole the items holding the Eucharist and desecrated the Blessed Sacrament by throwing it on the floor. Dębowska, 'Mariae-Vita', 163.

114 Ibid., 160–161.

115 Edward Warchoł, *Wybrane zagadnienia z historii mariawityzmu* (Radom: Wyd. Diecezjalne, 2007), 22.

116 'Jubileusz 50 – lecia istnienia Zgromadzenia Sióstr Mariawitek Nieustającej Adoracji Ubłagania 8.IX.1887–8.IX.1937', *KBNZ* 15 (1937): 2.

117 Even later opponents of Mariavitism praised the sisters for their charitable work and customs. Cf. Mazur, *Mariawityzm*, 18.

118 Kozłowska, 'Mariae-Vita', 101.

119 Tomasz M. D. Mames, *Oświata Mariawitów w latach 1906–1935* (Warsaw: Wyd. DiG, 2015), 22. Not even all the families of the sisters were informed of the formation of the Congregation. Cf. Dębowska, 'Mariae-Vita', 159.

120 Ibid., 173.

121 She wanted her daughter to join a more conventional convent, even if it was abroad. See Próchniewski, *Żywot*, 71.

the property in Warsaw and joined her daughter.[122] She eventually became a Mariavite nun, taking the name M. Hortulana. As in the case of Macrina (327–379) and Emmelia (d. 375), the daughter became the spiritual mother and teacher of her biological mother.[123] In the rules of the order established by Francis of Assisi, biological kinship was of no importance to the Poor Clares.[124] Thanks to her mother's financial assistance, Maria Franciszka was able to buy the property at 8 Dobrzyńska Street in 1894, where the sisters lived for several years.[125] The harsh living conditions were not the only problems faced by Maria Franciszka and her sisters. According to Antoni Julian Nowowiejski (1858–1941),[126] the nightly vigils, long fasts and mortifications, combined with the lack of supervision by the Church, made the sisters predisposed to raptures, visions, and mystical experiences.[127] Indeed, there are reports of supernatural phenomena occurring in the Congregation.[128] On the other hand, Kozłowska strongly opposed any symptoms of hysteria and exaltation among the sisters.[129] As in other convents, there were internal conflicts that sometimes ended in the departure or expulsion of some members.[130] But not all departures were accompanied

122 Warchoł wrote that she started living with the sisters in 1889. Cf. Warchoł, *Wybrane*, 23.

123 Anna M. Silvas, *Macrina the Younger: Philosopher of God* (Turnhout: Brepols, 2008), 2. Macrina lived in the fourth century in Caesarea in Cappadocia. Her younger brother was Gregory of Nyssa (c. 335–c. 394). She is considered a saint in the Catholic and Orthodox Churches.

124 Thompson (335–394), *Francis*, 40.

125 Gołębiowski, *Św. Maria*, 31–32.

126 In 1908, he became Bishop of the Diocese of Płock, and in 1999 Pope John Paul II beatified him. Nowowiejski admitted Przyjemski into the Franciscan Tertiary in the seminary. He was called to Mariavitism but rejected the proposal, becoming one of the movement's staunchest opponents. Some Mariavites believed that he embraced the Work of Great Mercy before his death, but this is not verifiable. Przysiecki rejected this view. Cf. Michał M. L. Jabłoński and Bronisław Dembowski et al., eds., *Dwustronna refleksja na temat podstawowych pism Matki Marii Franciszki Kozłowskiej dotyczących Dzieła Wielkiego Miłosierdzia* (Łódź – Włocławek: Wyd. ELWIT, 2006), 34–35.

127 Nowowiejski, *Płock*, 668.

128 Maria Franciszka's room was reported to have been full of light on some nights, and she was seen 'floating' (possibly levitating). See Kozłowska, 'Mariae-Vita', 107. However, these were the private observations of some sisters.

129 Przyjemski, 'Mariae-Vita', 217. It would be a mistake to make an analogy with members of the so-called 'New Prophecy' of the second century. We are told that one of their leaders, Montanus, used to fall into trance and ecstasy. He would go mad and talk nonsense while prophesying. Cf. Eusebius Pamphilus, *Ecclesiastical History I*, trans. Kirsopp Lake (London: William Heinemann, 1926), 475.

130 The overall rotation of sisters in secret congregations was quite high. See Joachim R. Bar, 'Z dziejów nowych form organizacyjnych stanów doskonałości w Polsce', *Prawo Kanoniczne* 3–4 (1965): 198.

Events Leading up to the 1893 Revelations

by hostility.[131] There were also a few attempts to replace Maria Franciszka in her leadership position.[132] All these conflicts have to be analysed individually, since the motivations of the sisters varied. Some of them came from other congregations where everything was done differently, others were not used to the strict lifestyle, and others may have felt that they were being treated unfairly.[133] One of the sisters who had left returned after a few years and was readmitted.[134] Despite the rotation and poor living conditions, the Congregation continued to grow and by 1892 numbered 18 sisters.[135]

---

131 One of the sisters returned later to ask for a blessing for her marriage. Cf. Dębowska, 'Mariae-Vita', 179.

132 Some sisters talked about it to Koźmiński behind Franciszka's back (Kozłowska, 'Mariae-Vita', 127) or, on other occasions, to Weloński. See Dębowska, 'Mariae-Vita', 180.

133 For example, Sister Jozafata had some health problems and was given some exemptions. Some sisters considered her useless and tried to get her expelled. Jozafata stayed until the end, proving herself to be a loyal and hardworking Mariavite. She later copied articles before they were printed and worked as a teacher, spending all her money on the Temple. Cf. Kozłowska, 'Mariae-Vita', 98–99.

134 Ibid., 99.

135 Dębowska, 'Mariae-Vita', 184.

Chapter 3

Mariavites in the Roman Catholic Church

This chapter begins with an analysis of arguably the most important moment in the history of Mariavites, namely, the revelation given to Kozłowska in 1893. This was understood as a foreshadowing of the fulfilment of the Apocalypse. Because the revelations were given by a woman, she was eventually understood as the 'woman clothed with the sun' (Rev 12:1), whose role was to fulfil God's will perfectly. We then focus on the spread of this movement in the Roman Catholic Church. Finally, we look at why it was finally condemned by the pope and the Catholic hierarchy in 1906. It is worth noting that many of the concepts of Mariavites that arose at that time were reinterpreted after the schism.

1. The Revelations of 1893

That response should not be, we deny the fact of your vision. It should be, Tell us the content of your vision. And then we will have to judge, not whether you had it or not, but whether we should follow it or not.

– J. D. Crossan, *The Birth of Christianity*

On 2 August 1893, Felicja Kozłowska attended a Mass at the St. John's seminary church in Płock. After the service, while praying in front of the painting of Mary Queen of Angels, Kozłowska is said to have suddenly found herself out of her senses and taken up into God's presence.[1] There she was shown the corruption of morality prevailing throughout the world. Responsibility for this deplorable state lay with immoral priests who were neglecting their religious duties.[2] As the world was approaching a just punishment, God decided to reach out with an offering of mercy, which could be obtained through devotion to the Blessed Sacrament and the intercession

---

1 She was believed to have entered the unapproachable light mentioned in 1 Tim 6:16. Próchniewski, *Żywot*, 125.

2 The sins and weaknesses of priests were also supposed to have been seen in the revelations to Wanda Malczewska (1907–2003). Czaczkowska, *Mistyczki*, 54–55.

of Our Lady of Perpetual Help.[3] To promote this initiative, known as the Work of Great Mercy, Kozłowska was instructed to found a religious group called the Mariavite Congregation,[4] consisting of Catholic priests. In addition to the Congregation of the Sisters of Adoration, the nuns also began an active Congregation of the Mariavite Sisters in 1893, based on the Third Rule of Saint Francis.[5]

From a social science perspective, it was not surprising that it was believed at the time in Poland that revelations had been received. People quite often had visions in periods of political and religious oppression or social upheaval.[6] The Poles, humiliated by a more powerful neighbour and unable to practise their Catholicism freely, tried to find ways to make their voice heard. In the second half of the nineteenth century, there were many reports of apparent apparitions of Mary or other Christian saints among Polish peasants.[7] Such apparitions were also known in other Catholic countries, above all in France (La Salette 1846, Lourdes 1858, Pontmain 1870; Tilly-sur-Seulles 1896–1899), but also in Germany (Marpingen 1876), Ireland (Knock 1879) or, a little later, in Portugal (Fatima 1917).[8] Mysticism, however, did not mean a severance of ties with Catholic tradition. Not only did political oppression not weaken the position of the Church, but it gave birth to a new awareness of Polish national identity, which was 'inseparable from traditional religiosity'.[9]

The revelations to Maria Franciszka were aimed at improving the deplorable state of the Catholic Church at the turn of the twentieth century, with their seemingly pretentious demand for the restoration of the

---

3   A certain similarity can be found in the vision given to Dominic Guzman (1170–1221), founder of the Dominican Order, who was believed to have seen an angry Jesus planning the annihilation of the world because of people's sins. He was appeased only when Mary introduced both Dominic and Francis to Jesus, convincing her Son that they would reform the Church. Cf. Philip H. Wiebe, *Visions of Jesus* (Oxford: Oxford University Press, 1997), 18.

4   Felicja M. F. Kozłowska, 'Początek Zawiązku Zgromadzenia Kapłanów', *DWM*, 5.

5   Mames, *Eucharystia*, 14.

6   Richard Heinberg, *Memories and Visions of Paradise: Exploring the Universal Myth of a Lost Golden Age* (Los Angeles: Jeremy P. Tarcher, 1989), 242. Heinberg is drawing on the work of Norman Cohn.

7   Ramet, *The Catholic*, 64.

8   Mary Heimann, 'Catholic Revivalism in Worship and Devotion', in *The Cambridge History of Christianity*, vol. 8, ed. Gilley and Stanley, 78.

9   Gabriel Adrianyi and Jerzy Kłoczowski, 'Catholic Nationalism in Great Hungary and Poland', in *The Cambridge istory of Christianity*, vol. 8, ed. Gilley and Stanley, 276. The Mariavites later criticised those Poles who treated religion merely as a tool to defend their national identity. Cf. 'Akt wiary czy demonstracja polityczna', *GP* 22 (1936): 170–172.

Eucharist-oriented devotion and reverence for Theotokos.[10] On the other hand, Marian devotion had experienced a revival in Catholic countries since the proclamation of the dogma of the Immaculate Conception in 1854.[11] As for the Eucharist, the first congresses entirely devoted to it were held in France in 1881, initiated by Emile Tamisier (1834–1910). Furthermore, Pius IX had already encouraged the Catholics, especially monks, to support the idea of perpetual adoration since 1851.[12] It is true that the Church in Congress Poland may have lagged behind due to the threatening political situation, but the oracles transmitted by Kozłowska were intended to reform the Catholic Church as a whole.[13] So what did the 1893 revelations bring that was new in the view of the Mariavites? Three points are worth mentioning. First, comparisons between the redemptive work of Jesus and the Work of the Great Mercy began to appear quite early.[14] Jesus was believed to have come at a time of incomparable moral decline.[15] Similarly, Mariavitism emerged, it was said, when the world was facing enormous corruption.[16] In both cases, we seem to be dealing with the typical exaggerated claims found in certain religious groups.[17] Such rhetoric can be used as a tool to help capture social or religious watershed moments, with biblical justification always available.[18] Second, the Mariavites were not the only ones to highlight the moral and religious crisis of the nineteenth century. Mickiewicz, for example, believed that the theologians and hierarchy of the Catholic Church were responsible for the moral decline in the Western world.[19] Mariavites followed him in his

10 Górecki, *Mariawici*, 26.
11 Societies dedicated to Mary flourished especially in Spain and Portugal in the second half of the nineteenth century. William J. Callahan, 'Spain and Portugal: The Challenge to the Church', in *The Cambridge History of Christianity*, vol. 8, ed. Gilley and Stanley, 391.
12 Banaszak, *Historia*, 376.
13 'DMHM IV', *MCPS* 22 (1907): 352.
14 Kozłowska, 'Początek', 28.
15 'Nowy Testament, Wstęp', *MCPS* 25 (1907): 389–392. The anonymous author of the second-century epistle to Diognetus wrote that unjust way of life came to fruition and human wickedness reached its peak. See 'Epistle to Diognetus 9', in *The Apostolic Fathers II*, ed. and trans. Bart D. Ehrman (Harvard: Harvard University Press, 2003), 149.
16 'DMHM. Wstęp', *MCPS* 6 (1907): 94–96.
17 Modern research tempers such radical conclusions about the social background of events taking place in the first century. Cf. Bart D. Ehrman, *The Triumph of Christianity: How a Forbidden Religion Swept the World* (New York: Simon & Schuster, 2018), 74–105.
18 For example, as the Bible states: 'The people walking in darkness have seen a great light; on those living in the land of deep darkness a light has dawned' (Isa 9:2).
19 Adam Mickiewicz, *L'église et le messie II* (Paris: Comptoir des Imprimeurs-Unis, 1845), 16–17: 'C'est ainsi qu'après les apôtres et les thaumaturges vien nent les théologiens et les casuistes …. Ainsi a fini le monde grec, ainsi finit le monde occidental'.

ideas that the Catholic Church had lost its connection to heaven and that only courageous individuals, including some outside the Catholic Church such as Martin Luther or Emanuel Swedenborg (1688–1772), sought to find the unity of matter and spirit. This unity was the sine qua non for the introduction of the Kingdom of Heaven on earth.[20] Third, although the Mariavites acknowledged the reforms in the Catholic Church, they thought those reforms lacked the Spirit of God.[21] Despite Leo XIII's reforms, the majority of Poles only received communion during major religious feasts, mainly because of the cumbersome preparations preceding admission to communion and the assumption that the Eucharist was a reward for a good life rather than a remedy to help people in their faith.[22]

The Mariavites classified revelations according to the model promoted by the Jesuit G. B. Scaramelli (1687–1752).[23] They distinguished between corporeal, imaginary, and intellectual visions.[24] Only the latter are immune

---

20 Mickiewicz expected the Holy Spirit to take possession of the earth again and placed great emphasis on direct contact between God and humans. 'Maryawityzm Mickiewicza', *WDM* 20 (1909): 153–155. He was inspired by representatives of French Utopianism as well as by J. G. Fichte (1762–1814) and F. W. J. Schelling, and their philosophical theory of *intellektuelle Anschauung*, which claimed that the mind is able to grasp knowledge without the mediation of the senses. See Xavier Tilliette, *Untersuchungen über die intellektuelle Anschauung von Kant bis Hegel* (Stuttgart and Bad Cannstatt: Frommann-Holzboog, 2015).

21 The Eucharistic Congresses were seen by the Mariavites as primarily tools for manifesting political identity. However, they later claimed that, to some extent, the congresses reflected the Work of Great Mercy. Cf. 'Święty Franciszek – Matka Marja Franciszka', *GSK* 34 (1938): 530. When necessary, the Mariavites were ready to defend the events. For instance, when Czesław Lechicki (1906–2001), a Polish publicist, became a member of the Evangelical Lutheran Church, the Mariavites applauded his courage in manifesting his religious convictions but criticised him for misrepresenting the Catholic understanding of the Eucharist and attacking the Congress. See Roman M. J. Próchniewski, 'Kongresy Eucharystyczne', *GSK* 25 (1938): 385–387.

22 In fact, the frequency of receiving the Sacrament varied. In the sixteenth century, due to the activities of the Jesuits, the frequency slightly increased (Sanak, 'Kult'). In later centuries, however, it was not very high. It seems that from the twelfth century on, Christians focused more on the cult of the Eucharist, e.g. kneeling before it rather than receiving it, feeling unworthy. Cf. Janusz Gręźlikowski, 'Przechowywanie i kult Eucharystii w ustawodawstwie synodalnym Polski przedrozbiorowej', *Prawo Kanoniczne: kwartalnik prawno-historyczny* 55 (2012): 115.

23 It was most likely based on the model developed by Augustine (354–430) in his *Literal Meaning of Genesis*, in which he distinguished between corporeal visions (seen with physical eyes), spiritual visions (seen with inner eyes) and intellectual visions (seen with the eyes of the intellect). See Emmanuel Bermon, *Le cogito dans la pensée de saint Augustin* (Paris: Librairie Philosophique Vrin, 2001), 156.

24 It is important to note that the classification was considered to have been given by God to Mateczka. Cf. Felicja M. F. Kozłowska, 'Wyjątki z Objawień w roku 1899 i 1900', *DWM*, 35.

to illusions. According to the Mariavites, these were the visions Mateczka had most often.[25] Intellectual visions are said to be transmitted by the Deity directly to the mind of the recipient. They are allegedly used in communication between God and angels or souls residing in heaven. It is also believed that they were employed in paradise before the Fall.[26] Because they leave permanent traces in the memory of the recipient, it is not necessary to write them down immediately.[27] Most saints received such visions in a state of ecstasy (*in exthasi*) or rapture (*in raptu*).[28] Like Mary, Mateczka was said to have known God's will without being in either state.[29] The recipient can reject the revelations or disregard their content. Maria Franciszka allowed the idea that she was delusional and did not consider herself worthy of the revelations, which allegedly led Jesus to reprimand her.[30] A similar fate befell Angela Merici (1474–1540), who was also said to experience visions of an angry Jesus when she disregarded the message she had received.[31]

Mateczka's revelations contained some ambiguous terms without adequate explanation. Particularly difficult to understand was the reference to the end times.[32] It was quickly juxtaposed with eschatological passages in the New Testament, such as Mt 24:12 ('Because of the increase of wickedness, the love of most will grow cold'), Mt 24:21 ('For then there will

---

25 'DMHM II', *MCPS* 11 (1907): 175. It was, however, believed that she had experienced all types. See Tomasz M. D. Mames, 'Maria Franciszka Kozłowska, osobowość mistyczki', *PNS* 23 (2001): 8–15. The idea of mixing authentic and inauthentic visions can already be found in the Apostolic Fathers. Cf. Hermas, 'Shepherd of Hermas', in *The Apostolic Fathers II*, 285.

26 'Pismo Święte. Księga Rodzaju. Uwagi do Rozdziału III', *MCPS* 6 (1907): 87–88.

27 Mateczka was believed to invariably repeat the revelations. See Kowalski, 'Krótki', 92. This was in line with the ancient belief that the words of authentic oracles must not be forgotten. Cf. Eusebius, *Ecclesiastical History I*, 461.

28 Paul, for example, described the vision *in raptu* (and probably in *exthasi*) in 2 Cor 12:2-4. See Próchniewski, *Żywot*, 113.

29 Ibid., 113. However, in 1907, the statement that she had been out of her senses was understood to indicate a rapture. It was also reported that she was in a state of ecstasy. Cf. 'DMHM II', *MCPS* 11 (1907): 173–174. Mariavite nuns claimed that they were unable to determine when she received the revelations, and for many years they did not even know that she had had them. See Konrad M. P. Rudnicki, 'Współczesne objawienia', *PNS* 20 (2001): 23.

30 Kozłowska, 'Początek', 14. The Mariavites did not think that Mateczka seriously doubted the authenticity of the vision, but, being humble, she could not understand why she had been chosen. Similarly, Mary could not believe that God had chosen her to be the mother of Jesus because of her humility. Cf. 'Niepokalana Marya', 793.

31 Wiebe, *Visions*, 18. Merici founded the Company of St Ursula and is recognised as a saint in the Catholic Church. She was canonised in 1807 by Pope Pius VII (pontificate 1800–1823).

32 Kozłowska, 'Początek', 5.

be great distress, unequaled from the beginning of the world until now') and Mt 24:15 ('So when you see standing in the holy place 'the abomination that causes desolation', spoken of through the prophet Daniel').[33] The Mariavites most likely believed from the very beginning that the end times did not refer to the literal destruction of the planet but were allusions to:

1. The corruption of morality and departure from God;
2. The mercy that God wanted to bestow on people to make them spiritually reborn;
3. The fulfilment of the book of Revelation.[34]

They were convinced that the Apocalypse could not be sufficiently explained without the Work of Great Mercy.[35] Depending on how one reads 2 Thess 3:10 ('The one who is unwilling to work shall not eat'), it can be argued that Paul objected to those who believed that the literal destruction of the planet was imminent and there was no longer any reason to continue with physical labour.[36] Similarly, the Mariavites did not expect rapid destruction because they immediately began to build many religious and social institutions.[37] If they believed that the world was coming to an end, they would most likely have focused their efforts on other activities, such as increased prayer or missionary efforts. It is worth noting that the Mariavites found confirmation of their ideas in the literature of other Christians. For example, after their union with the Old Catholics in 1909, they discovered that Johannes Heijkamp (1824–1892), the Old Catholic archbishop of Utrecht from 1875 to1892, published a book called *Znaki Czasu* (The Signs of the Time) in which, based on prophecies from the New Testament, he tried to demonstrate that the end times had already come.[38]

Finally, one might venture to say that the biggest problem with the revelations lay not in their content but in the fact that they were

---

33 The last verse was understood to refer to the priests. Cf. 'DM', *MCPS* 1 (1907): 12–13.

34 'DMHM II', *MCPS* 12 (1907): 191. The same interpretation was put forward in the 1940s, meaning that it was widely accepted. Próchniewski, *Żywot*, 120.

35 Próchniewski, *Żywot*, 120. They followed Justin Martyr (100–165), who claimed that prophets from time to time uttered oracles that were fulfilled centuries later. Cf. Justin Martyr, 'The First Apology', in *Writings of Saint Justin Martyr*, trans. Thomas D. Falls (Washington: The Catholic University of America Press, 1948), 78–79.

36 There are good reasons to read this as a social problem rather than an eschatological one, but there are many different opinions. See Ronald Russell, 'The Idle in 2 Thess. 3.6-12: An Eschatological or a Social Problem?', *NTS* 34 (1988): 105–119.

37 Mazur, *Mariawityzm*, 42–45.

38 'Historya Kościoła w Holandyi', *KM* (1910): 87–88.

communicated by a woman.[39] This can be illustrated by several examples. At Koźmiński's behest, Maria Franciszka kept a diary in which she recorded her inner experiences. On 15 August 1893, Jesus promised that she would receive authority (*moc*) over the priests, but she was afraid to put this information in the diary, knowing that such power was not expected from a woman.[40] Felicjan M. Franciszek Strumiłło (1861–1895), the first Mariavite, wondered whether there had ever been an instance in the history of the Church when a woman had been placed above men spiritually.[41] When Kozłowska presented her doubts to God, God revealed to her that Jesus had been under Mary's protection as a child.[42] Her authority was not to be the same as that of the bishops but was to be limited to spiritual guidance.[43] She was to be known as the Mistress and Mother.[44] This issue troubled Koźmiński for some time, but eventually he was able to find cases from the past that alleviated his concerns. For example, the Rule of the Poor Clares edited by Pope Urban VIII (pontificate 1623–1644) contained a clause ordering the chaplain to vow obedience to the mother superior of the convent because 'mulieres non sunt capaces potestat (is) ordinis, sed non iurisdictionis' ('women cannot be ordained as priests, but can have jurisdiction, i.e., spiritual authority').[45] This was not enough, however,

---

39 As rightly pointed out by Marzia A. Coltri, even new religious movements (and the Mariavites can be counted among them) have often excluded women from leadership roles. Cf. Marzia A. Coltri, 'Women and NRMs: Location and Identity', *in Female Leaders in New Religious Movements*, ed. Christian Giudice, Inga B. Tøllefsen (Cham: Palgrave Macmillan, 2017), 11–28. However, the same book discusses the cases of Ellen G. White, Elizabeth Clare Prophet and Mary Ann de Grimston, which challenge these conclusions.

40 This information was contained in a letter written by Kozłowska between 5 and 11 November 1893. See Felicja M. F. Kozłowska, 'List drugi', *PNS* 7 (1998): 17–18. The noun *moc* is often translated as 'power', 'force', and 'mightiness'. 'Moc', https://dictionary.cambridge.org/pl/dictionary/polish-english/moc. In my view, the word 'authority' best fits the context.

41 He was appointed to deal with economic matters at the Płock seminary. He called Maria Franciszka the dove with an olive branch from Noah's ark, a symbol of peace given to the whole world. Strumiłło died prematurely in Gorizia on 25 November 1895. Przyjemski, 'Mariae-Vita', 222–238.

42 She was also told that many priests follow ungodly women and that they could follow pious ones for a change. Felicja M. F. Kozłowska, 'Pierwotny tekst Objawień Mateczki', *DWM*, 123–125.

43 Kozłowska, 'Początek', 15–16.

44 She was called Mistress because her role was to teach the principles of monastic life and Mother because she gave birth to the Congregation. 'DMHM II', 192.

45 Both Colette of Corbie (1381–1447) and Teresa of Avila (1515–1582) were to be obeyed by priests; Catherine of Siena was to guide her confessor spiritually; Francis de Sales (1567–1622) would open his conscience to Joanna de Chantal (1572–1641); and

to change the general attitude of the Poles living in Congress Poland who constituted a traditional society for the most part and were suspicious of changes.[46] Therefore, when Weloński began to publicly accuse Mariavite priests of listening to a woman, they were subjected to derision from both the laity and other clergy.[47] Their attempts to defend themselves by citing the example of Bridget of Sweden (1303–1373), who founded the Order of the Most Holy Saviour (informally known as the Bridgettine Order) which also included monks, did not have the desired effect.[48] It is said that the Bishop of Płock, Jerzy Józef Szembek (1851–1905), contemptuously remarked that Jesus visited Ms Kozłowska for a cup of tea.[49] Rev. Jan Gajkowski published a pamphlet *Gdzie Dyabeł nie może, tam babę pośle* (Where the devil cannot go himself he sends a woman) in 1909.[50] The title referred to the Polish expression that women were more capable of leading men into sin than the devil, which certainly echoed ancient religious ideas about the danger of women.[51] The idea that a woman could be the head of the church was ridiculed even by children.[52] Agnieszka Graff was probably right when she stated that most Poles viewed women in leading roles in

---

finally Francis of Assisi consulted Clare (1194–1253) on religious matters (1194–1253). Cf. Kozłowska, 'Początek', 21.

46 For example, when iron ploughs appeared in the Polish countryside at the turn of the twentieth century, many peasants believed that this could bring vengeance from the soil. Cf. Andrzej Szyjewski, *Etnologia religii* (Krakow: NOMOS, 2008), 52.

47 He is said to have called Mateczka Satan because she would lead many priests astray. See Warchoł, *Wybrane*, 18.

48 Its statutes contained a point stating that the abbess had the prerogative to supervise monks. Cf. 'DMHM III', *MCPS* 17 (1907): 270.

49 'DMHM IV', *MCPS* 23 (1907): 364.

50 Gajkowski acknowledges that there were many holy women but states that some were Lucifer's equal in evil. See Jan Gajkowski, *Gdzie Dyabeł nie może, tam babę pośle* (Sandomierz: Drukarnia W. Byrzyński, 1909), 1. He also published a second pamphlet against Maria Franciszka and the Mariavites: *Prawda o Kozłowitach, albo mankietnikach ku przestrodze tym, którzy jeszcze rozumu i wiary nie stracili* (The Truth about Kozłowici, or Wearing Cuffs as a Warning to Those Who Have Not Yet Lost their Reason and Faith). He was sentenced to three weeks in jail for these works. See Gołębiowski, *Św. Maria*, 64.

51 James G. Crossley, 'History from the Margins: The Death of John the Baptist', in *Writing History, Constructing Religion*, ed. James G. Crossley, Christian Karner (Aldershot: Ashgate, 2005), 149–153.

52 Leszek Radzikowski, 'Motywy mariawickie w pamiętnikach Leszka Radzikowskiego', PNS 16 (2000): 14. Czernohorski-Fehérváry (1917–1984), a convert to Mariavitism from Hungary, admitted that the most difficult thing for him was to accept the idea that a woman founded the Church. But it was explained to him that it was Jesus who founded the Church and Mateczka was only called to found the Congregation. See Juliusz M. O. Czernohorski, 'Z misji Marjawickiego Kościoła na Węgrzech'm *GSK* 32 (1939): 510–511.

Christian churches to be a travesty.⁵³ They were not sufficiently qualified to deal with serious religious concepts.⁵⁴ This was due to the fact that they were not taught Latin or Greek, which rendered them unable to understand the Mass or study critical editions of the Bible.⁵⁵ The only way in which women could exercise religious authority was informally behind closed doors.⁵⁶ The public domain was reserved exclusively for men.⁵⁷ Unsurprisingly, some scholars have attributed the reasons for the development of Mariavitism to 'the persistence and devotion of peasant women who resisted pressure from both the Catholic Church and other lay Catholic believers'.⁵⁸

2. The Spread of the Congregation

Despite some doubts as to the authenticity of the revelations, Koźmiński allowed Kozłowska to continue forming the Congregation.⁵⁹ In 1893, only two priests were admitted. The first was Strumiłło, confessor of the Poor

---

53 Agnieszka Graff, *Świat bez kobiet. Płeć w polskim życiu publicznym* (Warsaw: Wyd. W.A.B., 2001), 35.

54 The view that women in Congress Poland were merely passive recipients has been challenged by some researchers who have pointed to their religious creativity. Cf. Włodzimierz Mędrzecki, 'Konwenans wiejski i nowe wzorce zachowań kobiet na wsi w Królestwie Polskim na przełomie XIX i XX wieku', in *Kobieta i kultura życia codziennego: Wiek XIX i XX. Zbiór studiów*, ed. Anna Żarnowska and Andrzej Szwarc (Warsaw: Wyd. DiG, 1997), 85–86.

55 Maria Franciszka, undoubtedly a very pious woman who attended church regularly, could not understand all the readings from the Bible or the sermons preached at Mass. See Kozłowska, 'Początek', 7. She knew some Latin, but very little: she could quote a few Latin phrases and say a few prayers in Latin. Cf. Konrad M. P. Rudnicki, 'Niezwykła książka o mariawityzmie', *PNS* 43 (2006): 22.

56 One priest is said to have abandoned Mariavitism because his biological mother forbade him to remain in the Congregation. It was believed that other women had supreme authority in some parishes but could only exercise influence in secret. Cf. Kowalski, 'Krótki', 145.

57 Many women at that time treated their spouses mainly as guardians rather than equal partners. See Agnieszka Lisak, *Miłość, kobieta, małżeństwo w XIX wieku* (Warszawa: Bellona, 2009), 26.

58 Dominik Gruziel, *At the Crossroads of New Catholicism and the 'Woman Question': Polish Roman Catholic Laywomen's Social Activism on Behalf of Women in the Three Zones of Partitioned Poland, 1878–1918* (Budapest: Central European University, unpublished PhD Thesis, 2012), 61.

59 Initially, he called these revelations 'diabolical illusions given to justify Kozłowska's sins'. Cf. Kozłowska, 'Pierwotny', 124. But a year later, he reportedly claimed that they came from God. Przyjemski, 'Mariae-Vita', 233.

Clares since 1888.⁶⁰ The second was Kazimierz M. Jan Przyjemski (1868–1920), who proved to be a zealous missionary, attracting many new members, also from outside the diocese of Płock.⁶¹ Those who joined did not receive information about other associates, and many had never heard of Maria Franciszka and her revelations.⁶² This was primarily due to the fear of political repercussions as well as the belief that not everyone was ready to receive solid food without adequate preparation.⁶³ More fundamental at this point was the encouragement of a large number of lay priests to transform their lives according to the paths set out by the monks. Mateczka was fully aware that it was not possible to implement all the precepts of the Franciscan First Rule, since a lay priest simply could not function without property. Nevertheless, she allegedly obtained a certain dispensation from Jesus.⁶⁴ It should be noted that not all priests responded favourably to the call, believing that Maria Franciszka was unable to legitimise her actions.⁶⁵ These individuals posed a double threat to the movement. First, they could have disclosed the entire initiative to others, potentially in a distorted form. Second, if the information had reached the ecclesiastical authorities, they might have put a stop to it because of a well-founded fear of the secular

---

60 Warchoł, *Wybrane*, 23. Mateczka thought he would become director of the Congregation, but his health prevented him from taking up the position. See Edward Warchoł, *Reakcja biskupa Jerzego Szembeka na formowanie się ideologii religijnej i kształtowanie się struktury organizacyjnej mariawitów* (Radom: Wyd. Diecezjalne, 2006), 15.

61 After graduating from St Petersburg Academy, he became a professor at Płock seminary. He made the decision to join the Congregation after hearing an inner voice and had previously considered joining the Jesuits. Cf. Przyjemski, 'Mariae-Vita', 225. He is sometimes referred to – although anachronistically – as the first supervisor.

62 As late as 1900, most of Mariavite priests in the diocese of Warsaw knew nothing about Mateczka. See Kowalski, 'Krótki', 143.

63 Gradual disclosure, of which the Mariavites were aware, was known in ancient Christianity. For example, Origen (c. 185–c. 253), drawing on 1 Cor 3:2-3, wrote that some truths are concealed if the hearers are not yet prepared to receive them. Cf. Origen, *Contra Celsum 3:51-54*, trans. by Henry Chadwick (Cambridge: Cambridge University Press, 1953), 163–165. The Polish messianists were not given all the secrets at once until they could fully understand them. The example of Jesus receiving first virgin milk and only later solid food was used as an explanation for such a procedure. See Kowalski, 'Słowo wstępne na Wykład Apokalipsy', 715–716.

64 It was believed that, as the author of the Rule, Jesus could modify it to suit new circumstances. Cf. Kozłowska, 'Początek', 23.

65 Kozłowska, 'Pierwotny', 132. She could only refer to moral changes in the lives of the priests, which was reminiscent of the Christian apologetic tactics of the second century, known as 'the triumphal song of the apologists'. Apologists attempted to affirm the authenticity of Christianity by drawing attention to the sudden change in the morals of believers after conversion. Cf. Justin Martyr, 'The First Apology', 47.

authorities.⁶⁶ Apart from occasional taunts, however, the first years of the Congregation's existence did not bring any major obstacles.⁶⁷

Like any organisation, the Catholic Church is not free of internal factions vying for greater influence. One group that found itself in opposition to the Mariavites was centred around Aleksander Zaremba (1857–1907) and Nowowiejski.⁶⁸ Both believed that the house of the Mariavite nuns was a hub of unwanted gossip and that Mateczka interfered too much in the internal affairs of the diocese.⁶⁹ In the opinion of the Mariavites, Nowowiejski had other reasons for opposing them. He was reportedly involved with Jakobina Łabanowska, who initially remained under Koźmiński's supervision but later, together with Nowowiejski, established Zakład Anioła Stróża (The Institution of the Guardian Angel) for girls in need of material and moral support.⁷⁰ Her disloyalty to Koźmiński was openly criticised by Kozłowska.⁷¹ Indeed, there were some disagreements between Nowowiejski and Koźmiński regarding secret congregations.⁷² It is worth noting that Przyjemski was accepted into the Third Order of Saint Francis by Nowowiejski already when the former was in seminary.⁷³ By uniting with Kozłowska, Przyjemski became associated with Koźmiński,

---

66   If the hierarchs had learned prematurely that the idea had become public knowledge, they would certainly not have risked supporting it. They acted cautiously with regard to all secret congregations. See Werner, *O. Honorat*, 529.

67   On one occasion, for example, Mariavite nuns found a three-year-old boy abandoned on the steps of their house. On Weloński's advice, Maria Franciszka took care of the child but after some time gave him to a charitable home. This gave rise to hostile rumours that it was the child of Przyjemski and Kozłowska. Cf. 'Sprostowanie fałszywych wiadomości o Maryawitach', *WDM* 34 (1907): 271.

68   Mateczka wanted to involve Zaremba in this initiative, but Jesus reportedly forbade her to do so. See Kozłowska, 'Początek', 9. Nowowiejski criticized Mateczka as early as 1894. Cf. Kozłowska, 'Pierwotny', 134.

69   Przyjemski, 'Mariae-Vita', 242. Mateczka resolutely objected to the sisters spreading rumours. This means that some of them were indeed responsible for it, but they acted without the Superior's permission. See Felicja M. F. Kozłowska, 'Notatki, jakie Mateczka sobie poczyniła, mając mieć konferencję do Sióstr', in *Ku Królestwu*, 84. The notes are not dated and were most likely written after the break with Rome, but the general principle seems to predate this event.

70   The Institution of the Guardian Angel was incorporated in 1899 into the Congregation of the Sisters of Our Lady of Mercy (Congregatio Sororum Beatae Mariae Misericordiae), of which Faustina Kowalska (1905–1938) later became a member. The revelations given to Kowalska, which also concerned God's mercy, are understood by some Mariavites to be similar to those received by Kozłowska. Cf. Konrad M. P. Rudnicki, 'Porównanie różnych Objawień Miłosierdzia Bożego', in *Teologia Miłosierdzia Bożego*, Konrad M. P. Rudnicki et al., eds. (Płock: KSM, 2003), 185–194.

71   'DMHM IV', *MCPS* 22 (1907): 349.

72   Koźmiński even called Nowowiejski his fiercest enemy. See Górecki, *Mariawici*, 34.

73   Przyjemski, 'Mariae-Vita', 223.

something Nowowiejski certainly did not appreciate. Divisions in the Church caused by the Mariavites were one reason why some clergymen disliked them.

Nevertheless, occasional disputes and quarrels could not stop the Congregation from growing. The third priest to join was Gołębiowski in 1894. Two years later, Ignacy M. Tomasz Kłopotowski (1866–1931) became the first Mariavite in the diocese of Lublin.[74] It was mainly due to his involvement in charitable activities that the Mariavite Sisters were able to establish collaboration with the Lublin Charity Society and carry out their activities in Łowicz.[75] The aforementioned Próchniewski was also recruited from the diocese of Lublin in 1896. By 1897, there were already 20 Mariavite priests, valued by the hierarchy for their pastoral work, and about 40 nuns.[76] As their numbers increased, the Mariavites decided to adopt somewhat more rigid organisational forms.[77] Problems soon began to appear on the horizon, however. In April 1897, Mateczka had a vision of Satan's legions ready to attack, and at the same time God revealed to her that some priests would leave the Congregation.[78] The first public controversy erupted when Weloński began to publicly accuse the Mariavites from the pulpit. His motives are not entirely known, and this was not the first time he did this.[79] The Mariavites believed that he had become jealous after discovering that he had not been elected superior of the female convent. He was also certainly disturbed by the fact that a secret organisation of priests

---

74 He left the Congregation in 1904 and later founded Zgromadzenie Sióstr Matki Bożej Loretańskiej (the Congregation of the Sisters of Our Lady of Loretto) and was beatified in 2005 with the approval of Pope Benedict XVI (pontificate 2005–2013). Surprisingly, some contemporary authors not only fail to mention that Kłopotowski was once a Mariavite, but they also present him as an uncompromising opponent of a 'sect' that 'spread unbelief through the villages and slandered the Roman Catholic Church'. He is portrayed as a defender of the Catholic faith and Polish nationality, which assumes that the Mariavites opposed both. See Józef Warzeszak, 'Wartości religijno – patriotyczne w piśmiennictwie Sługi Bożego ks. Ignacego Kłopotowskiego (1866–1931)', *Warszawskie Studia Teologiczne* 17 (2004): 253–254.

75 Gołębiowski, *W obronie*, 66.

76 Rybak, *Mariawityzm*, 11. Stanisław Gall (1865–1942), a vice-rector of the Warsaw seminary and future bishop, was keen to use the Mariavites as retreat preachers. Cf. Dorota Sobala, 'Mariawici spowiednikami w Kościele Rzymskokatolickim', *PNS* 42 (2006): 5.

77 Each diocese chose a spiritual supervisor. Przyjemski was chosen for Płock, Kłopotowski for Lublin, and Boleslaw M. Łukasz Wiechowicz (1869–1924) for Warsaw. See 'DMHM III', *MCPS* 16 (1907): 251.

78 Ibid., 251.

79 He had previously publicly criticised Łabanowska, also from the pulpit, and threatened Nowowiejski with removal from the seminary. Cf. 'DMHM IV', *MCPS* 22 (1907): 349.

had been established on his premises without his knowledge or consent.⁸⁰ Consequently, he demanded that Kozłowska return the money he had lent her to buy a house for the nuns.⁸¹ The whole situation probably attracted the attention of the Russian authorities and became a stumbling block in relations between the Catholic hierarchy and the Mariavites.⁸² A process of transerring priests to the remotest parishes began in order to sever the ties linking them to Maria Franciszka. This, however, only led to the spread of their ideas.⁸³ The deteriorating situation did not stop the enthusiasm of the Mariavites, who still planned to go to Rome to inform the pope of their existence.⁸⁴

Knowledge of the existence of the Congregation was not equivalent to knowledge of the revelations.⁸⁵ Only a relatively small group of people knew about them. The Mariavites from the beginning tried to inform the hierarchy but did not want to expose anyone to political consequences. Koźmiński advised that the matter should be presented to the bishops only after the Congregation had been internally regulated.⁸⁶ Przyjemski went to Bishop Michał Nowodworski (1831–1896) on 15 February 1894 to inform him about the changes he had made in his life.⁸⁷ At their next

---

80   The whole initiative was so secret that even the Mariavite sisters were not informed of the existence of the men's Congregation. Some of them mistakenly assumed that Przyjemski had been singled out to take control of them, as he had attended one of their meetings. One of the sisters soon reported this to Weloński who had also received information about the Congregation from a former Mariavite priest. See 'DMHM III', *MCPS* 16 (1907): 252.

81   Kozłowska, 'Protokół', 26–27.

82   Mateczka became known internationally; cf. Kozłowska, 'Początek', 24. According to the Mariavites, two priests, Czaplicki, a prelate of the Płock Chapter, and Szulborski, dean in Janowo Podlaskie, denounced them in 1897 to the governor-general in Warsaw. As a result, the Mariavites were closely watched by the Russian authorities. See Próchniewski, *Żywot*, 167. The reader must be cautious about accepting such testimonies uncritically, as they could be based on gossip. In addition, Koźmiński stated that the Russian authorities tolerated secret assemblies for many years, so even if they had known about the Mariavites, they would not necessarily have acted by force immediately. Cf. Werner, *O. Honorat*, 524.

83   Górecki, *Mariawici*, 61–62.

84   Koźmiński told them that such action would be premature. See Roman M. J. Próchniewski, 'Mariae-vita: Pamiętniki Brata Biskupa Jakóba', *KBNZ* 10 (1931): 75.

85   Stobiecki claimed that Mariavitism may have been known, to varying degrees, in about 70% of all dioceses in Congress Poland. Cf. Ignacy Stobiecki, 'Próba oceny', *PNS* 9 (1998): 25.

86   As an example, he cited the Association of Secular Priests, which operated in secret for many years until they notified the bishops and the pope of their existence and were approved. See Kozłowska, 'Początek', 22.

87   This was met with a positive response from the hierarchy. Cf. Przyjemski, 'Mariae-Vita', 229.

meeting, on 13 November 1895, Przyjemski went a step further, telling the bishop that a penitent had come to him with some visions and even read extracts from the revelations to the bishop. Nowodworski replied that they contained good things but were too general. Maria Franciszka visited the bishop in person on 3 December 1895, but it is not certain whether they discussed anything more than the statutes of the Congregation of Sisters. Wincenty Petrykowski (1845–1927), who administered the Płock diocese for several years after Nowodworski's death, received the revelations to read in 1896.[88] He recognised them as God's work, but found some passages too vague and decided not to join the Congregation.[89] The revelations were recognised as authentic by the Jesuit priest Henryk Pydynkowski (1847–1936), whose retreat Kozłowska had attended in Warsaw in 1896.[90] When it became known that Bishop Franciszek Albin Symon (1841–1918), rector of the theological school in St Petersburg, was being considered for a vacancy in the diocese of Płock, Przyjemski travelled to Russia to meet the possible superior and acquaint him with Mariavitism. Symon praised the idea of the Congregation but did not like some of the passages contained in the revelations. He pointed out that they contained contradictory statements regarding the role of bishops.[91] He also disliked the idea of a woman interfering in the lives of priests.[92] Eventually, Symon failed to obtain a position in Płock and was exiled by the Russian authorities to Odessa because of a conflict caused by the use of the Russian language during religious services.[93] The Auxiliary Bishop of Warsaw, Kazimierz Ruszkiewicz (1836–1925), was informed about the Mariavite statutes on 27 February

---

88 The Diocese of Płock had no bishop for five years (1896–1901). See Górecki, *Mariawici*, 30.

89 One possible reason would be to disrupt the hierarchy. He would have had to take religious orders from his subordinate'. Nevertheless, he expressed positive feelings towards the Mariavites even afterwards, assuring them that he would not betray their cause. Cf. Przyjemski, 'Mariae-Vita', 240–242.

90 Próchniewski, *Żywot*, 129.

91 There are some seemingly contradictory statements in early Mariavitism regarding obedience to Polish bishops. Maria Franciszka may, however, have been misunderstood in this regard. See Krzysztof Mazur, 'Refleksje po lekturze książki ks. Edwarda Warchoła "Reakcja biskupa Jerzego Szembeka na formowanie się ideologii religijnej i kształtowanie się struktury organizacyjnej mariawitów"', *PNS* 52 (2009): 34–35.

92 Maria Franciszka was advised to deal exclusively with the sisters, while the priests could form the Congregation on their own. Despite the presence of a woman, Symon felt that the initiative was taken in the right spirit. Cf. Krzysztof Mazur, 'Marii Franciszki Kozłowskiej zmagania z nieteologiczną rzeczywistością', in *MD I*, 211.

93 Banaszak, *Historia*, 306.

1899 and blessed them.[94] The five-year period without a bishop in Płock ended in 1901, when Szembek was elected the new Ordinary of the Płock diocese. On the second day after his investiture, he was told by Przyjemski about the Work of Great Mercy.[95] Despite his supposedly positive attitude towards the Mariavite priests, he soon declared finis mysticorum. This is understood by the Mariavites as a declaration of the end of the movement, at least in the Catholic Church. Consequently, Szembek is regarded as one of the leading figures that led to the condemnation of Mariavitism.[96]

3. Attempts to Obtain Official Approval in Rome

In December 1902, Maria Franciszka wrote down her revelations with the intention of passing them on to the bishops.[97] Kowalski, Gołębiowski, and Próchniewski were asked to make copies of the revelations and deliver them to the three hierarchs in January 1903. Kowalski went to the Warsaw Archbishop Popiel, but the latter did not accept the text, presumably fearing repercussions. Ruszkiewicz did so on his behalf.[98] Próchniewski went to the Bishop of Lublin, Franciszek Jaczewski (1832–1914), who also refused to accept it. The only person who officially received the text was Szembek. Together with the professors of the Płock seminary, he familiarised himself with its content and handed it to Zaremba for translation into Latin.[99] Controversy later arose over the reliability of the text. According to

---

94   Konrad M. P. Rudnicki, 'Tablica Chronologiczna Rozwoju Dzieła Miłosierdzia wewnątrz Kościoła Rzymskokatolickiego', *PNS* 54 (2009): 25.

95   Within a few days, the bishop was informed about the precepts of Mariavitism, Kozłowska's life, and most probably about the revelations. Szembek replied that the matter, at least in general, had already been disclosed to him by the secular authorities. See Przyjemski, 'Mariae-Vita', 303–304. It is noteworthy that as early as 1900, the Department of Internal Affairs of the Russian government requested information from the Polish bishops about the Mariavites. Cf. Górecki, *Mariawici*, 75–76.

96   Mazur, 'Marii', 215–226.

97   She claimed she wrote it at the request of Jesus. This is how the text known as *Początek Zawiązku Zgromadzenia Kapłanów* was written. According to Wojciechowski, this is the authoritative version of the revelations. See Józef M. R. Wojciechowski, 'Nie – dla 'grzeszności' Mateczki', *PNS* 8 (1998): 6.

98   He allegedly read it and praised Mariavite lifestyle but also found some parts of the revelations questionable. For example, he believed that the claim that mystical theology was not taught in seminaries was inaccurate. The Mariavites responded that he had confused lectures on asceticism with mystical theology. Cf. 'DMHM IV', *MCPS* 23 (1907): 364. Indeed, during the Partition period, the teaching of ascetical and mystical theology was below par. See Edward Warchoł, *Starokatolicki Kościół Mariawitów w okresie II Rzeczypospolitej* (Sandomierz: Wyd. Diecezjalne, 1997), 14.

99   Rudnicki, 'Tablica', 27.

Seweryniak, Gołębiowski omitted some controversial passages to increase the chance of a positive reception.[100] But this would imply that the Mariavites were naive and wanted to harm their own cause by providing different texts to different hierarchs and the pope.[101] For their part, the Mariavites accused Bishop Szembek and Nowowiejski of falsifying the text of the apparitions.[102] The matter is far from being settled.[103] On 13 February, Piotr Borniński (1862–1936), a priest in charge of finances, faith, and practice in the Diocese of Płock, sent a letter to the bishop's court in which he reported that a certain woman had revelations contrary to Catholic faith and practice. He accused her of assuming the position of mother and teacher of priests she considered the most noble. Her Congregation, armed with the grace of God, was considered by her followers to be the only one capable of reforming the whole Church. Moreover, she intended to absorb all other secret congregations.[104] It is puzzling why Borniński decided to write the letter at precisely this time since he must have known about the Mariavites beforehand.[105] As a result, Gołębiowski was summoned to testify before the bishop's court on 22 April and Maria Franciszka on 28 May.[106] It is interesting to note that Kozłowska was treated as a nun during the trial, despite

100 He found a translation of a Polish text allegedly written by Gołębiowski in Rome, but this has not yet been verified by graphological analyses. Cf. Henryk Seweryniak, 'Sprawa manipulacji w tekście "Początku związku …" w świetle archiwaliów przechowywanych w Kongregacji Nauki Wiary', *PNS* 53 (2009): 18–20. His theory is based, at least in part, on the problematic assumption that contemporary authors know what might have been scandalous for the early Mariavites. Similarly, some contemporary scholars are trying to decide what might have been embarrassing to early Christians. This approach has been recently criticised. See Rafael Rodríguez, 'The Embarrassing Truth about. Jesus: The Criterion of Embarrassment and the Failure of Historical Authenticity' in *Jesus, Criteria, and the Demise of Authenticity*, eds. Chris Keith and Anthony Le Donne (London: T&T Clark, 2012), 132–151.

101 It is not known what happened to the texts delivered to Jaczewski and Popiel. Gołębiowski did not know that they would not accept the documents. Did they also contain omissions? And if not, why would the Mariavites provide different versions of the revelations to different hierarchs? It would have been a very risky move on their part. Cf. Sławomir Gołębiowski, 'Moje votum separatum', *PNS* 59 (2010): 20.

102 'DMHM IV', *MCPS* 23 (1907): 366.

103 Sławomir Gołębiowski, 'Kto dokonał zmian w tekście objawień Marii Franciszki Kozłowskiej przesłanych do Rzymu?', in *MD I*, 257–269.

104 Warchoł, *Reakcja*, 83–84.

105 It is possible that he was acting at the request of Szembek, who was trying to collect all the documents before sending them to Rome. Since the existence of the Mariavites had been known and quietly tolerated in the diocese for many years, a passive attitude towards them would certainly have caused problems for the hierarchy. Mazur, Cf. 'Marii', 222–225.

106 Unexpectedly, the procedures used in heresy trials were used against them. See Michał M. L. Jabłoński and Bronisław Dembowski et al., eds., *Ze źródeł kwestii mariawickiej: nieznane dokumenty z lat 1903–1906* (Płock: Płocki Instytut Wydawniczy, 2011), 24–51.

her irregular status.[107] When all the documents were collected, they were sent to Rome. On 1 June 1903, Popiel sent a separate letter to Domenico Ferrata (1847–1914) – the Cardinal Prefect of the Congregation of Bishops and Regulars (Sacrae Congregatio pro consultationibus Episcoporum, Regularium et aliorum Praelatorum) – informing him of the existence of a secret society of priests. They were characterised by good practice and asceticism, but their secret activities could prove dangerous, especially in light of the current political situation.[108] Most incomprehensible to Popiel was the fact that the priests tolerated being led by a woman.[109]

In July 1903, a delegation of Mariavite priests, together with Mateczka and Sister Honorata Klichowska (1878–1962), set off for Rome with their own translation of the revelations into Latin and a brief history of the Congregation.[110] They decided to present the case directly to the pope because their situation in Poland was deteriorating.[111] While still on their way to Rome, they learned of the death of Leo XIII, whom they considered their potential ally.[112] On 6 August 1903, in Rome, the Mariavites elected Kowalski as their first Minister General.[113] A meeting with the newly elected

---

107 The monastic names were used to refer to her in official documents. Cf. Ignacy Stobiecki, 'Założycielka przed rzymskim sądem', *PNS* 51 (2008): 18.

108 This was the earliest letter sent to Rome regarding the Mariavites. See Górecki, *Mariawici*, 79.

109 Mazur, 'Marii', 218.

110 The translation was prepared by Próchniewski. Cf. Warchoł, *Wybrane*, 13. The document was called *Initia Congregationis Sacredotum* and the fate of the manuscript is unknown. See Konrad M. P. Rudnicki, 'Fałszerstwo tekstu 'Początek zawiązku zgromadzenia kapłanów', *PNS* 51 (2008): 27.

111 Mariavite priests were removed from the Warsaw seminaries, and some were transferred to distant parishes. According to the Mariavites, this was due to their devotion to Our Lady of Perpetual Help, which was considered too excessive. See 'DMHM VI', *MCPS* 28 (1907): 443. Some Catholics felt that such a representation of Mary was too closely associated with the Orthodox Church; cf. Kowalski, 'Krótki', 155. It is believed, however, that the icon of the Black Madonna of Częstochowa came to Poland from Constantinople via Ukraine. See Zenon Zawada, 'The Black Madonna', https://web.archive.org/web/20080126124229/http://www.ukraine-observer.com/articles/217/814.

112 His encyclical on the Eucharist, called *Mirae caritatis*, was published in 1902. Gołębiowski quickly translated this work into Polish so that the Mariavites could use it to legitimise their devotion to the Sacrament. The English translation can be found at Leo XIII, 'Mirae caritatis', http://www.vatican.va/content/leo-xiii/en/encyclicals/documents/hf_l-xiii_enc_28051902_mirae-caritatis.html. Leo XIII also introduced certain devotional practices in the Church, such as the recitation of the rosary in October, which were maintained by the Mariavites even after their break with the Roman Catholic Church. Cf. Ignacy Stobiecki, 'Dlaczego Rzym rozwiązał Zgromadzenie Mariawitów', *PNS* 23 (2001): 31–33.

113 It is possible that they acted pragmatically because they knew their cause would be more likely accepted if they had a male leader. After the election, Mateczka solemnly swore obedience to the minister. However, neither her role nor the fact that Kowalski was only

Pius X (pope 1903–1914) took place seven days later, on 13 August. The pope received St Peter's pence, a handwoven carpet, and a text with the revelations. He accepted the gifts and blessed the Mariavites.[114] After the meeting, Kowalski, Próchniewski, Gołębiowski, Kozłowska, and Klichowska remained in Rome for some time, trying to establish contacts with important church dignitaries. They met with, among others, José de Calasanz Vives y Tuto (1854–1913), Rafael Merry del Val (1865–1930), and Pius de Langogne (1850–1914).[115] Gołębiowski also confronted Szembek, accusing the hierarchs of insincerity and fabrications.[116] Assured of the papal blessing and permission to lead their monastic life, they decided to return to Poland on 5 September, expecting official recognition soon.[117]

On their return, they learned that Kowalski had been transferred to another parish.[118] Apparently, the visit to Rome had not been met with enthusiasm by the hierarchy, who apparently felt ignored and left out.[119] The consequence was that the Archbishop of Warsaw issued a document on 25 September in which he informed the clergy of his diocese that he considered the Mariavites to be pious but insubordinate priests who had introduced many devotional practices without the approval of the hierarchy. They placed too much emphasis on the cult of Our Lady of Perpetual Help (e.g., consecrating new altars to her, distributing or selling medallions with her image), encouraged nightly adoration of the Blessed Sacrament, avoided eating meat and were absent from their parishes too often.[120] The Mariavites denied all these accusations. They claimed that they never conducted nocturnal adoration or sold medals. Furthermore, they neither objected to other representations of Mary nor removed her icons or images

---

elected in Rome was concealed in the audience. See Próchniewski, 'Mariae-Vita', *KBNZ* 52 (1931): 411.

114 Rybak, *Mariawityzm*, 14.

115 Cardinal Vives y Tuto was a member of the Capuchin order, the personal confessor of Pope Pius X and prefect of the Congregation for Religious from 1908. Merry del Val was Cardinal Secretary of State from 1903 to 1914. His canonisation process began in 1953 and bears the title of Servant of God. De Langogne was Superior General of the Capuchin order and confessor to Pius X. Cf. Henryk Seweryniak, *Święte Oficjum a mariawici* (Płock: Płocki Instytut Wydawniczy, 2014), 19–27.

116 Rudnicki, 'Tablica', 22.

117 Rybak, *Mariawityzm*, 14. Mazur points out that the Roman hierarchs could not have known all aspects of the case. Mazur, *Mariawityzm*, 31.

118 'DMHM IV', *MCPS* 28 (1907): 444.

119 Kowalski, 'Krótki', 184.

120 According to the hierarch, the distribution of medals during confession may have led people to think that it was an integral part of the sacrament of confession. Cf. Warchoł, *Starokatolicki*, 28–30.

from their churches. As for leaving the parishes, they only did so when they had found a replacement for their absence and when they were needed by others.[121]

On 15 December 1903, Mateczka founded the Catholic Union of Perpetual Propitiation Adoration, which included:

1) a congregation of priests following the 1st Rule of Francis;
2) a congregation of sisters following the 2nd Rule of Francis;
3) male and female tertiaries following the 3rd Rule of Francis;
4) a confraternity–everyone else who was not obliged to follow the rule but to put its ideas into practice through membership in the confraternity and adoration of the Blessed Sacrament.[122]

On the same day, she claimed that Jesus told her that the revelations would not be accepted by the hierarchs in Rome because 'their faith is dead and requires reform'.[123] This has led some scholars to claim that the Mariavites acted insincerely because it had been revealed to them that their efforts would be rejected and they only feigned surprise when this happened.[124] But this does not seem to be an entirely justifiable perspective. First, it should be noted that Jesus' disciples were also informed several times of the impending death of their Master and were still shocked when it took place.[125] Similarly, the Mariavites admitted that they did not always understand the revelations.[126] Second, the case concerned only the rejection of the revelations. The fact that the Union itself was condemned and the intensity of the event surprised even Mateczka.[127] Third, the Mariavites did not blindly believe in Mateczka's understanding of the revelations. They allowed for the possibility that deficiencies in her theological education might lead to her misunderstanding them.[128] Finally, there was always the possibility that God would change the course of events, as in the case of Nineveh (Jon 3:10).[129]

121 'DMHM IV', *MCPS* 28 (1907): 447.
122 Rybak, *Mariawityzm*, 15–16.
123 Kozłowska, 'Wyjątki', 49–50.
124 Górecki, *Mariawici*, 99.
125 It has long been noted that the disciples were portrayed unfavourably, especially in the Gospel of Mark. They were blamed for betraying Jesus, abandoning the mission, and constant misunderstandings. See Brian J. Incigneri, *The Gospel to The Romans, The Setting and Rhetoric of Mark's Gospel* (Leiden: Brill, 2003), 346.
126 Kowalski, 'Krótki', 176.
127 Felicja M. F. Kozłowska, 'Uzupełnienia Objawień Mateczki z Maryawity', *DWM*, 61.
128 Kowalski, 'Krótki', 209.
129 'Odpowiedzi Redakcyi', *WDM* 20 (1908): 159. The Mariavites also drew parallels with the story of Pharaoh, whose heart was hardened by God but who eventually allowed

Meanwhile, the case was being analysed in Rome. In January 1904, after evaluating all the documents provided by the Mariavites, de Langogne concluded that some important parts were missing, such as the statutes of the Congregation and the recommendations of the bishops. Their absence would make it difficult to give the final decision.[130] In March of that year, Szembek wrote two letters. The first was addressed to Ferrata, informing the cardinal that the Congregation was functioning without the approval of the bishops on the basis of 'a certain doubtful approval' from Rome concerning secret congregations.[131] The second was addressed to Pius X, informing him that Szembek considered the revelations to be superstitions. The Polish bishop also mentioned the insubordination of the priests and asked the pope to respond, since it was not up to him to give a final verdict on the matter.[132] Oddly enough, he made allusions to passages of the revelations that were either completely lost or strangely interpreted.[133] Archbishop Denis Alphonse Steyaert (1827–1910) published *De visionibus et revelationibus Feliciae Kozłowski* in June 1904. The text contained critical and negative assessments of the visions.[134] In the opinion of the Mariavites, he reached his conclusions on the basis of a corrupt translation of the revelations.[135] Furthermore, Steyaert never personally examined

---

the Hebrews to leave Egypt. Cf. Felicja M. F. Kozłowska, 'List Mateczki do Papieża', trans. Henryk Seweryniak, *PNS* 58 (2010): 20.

130 Nevertheless, he was rather negative about the content of the revelations, stating that they were filled with ecstatic experiences and visions. He considered some passages theologically questionable, such as those concerning the similarities between Mary and Maria Franciszka. Cf. Seweryniak, *Święte Oficjum*, 27. De Langogne was informed by Próchniewski in August 1903 that the text of the revelations in his possession contained some fabrications. These included the proper relationship between Mary and Maria Franciszka. See Rudnicki, 'Tablica', 28.

131 According to Szembek, the only official decree issued by the Congregation for Bishops and Regulars on 11 August 1889 raised the role of bishops in setting up and monitoring secret congregations. Cf. Warchoł, *Reakcja*, 58.

132 He referred to the constitution of Leo X (pontificate 1513–1521) called *Supreme Maiestatis* of 1575, according to which only the pope has the authority to deal with such matters. Cf. Górecki, *Mariawici*, 95. But either they were published during the pontificate of Pope Gregory XIII (1572–1585), or Szembek made an error in attribution or date.

133 He claimed that the revelations stated that some people who were still alive at the time would be eternally damned by Jesus. Warchoł, *Reakcja*, 57.

134 It can be seen as a kind of dossier that the 1904 decree dissolving the Mariavite Congregation was mainly based on. Cf. Seweryniak, *Święte Oficjum*, 25.

135 He used a translation known as the *Prima initia congregationis Sacerdotum*. This was not the same text that the Mariavites had personally presented to the pope on 13 August 1903. It was missing some important passages, such as the fact that Mateczka was a 'great sinner' and that she was instructed to imitate Mary as Francis had imitated Jesus. See Rudnicki, *Fałszerstwo*, 27–29.

Kozłowska and used many humiliating terms regarding her and her mental state.[136]

On 3 August 1904, Gołębiowski and Próchniewski had an audience with Pius X, during which they handed him the statutes of the Union and reminded him of their last visit.[137] They also gave him a letter from Mateczka written on 9 June. In the document, Maria Franciszka notified the pope that she was aware of the negative opinions about the Work of Great Mercy in Rome, which had privately been communicated to Szembek.[138] The pope allegedly confirmed that he considered the initiative to be divinely inspired and encouraged the Mariavites not to be afraid despite the negative reaction of the Polish bishops.[139] It is likely that, at this point, the Roman dignitaries did not yet know how to approach the problem.[140] If they had indeed believed that the revelations contained manifestly heretical content, they would probably have reacted more quickly. A decision had to be made, however. In the same month, on 31 August 1904, in a special meeting, the Supreme Sacred Congregation of the Roman and Universal Inquisition adopted a decree abolishing the male branch of the Mariavite Congregation.[141] The document was signed on behalf of Pius X by Cardinal Serafino Vannutelli (1834–1915) on 4 September. The Mariavites could not come to terms with the fact that the decree called Mateczka's revelations hallucinations without examining her personally.[142] This surprised them to such an extent that they even questioned its authenticity.[143] Nevertheless,

---

136 He considered the possibility that Mateczka had been manipulated by Satan or that she may have been mentally unstable and needed a good confessor. Cf. Edward Warchoł, *Proces wydzielania się Związku Mariawitów Nieustającej Adoracji Ubłagania z doktrynalnych i organizacyjnych ram Kościoła rzymskokatolickiego* (Radom: Wyd. Diecezjalne, 2006), 43.

137 The statutes were completed on 8 June 1904. See 'DMHM IV', *MCPS* 29 (1907): 461.

138 She expressed the hope that the pope would take the statutes into consideration before issuing a final verdict, assuring him of her obedience. Cf. Kozłowska, 'List Mateczki do Papieża', 17.

139 Próchniewski, 'Mariae-Vita', KBNZ 16 (1932): 124.

140 They could not make any decision for a year. Mazur, *Mariawityzm*, 31.

141 For convenience, the author continues to refer to them as the Mariavites in the later part of the work, even though the Congregation was dissolved.

142 Przedpełski, 'Powstanie', 35. It is also surprising that Rome ignored the fact that there were two different versions of the translations of the revelations. See Gołębiowski, *Moje votum separatum*, 24. The visions of Teresa of Ávila were also referred to as hallucinations. Cf. Felicja M. F. Kozłowska and Roman M. J. Próchniewski, 'Dzieło Miłosierdzia: Życie Duchowne. Wstęp', *MCPS* 21 (1909): 330.

143 They pointed out that it looked like a private letter to Bishop Szembek, which only dealt with the Płock diocese. It had no official signatures or seals and contained errors, such

they signed it, encouraged by Mateczka to show obedience.[144] What Jesus said in the visions and the opinions of some Roman hierarchs led them to believe that the situation was only temporary.[145] Strikingly, the document did not mention heresy or any breach of doctrine, but the Mariavite priests and Maria Franciszka were asked to affirm the confession of faith.[146]

4. After the Decree Abolishing the Congregation

After the decree, the Mariavites continued their ascetic practices, but only in private.[147] They encouraged parishioners to frequent communion and the adoration of the Blessed Sacrament. People willingly attended their churches, even if they did not formally belong to their parish. This provoked hostile reactions from other clergymen, who wrongly called them heretics, referring to the verdict of the cessation of the Congregation.[148] In some cases, sacraments were denied to people who openly supported the Mariavites.[149] False rumours that they had been excommunicated also made the rounds.[150] The bishops, for their part, began to transfer Mariavite priests to other parishes, accusing them of insincerity and disloyalty. This situation further alienated both sides, forcing the Mariavites to turn to Rome. Paweł M. Dominik Skolimowski (1864–1921) a graduate of the University of Rome, was considered the most suitable person to mediate between the Mariavites and the Roman hierarchy. He was sent to Rome in

---

as the Mariavites being called Marianists (Congregationi Marianitarum). Moreover, how could Rome dissolve a congregation that had never been officially approved? Cf. 'DMHM VII', *MCPS* 31 (1907): 494. As for the name, this was most likely a mistake, as the preparatory materials on which the final document was based contained the word *mariavitarum*. See Górecki, *Mariawici*, 100.

144 Felicja M. F. Kozłowska, 'List do O. Jana Przyjemskiego (19.11.1904)', in *Ku Królestwu*, 57.

145 Mateczka was assured by Jesus that her authority was not completely taken away but only temporarily suspended. Cf. Kozłowska, 'Wyjątki', 52. Vannutelli allegedly informed the Mariavites that the decree was only a test of obedience; see 'DMHM VIII', *MCPS* 33 (1907): 527. Vives y Tuto encouraged them to wait for the resurrection of their Congregation; cf. 'DMHM VIII', *MCPS* 35 (1907): 557.

146 Zbigniew Pasek, 'Geneza Mariawityzmu i Przyczyny Jego Podziału', *Studia Religiologica* 24 (1991): 46–47.

147 Vives y Tuto assured them that there was nothing wrong with wanting to maintain devotional practices for their individual benefit; see 'DMHM VIII', *MCPS* 35 (1907): 557.

148 The accusations of heresy probably stemmed from a misrepresentation of the beliefs of the Mariavites. For example, it was believed that they preached that there was no Holy Spirit, but in fact they were only saying that some corrupt priests were not acting in accordance with the Spirit of God. See Mazur, *Mariawityzm*, 29.

149 'Najprzewielebniejszy Ojciec Jan Marya Michał Kowalski', *KM* (1910): 91.

150 'DMHM VIII', *MCPS* 33 (1907): 528.

January 1905.[151] All the dignitaries he met with praised the Mariavites for their obedience to the decree and their personal piety.[152] Archbishop Symon was even said to have criticised the Polish bishops for their inept action towards the Mariavites, indicating his readiness to become the supervisor of the Congregation if it was to be reactivated.[153] The most significant meeting was with the pope on 27 January 1905. Skolimowski asked Pius X to allow the Mariavites to gather once a month for spiritual exercises and retreats. The pope gave his blessing to both the Mariavites and Mateczka and promised protection, but no official decisions were made.[154] The decree did not put an end to the Mariavite Congregation of sisters. Nowowiejski and Borniński were appointed to detach the sisters from Mateczka and modify their Rule. Their proposal was decisively rejected since the new Rule in no way resembled the one the sisters had kept up to that time. Nowowiejski was remembered as having treated Mateczka harshly when he tried to convince her to leave the house she owned. As of 14 February 1905, Mariavite sisters could no longer call themselves nuns.[155] The Italian priest Antoni Pagani, director of the Istituto Paterno Ippolitto Piendemonte on the Via Rosa in Rome, encouraged the Mariavite sisters to relinquish their status as nuns and become lay workers under Mateczka's direction.[156] They agreed, but Maria Franciszka remained estranged from them until August 1905.[157]

The years 1904–1906 were regarded by Mateczka as particularly significant. She looked forward to the separation of the good from the bad, knowing that Mariavite priests were ready for any punishment in defence of the Blessed Sacrament and the monastic Rule.[158] Around 1903, she

---

151 He had most likely an influential protector in Rome; otherwise, he would not have been able to study there and gain access to the highest hierarchs so easily. Cf. Stobiecki, 'Dlaczego', 31–33.

152 The general of the Dominican order called the fasting of the Mariavites eccentric, although Dominicans were also asked not to eat meat. He felt that Mateczka's directives were behind the times and advised the Mariavites to join other congregations. But even he praised their obedience and religious behaviour. See 'DMHM VIII', *MCPS* 33 (1907): 525–526.

153 Ibid., 525–526.

154 Ibid., 526.

155 'DMHM VII', *MCPS* 32 (1907): 507–512.

156 Rudnicki, 'Tablica', 31. According to Seweryniak, he probably went to Poland, where he met Kozłowska in unclear circumstances. Pagani may have been a member of the Congregation; cf. Seweryniak, *Święte Oficjum*, 57.

157 Kowalski, 'Krótki', 188.

158 Felicja M. F. Kozłowska, 'List do O. Jana Przyjemskiego (1905)', in *Ku Królestwu*, 58.

received a revelation in which, she claimed, Jesus revealed to her the meaning of the two beasts mentioned in Revelation 13. The first beast signified Freemasonry.[159] The Antichrist was expected to come out of it.[160] The second beast referred to the corrupt clergy. Initially, they were expected to persecute those responsible for adoration of the Blessed Sacrament under the guise of zealotry but were later expected to openly rebel against God by uniting forces with the first beast. The good were expected to prepare the way for the Second Coming of Christ and the bad for the coming of the Antichrist.[161] In 1904, Mateczka claimed that Jesus showed her the New Jerusalem and the new church that would rise out of the present Church. She also saw the fall of Rome.[162] However, it is a serious mistake to read such visions through the prism of later events. The new church growing out of the existing Church did not necessarily refer to a schism but could signify renewal. The fall of Rome could have indicated a restructuring of the Church or signified an imminent spiritual or even political change.[163] Besides, the vision of the fall itself did not determine Mateczka's attitude towards Rome or the papacy.[164] These ideas, although somewhat reinterpreted, later formed the foundation of the Mariavites' teaching on the Kingdom of God on earth.

159 Kozłowska, 'List do O. Jana Przyjemskiego (1904)', in *Ku Królestwu*, 63. In another version, the first beast symbolised the masses of people representing various nations who abandoned God and blasphemed the Eucharist. Cf. 'DMHM VI', *MCPS* 29 (1907): 461.

160 In 1906, a rumour circulated that the Mariavites believed that Mateczka would give birth to the Antichrist. It probably first appeared in written form in a pamphlet by Honorat Koźmiński, *Prawda o 'Maryawitach'* (Warsaw, 1906), 42. The emergence of this rumour certainly preceded the latter, however. Peterkiewicz wrote that the Mariavites did not deny this belief but thought that God had changed his plan. See Jerzy Peterkiewicz, *Third Adam* (Oxford: Oxford University Press, 1975), 60. Mateczka's vision of 1903 seems to challenge such a bizarre claim.

161 Kozłowska, 'List do O. Jana Przyjemskiego (1904)', 63.

162 Kozłowska, 'Wyjątki', 51.

163 Our Lady of La Salette is believed to have predicted that Rome would abandon the faith and become the seat of the Antichrist. According to some Catholic authors, this could mean that the Antichrist would become the head of state, openly persecuting the Church, while the pope would run the Christian world underground, just as Peter allegedly did in Rome in the first century. In other words, the fall of Rome had nothing to do with the fall of Catholic Christianity. See Jimmy Akin, 'La Salette: Sorting Fact from Fiction', https://www.catholic.com/magazine/print-edition/la-salette-sorting-fact-from-fiction. The Mariavites later used La Salette's revelations to minimise the significance of the anathema imposed on them. Cf. 'Prawowite bezprawie', *WDM* 72 (1909): 570.

164 Słowacki also wrote about the fall of Rome and openly criticised it, but his words are also difficult to decipher, and his ideas susceptible to change. See Juliusz Słowacki, *Dzieła Juliusza Słowackiego tom I*, ed. Bronisław Gubrynowicz (Lwów: Księgarnia W. Gubrynowicza, 1909), 57.

In June 1905, three peasants representing 150,000 adorers of the Blessed Sacrament went to Rome to ask for the retention of Mariavite priests in their parishes.[165] Before going to the pope, they tried to communicate with the Polish bishops but without success.[166] The petition contains several examples of misconduct by priests. Pius X sent the document to the Inquisition, which forwarded it to the bishops, presumably for an explanation. Eventually, the document went to the priests themselves, who, in retaliation, allegedly began to treat the adorers more harshly.[167] The Mariavites were immediately accused of preparing the document in order to incite the people against their pastors.[168] In fact, the Mariavites were collecting examples of the ethical and religious abuses of their clerical colleagues at the time in accordance with the alleged requests by Vannutelli and Ruszkiewicz.[169] This was certainly a tactical error on the part of the Mariavites, who naively thought that by providing clear evidence of the wrongdoing of others, they would legitimise their own message in the eyes of the hierarchy.[170] They modelled themselves on the apostle Paul, who publicly exposed the sin of a man in Corinth who was accused of sleeping with his father's wife (1 Cor 5:1).[171] Archbishop Popiel acknowledged

---

165 They could not understand why the Mariavites who promoted Catholic devotional practices were being punished while there were many openly anticlerical and anti-religious groups trying to distance people from the Church. See 'Skarga włościan na duchowieństwo rzymskokatolickie w Polsce', in Warchoł, *Proces*, 112.

166 'DMHM VIII', *MCPS* 33 (1907): 543.

167 'Najprzewielebniejszy', 91–92.

168 In a letter to the Secretary of the Holy Office, Nowowiejski claimed that the document was created by Mariavite priests because the people did not know Latin; Górecki, *Mariawici*, 111–112.

169 Both later denied that they had given such an order. For Vannutelli, see 'DMHM VIII', *MCPS* 35 (1907): 556; and for Ruszkiewicz, see 'DMHM IX', *MCPS* 38 (1907): 605.

170 Stobiecki, 'Próba oceny', 25. There was a long-standing tradition in the Catholic Church that such issues could only be resolved with God's help and that people should not try to change them, especially if they were not bishops. For example, Federico Borromeo (1564–1631), an Italian cardinal and Archbishop of Milan, believed that exposing the sins of Church officials could only lead to unnecessary scandal. Paradoxically, his mere mention of the existence of sins could damage the interests of the Church; cf. 'Port Royal: Próba reform Kościoła w XVII w', *KM* (1910): 21.

171 It should be pointed out that he was a regular churchgoer and not a member of the clergy, but ministry in the Pauline churches may have belonged to everyone, not just a select few. See James D. G. Dunn, *Unity and Diversity in the New Testament: An Inquiry into the Character of Earliest Christianity* (London: SCM Press, 1977), 109–111. This man's identity was concealed, and he was probably known only to members of the church, but Paul did not need to mention his name in a letter that was potentially to be read by all Christians. It is worth recalling that Paul – who met opposition from his former co-religionists, by members of other Christian sects and by the Roman authorities – was in a particularly difficult

that there are sinful priests but accused the Mariavites of making sweeping generalisations.[172]

The conflicts followed different courses in different dioceses. In Płock, Bishop Apolinary Wnukowski (1848–1909), who succeeded Szembek, issued a resolution on 4 August 1905 forbidding the Mariavites to preach and hold religious services.[173] As a result of a misunderstanding, the Mariavites were convinced that the decision had been revoked and gathered on 8 December in Radyzmin to help Czesław M. Maciej Czerwiński prepare the Feast of the Immaculate Conception. In response, the bishop declared that the decision made in August was still in force.[174] In Warsaw, Kowalski, Wiechowicz, and Wawrzyniec M. Franciszek Rostworowski (1874–1956)[175] sent a memorandum to Popiel on 10 August in which they assured him of their conviction that the Catholic Church was the only legitimate teacher of truth and that they wished to remain obedient to its doctrine.[176] They asked the hierarch to justify the penalties imposed on them as they followed the decisions of the 1904 decree.[177] The Mariavites argued that adoration and other spiritual exercises were not forbidden by the document and were prepared to give up their meatless diet if they were ordered to do so. They could not understand why other priests calling them heretics was tolerated. They finally asked the hierarch for clear instructions on what to do but received no official answer.[178] Driven by the instinct of self-preservation, they decided to continue collecting evidence of the priests' immorality in order to protect themselves if they were summoned to Rome for trial. On 14 September, the Warsaw Consistory accused them

---

situation. He was clearly more concerned with the ethical integrity of his church than with eliminating potential accusations coming from the mouths of his opponents.

172 Nowowiejski added that some priests were in fact innocent, and their only fault was that they derisively called the Mariavites mystics. Cf. Górecki, *Mariawici*, 112.

173 Pasek, 'Geneza', 47.

174 'DMHM X', *MCPS* 43 (1907): 685.

175 He was Popiel's cousin and his private chaplain; cf. Mazur, 'Marii', 220.

176 Warchoł, *Proces*, 24–25.

177 According to them, they strictly obeyed decisions from Rome – contact with Mateczka was severed, apart from the occasional purchase of necessary ecclesiastical items from her workshop; the Mariavites remained in contact, but only to help each other with pastoral duties; all structures and leadership functions were abolished; monastic vows were terminated, and the profession of poverty was treated as a personal virtue; there was no separation from other clergy or disobedience to bishops. See 'DMHM VIII', *MCPS* 36 (1907): 571–575.

178 They probably asked for clear instructions to prove their innocence in Rome. Cf. Kowalski, 'Krótki', 192–193.

of false obedience to the bishops.[179] At the end of the month, two Mariavites were suspended, and six others were transferred from Warsaw to provincial parishes.[180] In an attempt to stop further actions, Kowalski declared that the Mariavites were prepared to cease their religious practices. Indeed, they stopped encouraging people to seek the protection of Our Lady of Perpetual Help, receive the Eucharist frequently, or adore the Blessed Sacrament.[181] They did so despite their conviction that there was no basis in canon law for suspensions and other punishments.[182] This did not improve the situation, and in early January some priests were permanently removed from their posts.[183] With nowhere else to go, they went to Kowalski who offered them temporary accommodation but did not allow them to conduct any liturgical activities.[184] This resulted in his suspension on 27 January.[185] Seeing no other options, the Mariavites decided to denounce obedience to the bishops and appeal directly to the pope.[186]

5. The Termination of Obedience

The Mariavites of Warsaw submitted documents announcing their decision on 1 February. The priests of the diocese of Płock did the same on 8 February.[187] They attempted to justify their termination of obedience on linguistic grounds, pointing out that they were not taking an oath of obedience but only a promise of obedience (*promitto obedientiam*) solely related to the spreading of Catholic devotions. They viewed obedience to an unjust episcopate as sinful, which was somewhat in line with the opin-

---

179 The Mariavites were also said to act independently, slandering non-Mariavites and inciting parishioners against priests; see 'DMHM IX', *MCPS* 37 (1907): 592.

180 Mames, *Mysteria*, 26.

181 Mariavite priests also stopped communicating with each other; cf. 'DMHM IX', *MCPS* 39 (1907): 624.

182 'DMHM IX', *MCPS* 40 (1907): 640. This was also the opinion of Father Lasocki, one of the judges of the Płock Consistory, who nevertheless encouraged them to obey. See Rudnicki, 'Tablica', 30.

183 This happened, for example, to Czesław M. Polikarp Kahl (1878–1914), Józef M. Stanisław Szymanowski (1878–1945), Roman M. Augustyn Gostyński (1875–1964), Edward M. Serafin Marks (1874–1955), Józef M. Czesław Poradowski and Józef M. Wawrzyniec Pągowski (died 1948). Cf. Warchoł, *Proces*, 27.

184 Kowalski, 'Krótki', 195.

185 'DMHM X', *MCPS* 42 (1907): 670.

186 The 1910 Mariavite calendar states that the Congregation was officially reestablished on 30 January 1906 in Płock, and Kowalski was reappointed Minister General, but only informally. His official appointment to this position followed their break with the Catholic Church. Cf. 'Najprzewielebniejszy', 93.

187 Rybak, *Mariawityzm*, 26.

ion expressed by Cyprian of Carthage (200–258).[188] Since the Mariavites were chastised for promoting adoration of the Sacrament, communion, and confession, their *promitto obedientiam* was no longer binding.[189] It is worth mentioning that this was not the first time in Christian history that monks broke or suspended Eucharistic communion with the bishops of the local church.[190]

As for the parishioners, they were given freedom to choose. They could either follow the Mariavites or remain loyal to the bishops.[191] Only at this point did they find out about the revelations.[192] It is difficult to calculate how many people followed the Mariavites, but it is estimated that between the beginning of February and mid-March, 16 parishes totalling about 60,000 people separated from the bishops.[193] Since most of these people came from the lower social classes, it was assumed that the Mariavites only attracted illiterate and 'backward' people who were deficient in theological education.[194] In fact, there is no reason to claim that the people who followed the other side were better educated. It seems that the accusations were part of a well-known strategy to discredit opponents by attacking

---

188 'Let not the people flatter themselves as if they could be safe from contagion of sin, communicating with a sinful priest and yielding their obedience to the unjust and unlawful episcopacy of their leader, when the Divine Censure threatens through the Prophet Hosea and says: Their sacrifices shall be like the bread of mourning: all who eat them shall be defiled, teaching obviously and showing that all are, indeed, involved in sin who have been contaminated by the sacrifice of a blasphemous and unjust priest.' See Cyprian of Carthage, *Letter 67*, trans. Rose B. Donna, C. S. J (Washington: The Catholic University of America Press, 1964), 233.

189 The bishops' guidance conflicted with their conscience and pastoral duties, not to mention their religious vows. Cf. 'Sprostowanie', *WDM* 5 (1907): 40.

190 The Studites broke communion with the Ecumenical Patriarch, Nikephoros I (patriarch 806–815) and all the bishops loyal to him. See Marie-France Auzépy, *La Vie d'Etienne le Jeune par Étienne le Diacre: Introduction, édition et Traduction* (New York: Routledge, 2016), 9.

191 The Mariavites believed in the idea of free will, so parishioners of at least 14 years of age had to decide for themselves who they wanted to follow. See 'Sprostowanie', *WDM* 12 (1907): 95.

192 Until then, they knew nothing about them. Devotional practices were explained in various ways by, for example, referring to Leo XIII's encyclical *Mirae Caritatis*. Cf. Kowalski, 'Krótki', 197–198. There is a possibility that not even all Mariavite priests and nuns knew everything until then. See Mazur, *Mariawityzm*, 35.

193 'DMHM X', *MCPS* 49 (1907): 781.

194 'Do Maryawityzmu przechodzi sama ciemna masa', *WDM* 20 (1909): 158–159. However, the same arguments could be used against lower-class Orthodox parishioners who once followed their priests into union with Catholicism. In reality, their situation was much more complex. See Chadwick, *A History*, 412.

their intellectual abilities.[195] People followed the Mariavites because they appreciated their religious piety and service.[196] They disagreed with the bishops, who were allegedly more interested in having obedient subordinates than priests characterised by religious zeal.[197]

When the final decision was made, each parish sent documents to the governor general, declaring that it had become independent from the Catholic bishops, at least temporarily, and asked the local administration to keep records. This led to accusations of national treason, as it had been the job of Catholic priests until then.[198] From the perspective of the Mariavites, this was motivated by fear of military involvement by the authorities.[199] The takeover of parishes varied. In some churches, the Mariavites were the parish priests, and the transition was relatively smooth, at least until the Catholics came to reclaim the church. In other places, however, the Mariavites never had a parish priest or even a vicar, so the transition was difficult. The dismissed priests did not want to leave the churches voluntarily and sought protection from the secular authorities.[200] The Mariavites tried to justify their actions by referring to one of Gregory VII's (pontificate 1073–1085) encyclicals, in which the pope encouraged people to expel lewd priests.[201] The autonomy of the parishes was considered temporary until the matter could be dealt with by Rome.

---

195 This is similar to the accusations made by Celsus, who believed that most ancient Christians were uneducated and ignorant slaves, women, and children, so their opinions do not even merit serious examination. Cf. Origen, Contra Celsum, 158–159.

196 If Przyjemski's testimony is to be believed, the bishops did not necessarily think that people needed to engage in frequent adoration or receive communion. According to the Mariavites, this was one of the reasons why they decided to denounce obedience. The salvation of the soul, inseparable from the Eucharist, was considered the most fundamental issue for Christians, and priests should be prepared to rebel against both 'earth' and 'heaven' to provide it. Cf. 'Sprostowanie', *WDM* 12 (1907): 95.

197 Gołębiowski testified that Wnukowski told him that he preferred corrupt priests to the Mariavites because they did not go beyond the decisions of church officials. See 'Sprostowanie', *WDM* 8 (1907): 64.

198 The Mariavites responded that the civil registers were mainly kept for the government, effectively making Catholic priests officials of the Russian authorities. Furthermore, it was pointed out that, in countries where the Catholics were a minority, registers are kept by civil officials. Cf. 'Sprostowanie', *WDM* 10 (1907): 77–80. The Mariavites, unlike the Catholics, did not make money from issuing civil status certificates. See 'DMHM X', *MCPS* 43 (1907): 688.

199 Kowalski, 'Krótki', 198.

200 In Zgierz, for example, parish priest Roman Rembieliński called in the army to help him remove parishioners from the church and cemetery; 'cf. DMHM X', *MCPS* 44 (1907): 704.

201 'Sprostowanie', *WDM* 12 (1907): 94.

Kowalski and Próchniewski went to Rome in February. This time they decided to take a much firmer stand since they fed up with 'meaningless blessings' and 'empty promises'. On arrival, they sent an official letter to the pope demanding the withdrawal of the suspensions, the acceptance of the revelations, and the recognition of Mateczka's mission.[202] They felt that the hopeless situation required them to take radical steps. On 15 February, de Langogne, who had become an intermediary between them and the Pope, admitted that the suspensions were contrary to canon law, and assured them that the pope would deal fairly with their case.[203] He advised them, however, to take a different tone, as their present one might adversely affect their aims.[204] Although de Langogne had previously given an unfavourable assessment of the revelations, Kowalski tried to convince him that he had been using a corrupt translation and that the passages he believed to be false were not included in the authentic version.[205]

The meeting with the pope took place on 20 February. During the audience, Pius X stated ambiguously that things had taken a disastrous turn.[206] Kowalski and Próchniewski swore obedience to him on behalf of all Mariavites.[207] Before they left, however, Kowalski handed him a sheet of paper citing God's promise that he would punish Eli and his family for their sins (1 Sam 3:1-18). This was meant to be a warning, showing that even the high priest could be rejected by God.[208] Despite the incident, both sides seemed to feel that the audience was successful.[209]

When the priests returned to Poland, they learned to their great dismay that the Mariavites had been openly branded as heretics, and the Catholic press began spreading false information that they had signed a new document in Rome confirming the dissolution of the Congregation.[210]

---

202 Kowalski, 'Krótki', 199.

203 He told them that the planned papal decree on the possibility of daily communion would be their success and the failure of the Polish bishops; Cf. Rudnicki, 'Tablica', 31.

204 Without revoking their demands, the representatives of the Mariavites wrote to the pope again, apologising for the tone of their first letter. See Warchoł, *Proces*, 20.

205 Kowalski, 'Krótki', 201.

206 Kowalski and Próchniewski thought he meant the actions of the bishops and clergy against the Mariavites and the Blessed Sacrament, but it turned out that he meant the denunciation of obedience. See 'Z niedalekiej przeszłości', *KM* (1908): 23.

207 At first, they only swore obedience to the Will of God, but when they were forced to swear obedience to the pope as well, they agreed, convinced that he was on their side; cf. 'DMHM XI', *MCPS* 52 (1907): 830.

208 Ibid., 830.

209 Warchoł, *Proces*, 59–60.

210 Mazur, *Mariawityzm*, 36. It is worth noting the example of Bishop Jaczewski, who advised priests against unnecessary verbal attacks on the Mariavites. See Franciszek

On 14 February, the Warsaw Consistory issued a circular against the Mariavites.[211] It contained some interesting accusations. It stated, for example, that they believed that the Antichrist was already three or four and a half years old. According to the Mariavites, the whole misunderstanding came from the pamphlet *Ostateczne Czasy* (The End Times), published by the nobleman Michał Piotr Radziwiłł (1853–1903).[212] Citing Joséphine Lamarine (1787–1850), he claimed that the enemy of Christ had appeared on earth in 1900.[213] His ideas were also based on the first encyclical of Pius X, which claimed that 'the 'Son of Perdition' of whom the Apostle speaks may already be in the world'.[214] Because the pamphlet was approved by the Warsaw Consistory, the Mariavites responded that it was rather the officials of the Catholic Church who believed all this about the Antichrist.[215] It was mainly because of this circular that the Mariavites came to be known as heretics.[216] Since this took place before Rome's final decision, it is not surprising that the Mariavites considered such statements to be non-canonical. In the first millennium, each local church had the prerogative to call its subjects heretics and excommunicate them, but the Catholics in the Middle Ages had developed a structure in which the pope had the last word in a conflict, especially if both sides appealed to him.[217] In the early twentieth

---

Jaczewski, 'List biskupa Jaczewskiego do proboszcza parafii w Grębkowie', in Warchoł, *Proces*, 203.

211 The document was signed by Borniński. Cf. Górecki, *Mariawici*, 123.

212 There is no evidence that Radziwiłł supported the Mariavites. He died in 1903, so it is highly unlikely that he knew anything about the revelations given to Kozłowska. *Ostateczne Czasy* was published after his death. Cf. Materiał Partnerski, 'Michał Piotr Radziwiłł: Mecenas i konserwatysta z artystyczną duszą', https://www.se.pl/wiadomosci/polska/michal-piotr-radziwill-mecenas-i-konserwatysta-z-artystyczna-dusza-aa-NEHp-CNc1-6Eyi.html.

213 Lamarine prophesied that the Antichrist would come from Jerusalem, be born of Muslim parents, and reign in Rome after killing the pope. See Michał P. Radziwiłł, *Ostateczne Czasy* (Warszawa: Wyd. Księgarni Nakładowej M. Szczepkowskiego, 1905), 42.

214 Ibid., 37. Pius X, 'E supremi apostolatus', http://www.vatican.va/content/pius-x/en/encyclicals/documents/hf_p-x_enc_04101903_e-supremi.html.

215 Approval was only withdrawn after the 7th edition; cf. 'DMHM XI', *MCPS* 50 (1907): 800.

216 'DMHM XI', *MCPS* 51 (1907): 816. Koźmiński, once Kozłowska's superior, also began to uncritically repeat preposterous claims about the Mariavites. He claimed, for example, that Mateczka had ordained a bishop for them and was considered the mother of the Antichrist. Cf. Górecki, *Mariawici*, 182–184.

217 One exception may be the canons of the local Council of Serdica (342/343). Orthodox theologians believe that the Council's disciplinary decisions applied only to Churches under the jurisdiction of the pope. In 1906, the Mariavites tended to agree with the Catholic rather than the Orthodox view but later reconsidered this. For example, they referred to the fact that the African bishops had warned their clergy at the Council of

century, the hierarchical aspect of the Church was strongly emphasised in Poland.[218]

Despite the difficult situation, Kowalski asked the Mariavite priests to obey the bishops, to stop removing priests from their parishes, and to try to make peace, calmly waiting for decisions from Rome.[219] At the same time, they were to continue to spread devotion to the Blessed Sacrament and Our Lady of Perpetual Help and to encourage people to confess their sins, adore Jesus, and receive communion frequently. The dismissed priests were not allowed to return to the churches before Rome's verdict. The laity were instructed to distance themselves from the priests who openly resisted the practice of adoration and to find a priest, not necessarily a Mariavite, who would not oppose such practices.[220] In light of the hostile reaction from the public, the Mariavites decided to go to St Petersburg on 28 February to secure a legal basis to defend their own interests. As in the case of record-keeping, this was used against them to prove their alleged anti-Polish stance.[221] In fact, the statutes they presented to the Russian officials contained a paragraph declaring their allegiance to the pope.[222] On the same day, Bishop Wnukowski appealed to the Governor-General to confine Przyjemski and Ludwik M. Alfons Ryttel to the monastery, thus confirming the legitimacy of Mariavites' actions in St. Petersburg.[223] From the beginning of March, the bishops called on the Mariavites to see if they were prepared to comply with the 1904 decree, but at the same time they did not

---

Milevum in the fifth century that whoever appealed to Rome against their decisions would be excommunicated. See Roman M. J. Próchniewski, 'Przeniesienie Stolicy Apostolskiej', *MMN* 4 (1924): 2.

218 Górecki, *Mariawici*, 87–88.

219 According to the Mariavite sources, more parishes came forward expressing a desire to separate from the Catholic hierarchy but were met with refusal; cf. 'Najprzewielebniejszy', 92.

220 Kowalski assured people that the pope would never oppose these devotional practices. See Jan M. M. Kowalski, 'Odezwa ks. Jana Kowalskiego do księży i wiernych świeckich – mariawitów', in Warchoł, *Proces*, 124–125. It is worth mentioning that Bishop Jaczewski encouraged his subordinates to imitate the Mariavites in all that was good; for example, he recommended that priests listen to confessions long and patiently.

221 Similarly, when Orthodox believers converted to Catholicism, they were accused first of betrayal of a political nature and only then of a religious one. Barbara Skinner, 'The Irreparable Church Schism: Russian Orthodox Identity and Its Historical Encounter with Catholicism', in *Polish Encounters, Russian Identity*, 26.

222 'DMHM XI', *MCPS* 1 (1908): 13. The Russian authorities refused to recognise them because they did not want to aggravate relations with the Catholic Church; cf. Rudnicki, 'Tablica', 31.

223 After two days, he asked for other Mariavites to be locked up as well. Surprisingly, this appeal was not considered a betrayal. See 'Sprostowanie', *WDM* 11 (1907): 87–88.

want to enter into any dialogue with them.²²⁴ On 4 March, Kowalski and Próchniewski sent a letter to Pius X, informing him that Mariavite priests were still under suspension and that Mateczka, together with their sisters, were publicly ridiculed.²²⁵ For example, Maria Franciszka was mockingly portrayed in a Catholic newspaper in February as an Orthodox nun.²²⁶ The dispute went to court and had an unpleasant course.²²⁷ The court did not rule in favour of either side, but the press falsely reported that the guilt of the Mariavites was proven.²²⁸ On 7 March 1906, de Langogne recommended that the bishops of Warsaw and Płock show a spirit of moderation towards the Mariavites, especially since they had been punished for observing the piety long established in the Catholic Church. He had serious reservations about Popiel, who falsely claimed that the situation was becoming stabilised.²²⁹ De Langogne wanted Kozłowska to be sent to Rome, where she would be persuaded to influence the Mariavites not to take further steps.²³⁰ For his part, Pagani advised sending an apostolic emissary to Poland to investigate the matter on the spot.²³¹ On 19 March 1906, Kowalski sent an official letter to Popiel demanding that the hierarch withdraw the suspension, publicly recognise the Mariavites as non-heretics, allow them to continue their devotional practices, let Mariavite priests to remain in churches where parishioners demanded their presence, and condemn incitement to violence.²³² On 21 March, he personally visited the bishop, assuring him that the Mariavites were ready to obey.²³³ Popiel, however, decided to wait for the decision from Rome.

---

224 Mazur, *Mariawityzm*, 36.

225 The situation reached such a critical level that the Mariavites were almost forced to seek protection from the secular authorities. Cf. Górecki, *Mariawici*, 139.

226 'Sprostowanie', *WDM* 31 (1907): 248. This was a clever scheme, as the prevailing religion in the Russian partition was Orthodoxy. The court would not have been able to pass a guilty verdict, which would have been tantamount to an opinion that the depiction of Kozłowska in the garb of an Orthodox nun was reprehensible. See Gołębiowski, *W obronie*, 53.

227 Some witnesses lied without embarrassment. For example, the testimony of a certain Mrs Goczalska was cited. She was Kowalski's alleged housekeeper and had been allegedly made pregnant by him and forced to have an abortion. The problem was that no Mariavite had ever known her. Cf. 'Sprostowanie', *WDM* 35 (1907): 279–280.

228 During the trial, the public continually insulted the Mariavites. The latter had to leave the court building via side exits. Cf. 'Sprostowanie', *WDM* 36 (1907): 287–288.

229 Warchoł, *Proces*, 61–62.

230 Górecki, *Mariawici*, 145.

231 Warchoł, *Proces*, 60–62.

232 'DMHM XI', *MCPS* 1 (1908): 13–14.

233 Próchniewski, 'Mariae-Vita', *KBNZ* 4 (1933): 27–28.

6. The Final Break with Rome

A great deal of time had passed since the visit to Rome, but a decision was not forthcoming. The matter of the Mariavites was to be investigated in earnest, but they began to feel cheated again.[234] The Polish hierarchs did not want to communicate other than from a position of power, and secular authorities refused to interfere in the internal affairs of the Catholic Church.[235] As a result, Kowalski decided to visit the parishes that espoused Mariavitism and explain Mateczka's role to them.[236] He called her the Spouse of Jesus and the Mother of Mercy, similar in holiness to Mary. These points may certainly have sounded controversial and needed further clarification. The Spouse of Christ was a well-established title in the history of the Church, and the Mariavites were aware of it.[237] To give a classic example, the Church Father Caesarius of Arles (468/470–542) wrote that 'the souls not only of nuns but also of all men and women, if they will guard chastity of the body and virginity of heart […] should not doubt that they are spouses to Christ.'[238] Many people in the Middle Ages were seen as saints, capable of performing miracles and interceding before God for others, even during their lifetime. The most well-known was Francis of Assisi.[239] Similar instances can be found in older traditions.[240] It should be noted that the Mariavites did not use the term saint according to the official teaching of the Catholic Church:[241] following Vincent Ferrer (1350–1419),

---

234 Surprisingly, despite his sense of abandonment, Kowalski continued to trust the pope, telling parishioners that they should follow the pope in the case of condemnation. Cf. Kowalski, 'Krótki', 209.

235 The czar regarded the pope as his ally against the socialists. See Mazur, *Mariawityzm*, 36.

236 One of the reasons why the Mariavites decided to reveal the identity of Mateczka and her revelations to the laity was the fear of misrepresentation by opponents. Cf. Józef M. R. Wojciechowski, *Pisma Wybrane: Dzieło Bożego Ratunku, Mariawicki znak czasu* (Felicjanów: KKM, 2003), 54.

237 'DMHM VI', *MCPS* 30 (1907): 479.

238 Bernard McGinn, *The Presence of God: A History of Western Christian Mysticism*, vol. II: *The Growth of Mysticism* (New York, NY: The Crossroad Publishing Company, 1994), 31.

239 Thompson, *Francis*, 131. He himself considered his fellow friar, Rufinus, to be a saint, believing that the latter had already been sanctified by God during his lifetime. Cf. 'Synowie Królestwa' Kwiatki świętego Franciszka z Asyżu', *KBNZ* 16 (1932): 127.

240 For example, Abraham of Clermont (died c. 479) was called a saint and a perfect dwelling (tabernacle) of Jesus by his bishop long before his death; 'Synowie Królestwa: Żywot św. Abrama Pustelnika', *KBNZ* 35 (1929): 279. When Kowalski saw Mateczka for the first time, he also called her a tabernacle; see Kowalski, 'Krótki', 91.

241 Maria Franciszka forbade the introduction of canonisation into the Church of Mariavites. B. Stanisław, 'Z powodu kanonizacji Andrzeja Boboli', *GSK* 24 (1938): 369.

they claimed that a saint was one who perfectly observed the Rule of Francis.[242] Maria Franciszka, on the other hand, strongly protested when Kowalski called her a saint.[243] The title Mother of Mercy first appeared, in all probability, in 1901.[244] This mercy, however, was not confined to Maria Franciszka, and one might venture to say that her only privilege was that she was chronologically the first to receive it. She was believed to have received mercy in the highest degree but still only as a semi-passive recipient. Over time, however, the Mother of Mercy came to be understood by some Mariavites as an official title. It is possible that the emphasis on Mateczka's role expressed a desire to undermine the position of the pope, who was presented by Catholic theologians as 'the father appointed for deliverance of all the faithful'.[245] As far as the resemblance to Mary is concerned, the Mariavites never claimed that Maria Franciszka had replaced the Theotokos. They believed that Mateczka's mission not only did not diminish Mary's significance but actually elevated her status. To plead for mercy, Kozłowska always offered her prayers through the intercession of the Mother of Jesus.[246] Her similarity in holiness to Mary was due to her mission and not her private merits. Just as Mary offered Jesus to humanity through birth, so Maria Franciszka was to offer Jesus to humankind by emphasising His presence in the Blessed Sacrament. The likeness to Mary was reflected in Kozłowska, just as the likeness to Jesus was reflected in Francis of Assisi.[247]

The decision from Rome came on 5 April, when the encyclical *Tribus circiter* was issued. It was read in the churches a few days later, on Maundy Thursday, that is 12 April. The document called the Mariavites mystics, which was a derogatory name given to them by their opponents. It claimed that they believed that Felicja Kozłowska had been given to people in the end times to save the world.[248] In fact, they maintained that only the Eucharist and Mary's intercession could save the world, and Mateczka had only been

---

Canonisation is, of course, not the 'production' but only the 'recognition' of someone's holiness. It was revealed to Mateczka, however, that only God can recognise a saint; see Kozłowska, 'Początek', 9.

242 Felicja M. F. Kozłowska, 'List 1', in *Ku Królestwu*, 54.

243 Kowalski, 'Krótki', 163. Similarly, Francis thanked the bishop for not calling him a saint. Cf. Thompson, *Francis*, 42.

244 Kozłowska, 'Wyjątki', 47.

245 The pope was called 'Sanctissimus Dominus Noster', and Roman dignitaries referred to themselves as 'most holy' or 'angelic people'. See 'DMHM XI', *MCPS* 5 (1908), 78.

246 'DMHM IV', MCPS 21 (1907): 335–336.

247 'DMHM XI', MCPS 51 (1907): 816.

248 Pius X, 'Tribus circiter', in Warchoł, *Proces*, 145–146.

given revelations on renewing proper piety.[249] Pius X acknowledged that the Mariavites promoted traditional Catholic practices but accused them of doing so too nonchalantly, without properly assessing the disposition of the faithful. They were also accused of claiming that the Holy Spirit had left the Church and of insincere obedience to bishops.[250] The encyclical upheld the 1904 decisions and warned that prolonged insubordination would be met with severe consequences.[251] The document did not, however, call the Mariavites heretics.[252]

The day after the encyclical was read in churches, the confession of faith erroneously known as *the Mariavite creed* (Latin: *Mariavitae credunt*) came out.[253] It contained four points, stating that the Mariavites believe

1. Everything the Catholic Church teaches;
2. Mateczka received the highest degree of holiness from God (literally: 'God has made her the holiest') and was given the same gifts of grace as Mary;
3. Mercy for the whole world has been placed in Mateczka's hands, and no one can receive it without her help and mediation;
4. Prayer to Maria Franciszka is not only beneficial but necessary to fend off the temptations of Satan and to become confirmed in grace.[254]

There are several problems with the text in terms of purpose, content, and interpretation. First, some versions of the document were called

---

249 'DMHM X', *MCPS* 3 (1908): 47.

250 Pius X, 'Tribus circiter', 146–148.

251 Ibid., 149–150.

252 It mentions the request of the Mariavites to recognise Maria Franciszka as the Mother of Mercy, who had received the highest degree of holiness from God. Pius X calls this a deceptive illusion but not a heresy; cf. Krzysztof Mazur, 'Tworzenie zrębów mariawickiej struktury eklezjalnej', *PNS* 41 (2006): 47. According to the Catholic theologian Father Wojciech Różyk, the whole of Maria Franciszka Kozłowska's theology, apart from the interpretation of primordial justice, fell within Catholic orthodoxy; see Wojciech Różyk, *'Objawienia' Marii Franciszki Kozłowskiej według rękopisu z archiwum watykańskiego: studium teologiczne* (Świdnica: Świdnicka kuria biskupia, 2006), 211. According to Mames, Różyk's work on heterodoxy in interpreting the essence of original sin relied on only one text by Mateczka, and it is difficult to agree with his conclusions. Cf. Tomasz D. M. Mames, 'O objawieniach Mateczki sto lat za późno', https://www.ekumenizm.pl/ekumenizm/o-objawieniach-mateczki-sto-lat-za-pozno/.

253 At the time of its promulgation, Kowalski knew nothing about the encyclical, so neither he nor the other Mariavites who signed it regarded it as an alternative creed opposed to the faith of the Catholic Church; see Kowalski, 'Krótki', 209. The points contained in the creed had already been announced during Kowalski's visitation to the parishes.

254 Jan M. M. Kowalski, 'Okólnik ks. Jana Kowalskiego (13.04.1906)', in *Wyznania wiary*, 172. The text is quoted in *Przegląd Katolicki* 18 (1906): 261.

'Kowalski's circular', despite the fact that he had no formal authority to impose his beliefs on others at the time.[255] Second, one version included a continuation about the organisation of an independent Mariavite parish, which slightly alters the purpose of the text.[256] Third, there are serious problems with the signatures.[257] Fourth, there are different versions of the fourth point, each of which radically changes the meaning. In some sources, there is a prayer 'by' Mateczka, while others have prayers 'to' her.[258] Fifth, in the Mariavite Congregation that was revived after 1907, the text was not officially endorsed in any version, so elevating it to the Mariavite confession of faith is, to put it mildly, a misunderstanding.[259]

Interpretation requires an individual approach to each point. Regarding the first point, even the Catholic synod of the diocese of Przemyśl convened in 1908 stated that the Mariavites had not formulated a separate confession of faith at that time.[260] The second point has already been discussed.[261] The biggest problem with the third point was the correct interpretation of the

---

255 Kowalski is also referred to as the head of Mariavites, but after the 1904 decree he officially ceased to be its Minister General. This is not a contemporary mistake, however, because, as early as September 1906, Zenon M. Szymon Kwiek (1868–1949) referred to the document as such. See Edward Warchoł, ed., *Ważniejsze dokumenty na temat Mariawitów i Mariawityzmu (1903–1906)* (Radom: Wyd. Diecezjalne, 2009), 337. On the other hand, one of the versions does not mention Kowalski at all; cf. Nowowiejski, *Płock*, 669.

256 The struggles over churches required tools to establish the number of the Mariavites in each parish. In these circumstances, the text was not regarded as a creed opposed to the doctrine of the Catholic Church but as designed to help normalise the situation in the local Catholic parish. See Tatiana Romenko, 'Mariawici wierzą – czym jest ten tekst?', *PNS* 52 (2009): 26.

257 The version given by Nowowiejski is signed by the Mariavites with their monastic names. Until the final schism with Rome, however, they commonly used lay names and the title 'priest' instead of 'father'; see Sławomir Gołębiowski, 'Mariavites credunt – Mariawici wierzą', *PNS* 53 (2009): 23. The signature of one of Mariavite priests differed significantly from his other authentic signatures; cf. Sławomir Gołębiowski, 'Glosy mariawickie', *PNS* 54 (2009): 15–16. Finally, the Latin translation of the text, allegedly dated April 1906, included an unknown priest (Tomasz Kraśkiewicz) and one who joined the Congregation a year later (Henryk M. Fabian Jarzymowski); cf. Sławomir Gołębiowski, 'O rzetelność i prawdę', *PNS* 65 (2012): 23–25.

258 Gołębiowski, 'Mariavites credunt', 24. Years later, Kowalski attested to the 'to' version; cf. Jan M. M. Kowalski, 'Kielich Mateczki', *KBNZ* 10 (1931): 73. But this does not exclude the possibility that the content of the creed was not uniform in 1906.

259 Gołębiowski, *W obronie*, 37.

260 They were accused of challenging the hierarchical authority and primacy of the pope. Porter, *Catholicism*, 13. As we shall see, this was only partly accurate. The primacy of the pope was of course part of the doctrine of the Catholic Church, but the issue was more complex.

261 Romenko added the case of Koźmiński who was called a saint when he was still alive by a French Capuchin friar. See Romenko, 'Mariawici wierzą', 28.

term 'mercy'. For the Mariavites, it referred to the Work of Great Mercy, which was given to Maria Franciszka in the 1893 revelations.[262] In other words, Mateczka was understood as the Mother of the Work of Great Mercy, the person who took the initiative at God's behest. This did not in any way threaten the salvation of others who were not Mariavites. Those who chose to remain in the Catholic Church could be saved as long as they obeyed God's commandments, received the sacraments, and acted according to their conscience.[263] It was believed that salvation was attainable even for those who were not baptised. But the conscious rejection of the sacraments could have certain spiritual consequences that did not necessarily amount to condemnation.[264] In the opinion of the Mariavites, only humans could bring condemnation down on their heads because God wants everyone to be reconciled to Him. Regarding the fourth point, assuming that the 'to' version is correct, the Mariavites knew that prayers to the saints during their lifetime were recognised in the history of the Church.[265] Maria Franciszka never consciously encouraged anyone to pray to her during her lifetime and protested vehemently when others did so.[266] After reading the text of the creed, Mateczka ordered it to be destroyed, so we only know about it from various copies.[267]

After becoming acquainted with the encyclical, the Mariavites did not know how to react.[268] The importance of further steps can be seen from the

---

262 Mercy could be received by people who have never heard of Mateczka. Cf. ibid., 27–28.

263 'Odpowiedzi Redakcyi', *WDM* 25 (1908): 199. This was contrasted with some of the opinions of the popes. Boniface VIII (pontificate 1294–1303) stated in 1302 that it was 'absolutely necessary for salvation that every human creature be subject to the Roman Pontiff'; cf. Boniface VIII, 'Unam sanctam', https://www.papalencyclicals.net/Bon08/B8unam.htm, in his 1856 encyclical (or allocution), 'Singulari quadam', Pius IX reiterated this claim, writing that 'there is only one true, holy, Catholic church, which is the Apostolic Roman Church. There is only one See founded in Peter by the word of the Lord, outside of which we cannot find either true faith or eternal salvation'. Pius IX, 'Singulari quadam', https://www.papalencyclicals.net/Pius09/p9singul.htm.

264 'Odpowiedzi Redakcyi', *WDM* 22 (1909): 174. Even in 1931, Kowalski maintained that Mk 16:16 does not explicitly say that whoever is not baptised will be condemned; see Jan M. M. Kowalski, 'O 120.000 złotych nagrody', *GP* 7 (1931): 59.

265 In addition to Francis, there was also example of Padre Pio (1887–1968). Cf. Romenko, 'Mariawici wierzą', 28.

266 Tatiana Romenko, 'Proces usuwania Mariawitów z Kościoła rzymskiego', *PNS* 33 (2004): 22–23.

267 Ibid., 28.

268 Kowalski, 'Krótki', 210. Maria Franciszka was still worried in October that the Mariavites were cut off from the Church, but it was revealed to her that they would remain in communion with the Church, though not dependent on it. See Kozłowska, 'Wyjątki', 53.

fact that, at the time, deviation from the Catholic Church and 'its organic spiritual hierarchy' headed by the pope was understood as an abandonment of God.[269] On the other hand, the Mariavite movement drew on the ideas of Francis of Assisi from the very beginning. Franciscans held the view that when there was a contradiction between the inner voice of God and the command of the Church, obedience was owed to the former.[270] In the end, belief in the authenticity of the revelations prevailed, and the Mariavites informed the bishops and Pius X that 33 priests and some 45,000 people had decided to leave the Catholic Church.[271] Only one priest, Kwiek, renounced his affiliation with the Mariavites, but he did so only after a long internal struggle.[272]

Meanwhile, the battles for the churches continued and many people were wounded and some even killed. One of the most famous battles took place in the village of Leszno, where, in April 1906, some ten thousand Catholics marched to reclaim the church.[273] Mariavite nuns residing in Płock were not spared persecution. Potential clients were banned from using their services in order to deprive them of their livelihood and force them to leave the city. Their telephone wires were cut and their house was constantly pelted with stones, to the point where it was pointless to put in new windows.[274] Because of her health, Maria Franciszka did not leave

---

269 Porter, *Catholicism*, 16.

270 Paul Sabatier, *Życie świętego Franciszka z Asyżu*, trans. Paweł Hulka-Laskowski (Cieszyn: Wyd. B. Kotula, 1927), 264.

271 The number of adherents may have been higher. Wojciechowski estimated that around 90,000 people secretly followed Mariavitism; cf. Wojciechowski, *Pisma*, 63. Most of them continued to attend the Catholic Church, considering themselves its members; see 'Z listów do Redakcyi', *WDM* 20 (1909): 159–160. Similarly, in the second century, Valentinians attended Orthodox churches because the boundaries were not clearly marked. Cf. John Behr, *Irenaeus of Lyon: Identifying Christianity* (Oxford: Oxford University Press, 2013), 28.

272 He even claimed that he would have become a Mariavite again if the pope had recognised the Congregation. His association with the Mariavites was never forgotten, and it hindered his career in the Catholic Church. Cf. Krzysztof Mazur, 'Rozterki Ojca Zenona M. Szymona Kwieka, próba rekonstrukcji', *PNS* 57 (2010): 18–28.

273 Initially, it was the Mariavites who were accused of attacking the 'peaceful procession', but in 1913 the roles were reversed, and it was the Catholics who were accused of causing the riots. The situation was tragic for other reasons as well. Around 100 families were dismissed from their jobs simply because they had joined the Mariavites. Some were forced to emigrate, even to the United States, where their religious ideas were slowly forgotten; see 'Leszno', *KM* (1914): 65–77.

274 The situation was repeated almost every Sunday. To encourage the vandals, Mt 24:2 was quoted. 'Założenie kamienia węgielnego i poświecenie fundamentów pod kościół katedralny Maryawitów w Płocku', in *KM* (1912): 24.

her sister's house for four years (1905–1909).²⁷⁵ The praiseworthy Polish religious tolerance had somewhere disappeared when it came to attitudes towards Mariavites.²⁷⁶ Missionaries were sent to towns and cities where the Mariavites had gained popularity and convinced the people that their sacraments were invalid, which, by the way, was contrary to the Catholic Catechism.²⁷⁷ Sometimes the medallions of Our Lady of Perpetual Help were forcibly taken from the Mariavites and buried in the ground or tied to bull horns.²⁷⁸

This only strengthened the Mariavites' conviction that they were fighting for a just cause.²⁷⁹ It also forced them to seek protection from the Russian government.²⁸⁰ As in previous cases, they were immediately accused of national treason. In fact, they needed a legal means of defence from the secular authorities since they were an informal group without

275 Mames, *Mysteria*, 33.

276 At the time of the Counter-Reformation, Skarga could only deplore the fact that the Catholics were marrying 'heretics', engaging in religious dialogue, attending Protestant funerals, and even sending their children to 'heretical' schools; see Janusz Tazbir, 'Specyfika polskiej tolerancji', in *Naród, Kościół, Kultura: Szkice z historii Polski 2*, ed. Adam Chruczewski et al. (Lublin: Wyd. KUL, 1986), 65. Some opponents, despite their initial negative attitude, changed their opinions after learning about the case. For example, J. Bandrowski, writing for *Kurier Warszawski*, called the Mariavites blind heretics, but after visiting their establishments, he changed his mind. It turned out that Mateczka was not worshipped and had no special throne in the chapel. See Górecki, *Mariawici*, 246–248.

277 According to the teachings of the Catholic Church, a validly ordained priest cannot cease to be ordained and his sacraments are valid, even if he becomes a schismatic or heretic. Cf.'Sprostowanie', *WDM* 1 (1907): 7. The decrees of the Council of Trent (1545–1563) state that 'as in the sacrament of Order, as also in Baptism and Confirmation, a character is imprinted, which can neither be effaced nor taken away; the holy Synod with reason condemns the opinion of those, who assert that the priests of the New Testament have only a temporary power; and that those who have once been rightly ordained, can again become laymen, if they do not exercise the ministry of the word of God'; See 'Chapter IV of The Twenty-Third Session: On the Ecclesiastical Hierarchy, and on Ordination', in *The Canons and Decrees of the Sacred and Oecumenical Council of Trent*, ed. and trans. by James Waterworth (London: Dolman, 1848), 172.

278 'DMHM IV', *MCPS* 28 (1907): 448. It would be a mistake, however, to think that the Polish Catholics were opposed to such a representation of the Mother of God. For example, the Redemptorist Bernard Alojzy Łubieński (1846–1933), who initially supported Kozłowska's mission, shared a devotion to Our Lady of Perpetual Help with the Mariavites even after 1906. See Władysław Szołdrski, 'Les Rédemptoristes polonais dans l'empire Russe de 1905 à 1910', *Spicilegium Historicum: Congregationis Ssmi Redemptoris* 53 (2005): 394–395.

279 'Z niedalekiej', 27. Later, the Mariavites interpreted the persecution mystically, comparing it to the Jews' persecution of. Citing Cieszkowski, the Mariavites claimed that the enemies could not tolerate the vision given to the Great Daughter of the Polish Nation. See Próchniewski, *Żywot*, 15–16.

280 Mazur, 'Tworzenie', 47.

any protection.[281] The Roman hierarchs tried to hinder their legalisation by convincing the Russians that the Mariavites were a threat to the state.[282] If the officials had taken these denunciations seriously, especially after the social revolutions of 1905, the Mariavites would have faced serious consequences.[283] Eventually, the government acceded to the Mariavites' request and recognised them as a legally protected religious sect on 28 November 1906.[284] This would not have been possible without the act (*ukaz*) of 17 April 1905, which liberalised religious law in the Empire.[285] The act of 28 November gave the Mariavites legal permission to profess their ideas and hold religious services. It allowed them to build churches, cemeteries and organise autonomous parishes.[286] Priests had to be approved by the governors and were only financially supported by the faithful. All churches taken over by the Mariavites had to be returned to the Catholic Church, including those that had been built or completely renovated after the denunciation of obedience in February.[287] In addition, they were forced to pay all financial dues to the Catholic parishes that had been accumulated before the official legalisation of Mariavitism.[288] Although it was legally decided that the churches belonged to the Catholic Church, the Mariavites saw this as a

---

281 They were even called traitors because the Russians forbade their opponents to use the telegraph system and railways to attack them. Cf. Górecki, *Mariawici*, 199–200.

282 'Kowalski czy Kucharski', *GP* 35 (1932): 276. Pius X also claimed that they were in competition with the Orthodox Church. See Górecki, *Mariawici*, 202.

283 Ignacy Stobiecki, 'Stanisławowi Janowi Rostworowskiemu ku rozwadze', *PNS* 12 (1999): 28. Popiel and Wnukowski allegedly reported to the General Governor that the Mariavites maintained regular and close contacts with socialists. See 'Sprostowanie', *WDM* 11 (1907): 88. These and other denunciations led to unexpected overnight visits; cf. 'DMHM XIII', *MCPS* 49 (1908): 782–783.

284 The full text of the *ukaz* was given after *Warszawskij Dniewnik* in 'Wiadomości bieżące', *WDM* 5 (1907): 35.

285 'Already in the late nineteenth century, pressure had been building for religious reform, especially as regards 'recalcitrants' and 'apostates' seeking affiliation with Catholicism, Lutheranism, or Islam, and by December of 1904 the autocracy agreed to eliminate 'all constraints on religious life not established by law'. Based on a decision by the czar, the new law came into force on 17 April 1906. Cf. Paul W. Werth, *Freedom of Conscience and the Redefinition of Confessional Boundaries in Imperial Russia, 1905–1914* (Washington: The National Council for Eurasian and East European Research, 2002), 3.

286 They were only allowed to form a confederation of autonomous parishes, each of which had to regulate its statutes with the secular authorities. See Warchoł, *Starokatolicki*, 37.

287 Popiel appealed in May to the Russian authorities to return the churches to the Catholics. Cf. 'Sprostowanie', *WDM* 11 (1907): 87.

288 As many parishioners terminated their obedience to the bishops in February, they had to pay all dues from then until 28 November. See 'Z życia maryawickiego', *WDM* 34 (1907): 268.

gross injustice.[289] A few years later, Mateczka compared their situation to the exodus of the Hebrews from Egypt. One puzzling passage in the Bible says that the Jews asked the Egyptians for certain articles and took them with them when they left (Ex 12:35–36). Clement of Alexandria, whose works Mariavite priests knew and read, believed that they were entitled to these goods because they had not been properly rewarded for their work.[290] Similar logic must have guided the Mariavites.[291] The army and Cossacks were occasionally used to remove the Mariavites from the churches. The physical abuse probably did not strengthen the argument about their alleged collaboration with the political occupier.[292] In some places, they solemnly abandoned the churches, carrying the Blessed Sacrament to village huts where temporary chapels were set up.[293] The churches taken from the Mariavites were reconsecrated, even though they had been seized before the official anathema.[294] The Mariavites saw an analogy here with the so-called Donatists of the fourth century, who also considered churches taken from the Catholics to be desecrated.[295]

---

289 They believed that the Dutch government acted more justly in the sixteenth century, because it acted on the assumption that the churches belonged to the people. When the majority of parishes adopted the Reformed view, the church with all its property was given to the Protestant Church. If the majority remained Catholic, it was not taken away. See 'Historya', 74.

290 Clement, *Stromateis*, 139.

291 They even tried to defend the actions of the Hebrews. See 'Uczył Kuba Marcina', *GP* 14 (1930): 29.

292 Cossacks beat the Mariavites who refused to leave the churches with sticks. See Ignacy Stobiecki, 'Prostaczka rozważania z siostrami betankami w tle', *PNS* 47 (2007): 8. Some researchers believe that this was a deliberate tactic on the part of the Russians to deepen the antagonism between the Catholics and the Mariavites and further weaken the influence of the Catholic Church. Cf. Stanisław J. Rostworowski, 'Socjologiczna metoda ujęcia Mariawityzmu', *Nasza Przeszłość* 88 (1997): 403. But this seems to be purely out of prejudice against the Mariavites and not the result of sound historical analysis. It could just as well be said that the Romans persecuted the early Jesus movement with the sole purpose of weakening its relation to other Jewish groups.

293 This was compared to the biblical scenes of carrying the Ark of the Covenant (e.g., Josh 3:3) and the descent of the first Christians into the catacombs. See 'Z niedalekiej', 33–36.

294 The Mariavites felt that this was contrary to canon law because they had not been defiled. For example, no one was murdered there. Cf. 'Sprostowanie', *WDM* 7 (1907): 56. There are Christian churches, notably the Ethiopian Orthodox Tewahedo Church, where even entering a church wearing shoes can be understood to be a defilement. See Sevir B. Chernetsov, 'On the Reasons of Empress Taytu's Anger Which Come Down upon Afawarq Gabra Iyasus in 1894', in *Proceedings of the XVth International Conference of Ethiopian Studies*, ed. Siegbert Uhlig (Wiesbaden: Harrassowitz Verlag, 2006), 218–219. In the Polish context, however, this was atypical.

295 'DMHM XI', *MCPS* 8 (1908): 126.

The Polish bishops and clergy demanded a swift excommunication for the Mariavites.[296] Eventually the decree was issued on 5 December. It reiterated the earlier accusations, adding erroneously that the Mariavites believed that no one could be saved without the help of Maria Franciszka.[297] Kozłowska and Kowalski were immediately excommunicated, and the rest were given twenty more days to think about the situation.[298] In the mentality of most Poles at the time, excommunication was tantamount to condemnation at the Last Judgement.[299] But if the Mariavite sources are to be believed, not a single person backed down, and *Te Deum* was sung to celebrate the decision and to give encouragement.[300] This was not motivated by pride, but by a strong conviction that they were innocent and that even the power of Rome would not harm their mission.[301] They were quick to draw parallels between their condition and the early Christians who had been unjustly expelled from the synagogues (Jn 12:42).[302] Jesus was never reported as using interdicts, censure, or excommunication, and the Mariavites put themselves in line with Girolamo Savonarola (1452–1498), Jan Hus (1369–1415), and Thomas Connecte (d. 1434).[303] The whole situation taught them that the end times mentioned in the 1893 revelation had

---

296 In September and October, Popiel sent letters to Rome demanding a speedy excommunication for all Mariavites. One Polish priest who was in Rome, Skirmunt, wrote a report on 17 September demanding Mateczka be excommunicated. See Górecki, *Mariawici*, 159. The Mariavites believed that the pope had to sacrifice them in order to appease the Polish bishops and avoid a split in the Polish Church. Cf. 'Odpowiedzi Redakcyi', *WDM* 4 (1908): 32. The Mariavites thought that it was the actions of Bishop Stanisław Zdzitowiecki (1854–1927) that led to the publication of the decree. Cf. 'DMHM XIII', *MCPS* 7 (1909): 111.

297 It was also erroneously assumed that Mateczka had appointed Kowalski to the post of Minister General. See 'Dekret Świętej Rzymskiej i Powszechnej Inkwizycji', in Warchoł, *Proces*, 153. The decree was read out in Polish churches on 30 December.

298 The Mariavites believed that this may have been the first case in the history of the Catholic Church of a woman being excommunicated by a pope. However, this depends on the nature of the anathema imposed on Anne Boleyn (1501–1536) or Queen Elizabeth I (reigned 1558–1603). See Marcin Karas, 'Kapłaństwo kobiet w felicjanowskim odłamie mariawityzmu na tle jego założeń teologicznych', *Przegląd religioznawczy* 4 (2000): 92. Kozłowska was subjected to excomunica maior; Cf. Gołębiowski, 'Glosy', 16.

299 Warchoł, *Proces*, 65.

300 'Założenie kamienia', 25–26.

301 Following Pope Innocent III (pope 1198–1216), the Mariavites believed that acting against conscience was a grave sin and it was better to receive excommunication than to oppose conscience. See Krzysztof Mazur, 'Dwie figury', *PNS* 42 (2006): 8. Later, they also referred to the case of Pope Eugene III (pontificate 1145–1153), who imposed an interdict on Poland and cursed the Polish hierarchs for political reasons but was ignored. See Kowalski, 'Słowo wstępne na Wykład Apokalipsy', 747.

302 'Odpowiedzi Redakcyi', *WDM* 20 (1908): 159.

303 'Prawowite bezprawie', *WDM* 72 (1909): 569–570.

indeed come and that the pious 'who refused to worship the image [of the beast]' (Rev 13:15), which for them was tantamount to abandoning devotion to the Blessed Sacrament, would be separated from the ungodly. The Mariavites did not expect the schism, but, when it happened, they viewed it through the prism of the book of Revelation. Kowalski, for example, stated that, when he read the encyclical written against the Mariavites by the pope, he concluded that this man was not the Vicar of Jesus but the Antichrist.[304]

---

304 Kowalski, 'Krótki', 211. Such claims, however, need to be put into context. It is doubtful that they mean that Kowalski literally believed that the pope was the Antichrist. Rather, it is a statement designed to demonstrate unequivocally that the pope was acting against the will of God.

Chapter 4

From the Schism with Rome to Mateczka's Death

This chapter will focus on the years after the schism until the death of Mateczka. These were pivotal times for the formation of the Mariavite identity and their ecclesiology. The reader will have the opportunity to look at the problems they faced in trying to understand how the Catholic Church could become Babylon the Great (Rev 17:5) and yet remain the Bride of Christ. One will also see how the Mariavites lived through the serious dilemma of establishing criteria that would help them recognise authentic revelation. This proved particularly important when a woman began to claim to be the recipient of new divine oracles that challenged Mateczka's authority. Finally, the reaction to the news of the cessation of the valid Eucharist in the Catholic Church and the appearance of the Book of Life (Rev 3:5, 13:8, 17:8, 20:12) will be examined.

1. The First Years after the Schism and Problems with Self-Identification

Deprived of churches, the Mariavites vigorously began to build their own places of worship and other facilities where culture and education could flourish.[1] Schools were established not only to impart knowledge of the new faith but also because the Mariavite children were not admitted to the various educational institutions.[2] In an effort to help adults who had been dismissed from their jobs for their religious beliefs, low-cost shops,

---

[1] By the end of 1909, the Mariavites had built 38 churches and 34 chapels. See Pasek, 'Geneza', 50. In 1910 they had 44 churches, 166 house chapels, 35 shelters, 16 schools, 32 craft workshops, five community shops and a printing press; Rybak, *Mariawityzm*, 43.

[2] The problem of funding these schools arose immediately. The Mariavites contributed as much as they could, but it was not enough. Around 1913 they received some financial help from the government and were exempted from the school tax. But this was not a privilege, as other religious minorities, including Orthodox, Protestants and Jews, were treated in the same way. See 'Kościół Maryawicki w roku 1913', *KM* (1914): 59.

bakeries, union shops, and workshops were opened.³ Lay people were encouraged to take responsibility for their less fortunate brothers and sisters.⁴ The Mariavite priests tried to set an example of modest living for the laity and thus did not live in separate houses but in small monastic cells above the sacristy.⁵ All this made the movement very popular, and even the opponents had to admit that the influence of the Mariavites on society was enormous.⁶ Success, of course, had its negative side. It quickly attracted fraudsters who wanted to take advantage of the complex situation to enrich themselves.⁷ Moreover, this provoked anger among some fanatical Catholics who wanted to destroy the Mariavites at all costs. Certainly, the Catholic hierarchy cannot be held responsible for all the incidents that took place, but some priests actively encouraged their parishioners to distance themselves from the Mariavites, even if family members were involved.⁸ Systematic pogroms did cease after 1909, but slander, boycotts, and occasional strikes continued.⁹ There were people who tried tirelessly to end the schism, but their efforts proved futile.¹⁰

The schism with Rome did not mark the end of the spiritual battle. It was expected that the worst was yet to come. On 9 August 1907, it was revealed to Mateczka that a world war would break out[11] as a consequence

---

3   'Z niedalekiej', 40.
4   The faithful believed that they were one body. See Jan M. M. Kowalski, 'List pasterski (31.12.1909)', *MCPS* 4 (1910): 58. The poor and homeless could find shelter in so-called parish houses.
5   'Życie wewnętrzne Kościoła Maryawickiego', *KM* (1911): 76.
6   *Z Papieżem czy bez Papieża? Pytanie do odpowiedzi dla katolików i maryawitów* (Warsaw: Druk 'Polaka-Katolika', 1911), 28. According to the Mariavites' calculations, they had around 122,000 adherents in 1908; the Russians estimated their number at 128,000. See Mazur, *Mariawityzm*, 41. In 1909, religious processions in Łódź, Warsaw, and Zgierz attracted several thousand participants. Cf. 'Rok 1909', 100. According to the 1911 Catholic Encyclopaedia, the number of the Mariavites reached over 160,000, which seems somewhat exaggerated. Mariavite sources went even further and recorded 200,000 members a year later. See 'Założenie kamienia', 26.
7   'Wiadomości bieżące', *WDM* 4 (1907): 28. Some pretended to be the Mariavites to collect money even in territories where Mariavitism had no representatives, such as Prussia or eastern Russia. Cf. 'Odpowiedzi Redakcyi', *WDM* 9 (1909): 72.
8   Wacław Legański, 'List do Redakcyi', *WDM* 16 (1908): 126.
9   During the procession, stones were thrown and the Blessed Sacrament was desecrated. There were cases where people were dismissed from their jobs. This forced them to migrate to places where Mariavitism was not present. Some of them stopped being Mariavites over time, so this was an effective strategy. See 'Rok 1909', *KM* (1910): 108–110.
10 For example, Pagani sent a letter to Kowalski in 1909, encouraging him to return to the Catholic Church, promising that the Congregation would be recognised. Cf. Mazur, *Mariawityzm*, 58.
11 Kozłowska, 'Wyjątki', 53.

of the rejection of God's mercy and punishment for sins.[12] The fact that the Mariavites interpreted current events in connection with the revelations should not come as a surprise. It was firmly believed that they had been entrusted with a certain mission. They were supposed to represent the Kingdom of God on earth, i.e., a community of holy people united with God through the Eucharist.[13] But, although Jesus defeated Satan, the latter still had the power to tempt Christians into sin until the coming of the end times.[14] These times were fast approaching. All the means to establish the Kingdom of God on earth had been given, and the role of the Mariavites was to put them into practice.[15] This did not mean that the early Mariavites knew how and when the Kingdom would eventually be revealed in full force. They anticipated the imminent reconfiguration of relationships between people representing different nations, languages, and even religions.[16] In 1912, a certain discouragement became noticeable. After all, the formation of any religious group is often accompanied by an initial excitement that gradually fades. It was no different for the Mariavites. The clergy began to feel that they were devoting too much energy to building new places of worship and social institutions, somewhat to the neglect of their religious duties. To rectify this situation, solemn retreats were introduced in all Mariavite parishes. Their leitmotif was a combination of Mt 4:17 ('Repent, for the kingdom of heaven has come near') and Lk 13:5 ('Unless you repent, you too will all perish').[17] The idea of establishing the Kingdom of God on earth called for greater religious commitment.

In the early years of their independent existence, the Mariavites encountered serious problems in trying to establish their own identity. From the

---

12   Próchniewski, *Żywot*, 120.

13   'Przenajświętsza Eucharystia', *MCPS* 24 (1908): 377. Opponents of the Mariavites realised that the Blessed Sacrament was at the centre of their theology and sought to discredit them in the eyes of the public, claiming that they had replaced the Eucharist with small images of Mateczka that were swallowed. Among those who attributed such practices to the Mariavites was the well-known Polish writer Jarosław Iwaszkiewicz (1894–1980). See Konrad M. P. Rudnicki, 'Komentarz', *PNS* 24 (2002): 29. In fact, it all stemmed from a misunderstanding. See Krzysztof Mazur, 'O łykaniu obrazków – glossa trzecia', *PNS* 24 (2002): 26–27.

14   'Ewangelia według św. Mateusza', *MCPS* 13 (1908): 197.

15   There were three periods of development of the Polish kingdom: the beginning, growth, and the end. Growth continued until the nineteenth century. Cf. 'Przenajświętsza Eucharystya', *MCPS* 13 (1908): 203.

16   All were to be animated by love. See 'Przyjdź Królestwo Twoje...', *KM* (1909): 18.

17   'Kościół Maryawicki w roku 1912', *KM* (1913): 49–50.

perspective of the state, they were merely a tolerated sect.[18] This term referred to a group of people who had separated from the legal Church and did not constitute an independent denomination, at least temporarily.[19] From the perspective of the Catholic Church and the majority of Polish society, they were schismatics or even heretics.[20] In their own eyes, however, they were neither sectarians nor schismatics, let alone heretics: they identified themselves as Catholics.[21] Indeed, the history of Christianity knows instances of many charismatic-mystical movements that have had their quarrels with the institutional Church but have not renounced the name Catholic.[22] According to the Mariavites, the term Catholicism meant more than blind obedience to bishops or even popes. It was a set of certain values and principles that not only had to be taught, but also implemented in daily life.[23] They pointed out that the word 'catholic' was introduced by Ignatius of Antioch (died c. 108 AD), a bishop who died a martyr's

---

18 Today we are accustomed to the term 'new religious movements', but in fact this term only began to be widely accepted in the 1970s as a replacement for older terms like 'cult' or 'sect'. See John A. Saliba, Understanding New Religious Movements (Oxford: Altamira Press, 2003), XI.

19 The Mariavites knew that the word had only a descriptive meaning and did not treat it in a derogatory manner, pointing to the fact that even the first Christians were called members of the sect (Acts 28:22). 'Z krainy obłudy i kłamstwa', *WDM* 25 (1909): 200. According to Philip Jenkins, most sociologists classify religious bodies as churches or sects. Churches are considered to be 'larger bodies, more formally structured in terms of hierarchy and liturgy, which appeal to better-off members of society; sects, in contrast, are smaller, less structured, and more spontaneous and draw their members from working-class or lower-class people. Members of churches are born into them; sects find their membership by recruitment and conversion'. Cf. Philip Jenkins, *Mystics and Messiahs: Cults and New Religions in American History* (Oxford: Oxford University Press, 2000), 16.

20 The Mariavites agreed that the schism was regrettable but denied having caused it. As for the term heretic, they never admitted to holding heretical views. See Jan M. M. Kowalski, 'List do Arcybiskupa Edwarda Roppa (17.11.1929)', in *Wymiana prywatnych listów między Biskupami Maryawickimi i Rzymskokatolickimi*, ed. Edward Warchoł (Sandomierz: Wyd. Diecezjalne, 2003), 32.

21 Mateczka was referred to as the Founder. But the Mariavites claimed that the only Founder of their church was Jesus as they remained Catholic. Cf. 'DMHM IV', *MCPS* 20 (1907): 320.

22 Stephen Bullivant drew my attention to the Fraternité Notre Dame, which is a traditionalist Catholic Marian movement founded in 1977 by Bishop Jean Marie Kozik, who received monthly visions, mainly of the Virgin Mary. There are, of course, some parallels with the Mariavites (i.e. revelations), but these occurred in different contexts. The fraternity may have been a response to the changes brought by the Second Vatican Council, while the Mariavites were responding, at least in the first phase, to the arguably weak condition of the Catholic Church in the Polish regions occupied by the Russian Empire. For more information about the Fraternité Notre Dame, see Benjamin E. Zeller, 'The Fraternité Notre Dame: From Emergence in Fréchou to Sojourn in Chicago', *Numen* 67 (2020): 191–225.

23 'DMHM X', *MCPS* 49 (1907): 784.

death in the early second century.²⁴ He held that 'wherever Jesus Christ is, there is also the universal (catholic) Church' ('ὅπου αν ἡ Χριστός Ιησούς, εκεί η καθολική Εκκλησία').²⁵ The Mariavites argued that since they have Jesus in the Blessed Sacrament and the validity of their sacraments cannot be questioned even under canon law, they remain Catholics. At the same time, they were not bothered by the fact that their opponents deprived them of this name, believing that people commonly used a distorted version of the word that was not identical with how Ignatius used it. They willingly adopted the name Mariavites because it pointed to the glorious principle of following the life of Mary.²⁶ Some of their opponents, however, were not even willing to call them this and instead derisively referred to them as Kozłowici, with a reference to Feliksa Kozłowska's surname.²⁷ In the Polish language, the word kozłowita is quite close to the word 'goat', and thus people would bleat when they saw Mariavites.²⁸ The latter even saw it as part of God's plan, claiming that they were 'the goats that lead the flock'.²⁹

It is worth recalling that the earliest Mariavites regarded the Catholic Church not only as part of the universal Church but as the only fully authentic Church. It was the Bride of Jesus who could establish the Kingdom of God on earth, but, because of her corruption, she was unable to fulfil this task.³⁰ The Mariavites did not want to replace the Catholic Church

24   'Odpowiedzi Redakcyi', *WDM* 21 (1908): 168.
25   Ignatius of Antioch, 'Letter to Smyrneans', in *The Apostolic Fathers I*, ed. and trans. Bart D. Ehrman (Cambridge, MA: Harvard University Press, 2003), 304–305. Ehrman translates ἡ καθολική εκκλησία as 'the universal church', while the Mariavites translated it as 'the Catholic Church'. Modern scholars have concluded that Ignatius did not use the term in a technical sense but most likely as an adjective. It could have been applied to other words such as resurrection or epistle. It also meant the wholeness and completeness of the faith. See Holmes, *The Apostolic Fathers*, 255.
26   'Odpowiedzi Redakcyi', *WDM* 21 (1908): 167.
27   Gołębiowski, *Św. Maria*, 10. The history of Christianity knows of countless instances in which opposing factions gave each other names based on their supposed leader. For example, the supporters of Pope Callixtus I (pontificate 218–222) were called Callixtians by their opponents, the supporters of (-anti) pope Hippolytus (170–235). The letter even accused the former of daring to call themselves the 'catholic' church. *Refutation of all Heresies*, trans. M. David Litwa (Atlanta: SBL Press, 2016), 657–659.
28   In these practices, the Mariavites saw the fulfilment of the prophecy in Jer 50:11 'neigh like stallions'. Cf. 'Odpowiedzi Redakcyi', *WDM* 9 (1908): 71. All this went on for a long time because, even in 1939, such bleating could still be heard during the funerals of the Mariavites. See Wacław M. B. Przysiecki, 'Kronika marjawicka: Wzmożenie uczuć religijnych', *GSK* 7 (1939): 108.
29   'Księga Jeremiasz Proroka 50:8', *PŚST II*, 299.
30   It was held that, because of the separation, other churches have not been able to enjoy all the gifts God bestowed on His Bride, for example, some Protestants have rejected

with their own.³¹ Like the Jews who did not accept Jesus, the Catholics remained the people of God. But, like their predecessors, they had committed adultery with false gods and symbolically became Babylon.³² Based on Jer 51:6, the Mariavites believed they had to abandon its structures. The Catholics held to correct dogma and orthodox teaching on the Eucharist but also placed dead law, obedience, and the lack of morality above the will of God. Because of that, they became the Mother of Harlots and of the Abominations of the Earth mentioned in Rev 17:5.³³ Such a situation could only occur at the end of time. For all these reasons, the Mariavites built their identity on the history of the Catholic Church. They relied heavily on the church fathers, but they also referred to popes, saints, and theologians whose authority was only recognised in the Western Church.

Their position towards Rome and the pope was ambiguous. It has already been mentioned that Maria Franciszka claimed that it had been revealed to her in 1903 that Rome was in need of reform, but this was not tantamount to questioning the position of the pope in the Church.³⁴ On another occasion, Kozłowska proposed that Peter may have been equal to the other apostles and that John was even superior to him in his understanding of the mysteries of faith.³⁵ Such opinions, however, were not unprecedented and can be found among the church fathers and theologians or could at least be interpreted in such a way.³⁶ For example, Jerome (347–420) argued that Peter was chosen to be a 'rock' over John only because of his age and

---

the real presence of Jesus in the Eucharist and have been deprived of this sacrament. See Kowalski, 'Stanowisko', 143. Mariavites have always wholeheartedly defended the real presence. Cf. 'Odpowiedzi Redakcyi', *WDM* 7 (1908): 54–55.

31 For a long time, the Mariavites did not consider themselves a separate Christian denomination but simply a Catholic movement that followed Jesus. See 'Odpowiedzi Redakcyi', *WDM* 32 (1908): 256.

32 Damiana M. B. Szulgowicz, 'Ideologia Mariawityzmu w Listach pasterskich i Odezwach arcybiskupa Jana Marii Michała Kowalskiego', in *Z dziejów*, 159. Mickiewicz also compared the priests of the Catholic Church to the ancient Hebrews, who had become corrupt. Cf. 'Notatki z tego, co Brat Adam Mickiewicz mówił na ogólnych zgromadzeniach do Siódemek, albo w prywatnych rozmowach', *GP* 7 (1937): 51. The Mariavites believed that the Jews would eventually convert and accept Jesus. It is very likely that they hold similar views about the Catholics. See 'Ewangelia według św. Mateusza', *MCPS* 32 (1908): 504.

33 Kowalski, 'Stanowisko', 142.

34 Similarly, Słowacki may have argued that the Rome had lost its status as Queen [of Churches] and compared union with it to a curse, but he did not deny its privileged position. See 'Synowie Królestwa: Juljusz Słowacki a Kościół Rzymski', *KBNZ* 52 (1931): 414.

35 Kowalski, 'Krótki', 209.

36 The Mariavites pointed out that Cardinal Nicholas of Cusa (1401–1464) claimed that all the apostles were equal to Peter with respect to authority. Cf. 'Błąd papiestwa', *KBNZ* 38 (1929): 300–301.

'Peter is an Apostle only, [but] John is both an Apostle and an Evangelist, and a prophet'.[37] The question of infallibility was not an issue even after the schism. In 1908, the Mariavites claimed that they did not reject the dogma nor even object to the title 'head of the Church' as long as it was properly understood.[38] They continued to believe that the pope was Peter's successor, whom the church fathers referred to as the prince, leader, or chief of the apostles.[39] Gradually, however, they came to the conclusion that this did not imply definitive and unquestionable authority, since other figures from the Bible were also elevated. Paul, for example, was called the chief and leader of the choir of saints by John Chrysostom (347–407).[40] Moreover, Peter's authority over the rest had certain limits. He could make mistakes and be admonished by others.[41] Likewise, his successors could make mistakes, as the cases of Pope Honorius I (pontificate 625–638) indicated.[42] They could even be excommunicated.[43] For example, Firmilian (died 269), Bishop of Caesarea Mazaca, wrote that Pope Stephen I (pontificate 254–257) cut himself off from ecclesiastical unity by becoming an apostate and schismatic.[44] Therefore, the Mariavites believed that the pope was infallible

---

37 Jerome, 'Against Jovinianus Book I', in *Jerome: The Principal Works of St. Jerome*, ed. Philip Schaff, trans. William H. Freemantle (Grand Rapids, MI: Eerdmans, 1954), 816. Cyril of Alexandria (376–444) called Peter and John 'equal in honor as apostles and holy disciples'; see Cyril, 'Third Letter to Nestorius', in *Cyril of Alexandria, Selected Letters*, ed. and trans. Lionel R. Wickham (Oxford: Clarendon Press, 1983), 19.

38 'Odpowiedzi Redakcyi', *WDM* 14 (1908): 111–112.

39 'DMHM V', *MCPS* 24 (1907): 381. Peter was given this title but with some reservation. For example, Gregory of Nyssa calls him the head of the apostles in whom all the apostles are remembered. James and John are also princes of the apostolic order. See *The Brill Dictionary of Gregory of Nyssa*, ed. Lucas F. Mateo-Seco, Giulio Maspero (Leiden: Brill, 2010), 711.

40 John Chrysostom, 'Homily XXXII on the Epistle to the Romans', in *Saint Chrysostom: Homilies on the Acts of the Apostles and the Epistle to the Romans*, ed. Philip Schaff, trans. by J. B. Morris and W. H. Simcox (Grand Rapids, MI: Eerdmans, 1925), 993. Elsewhere, Chrysostom favoured the authority of James, the Lord's brother, over that of Peter, stating that the former was 'invested with the chief rule'. John Chrysostom, 'Homily XXXIII on Acts', in *Saint Chrysostom*, 387.

41 He did not have to authorise Paul's missionary efforts. The latter rebuked Peter, as evidenced in the Epistle to the Galatians; see 'Odpowiedzi Redakcyi', *WDM* 9 (1908): 72

42 'Odpowiedzi Redakcyi', *WDM* 13 (1908): 102–104.

43 'Błąd papiestwa', *KBNZ* 2 (1930): 13.

44 Cyprian, *Letter 75*, 311. Similarly, Pope Gregory IV (pope 827–844) was threatened with excommunication by the Frankish bishops in the ninth century for interfering in the internal affairs of the kingdom and expecting the Frankish clergy to follow his example in these matters. See Jan M. M. Kowalski, 'List do Arcybiskupa Edwarda Roppa (21.11.1929)', 39. The context of this situation can be found in Thomas Noble, 'The Papacy in the Eighth and Ninth Centuries', in *The New Cambridge Medieval History*, vol. 2, ed. Rosamond McKitterick (Cambridge: Cambridge University Press, 1995), 584.

only if he did not contradict the deposit of faith.⁴⁵ It can be argued that they were willing to accept the position of the pope as long as he was on their side. It was somewhat more complex. First, the Mariavites referred to the testimony of Augustine, who emphasised that Peter was called blessed (Mt 16:17) as long as he followed the will of God, but when he began to follow his own understanding, he was called Satan (Mt 16:23).⁴⁶ Second, the very fact that the Mariavites continued to affirm the position of the pope after the schism was significant. They could have followed in the footsteps of Nectarios of Aegina (1846–1920) who tried to prove historically that Peter had never been in Rome and therefore could not have been the first pope.⁴⁷ They could have adopted the view of the Orthodox or the Old Catholics, but they did not, at least for some time. The situation changed after the reunion with the Old Catholics, but perhaps not as radically as one might think. In his first pastoral letter, Kowalski argued that no one had the right to call himself 'head of the Church'. The problem, however, lay not in the title itself but in certain prerogatives and honours attached to it, which could only be bestowed on Jesus.⁴⁸ The pope was not the only one who could be infallible; other bishops could also be infallible as long as they followed the Holy Spirit. The Holy Spirit's constant assistance, however, was given only to Jesus and could not be linked to any office.⁴⁹

The conclusion reached by the Mariavites in early 1909, that the pope is the man of lawlessness (2 Thess 2:3), the Catholic hierarchy collectively a false prophet (Rev 16:13) and the Catholic Church a synagogue of Satan (Rev 2:9), was only possible on the assumption that the Catholic Church is the Church of Christ.⁵⁰ Previously, it was expected that the Antichrist would come from Freemasonry; now it was emphasised that he could only manifest himself in the Church since he is said to be 'setting himself up

---

45   'Odpowiedzi Redakcyi', *WDM* 13 (1908): 102–104.
46   Jan M. M. Kowalski, 'List pasterski o nowym przekładzie Pisma Św. (23.08.1923)', in *Ku Królestwu*, 197. Augustine noted that 'Peter was built upon the Rock, not the Rock upon Peter'. According to the Mariavites, his successors could lose the gift of leadership if they did not follow Jesus, who is the Rock. Cf. 'DMHM XI', *MCPS* 52 (1907): 831–832.
47   Νεκτάριος Αιγίνης, Μελέτη ιστορική περί των αιτίων του Σχίσματος (Athens: Panagopoulos Nektarios, 1998), 12–40. He was canonised in 1961 by the Ecumenical Patriarchate of Constantinople. It is worth noting that modern research tends to favour the theory that there was not a single bishop in the Roman Church until the second half of the second century. See Peter Lampe, *From Paul to Valentinus. Christians at Rome in the First Two Centuries*, trans. Marshall D. Steinhauser (Minneapolis: Fortress Press, 2003).
48   Jan M. M. Kowalski, 'List pasterski (31.12.1909)', *MCPS* 3 (1910): 46.
49   Kowalski, 'List do Arcybiskupa Edwarda Roppa (17.11.1929)', 33.
50   Kowalski, 'Stanowisko', 142.

in God's temple' (2 Thess 2:4).[51] These two positions were not necessarily mutually exclusive as it was recognised that Rome had been in the grip of Freemasonry since the pontificate of Pius X.[52] This did not mean, however, that the Mariavites completely rejected the office of the pope, but it certainly meant that they believed it had been corrupted. According to them, there was a clear connection between the dogma of infallibility, the solemn language applied to the pope and the coming of the Antichrist.[53] The revelation was allegedly directed against the papacy in its present form.[54] These views softened somewhat after the Mariavites united with the Old Catholics.[55] The semantic boundaries of the term 'catholic' were noticeably broadened.[56] Since the churches in union with Rome did not have a monopoly on catholicity, the Antichrist could come from elsewhere. But this did not of course exclude the papacy.[57] In 1911, Jesus allegedly revealed to Mateczka that the dogma of infallibility was blasphemy and the idea of Roman primacy an error.[58] She maintained that the pope is Peter's successor and the first among equals, but both statements needed

---

[51] The Mariavites understood the temple of God to be the Church and identified the man of lawlessness with the Antichrist. Cf. 'List II św. Pawła Ap. do Tesaloniczan 2', *NTPP*, 584–585. The word Antichrist does not appear in the Second Epistle to the Thessalonians, so some biblical scholars are cautious about the identity of the man of lawlessness. But many still identify him with the Antichrist, and it seems that for the Mariavites these two characters always referred to one and the same person. Jeffrey A. D. Weima and Stanley E. Porter, *An Annotated Bibliography of 1 and 2 Thessalonians* (Leiden: Brill Publishers, 1998), 263.

[52] Dwojnych, Łętocha, *W stronę Królestwa Bożego*, 92.

[53] Kowalski, 'Stanowisko', 142.

[54] Kowalski, 'Słowo wstępne na Wykład Apokalipsy', 778.

[55] It was still maintained that the Roman Catholic Church was the Church of Christ, but this time it was only part of the universal (catholic) Church. As such, it could not become the embodiment of the Dragon in Revelation 12. Cf. *W Obronie Zasad Ewangelii* (Łódź: Wyd. OO. Maryawitów, 1910), 6.

[56] For example, the Mariavites began to refer to the ancient churches in the East as 'Catholic Eastern Orthodox Churches'. Cf. *Z podróży do ziemi świętej* (Płock: Wyd. OO. Maryawitów, 1927), 8. They officially adopted the name Old Catholic Mariavite Church because they wanted to hold on to the heritage of the undivided universal (Catholic) Church. Cf. Krzysztof Mazur, 'Mariawici piszą', *PNS* 40 (2006): 16.

[57] The Mariavites referred to the visions of La Salette, who said that Rome would become the capital of the Antichrist. See *W Obronie*, 8. Nevertheless, previous perspectives were never fully eliminated. Archbishop Wojciechowski could claim in 2003 that the theological error of Pope Liberius (pontificate 352–366) made the whole Church Arian for a time. Wojciechowski, *Pisma*, 53. He immediately added that the Catholic faith was defended by other eastern and western bishops who did not deny their belief in the divinity of Christ, but the fact that the pope's opinion could so influence the whole Church was significant.

[58] Felicja M. F. Kozłowska, 'Notatki Rekolekcyjne z r. 1911', in *DWM*, 76.

clarification.⁵⁹ The pope was useful from a pragmatic point of view because he could help resolve conflicts between churches, but he was certainly not irreplaceable and definitely did not shape Catholic identity.⁶⁰ His privileged position was due to the dominant position of Rome as the capital of the Roman Empire.⁶¹ He had no authority over the other bishops, but he did know how to take advantage of the fact that they all went to Rome at various times for different reasons.⁶² The Mariavites' change of opinion about the papacy was due not only to revelations but also to in-depth historical and theological research.⁶³ For example, they came to the conclusion that the Catholic hierarchy focused only on the positive aspects of the biblical figures from whom it derived its authority and neglected the critical comments.⁶⁴ From time to time, the Mariavites softened their position towards the Catholic Church, but acceptance of papal infallibility was, at least from 1911 onwards, off the table.⁶⁵ But this is not a problem that could not be overcome on the road to unity.⁶⁶ When the Mariavites proposed union

---

59 There were other successors to Peter who were not bishops of Rome (popes). For example, Ephrem the Syrian (306–373) named Basil of Caesarea as Peter's successor; cf. *W Obronie*, 94. For a precedent, the Mariavites referred to Jerome who argued that Peter was the first among the apostles, just as Plato was the first among the philosophers. Cf. ibid., 104.

60 Nowhere in his letters did Paul mention that one bishop should have authority over all the churches. See 'Bóg w Trójcy Świętej Jedyny', *MCPS* 27 (1910): 418. To paraphrase Ignatius of Antioch, the Catholic Church was where Jesus was, but not necessarily *ibi Christus ubi Roma*. See Jan M. M. Kowalski, 'List do Arcybiskupa Edwarda Roppa (31.10.1929)', in *Wymiana*, 22.

61 There were many apostolic sees in Christendom, although only one in the West. Traditions proclaiming that Barnabas preached in Milan and Mark in Aquileia have been challenged. Cf. 'Powszechne budzenie się Katolicyzmu', *KM* (1913): 91.

62 The Mariavites agreed with the Eastern Patriarchs that the term convenire in Irenaeus' book *Against Heresies* should be translated as 'to gather together', 'to assemble', but not necessarily 'to agree with'. Cf. 'Encyclical of the Eastern Patriarchs, 1848: A Reply to the Epistle of Pope Pius IX, to the Easterns', https://sourcebooks.fordham.edu/mod/1848orthodoxencyclical.asp. Irenaeus (c. 125–c. 202) claimed that the first Roman bishop was Linus (died 76). 'Bóg w Trójcy Świętej Jedyny', *MCPS* 34 (1910): 530.

63 Kowalski, 'List (31.10.1929)', 22.

64 For example, the Catholic hierarchy emphasised the connection between Peter and the rock (τῇ πέτρᾳ, Mt 16:18), but deliberately ignored Mt 13:5 and Lk 8:13, where the seed is said to fall on rocky ground (τὰ πετρώδη). The Mariavites noted the connection between the 'rocky ground' and the papacy but failed to see the connection between the name Peter and the rock depicted in the story. See Roman M. J. Próchniewski, 'Słowo Boże', *GSK* 7 (1938): 100.

65 Szulgowicz, 'Ideologia', 161.

66 The Mariavites knew that Jesus used harsh language in his criticism of the Pharisees. Cf. Jan M. M. Kowalski, 'Błyskawice, głosy i gromy', *KBNZ* 8 (1930): 57. Early Christians also sometimes used insults. The Ebionites, for example, were called poor in intelligence because their name meant 'poor' in Hebrew. See Eusebius, *Ecclesiastical History I*, 263.

with the Catholic Church in the 1920s, they openly stated that some issues would remain points of contention, including papal infallibility.[67]

2. The Significance of the General Chapter after 1907

The first General Chapter after the schism with Rome was held on 10 September 1907 and was attended by 32 priests and two lay delegates from each parish.[68] It was first decided that the General Chapter would be convened every three years during the octve of Pentecost. Kowalski was officially reappointed Minister General, and Próchniewski became his vicar. The office of Minister General was to be for life,[69] but this issue proved controversial in the later history of Mariavitism and was one of the main factors that led to the schism in 1935. The Minister General was given almost unlimited power, and there was no formal mechanism for removing him from office.[70] During Maria Franciszka's lifetime, this issue was not a problem because of her unquestioned authority. Moreover, she promoted the idea of collegiality by seeking the advice of others, notably Próchniewski, Gołębiowski, Skolimowski, Przyjemski, and of course Kowalski.[71]

The Congregation was divided into provinces governed by provincial ministers and their vicars. Provinces were divided into districts (*okręgi*) governed by curators and their vicars. Finally, districts were divided into parishes, which could set up their branches (*filie*). Each parish was to

---

67   'Z prasy przeciwmaryawickiej. Niesłuszne oskarżenie', *KBNZ* 5 (1930): 37–38. Some Catholic theologians claim that the dogma of infallibility has not been fully defined and is therefore not formally binding. This was the view of, among others, Lucjan Balter (1936–2010), who also saw nothing heretical in the revelations of Maria Franciszka. See 'Ksiądz Lucjan Balter', *PNS* 58 (2010): 25.

68   The Mariavites intended to emulate the Jerusalem council at which the apostles met with the elders (Acts 15:6). According to them, the former represented the clergy and the latter the laity. Cf. 'Pierwsze zebranie ogólne księży maryawitów', *KM* (1908): 71. According to Gołębiowski, because lay representatives of parishes outnumbered priests in attendance, it was in fact a form of synod. See Gołębiowski, *W Obronie*, 47.

69   Future Ministers General were to be appointed by a two-thirds majority of provincial ministers and curators in a secret ballot. Cf. ibid., 72.

70   Previous statutes of the Union had delegated all authority to the pope, but after the schism, chapter 10 on this issue was simply removed without being replaced by anything else. Cf. Konrad M. P. Rudnicki, 'Myśli o mariawityzmie I. O rozłamie w roku 1935', *PNS* 60 (2010): 25. The original statutes also provided for recourse to the cardinal protector. It was not replaced by anything else either. See Konrad M. P. Rudnicki, 'Uwagi o ustawach Związku Katolickiego Nieustającej Adoracji Ubłagania', *PNS* 24 (2002): 47.

71   Ignacy Stobiecki, 'Dwugłos o arcybiskupie Janie M. Michale Kowalskim', *PNS* 25 (2002): 19.

have a parish priest and could also have a deacon if needed. The Minister General was to appoint all offices, but in the case of the parish priest he had to discuss this with the parishioners. The Mariavites wanted to give the laity more of a voice, following the example of the early Christian communities.[72] They were also given the option of dismissing their priests on presentation of reasonable arguments.[73] This was introduced to prvent the parish priest from becoming an autocrat. The Mariavites wanted parishioners to take responsibility for the local church. Each parish had four purposes: religious, moral, educational, and charitable.[74]

The general assembly of all parishioners, in addition to electing and dismissing the priest, could elect and dismiss the members of the board of trustees, who were elected for three years with executive and representative functions. The general assembly could decide on financial matters relating to the acquisition and management of parish properties and taking loans. It was to be convened once a year or more often if warranted.[75] Finally, it should be noted that general assembly could deprive some of their members of the right to vote at meetings. However, this was not the same as excommunication, which did not exist in Mariavitism.[76] They justified their decision by referring to Pope Gregory I (pontificate 590–604), who argued that the ban could only be applied to sinful acts but not to people.[77] Furthermore, as followers of Francis of Assisi, they could not ignore the fact that he was not in favour of excommunication.[78]

The participation of the laity was reconsidered not only at the level of decision-making, but also at the level of conducting religious services. The

---

72 For example, the author of the *Didache* wrote that the local congregation elected bishops (most likely a synonym for presbyters) and deacons for themselves. Cf. 'Didache', in *The Apostolic Fathers I*, 441.

73 'Pierwsze', 72. In fact, only the Minister General could dismiss priests at the request of parishioners, so the situation differed from that existing in the early community of Corinth, where younger men themselves expelled their presbyters/elders, even if the latter were honourable and blameless. See Andrew Gregory, '1 Clement: An Introduction', in *The Writings of the Apostolic Fathers*, ed. Paul Foster (New York: T&T Clark, 2007), 24–25.

74 'Organizacya parafii mariawickich', *WDM* 68 (1909): 537–539.

75 'Organizacya parafii mariawickich', *WDM* 70 (1909): 553–554.

76 Modern research tends towards the view that the idea of formal excommunication may have been alien to the early Christians. According to Behr, formal excommunication did not exist in the second century. Cerdo, Marcion, and Valentinus were never formally excommunicated. Even in the case of the famous Paschal conflict, when the Roman bishop Victor (pontificate 189–199) threatened to 'cut off from the common unity all the communities of Asia', it may have been an internal conflict in Rome that suspended the exchange of Eucharistic gifts. Cf. Behr, *Irenaeus*, 24–57.

77 'Prawowite bezprawie', *WDM* 72 (1909): 569–570.

78 Thompson, *Francis*, 74.

celebration of Mass was understood in a collective way, where the laity were understood as co-concelebrants.[79] For this reason, Mariavite priests tried to make all services comprehensible. As early as 16 January 1907, it was decided that all of them, with the exception of the Mass, would be celebrated in Polish.[80] A further step was taken at the first General Chapter, which decided to introduce the vernacular for the Mass as well, and the first one was celebrated in Polish on Christmas Day 1907.[81] A year later, Kowalski celebrated Mass in Lithuanian.[82] This was the first reform, apart from giving the laity the possibility to choose their own priest, that clearly distinguished the Mariavites from the Catholics. The former, however, strongly emphasised that they had not introduced anything new. The Mariavites were proponents of the hypothesis that Christianity was first brought to Poland by the Czechs, who celebrated the Slavic liturgy introduced by Cyril and Methodius. It was only later that the Germans introduced foreign Latin rites.[83] Queen Jadwiga of Poland (reigned 1384–1399) allegedly attempted to reintroduce the Slavic language by bringing Slavic Benedictines from Prague in 1390, but her premature death thwarted these plans. In 1555, the Polish states demanded that King Sigismund II Augustus (reigned 1548–1572) introduce the Polish language in religious services. The idea gained the support of the Archbishop and Primate of Poland Jakub Uchański (1502–1581), but did not meet with the approval of Pope Paul IV (pontificate 1555–1559).[84] The introduction of the Polish language was defended on many different levels. The Mariavites invoked Rom 14:11, where it is stated that 'every tongue will acknowledge God'. They argued that local liturgies had been celebrated in different languages since ancient times, such as Armenian, Greek, and Coptic, which allowed people to participate actively in the mysteries. They pointed out that a local synod in Frankfurt in 794 decided that God must be praised in all

79 The Mariavites wanted to emphasise the active role of the laity in liturgical life. The Greek word λειτουργία is composed of the words λαός (people) and ἔργο (work) and can therefore be understood as work of the people or work for the people. Cf. Pierre Chantraine, *Dictionnaire étymologique de la langue grecque* (Paris: Klincksieck, 1999), 1447.

80 'Z życia maryawickiego', *WDM* 5 (1907): 37. For a while, the Mass continued to be celebrated in Latin as the Mariavites wanted to avoid chaos and needed time to prepare the necessary translations.

81 'Z życia maryawickiego', *WDM* 51 (1907): 405.

82 'Najprzewielebniejszy', 95.

83 It is worth noting that Kowalski encouraged the Russian bishops to conduct services in Russian rather than Old Church Slavonic. Cf. 'Msza Polska', *WDM* 15 (1908): 113–114.

84 Ibid., 114. From the seventeenth to the nineteenth century there was also part of the Mass during the distribution of the Eucharist conducted in Polish. See Kozłowska, Próchniewski, 'Dzieło Miłosierdzia IV', *MCPS* 30 (1910): 479.

languages. Moreover, as late as the 17th century, the Jesuits received permission from Pope Paul V (pontificate 1605–1621) to celebrate Mass in Chinese, which may have helped them attract new converts.[85] The use of vernacular languages had been introduced in Mariavitism long before the union with the Old Catholics and did not influence their decision in this regard.[86] It is worth noting that, around the same time, voices were raised in the Catholic Church, most notably by the Belgian Benedictine monk Lambert Beauduin (1873–1960), to make a full translation of the Mass available to the laity.[87]

Several other issues were discussed during the General Chapter. It was decided that divorce would not be accepted. Like the Catholics, however, people could seek an annulment of marriage if they had a strong case.[88] Clerics were not to be sent to seminaries. After completing at least four years of middle school, they were to assist priests and observe them for four years. After this period, they would enter a one-year novitiate since it was intended that they become both priests and monks. Only then could they be ordained.[89] In 1908, the Mariavites claimed to have candidates for the clergy but did not know what to do with them. The fact that the Mariavites firmly believed that only bishops could validly ordain clergy left them with a fundamental problem.[90] At the time of the General Chapter, the Mariavites had no bishops. There have been exceptional occasions in Catholic Church history when ordinations were carried out in a non-canonical way and then recognised as valid by others.[91] Nevertheless, the Mariavites did not entertain the idea of breaking with tradition. Most likely, they hoped that some

---

85 'Msza Polska', 115.

86 The Dutch language was introduced in the Old Catholic Church in Holland in 1911. The Mariavites believed that this was one of the reasons for the increase in the number of believers in the Church. Cf. 'Z życia Kościołów Starokatolickich', *KM* (1913): 63.

87 Indeed, such translations had been prepared for some parishes in Belgium and Germany. These were met with criticism in conservative circles, which claimed that parishioners were attending Mass too loudly, depriving the service of mystery and solemnity. Chadwick, *A History*, 363.

88 'Pierwsze', 73–74. The early Mariavites were quite conservative and only allowed divorce in cases of adultery, but even then they encouraged reconciliation. Cf.'Ewangelia według św. Marka', *MCPS* 30 (1910): 470.

89 'Pierwsze', 76.

90 'Odpowiedzi Redakcyi', *WDM* 25 (1908): 200.

91 For example, Anglicans tried to defend the continuation of their ordination during the English Civil War (1642–1651), when the episcopal system was under serious attack and canonical ordination was hampered. Ecumenical Patriarch Meletius IV (in office 1921–1923) recognised the validity of Anglican ordination on behalf of his Orthodox Church, which was later accepted by some other Orthodox Churches. See Damian Cyrocki, Relacje anglikańsko – prawosławne od początku XIX w. do roku 1938 w perspektywie ważności

Catholic bishops would eventually join them. In 1909, they sent letters to Catholic bishops around the world, informing them of the aims and progress of Mariavitism, but this did not meet with a positive reception.[92] The matter was finally resolved after the union with the Old Catholics. On 10 October 1909, Kowalski was able to ordain Przysiecki and Feldman as subdeacons in accordance with canon law.[93] The first ordination of priests, however, took place on 15 August 1914, the day after the consecration of the Temple of Mercy and Charity.[94]

3. Union with the Old Catholics

After excommunication in 1906, the Catholic Union of Perpetual Propitiation Adoration became the Mariavite Union of Perpetual Propitiation Adoration. The organisation still had four departments, but the boundaries between them became increasingly blurred over time until they disappeared altogether.[95] Similarly, some of the statutes became redundant after a while.[96] It is extremely important to note that, for almost three years, the Mariavites did not exist as a separate church but only as an independent union.[97] Legally, they were a loose association of several independent parishes. Kowalski and Próchniewski therefore went to St Petersburg at the end of 1908 to deal with this unfavourable situation. Each parish could have seceded, and the Union would have lost all properties

---

święceń kapłańskich, (Krakow: Jagiellonian University, unpublished Bachelor's thesis 2001), 39–40.

92 Wojciechowski, 'Mariawityzm', 16.

93 Together with Feliks M. Mateusz Szymanowski and Michał M. Grzegorz Fortuna. Cf. 'Dzieło Miłosierdzia. Kronika Maryawicka', *MCPS* 6 (1910): 94. Eight days later, along with Franciszek M. Alojzy Gromulski, they were consecrated as deacons. See 'Z życia maryawickiego', *WDM* 83 (1909): 663.

94 Rybak, *Mariawityzm*, 47.

95 The Confraternity ceased to exist with the outbreak of the First World War. The Tertiaries disappeared, although not completely, during the Second World War. See Konrad M. P. Rudnicki, 'Liczba zgromadzeń w mariawityzmie', *PNS* 67 (2012): 27. The division became more conventional between clergy and laity. The introduction of the people's priesthood in the Catholic Mariavite Church was an attempt, albeit not entirely successful, to bridge this divide.

96 Rudnicki, 'Trzecie wydanie', 23.

97 It can be argued that they became a church when Kowalski was ordained bishop in 1909. But they did not gain full independence until a year later, when Gołębiowski and Próchniewski were also consecrated, as they had three bishops at that time. Cf. Jerzy Fidura, '100-lecie istnienia Starokatolickiego Kościoła Mariawitów (1906–2006)', *Studia Ełckie* 8 (2006): 105–106.

and assets.⁹⁸ The visit to Russia was partially successful, and the internal statutes of the parishes were formally recognised on 16 February 1909.⁹⁹ Autonomous parishes were able to elect their priests without interference from the Minister General. The parishioners could elect a board of trustees to manage finances on their behalf. Its activities were controlled by an assembly of all parishioners. Women and men had equal voting rights, but all elected board members were men. This was most likely for practical reasons, as the board members were supposed to represent the parish in its dealings with the secular authorities.¹⁰⁰ Nonetheless, the trip to Russia did not change the most important thing. Legally, the Mariavites were still considered a confederation of independent parishes.¹⁰¹ This was soon to change.

While in St Petersburg, the Mariavites met the Russian General Alexander Kirejew, rector of the Ecclesiastical Academy, who encouraged them to establish contacts with the Old Catholics.¹⁰² Until then, the Mariavites' knowledge of the Old Catholics was residual and even negative.¹⁰³ The Mariavites formed a Eucharist-centred union whose members advocated daily communion, while the Old Catholics were portrayed as very strict in this regard.¹⁰⁴ In reality, however, they were no different from other Catholics and were also inclined to modify their theology.¹⁰⁵ At the

---

98   In St Petersburg, the Mariavites discovered that their opponents, who had portrayed them in Poland as collaborators with Russia, had presented them to the Russian government as anti-Russian rebels. Cf. 'Delegaci Związku Maryawickiego w Petersburgu', *WDM* 4 (1909): 25–26. Attempts were made to associate the Mariavites with almost everyone, including their main opponents, the National Democrats, depending on whom the public considered to be the enemy. Cf. 'Z krainy obłudy i kłamstwa', *WDM* 6 (1909): 48.

99   Sławomir Gołębiowski, 'Wpływ prawa państwowego na kształtowanie organizacji mariawickich', *PNS* 41 (2006): 53.

100   To justify the practice of equal rights, at least in theory, the Mariavites referred to Gal 3:28. See 'Organizacya parafii mariawickich', *WDM* 66 (1909): 522.

101   Mazur, *Mariawityzm*, 48.

102   Ibid., 46. Kirejew participated in the famous Bonn Conference in 1874, which aimed to unite the Old Catholics with the Orthodox Churches. Cf. 'The Fourteen Theses of the Old Catholic Union Conference at Bonn A. D. 1874', https://ccel.org/ccel/schaff/creeds2/creeds2.vii.i.html.

103   For example, they regarded Jansenism, which is a theological movement strongly linked to Old Catholicism, as a heresy because it was fiercely opposed by Louis-Marie Grignion de Montfort (1673–1716). See 'DMHM III', *MCPS* 14 (1907): 223–224. The Mariavites believed that they were called to form the army of Mary prophesied by De Montfort. Cf. Kozłowska, 'Początek', 14.

104   Joseph Dougherty, *From Altar-Throne to Table: The Campaign for Frequent Holy Communion in the Catholic Church* (Maryland: Scarecrow Press, 2010), 15–16.

105   The idea that the Eucharist was a kind of reward for virtue rather than a medicine to help one overcome sin prevailed in most Western churches in the eighteenth century. Ralph

end of August 1909, Kowalski received an invitation to an Old Catholic congress in Vienna. There, both parties expressed their willingness to unite,[106] and on 5 October 1909, Kowalski was consecrated a bishop. The ceremony was held at St Gertrude's Church in Utrecht by the Archbishop of Utrecht, Gerardus Gul (1847–1920), assisted by Bishops Jakob van Thiel of Haarlem (1843–1912), Nicholas Spit of Deventer (1853–1929), Josef Demmel of Bonn (1846–1913) and Arnold Mathew (1852–1919) of London. A week before the event, pastoral letters were read out in Old Catholic churches in the Netherlands informing parishioners about Mariavitism.[107] After the consecration, new opportunities opened up for the Mariavites. Kowalski, for example, confirmed 1,342 people on 17 and 18 October.[108]

There were, however, some organisational problems. The Mariavites retained the monastic structure, and provinces and custodies instead of dioceses and deaneries.[109] Another problem concerned the relationship between the bishops and the Minister General.[110] The latter did not have to be a bishop and had certain prerogatives that placed him above the former.[111] It was the Minister General who was to be the chief consecrator of bishops in the Church of Mariavites; if he was not a bishop, he had to appoint a chief consecrator from among the available Mariavite bishops.[112] After 4 September 1910, when Próchniewski and Gołębiowski were

---

Gibson, *A Social History of French Catholicism, 1789–1914* (New York: Routledge, 1989), 257. The Mariavites acknowledged that, on careful reading, the so-called Jansenist errors turned out to be correct statements. See *W Obronie*, 34–37.

106 The congress and conference ran from 7 to 9 September. Cf. 'Międzynarodowy Kongres Starokatolicki w Wiedniu', *WDM* 77 (1909): 609–611.

107 'Konsekracja Biskupa Naszego w Utrechcie', *WDM* 81 (1909): 642–643.

108 'Z życia maryawickiego', *WDM* 83 (1909): 663.

109 Konrad M. P. Rudnicki, 'Czy mariawityzm może istnieć Zgromadzenia Mariawitów', *PNS* 37 (2005): 21.

110 A similar problem of authority already existed when the Mariavites were members of the Roman Catholic Church. When Petrykowski was considering joining the Congregation, he was the administrator of the Płock diocese. If he had joined the Congregation, he would have been in a sense responsible to Przyjemski, who had a lower position in the Catholic Church but was the informal leader of the Congregation. Przyjemski, 'Mariae-Vita', 243.

111 The consecration of a bishop had to be approved by the General Chapter, the Minister General, the clergy, the laity and other bishops who joined the Mariavites. The example of the Dutch Catholic Church was used to justify this practice. In the twelfth century, the bishop there was elected by both clergy and laity. Later, election was restricted to the priests of the cathedral church only. Conflict erupted when Rome began to claim the right to appoint bishops for Dutch Christians. Cf. 'Historya', 70–72.

112 'Konsekracya Biskupów', *KM* (1911): 89.

ordained as bishops, the Mariavites gained ecclesiastical independence.[113] The secular authorities were informed of the changes and decided to make legal amendments in the light of the new situation. On 22 October 1910, Kowalski was appointed by the Russian czar as administrator of all the Mariavite parishes, but, in reality, the latter were still considered a federation of independent entities. Próchniewski and Gołębiowski were officially appointed his administrative assistants in January 1911.[114] From a legal point of view, the Mariavites only became a church on 11 March 1912, when the Russian authorities finally granted them the same prerogatives as other churches.[115] In particular, the permission to keep civil records proved to be important, as officials sometimes registered the Mariavites as members of the Orthodox Church or referred them to Catholic priests who used this as an opportunity to try to convert them to the Roman Catholic Church.[116]

Apart from all the advantages, the union with the Old Catholics also had some disadvantages. The Mariavites never wanted to limit their activities to just one nation. Requests for Mariavite priests came from Odesa, the Volga area, St Petersburg, the Caucasus and even Sakhalin.[117] The Mariavites also attracted people who were not ethnically Polish, but an insufficient number of clergy and a limited budget meant they were unable to respond to the needs of all who asked for them.[118] In Lithuania, they had only two

---

113 The fourth canon of the First Ecumenical Council of Nicea (325) states that it is desirable for each bishop to be consecrated by all the bishops of the province. If this is not possible for legitimate reasons, the consecration may be done by three bishops with the written consent of the others. Finally, the consecration must be approved by the Metropolitan Bishop. Cf. 'Sobór Nicejski I', in *Dokumenty Soborów Powszechnych*, ed. Arkadiusz Baron, Henryk Pietras SJ (Krakow: Wyd. WAM, 2003), 29. But this canon did not claim that ordinations conferred by a single bishop were invalid, especially in extraordinary circumstances. See Szczepan Włodarski, *Siedem Soborów* (Warsaw: IW Odrodzenie, 1968), 44.

114 Warchoł, *Starokatolicki*, 38–39.

115 For example, priests were allowed to keep civil records, and divorces were to be settled by the Church. But divorce orders had to be recognised by secular authorities. See Gołębiowski, 'Wpływ prawa', 54.

116 'Delegaci', 26.

117 These requests were sent mainly by Poles living in these regions who had heard of priests celebrating services in Polish and wanted to attend. In the Congress Kingdom of Poland, the Mariavites were considered Russian collaborators, but to these people they were promoters of Polish culture. Financial matters made it impossible to send priests there. See 'Rok 1909', 100.

118 For example, in 1913 in Vilnius, after a rental agreement was concluded, the landlord demanded double the price, mainly because the windows were constantly broken, making it difficult to hold Mass. The Mariavites were forced to find another place to hold services. Cf. 'Wilno', *KM* (1914): 88–89.

priests, which severely limited missionary progress.[119] Nevertheless, they had some successes. For example, in 1910 they opened a chapel in Kyiv and in 1913 managed to organise a parish in Riga, the capital of Latvia.[120] In addition, they carried out a mission in France.[121] They were even known in Brazil, where the local Polish population encouraged them to come.[122] After the union, the Mariavites had to respect the local jurisdictions of the Old Catholic bishops and were not free to conduct missions in their territories.

4. Maria Czychlarzowa and Wacław Żebrowski

After the Mariavites began to ordain bishops, quarrels, and jealousy over positions began. The priest Wacław Żebrowski (1877–1931) was known for his oratorical skills, impeccable life, and diligence.[123] Despite this, according to the Mariavite sources, he could not accept the fact that his candidacy for bishop was not considered.[124] He joined forces with Maria Czychlarzowa, who introduced herself as Mary of Prague.[125] For several years, she tried to mediate between the Catholic hierarchy and the Mariavites, but when this proved unsuccessful, she decided to join the Church of Mariavites and offer her flat for use as a chapel. Żebrowski was appointed to hold services there, but Czychlarzowa only allowed people into her home whom she considered to be filled with the Holy Spirit.[126] Kowalski was forced to close this chapel after a while, but Żebrowski continued to maintain private contacts with Czychlarzowa. From the beginning of November 1910, he began to promote public confession in Warsaw

---

119 'Kościół Maryawicki w roku 1910', *KM* (1911): 59.

120 'Kościół Maryawicki w roku 1913', *KM* (1914): 56.

121 Mames, *Oświata*, 253–260. See also Tomasz M. D. Mames, 'Mariawici i Mariawityzm doby I Wojny Światowej. Przykład Austriackiej Okupacji Terenów Królestwa Polskiego', in *Prowincja Galicyjska Wokół I Wojny Światowej*, ed. Tomasz Pudłocki and Arkadiusz S. Więcha (Przemyśl: Wyd. Towarzystwo Przyjaciół Nauk, 2014), 83.

122 'Kościół Maryawicki w roku 1910', 63–65. Four Mariavite families were forced to migrate to Brazil from Leszno in 1912. A year later, there were already several Mariavite families in Paraná but no priest. Cf. 'Odpowiedzi Redakcyi', *WDM* 7 (1913): 112.

123 'Fakta mówią', *KM* (1909): 122.

124 Mames, *Mysteria*, 37.

125 Her name is spelt differently in different sources: Cyglar, Cyklar, Cychlarz, and Cyhlarz.

126 She herself also received communion directly from the ciborium, the metal vessel in which the Eucharist is stored. Cf. 'Wyjaśnienie', *WDM* 18 (1911): 137. It is possible that she even celebrated Mass with Żebrowski's knowledge and consent. Cf. Kowalski, 'Krótki', 234–235.

churches.[127] Mateczka strongly opposed this, arguing that not only did it not purify consciences, but it actually encouraged sin.[128] Moreover, after the revolution of 1905, all public gatherings were under police surveillance. Public confession was not only a violation of church penance but a social threat.[129] Żebrowski, however, ignored the admonitions and began to foment against the Mariavites, gathering Christians from other denominations, including Baptists, around him.[130] On 5 February 1911, he informed Mateczka that she had been abandoned by God and was no longer a Mariavite.[131] This information came from a private revelation given to Czychlarzowa who maintained that God had appointed her to replace Mateczka as Mother of Mercy. Kowalski ordered Żebrowski to break with Czychlarzowa, but the latter refused and was removed from the Church of Mariavites.[132] In retaliation, he began to incite people to demand the money they had given to build Mariavite churches and other social buildings be refunded. He sent his followers to all the parishes to incite revolts.[133]

The churches in Warsaw legally belonged to Żebrowski, who had acquired them with parishioners' money, but in his private name.[134] There was thus the threat that the Church of Mariavites would lose these establishments. Kowalski decided to appeal to the Russian authorities, who ruled in favour of the Mariavites in this conflict.[135] Paradoxically, they used a legal act here that had been passed against them in the past. The Senate – the highest executive body in the Russian Empire – decided on 7 December 1908 that the eviction of Mariavite priests from churches to which the Catholic Church claimed rights should take place on the basis of

127 He publicly confessed his sins, especially those concerning sexual matters. He also began to publicly attack other Mariavite priests for their alleged immorality. See Janusz Sobiech, 'Początki ruchu wolnych chrześcijan w Polsce do 1918 roku', *RTChAT* 59 (2017): 310.
128 Kozłowska, 'Notatki', 74.
129 Gołębiowski, *W Obronie*, 71.
130 'Wyjaśnienie', *WDM* 18 (1911): 138.
131 Kozłowska, 'Notatki', 75.
132 'Wyjaśnienie', *WDM* 18 (1911): 139. As already mentioned, he could not be excommunicated because this form of punishment did not exist in the Church of Mariavites. They believed that a person could condemn himself but could not be anathematised by others.
133 'Założenie kamienia', 26.
134 Kowalski, 'Krótki', 232. When the legal status of Mariavite parishes was regularised in 1909, they had an excellent opportunity to stabilise their financial situation, but they did not take advantage of it. See Sławomir Gołębiowski, 'Testament księdza Pągowskiego', *PNS* 50 (2008): 19.
135 This provided another argument the opponents of the Mariavites could use, i.e., that they were supported by the Russians. Bishop Józef Sebastian Pelczar (1842–1924) believed that the Mariavites were financially supported. Sobiech, 'Początki', 313–314.

administrative rather than civil law. The Russians did not want to antagonise relations with the Vatican, counting on its help in pacifying socialist tendencies. Kowalski, in applying to the authorities against Żebrowski, relied on the 1908 decision that had the effect of expropriating Żebrowski's churches.[136]

Some Mariavites believed that the scandal revolving around Czychlarzowa could have been initiated by representatives of the Catholic Church who wanted to introduce discord among the Mariavites and discredit them in the eyes of Polish society. Czychlarzowa was not the first person to use her private revelations to lessen Mateczka's authority. For example, Weronika Trafilska claimed to have experienced revelations, which she presented to Przyjemski on 3 November 1896.[137] She tried to replace Maria Franciszka as Superior of the Congregation but was removed. She then moved to Włocławek and was immediately accepted into another congregation, also founded by Koźmiński. The fact that no one consulted Maria Franciszka before her admission raises some suspicions, given that Trafilska was expelled on disciplinary grounds. Stobiecki speculated that Trafilska, like Czychlarzowa, acted on the orders of someone who was trying to discredit Mateczka among the Mariavites.[138] The two women acted in different contexts and may have been influenced by different people, but their aims and modus operandi overlapped.

An Austrian citizen, Czychlarzowa, was sent back to Austria by the Russian authorities. Żebrowski followed her but did not stay there long and soon moved to the United States, where he was consecrated as a bishop by Franciszek Hodur (1866–1953), Prime Bishop of the Polish National Catholic Church.[139] The problem was that the Polish National Catholic Church was a member of the Union of Old Catholic Churches, so he was in full communion with the Church of Mariavites at the time of Żebrowski's ordination. There were several other problems. Żebrowski did not belong to the church under Hodur's jurisdiction, and Hodur did not ask the opinion of his former superior, namely, Kowalski. Finally, Żebrowski did not repre-

---

136 Ignacy Stobiecki, 'Ważne wyjaśnienie', *PNS* 18 (2000): 35–37.
137 Ignacy Stobiecki, 'Tajemnicza siostra W…?!' *PNS* 62 (2011): 18–20.
138 Ibid., 20.

139 There are some ideas shared by the Church of Mariavites and the Polish National Catholic Church, i.e., relating to the understanding of the term 'catholic'. Both ecclesiastical bodies were established at about the same time. However, from the very beginning they emphasised different theological issues. See Edward Warchoł, *Podobieństwa i różnice między Starokatolickim Kościołem Mariawitów i Polskim Narodowym Kościołem Katolickim od ich powstania do końca okresu międzywojennego* (Sandomierz: Wyd. Diecezjalne, 2012), 39–50.

sent any parish, and according to Old Catholic theology, a bishop can only be ordained for a parish.[140] Żebrowski's subsequent fate is no less interesting. He returned to Poland, became a Baptist, was rebaptised and married, continuing to fight with the Mariavites over financial issues.[141]

The problems regarding Czychlarzowa, Żebrowski, and even Trafilska showed that the Mariavites did not accept revelations and visions uncritically.[142] They were aware that the Bible and ancient Christian documents warned against false prophets and teachers.[143] Moreover, their opponents quoted 1 Tim 4:1 against them, claiming that 'in later times some will abandon the faith and follow deceiving spirits and things taught by demons'.[144] All of this forced the Mariavites to come up with criteria to help them distinguish authentic visions from false hallucinations. This was not the first such problem in the history of Christianity. For example, Apollonius of Ephesus, a second-century bishop, claimed that an authentic prophet or prophetess did not receive gifts or money for his oracles, did not dye his hair, paint his eyelids, adore ornaments, or gamble.[145] According to the Mariavites, an authentic Christian prophet (προφήτης) plays the same role as a Hebrew *nabi* (נָבִיא). He is someone who proclaims something in the name of God.[146] A true seer is zealous for God's glory and diminishes his own role.[147] He does not reveal the content of the revelations unless commanded by God.[148] His oracles may be full of threats, but they always contain a glimmer of hope.[149] The Mariavites were sceptical of ecstatic experiences, believing that human souls should remain passive when receiving God's oracles.[150] Mateczka strongly opposed any rapturous

---

140 Mames, *Mysteria*, 37–38.

141 Marcin Karas, 'O pewnym 'reformatorze' mariawityzmu', *PNS* 18 (2000): 30–33.

142 'Bóg w Trójcy Świętej Jedyny', *MCPS* 30 (1909): 466.

143 For instance, *Didache* 11:8. Cf. Jan M. M. Kowalski, 'List do Arcybiskupa Edwarda Roppa (08.12.1929)', in *Wymiana*, 64.

144 The Mariavites noted that the Catholics mistranslated ὑστέροις καιροῖς as 'end times' rather than 'later times'. Cf. 'Odpowiedzi Redakcyi', *WDM* 38 (1908): 304.

145 Eusebius, *Ecclesiastical History I*, 491.

146 'Bóg w Trójcy Świętej Jedyny', *MCPS* 19 (1909): 286. Old Testament prophets were understood by early Christians as speaking in the name of the Father, Jesus, or the Holy Ghost on various occasions. See Justin Martyr, 'The First Apology', 73–76.

147 'Bóg w Trójcy Świętej Jedyny', *MCPS* 30 (1909): 467–469.

148 For example, Mary did not explain the nature of her pregnancy to others because she had no sign from God to do so. She waited for the angel of God to inform Joseph in a dream. See 'Ewangelia według św. Mateusza', *MCPS* 43 (1907): 679.

149 'Bóg w Trójcy Świętej Jedyny', *MCPS* 19 (1909): 287.

150 'Cuda Teresy Neuman', *GP* 5 (1931): 34–35. For this reason, they did not have a positive view of the Montanists. Cf. 'Bóg w Trójcy Świętej Jedyny. Dowody Istnienia Pana Boga', *MCPS* 18 (1909): 276.

experience and wanted to eradicate traces of hysteria in the Church.[151] Surprisingly, after the schism, the Mariavites were sometimes compared to Quakers, most likely because of their alleged susceptibility to exaltation and relationship to the Holy Spirit.[152] It was possible to induce artificial ecstatic states by various means, which made them ambivalent. They did not come from God, though they did in many cases result from a genuine desire to unite with the divine.[153] False prophecies usually contained inaccurate historical data, and their recipients claimed to have obtained them by dubious means.[154] Being filled with the Holy Spirit was the sin qua non of being an authentic prophet.[155] The Mariavites believed that every prophet could be recognised by the fruit he bore (Mt 7:16), even if he did not perform any miracles.[156] Finally, his oracles had to be in accordance with the prophecies contained in the Apocalypse.[157]

5. The Temple of Mercy and Charity

In 1902, Maria Franciszka purchased a house with a garden at 27 Dobrzyńska Street.[158] The location was important for several reasons. Dobrzyńska Street had been called Jerozolimska (Jerusalem) Street in the past, which automatically brought to mind the site where the Jewish Temple had once stood.[159] This was also the location of the church dedicated to Philip and Jacob and of the bishop's mansion until the eighteenth

151 Kowalski, 'Krótki', 166.
152 Górecki, *Mariawici*, 275. The idea may have been borrowed from Ronald Knox (1888–1957), an English Catholic priest and historian who, in his book *Enthusiasm*, grouped the second-century Montanists, the fourth-century Donatists, the twelfth-century Waldensians, the seventeenth-century Jansenists, and various Quaker and Methodist churches under the pejorative label 'enthusiast', applied to charismatic groups whose members claimed to be directly led by the Holy Spirit. Cf. Evelyn Waugh, *The Life of Right Reverend Ronald Knox* (London: Penguin Books, 2012), 274.
153 'Bóg w Trójcy Świętej Jedyny', *MCPS* 19 (1909): 285.
154 'Proroctw nie lekceważcie: Cel proroctw', *KBNZ* 3 (1928): 18–19.
155 'Bóg w Trójcy Świętej Jedyny', *MCPS* 18 (1909): 276.
156 The same criterion was applied to the authentic Church. See 'Bóg w Trójcy Świętej Jedyny', *MCPS* 29 (1910): 449. Miracles were only valid if they led to conversion. Cf. ibid., 452.
157 'Z życia maryawickiego', *WDM* 7 (1910): 54.
158 Gołębiowski, *Św. Maria*, 32.
159 This is why the Mariavite Youth Association, founded in 1932, was called the 'Templars'. This referred not only to the Poor Fellow Soldiers of Christ and the Temple of Solomon, known as the Knights Templar, but above all to the Temple of Mercy and Charity. Cf. Tomasz M. D. Mames, 'Związek Młodzieży Mariawickiej "Templariusze" (1932–1935)', in *Sborník příspěvků mezinárodní vědecké konference Evropské pedagogické forum 2* (Hradec Králové: Magnanimitas, 2012), 338.

century.¹⁶⁰ The house initially served as a convent for Mariavite nuns, but the Temple of Mercy and Charity was later built in its place.¹⁶¹ The cornerstone of the building was laid on 27 May 1911. For the Mariavites, it was a moment of triumph that reassured them of the rightness of the cause.¹⁶² Their opponents, however, refused to be forgotten. They began to claim that the choice of date was not accidental and marked the anniversary of the coronation of the Russian Emperoczar.¹⁶³ In fact, it was the date of Feliksa Kozłowska's fiftieth birthday.¹⁶⁴ Although the Mariavites did not have many followers in Płock, this city was the best place for them to build their Temple.¹⁶⁵ It was there that Maria Franciszka received revelations and organised the Congregation. The construction of the Temple required an enormous amount of money. It was another test for the fledgling Church as well as another opportunity for opponents to discredit the Mariavites. No one should be surprised by the allegations that the construction was allegedly financed by the Russian government, which was fighting the Poles and the Catholic Church at that time.¹⁶⁶ In reality, however, people underestimated the willingness of the Mariavites to make sacrifices. The Temple, whose construction cost 200,000 roubles, was built entirely because of the generosity of the faithful and supporters.¹⁶⁷ The plans for the project were prepared mainly by Kowalski, with the help of Maria Franciszka, Przysiecki, and Feliks M. Mateusz Szymanowski (1875–1943).¹⁶⁸

160 Dominik Stoszewski, *Dawne kościoły płockie* (Płock: Druk. K. Miecznikowski, 1912), 43–44.

161 Initially, the building was called the Cathedral of Perpetual Propitiation Adoration. It was not until 1918, as a result of a revelation, that the name was changed to the Temple of Mercy and Charity. See Stefan M. R. Żaglewski, *Świątynia Miłosierdzia i Miłości w Płocku – święte miejsce mariawitów* (Płock: Wyd. KSM, 214), 60.

162 'Założenie kamienia', 24–26.

163 Stefan M. R. Żaglewski, 'Co sądzili inni o budowie naszej Świątyni', *PNS* 47 (2007): 18–19.

164 'Założenie kamienia', 28–30.

165 Nowowiejski reported that there were only 188 Mariavites in Płock and only 3,000 in the whole diocese in 1917. Cf. Nowowiejski, *Płock*, 672. *Głos Płocki* of 1914 reported that the number of the Mariavites was slightly less than a thousand. Cf. Żaglewski, *Świątynia*, 61. The Mariavites reported that several hundred people attended Sunday Mass, but some were just onlookers. See 'DMHM XIII', *MCPS* 51 (1908): 813.

166 Żaglewski, 'Co sądzili inni', 19.

167 For example, M. Illuminata Nowakowska, who later became a nun, donated 30,000 roubles. See Próchniewski, *Żywot*, 375. Mariavites from distant parishes came to Płock to help with the construction, and parishes closer to Płock provided free food for the workers. Rybak, *Mariawityzm*, 47.

168 Szymanowski graduated with honours in mechanical engineering from the École Centrale Paris. He worked in France, Egypt, and the United States as an engineer on skyscrapers and bridges, and in Russia on the construction of the Trans-Siberian Railway.

Despite the fact that Jesus said that 'the true worshipers will worship the Father in the Spirit and in truth' and 'a time is coming when you will worship the Father neither on this mountain nor in Jerusalem' (Jn 4:21-3), Christians continually tried to establish the physical centre of their religion. In the beginning, it was located in Jerusalem, which was called the Mother of all Churches.[169] Later, mainly because of its political importance, Rome tried to take over this central position. This was accepted by some churches, especially in the West. When Constantinople was politically elevated as the new capital of the Roman Empire, Byzantium became the centre of Christianity for many Eastern Christians, although the role of the Patriarch was never the same for Orthodox Christians as that of the Pope for Catholics.[170] After the fall of the Byzantine Empire, the Orthodox monk Philotheus of Pskov (1465–1542) came up with the idea of Russia as the Third Rome, a new centre of Christianity that would defend the purity of the Orthodox faith.[171] There were other, though lesser, contenders. For example, in the second century, members of the New Prophecy believed that Pepuza (and Tymion) in Phrygia would become the New Jerusalem descending from heaven.[172] The idea of a Christian centre in Poland itself had also appeared earlier. Konstanty Ostrogski (1526–1608) planned to move the seat of the Patriarchate of Constantinople to Ostroh, which was once part of the Crown of the Kingdom of Poland, making it the symbolic 'See of Orthodoxy'.[173] The Mariavites' plan to establish a new capital for Christianity in Poland was thus not as revolutionary as it might initially appear. They believed that the Temple would gather the elect, who were called the New Jerusalem (Rev 21:2).[174] Only people without mortal sins could belong to the Kingdom of Christ, which was synonymous with the Kingdom of God (1 Cor 6:16-17; Eph 5:27).[175]

Cf. Thierry Claeys, 'Les Investissements Français en Russie de 1857 à 1914: Conseils, Expertises et Stratégies', *Quaestio Rossica* 4 (2015): 165–179.

169 'Council of Constantinople, A. D. 382, The Synodical Letter', in *The Seven Ecumenical Councils*, ed. Philip Schaff, trans. H. Wace, (Grand Rapids, MI: Eerdmans, 1952), 396.

170 John A. McGuckin, *The Orthodox Church* (Oxford: Blackwell Publishing, 2008): 32.

171 Бердяев, *Истоки*, 9–10.

172 William Tabbernee, 'Material Evidence for Early Christian Groups during the First Two Centuries C. E.', *Annali di Storia dell'Esegesi* 30 (2013): 288.

173 Antoni Mironowicz, 'Swoi czy Obcy. Prawosławni w dawnej Rzeczpospolitej', in *Latopisy Akademii Supraskiej 8: Cerkiew a asymilacja – Swój i Obcy*, ed. Marzena Kuczyńska (Białystok: Oikonomos, 2017), 213.

174 Żaglewski, *Świątynia*, 14–15.

175 'Ewangelia według św. Mateusza', *MCPS* 32 (1908): 503.

It was a movement of moral renewal so it was no surprise that nothing impure was allowed to enter the Temple or its environs.[176] It was imagined as a sacred place and axis mundi, that is, a place separating chaos from order and reflecting heaven.[177] It did so not because of its geographical location but because Jesus reigned there. It was the place from which the Work of Great Mercy would penetrate the whole world.[178] In 1918, it was revealed to Mateczka that Jesus, concealed in the Blessed Sacrament in the Temple, had taken dominion over the whole world into his own hands, depriving priests of their power over souls.[179] In other words, this was the beginning of the Kingdom of God on earth, but this interpretation only came with time.[180] Jesus promised to listen to all the prayers of the people in the Temple, as long as they were in accordance with God's will.[181]

6. The Cessation of the Eucharist and the Book of Life

The Mariavites, as has already been emphasised, constituted a Eucharist-oriented movement.[182] The Blessed Sacrament was at the centre of their religious existence. They believed that it was the only means by which they could renew the whole world and establish the Kingdom of God on earth.[183] Whenever the Mariavites were persecuted because of their devotion to the Blessed Sacrament, the belief that they were fighting for a just cause became stronger.[184] According to them, it was only through the Eucharist, and therefore union with Jesus, that people could become deified, which meant that they could 'participate in the divine nature' (2 Pet 1:4).[185] This was in line with Orthodox theology, where only God is fully

---

176 Kozłowska, 'Notatki', 79.

177 Mircea Eliade, *Sacrum a profanum* (Warsaw: Wyd. Aletheia, 2008), 27–48. On the mirroring of heaven, see Jan M. M. Kowalski, 'List pasterski o Królestwie Bożem na ziemi (21.04.1927)', in *Ku Królestwu*, 244.

178 Kozłowska, 'Początek', 13.

179 Kozłowska, 'Notatki', 78.

180 Jesus consecrated the Temple, giving it the complete forgiveness of all sins on that occasion. See ibid., 77–78.

181 Jan M. M. Kowalski, 'Wola Boża', *MMN* 1 (1924): 3.

182 Mateczka stated before her death that the foundation of the union between the Churches could only be the Blessed Sacrament. Besides, all Churches can cultivate their own customs and local traditions. Cf. Ignacy Stobiecki, 'Mateczka a ekumenizm', *PNS* 22 (2001): 4–5.

183 'Przenajświętsza Eucharystya', *MCPS* 13 (1908): 203.

184 Even the secular authorities sometimes forbade them to organise Eucharistic processions. Cf. 'DMHM XIII', *MCPS* 43 (1908): 686.

185 The Mariavites also referred to Jn 14:20 to justify their beliefs. Cf. 'Przenajświętsza Eucharysta', *MCPS* 47 (1908): 745.

holy and people can only participate in His holiness.[186] The idea of theosis is ancient and can be found as early as the second century in Irenaeus' *Against Heresies*.[187] The Mariavites followed this line of reasoning, claiming that people who continually receive the Eucharist and follow the will of God will eventually become children of God (Rom 8:16), which is tantamount to deification.[188] It was views such as these that formed the basis of later lofty perspectives on Mateczka. They also helped shape the concept of sinless people who would ideally follow the will of God and inhabit the Kingdom of God on earth. Finally, they became one of the reasons for Kowalski's introduction of the priesthood of the people.

Initially, there was no indication that the Mariavites would begin to question the validity of the Mass celebrated in the Catholic Church. Immediately after the schism, they shared the Catholic view that canonically ordained priests, even if they are schismatics or celebrate the Mass impiously, have the authority to consecrate the Eucharist.[189] They pointed out the need for moral change among the clergy but did not openly question the validity of the Mass. This was largely because the Mariavites had to fend off accusations that their Masses and sacraments were invalid. Some of their opponents even claimed that the devil was hidden in their Eucharist. This could, potentially have been just a rhetorical device, but some people took it literally, leading to occasional acts of desacralisation.[190] From the very beginning, the Mariavites were strongly influenced by passages in the Hebrew Bible which stated that some sacrifices were not pleasing to God

---

186 Siergiej Bułgakow, *Prawosławie. Zarys nauki Kościoła prawosławnego*, trans. Henryk Paprocki (Białystok and Warszawa: Orthdruk, 1992), 110.

187 '[F]ollowing the only true and steadfast Teacher, the Word of God, our Lord Jesus Christ, who did, through His transcendent love, become what we are, that He might bring us to be even what He is Himself'; Irenaeus, 'Against Heresies, Book 5', in *The Apostolic Fathers with Justin Martyr and Irenaeus*, ed. Philip Shaff et al. (Edinburgh: T. & T. Clark, 1867), 883.

188 'Przenajświętsza Eucharystya', *MCPS* 47 (1908): 747.

189 It is worth noting that similar opinions can be found among some Orthodox theologians. For example, Peter Mogila (1596–1647) argued in Trebnik that the priesthood seals a person's soul with an indelible stamp of spiritual power. Cf. Aleksander Naumow, 'Powroty do prawosławia', in *Latopisy 8*, 245. However, he was deeply influenced by Latin Christianity, so some of his ideas may have appeared strange to his co-religionists. Cf. 'Saint Peter Mogila', https://www.oca.org/orthodoxy/the-orthodox-faith/church-history/seventeenth-century/saint-peter-mogila.

190 Kowalski, 'Stanowisko', 142.

because the proper intention was lacking.[191] But Jesus' sacrifice largely put an end to this.[192]

As early as 1904, Mateczka revealed that Jesus would leave the house of those who would not receive mercy empty.[193] Nevertheless, to tie this to the idea of the cessation of the valid Eucharist would be an anachronism. It was simply an example of religiously ambiguous language that can be interpreted in different ways. A reference to Mt 23:38 can certainly be seen here, but this does not make Maria Franciszka's pronouncements any easier to understand. Similar pronouncements about leaving their house empty were revealed to Mateczka in November 1907.[194] However, they were still very ambiguous. The claim contained no information about the circumstances under which it was to be fulfilled and when. Moreover, this was a time when the Mariavites still believed in papal infallibility, albeit slightly modified, and taught people that they could be saved if they remained in the Catholic Church and obeyed God's commandments. They did not understand why they were persecuted for their devotion to the Eucharist, but they did not deny the presence of Jesus in the Catholic Church. The change in perception of this issue was gradual and linked to apocalyptic tendencies that influenced how the Mariavites understood the external situation.

The 46th issue of *Maryawita*, in which the Book of Life was mentioned, was published on 28 November 1907.[195] This was a reference to Rev 17:8, which reads: 'The beast, which you saw, once was, now is not, and yet will come up out of the Abyss and go to its destruction. The inhabitants of the earth whose names have not been written in the book of life [!] from the creation of the world will be astonished when they see the beast, because it once was, now is not, and yet will come'. The people whose names were mentioned in the Book were understood to be defenders of the Blessed Sacrament. The Mariavites maintained that if the Catholics did not stop blindly following their corrupt hierarchy, Jesus would leave their house. This was tantamount to being unlisted in the Book.[196] After unifi-

---

191 Among other things, Hos 6:6 was quoted. Furthermore, Abel's sacrifice pleased God, but Cain's did not because there was no good intention behind it. See 'Pismo Święte. Księga Rodzaju. Uwagi do Rozdziału IV', *MCPS* 10 (1907): 152.

192 We have testimonies by early Mariavites who believed that Jesus descended onto the altar, despite the sins of the priests, for the good of the people. Cf. 'Przenajświętsza Eucharystya', *MCPS* 10 (1907): 156–157.

193 This happened during the feast of Saints Peter and Paul. See Kozłowska, 'Uzupełnienia', 60.

194 Kozłowska, 'Wyjątki', 53.

195 'Niepokalana Marya', *MCPS* 48 (1907): 762.

196 'Odpowiedzi Redakcyi', *WDM* 1 (1908): 8.

cation with the Old Catholics, the apocalyptic elements associated with the Book were, at least temporarily, marginalised. They began to manifest themselves more strongly again from 1917 onwards, when the Mariavites began energetically to enrol people in the Book. It was noted that this idea was not only present in the Apocalypse (3:5, 13:8, 17:8, 20:12, 20:15, and 21:27) and other books of the Bible (e.g., Phil 4:3), but also that Francis of Assisi called his Rule the Book of Life.[197] The Mariavites also called it the Book of Adoration, which placed more emphasis on its connection to the Eucharist. It was placed under the monstrance in the Temple. All who believed in the real presence of Jesus in the Eucharist in the Temple were encouraged to write their names in it.[198] The Mariavites did not forbid Christians representing different churches to write their names in the Book of Life. Even non-Christians could do so, provided they honoured Jesus in the Eucharist.[199] Baptism was not required because it was believed that devotion to the Eucharist baptises people in the Holy Spirit and took precedence over water baptism.[200]

In 1918, Jesus revealed to Mateczka that the valid celebration of the Eucharist would cease in the Catholic Church. This was taken as a fulfilment of earlier warnings that their house would remain empty. This desolation was not to be immediate, however, as Jesus still had devout priests who did not celebrate Mass for money or in a state of mortal sin. There were also lay Catholics who loved him with all their hearts, and for their sake he decided to continue his descent to the altar.[201] Interestingly, the cessation of the valid Eucharist did not necessarily mean the cessation of the Holy Spirit's assistance, and it was not necessarily permanent.[202] Mateczka did not indicate the date of Jesus' final departure from the Catholic Eucharist but said it would begin in Rome on the day of the abolition of the Mariavite Congregation. This was to take place on 31 August 1904, but since the future tense was used in the 1918 revelation, the exact date remains unknown.[203]

197 Kozłowska, 'List 1', 53.
198 Kowalski, 'Wola Boża', 3.
199 Individuals from different countries were also registered. For example, several people from the United States were signed in. See Klemens M. F. Feldman, 'Dziennik z podróży do Ameryki', *KBNZ* 52 (1931): 414.
200 *Z podróży*, 30. In fact, an entry in the Book could be considered a baptism for non-Christians. Cf. Klemens M. F. Feldman, 'Zraniona bestya', *MMN* 5 (1924): 16.
201 Kozłowska, 'Notatki', 78.
202 Since the Church must exist, a complete cessation of the Eucharist is inconceivable; see Wojciechowski, 'Mariawityzm', 46.
203 Tatiana Romenko, 'Dwugłos o ustaniu ofiary: Co jest zapisane w objawieniach Mateczki?', *PNS* 65 (2012): 15.

This was not the first time in history when someone claimed that the Eucharist would become invalid. For example, after the non-canonical election of the Ecumenical Patriarch Nikephoros I (patriarch 806–815), who was a layman when he was elevated to the throne, a rigorous group about the Studites concluded that a valid hierarchy in Constantinople had ceased to exist and therefore the sacraments had become invalid.[204] Jan Hus argued that impious priests could not serve at the altar and that their actions had no effect.[205] Even the canon law of the Catholic Church, published in 1983, slightly modified the previous position and stated that a priest who is aware of having committed serious sins must first receive absolution before celebrating Mass.[206] The idea of depriving Catholic clergy of the ability to consecrate the Eucharist was familiar to the Polish messianists.[207] Mickiewicz wrote that the Holy Sacrament is as much in the hands of the Catholic priests as Poland is in the hands of the Muscovites.[208] High moral standards were expected of all priests, including the Mariavites, as the threat of cessation was quickly interpreted as applying to all clergy in all churches.[209] Mariavite priests were aware that Jesus would not descend at the consecration of the bread and wine if they were godless.[210] Although the power of the priests was severely curtailed, this did not mean that Jesus would abandon the Christians. In 1918, Mateczka was told that Jesus began to rule the whole world from the Temple in that year and took control of the souls from the godless priests.[211] In fact, this was the next step in the realisation of the Kingdom of God. Jesus was the sole ruler there, and all

---

204 They saw signs of the coming of the Antichrist in the patriarch's actions. Cf. H. Paprocki, *Focjusz*, 48. As for the validity of the ordination, it should be remembered that Ambrose was not even baptised when he was elected bishop by the people of Milan. See Neil B. McLynn, *Ambrose of Milan: Church and Court in a Christian Capital* (Berkeley: University of California Press, 1994), 2–3.

205 Stanisław Wieczorkowski, 'Glosy do recenzji', *PNS* 28 (2003): 21–25.

206 Marian Pastuszko, *Najświętsza Eucharystia według Kodeksu Prawa Kanonicznego Jana Pawła II* (Kielce: Wyd. Jedność, 1997), 77; 102–103.

207 The people gathered around Towiański, including Mickiewicz, believed that they had to receive the Eucharist from the hands of Catholic priests because they were unable to consecrate it themselves. But they hoped that when they became spiritually pure, God would take away the ability of the godless priests to consecrate the Blessed Sacrament and place it in their hands. Cf. 'Notatki z tego, co Brat Adam Mickiewicz mówił', *GP* 6 (1937): 45–46.

208 Adam Sikora, *Posłannicy słowa: Hoene-Wroński, Towiański, Mickiewicz* (Warsaw: Państwowe Wydawnictwo Naukowe, 1967), 317–324.

209 Wojciechowski, 'Mariawityzm', 45.

210 Only the Minister General had the authority to absolve Mariavite priests who were in a state of mortal sin. Cf. Jan M. M. Kowalski, 'O ustaniu Ofiary Mszy Świętej w Kościele Rzymskim. Objawienie Boże', in *Ku Królestwu*, 216.

211 Kozłowska, 'Notatki', 78.

people were equally subject to him through the Eucharist.[212] Cessationism was not the same as rejection but had pedagogical value, exhorting the Catholics to improve.[213] There were many different interpretations regarding the 1918 revelation. Some Mariavites believed that it referred to the changes made to the liturgy during the Second Vatican Council, when certain words spoken during the offertory were altered or omitted. Others pointed to Faustina Kowalska in 1929 or 1930. At one point, Jesus communicated to her that he would leave the house empty because there were things there that he did not like, which probably referred to the situation in the Church: the Host then left the tabernacle. Faustina placed the Host in the tabernacle three times, and it left three times. In the end, Jesus decided to stay because the nun did not want to let him out, and after this incident she adored the Blessed Sacrament.[214]

In 1924, however, the revelations had clear apocalyptic overtones. Kowalski announced that Jesus revealed to him that the sacrifice of the Mass had completely ceased in the Catholic Church.[215] From then on, it was believed that Jesus was only spiritually present there.[216] The archbishop urged the faithful to inscribe themselves in the Book of Life because he believed that a great world catastrophe was imminent.[217] The whole earth was to be burned with fire, and only the righteous, i.e., those whose names were written in the Book, were to be saved.[218] The rest were to be cast into the lake of fire (Rev 20:15). Kowalski elsewhere linked this to the parable of the net in the Gospel of Matthew, which is linked to the burning furnace (Mt 13:50) said to be the same as the lake of fire (Rev 20:15). The casting of the net signified the call to enter the Book of Life. The latter was symbolised by the baskets in which the good fish were gathered (Mt 13:48). The angels, whose role was to separate the wicked from the righteous (Mt 13:49) were said to be Mariavite priests and sisters.[219] The whole interpretation was imbued with symbolic language, in which the

---

212 'Ewangelia według św. Mateusza', *MCPS* 23 (1908): 357–360.
213 Szulgowicz, 'Ideologia', 138–139.
214 Romenko, 'Dwugłos', 18–19.
215 Kowalski, 'O ustaniu', 216. Kowalski was sentenced to one year in prison for this but remained at liberty after posting bail. See Szulgowicz, 'Ideologia', 137.
216 'Dysputa z panem Inspektorem', *GP* 38 (1932): 287.
217 Jan M. M. Kowalski, 'Wezwanie wszystkich aby się zapisali do Księgi Żywota', *MMN* 4 (1924): 16.
218 This did not mean that wicked people would be eternally condemned, but they would certainly not dwell in the Kingdom of God on earth. Cf. Jan M. M. Kowalski, 'Przede wszystkiem jedność z Panem Jezusem w Boskiej Eucharystyi', *MMN* 6 (1924): 8.
219 Kowalski, 'List pasterski (21.04.1927)', 225–226.

burning of the earth did not mean the literal destruction of the planet, but its renewal. After the sinners had been destroyed, the pious whose names were in the Book of Life would dwell on the renewed earth and inaugurate the Kingdom of God, which would never pass away.[220] The only condition for inclusion in the Book was belief in the real presence of Jesus in the Blessed Sacrament in the Temple and paying him spiritual honour. Non-Christians or Christians from other denominations could be enrolled, but in a different Book.[221] The fact that the pious would be saved, which meant being left on earth, did not mean eternal damnation for those who would be 'cast into the lake of fire'. The Mariavites believed that the fire must come because it is written in the Book of Revelation, but the fire symbolised the unbridled will to see God and live in the Kingdom.[222] Despite the belief that transformation must come according to biblical prophecy, the Mariavites did not stop praying for mercy for others, including their opponents.[223]

Another name given to the Book of Life was the Book of the Kingdom of God on earth. The idea of establishing God's Kingdom became paramount to Kowalski. He constantly encouraged the Mariavites to purify themselves since they were to constitute the group of the pious who would dwell in the Kingdom. Enrolling in the Book imposed certain obligations on them. As already mentioned, the most important of these was devotion to and adoration of the Blessed Sacrament. In 1928, Kowalski established new conditions to prepare the Mariavites for the coming of the Kingdom. Everyone had to obey the Ten Commandments and the precepts of the Church, which were contained in the Mariavite Catechism. Obedience to the archbishop was essential. People were limited in their possessions and, if their wealth was too much, they should share it with family members or the poor. Smoking and drinking vodka were not allowed. Young women were advised to wear modest clothing. All Mariavites were urged to learn to read and write, otherwise they would not be able to read the Bible. All quarrels were to be resolved by Mariavite clergy and not in secular courts.[224] Kowalski maintained that Satan's power to tempt would be taken away from him in the Kingdom of God.[225] After Jesus came to earth,

---

220 Ibid., 221.

221 Jesus commanded that non-Mariavites be recorded in a separate book. See Kowalski, 'Wezwanie', 16.

222 Kozłowska, Próchniewski, 'Dzieło Miłosierdzia II', *MCPS* 33 (1909): 527–528.

223 Jan M. M. Kowalski, 'List pasterski (24.12.1927)', *KBNZ* 1 (1927): 3.

224 Jan M. M. Kowalski, 'List pasterski o zapisie do Ksiąg Królestwa Bożego (22.04.1928)', *KBNZ* 20 (1928): 154–156.

225 Jan M. M. Kowalski, 'List pasterski o związaniu Szatana (19.07.1929)', *KBNZ* 31 (1929): 242.

Satan was defeated, but he could still tempt members of the Church.[226] Man fell in the Garden of Eden because of the woman, but Satan would similarly be defeated by a woman, i.e., Mateczka and the Work of Great Mercy, implemented by the Church of Mariavites, which was her symbolic seed.[227] Before the coming of the Kingdom, the Mariavites were tempted and sinned.[228] People could be removed from the Book for living unworthy lives and betrayal of the Work of Great Mercy.[229] Only the heavenly prototype of the Book remained perfect and unchanged, but the earthly one could be modified. Thus, some names were removed from it and later restored in case of repentance. All former Mariavites and those who broke the Rule were deleted from the Book.[230] The Book is currently kept in Felicjanów, and more names are still being added to it.[231]

7. Mateczka's Death

In 1920, Mateczka fell ill with dropsy.[232] Her ascetic lifestyle, fasts, mortifications, and previous illnesses had directly affected her health. From 1918 onwards, the Mariavites paid more attention to improving their spiritual life and prayer than to penance and mortification, which were abolished.[233] Maria Franciszka, however, continued her austere ascetic life, thinking of herself as a sacrifice to God. This is why she refused medical assistance but did not encourage the Mariavites to follow her in this regard. Her decision was certainly not unique. Francis of Assisi also adamantly refused any medical aid.[234] It was popular among nineteenth-century devout Christians

---

226 Satan could only tempt Jesus and Mary externally because he had no access to their inner being. In the case of Paul, who was most likely confirmed in grace, Satan could still tempt him and use his desires against him. Cf. 'Ewangelia według św. Mateusza', *MCPS* 14 (1908): 213.

227 Jesus told Maria Franciszka in a revelation that he would give her victory over the unclean spirit, which was Satan. See Kozłowska, 'Początek', 30.

228 Kowalski claimed that some were Mariavites in name only and did not follow God's will. See Kowalski, 'List pasterski o związaniu', 243.

229 Jan M. M. Kowalski, 'List pasterski o wykreśleniu z Księgi Żywota i z liczby członków Kościoła Maryawickiego (18.04.1931)', *KBNZ* 16 (1931): 121.

230 Warchoł, *Starokatolicki*, 54.

231 Wojciechowski, *Pisma*, 39.

232 After the end of the First World War, she contracted Spanish flu, which certainly weakened her physically. Cf. Gołębiowski, *Św. Maria*, 119.

233 Kozłowska, 'Notatki', 80. This was in line, for example, with the perspective of Augustine, who did not want his monks to be hungry, which would distract them from their spiritual development. See Hill, *Christianity*, 266–267.

234 When one of the nursing brothers tried to apply ointments or other soothing remedies, he resisted and complained that taking care of bodily needs interfered with his

in Russia to believe that a good death should be preceded by suffering, illness, and confession of sins.[235] The Mariavites knew that Jesus wanted Christians to bear their crosses. Suffering meant freedom and purification from sins.[236] Only the path of self-denial could lead to the Kingdom of God.[237]

The case of Mateczka, however, was somewhat different. She sacrificed herself for the sake of Poland and the Church during the invasion by the Bolsheviks on 19 August 1920.[238] From that moment on, she actively pursued her final union with Jesus, which involved sacrificing everything she owned, including her earthly body.[239] She thought she was doing it for the glory of God. Her mind was not perfectly united with the mind of Jesus until her last breath.[240] Before her death, she declared that she was convinced that the dogma of papal infallibility was blasphemy.[241] This did not mean that the Mariavites were to abandon their attempts to unite with the Roman Catholic Church; it only meant that they could not accept this dogma.[242] She promised to remain with her fellow believers even after her death.[243] This certainly brought to mind the promise that Jesus made to his disciples in Mt 28:20 and gave rise to various theological speculations concerning the Blessed Sacrament. It was believed that her death would open up the third heaven to which Paul had been taken (2 Cor 12:2-4).[244] As this

---

conscience. He only relented when one of the nursing brothers reminded him that he could not serve God without his body. Cf. Thompson, *Francis*, 113.

235 Wasilij Rozanow, *Ciemne oblicze: Metafizyka chrześcijaństwa*, trans. Henryk Paprocki (Warsaw: ENETEIA, 2006), 73.

236 'Niepokalana Marya', *MCPS* 24 (1910): 378.

237 'Ewangelia według św. Marka', *MCPS* 25 (1910): 391.

238 She believed that Jesus accepted her sacrifice. See Kowalski, 'Krótki', 301.

239 There are many cases of Christians from ancient times who actively sought martyrdom. One example is Eulalia of Barcelona (290–303), who at the age of just 12 ran away from her parents and went to see the Roman governor. Standing in his presence, she boldly confessed that she was a Christian, spat in his face, and kicked a pagan altar, which led to her execution. Cf. Hill, *Christianity*, 149.

240 Kowalski, 'Krótki', 163–164. Only in this way could she perfectly fulfil the will of God. See Wojciechowski, 'Mariawityzm', 81. Similarly, Ignatius of Antioch claimed that he could only be perfected in Christ through death; cf Ignatius, 'Letter to the Ephesians', in *The Apostolic Fathers I*, 223.

241 Kowalski, 'Krótki', 318.

242 Towiański, for example, openly criticised the doctrine of papal infallibility and even called it a sin against the Holy Spirit. However, this did not mean that he wholeheartedly rejected the Catholic Church. See 'Proroctw nie lekceważcie. 1 Tess. 5,20. Znieważenie stolicy', *KBNZ* 33 (1928): 259.

243 Kowalski, 'Krótki', 310.

244 The interpretation that it was Paul who was taken to the third heaven is ancient. Cf. Eusebius, *Ecclesiastical History* I, 251. According to Mateczka, the third heaven did

could not have happened before the perfect union of Mateczka and Jesus, it came to be believed that she was present with Jesus in the Eucharist after her departure.[245] As we will soon see, this played a certain role in the introduction of marriages between Mariavite clergy and nuns. A few hours before her death, Maria Franciszka asked Feldman to ensure that her name would not be added to the Hail Mary and that she would not be called Mother of Mercy because this title was misleading and led to erroneous conclusions.[246] She wanted to be remembered as the mother of the Work of Great Mercy, which was given by God through her.[247] On the other hand, she revealed that what Kowalski preached about her sainthood in 1906 did not contain serious theological errors but had to be correctly understood.[248]

Mateczka died on 23 August, most likely from liver cancer, diagnosed as dropsy.[249] For the Mariavites, this was an incomparable loss. They believed that no one in the history of Christianity had imitated Mary as she had.[250] The faithful continually gathered to take one last look at the body of their spiritual mistress. Kowalski claimed that it was only then that he understood what Mateczka had meant when she told him in 1902 that her body belonged to him and her soul to Jesus. The hierarch buried her in the Temple so that she could be with Jesus and the Mariavites at the same time.

---

not necessarily mean a place but a greater knowledge of God's mysteries. Felicja M. F. Kozłowska, 'List 3', in *Ku Królestwu*, 55. Later Mariavites believed that the second heaven was opened only after Mary's birth and the third heaven only after the marriage of Jesus and Mateczka. See Kowalski, 'Wykład', 141.

245 Kowalski, 'Krótki', 309. Mateczka's case was often contrasted with that of the pope. Some Catholic theologians believed that Jesus was only partly present in the Eucharist and partly in the pope. After the death of Pius XI (pontificate 1922–1939), his body was transferred to the Blessed Sacrament Chapel and the monstrance with the Eucharist was placed on a catafalque at his head. This was blasphemy for the Mariavites, but they too placed Mateczka in or near the Eucharist after her death. Cf. 'Zgon papieża Piusa XI', *GSK* 8 (1939): 125.

246 Mateczka was included in the Ave Maria prayer as early as 1906, when the Mariavites added the words 'and Bride of Christ' after the words 'Holy Mary, Mother of God', referring to Kozłowska. This continued for two years despite her protests. Eventually, Kowalski decided to remove the addition. He did, however, allow internal prayers to Maria Franciszka. See Szulgowicz, 'Ideologia', 178.

247 She was a mother to her congregation, just as others were fathers and mothers to the religious orders they founded. Cf. Wacław M. B. Przysiecki, 'Czy Towiański był fałszywym prorokiem', *GP* 44 (1937): 345.

248 Kowalski, 'Krótki', 163.

249 The credibility of some works on Mariavitism leaves much to be desired. For example, Emile Appolis wrote that Mateczka died in 1922. See Emile Appolis, 'Une Église des derniers temps: l'Église Mariavite', *Archives de sociologie des religions* 10 (1965): 55.

250 Mary received all the spiritual gifts because of the birth of Jesus, and Mateczka received them because of his death. Cf. Kozłowska, 'Wyjątki', 47–51.

He compared himself to a man who found a valuable treasure and buried it in his field.[251] The opponents of the Mariavites saw the whole affair differently and even at this point were unable to show respect for their beliefs.[252] At the time of her passing, Mateczka left three bishops, 30 priests, 244 Mariavite sisters, and 57 monks.[253] It is difficult to estimate how many faithful belonged to the church at the time of her death. Her will mentions about 42,000 souls, but the 1921 census gives a figure of 33,000.[254]

Maria Franciszka advocated minimal change. The Mariavites introduced vernacular languages into the liturgy, rejected the claims of the papacy, and had a slightly different understanding of the validity of the Eucharist. The Book of Life may have seemed controversial, but it was initially just a register of those who wanted to adore the Eucharist. The semantic boundaries of the term 'catholic' were broadened, and this influenced the Mariavites' exegesis of the book of Revelation. For example, the man of lawlessness in 2 Thess 3-4 – understood as the Antichrist – was for a time identified with the first beast of Rev 13:1 and was expected to come from within the Church.[255] Once the meaning of the word 'catholic' was expanded, it was concluded that the pope was not necessarily synonymous with the Antichrist, although he could still play that role. After the death of Mateczka, Kowalski became the unquestioned authority on matters of faith and morals in the Old Catholic Mariavite Church. Mariavitism began to be increasingly understood as the new Jerusalem (Rev 21:2) of which Isaiah had prophesied.[256] This idea was quickly juxtaposed with the Kingdom of God, also known as the third heaven, to which Paul the Apostle was taken.[257] It was not long before Kowalski decided to introduce certain reforms to hasten the coming of the Kingdom.

---

251 Kowalski, 'Krótki', 170.

252 A few hours after Mateczka's death, someone wrote on the walls of the monastery: 'Kozłowska is at the bottom of hell condemned'. See Mazur, *Mariawityzm*, 65.

253 Kowalski, 'Krótki', 321.

254 Pasek, 'Geneza', 53.

255 Initially, it was thought that the Antichrist would emerge from Freemasonry. See Kozłowska, 'List do O. Jana Przyjemskiego (1904)', 63.

256 See footnotes, 'Księga Izaijasza Proroka 59–62', *PŚST II*, 240–242.

257 Kowalski, 'Wykład', 123.

Chapter 5

Reforms in the Church of Mariavites

Due to the large amount of data, it is not possible to discuss in detail all the reforms introduced by Kowalski between 1922 and 1935. For this reason, three of the most important ones have been chosen: marriage between priests and nuns, the ordination of women, and the priesthood of the laity. The main reason for selecting these three is that they were inextricably linked to the idea of the Kingdom. At the outset, however, it is worth discussing how the figures of Maria Franciszka and Kowalski were perceived after 1921. In both cases, the reception of their personalities was determined by in-depth studies of the Apocalypse, ancient Christian sources, and Polish Romantic literature.

1. Mateczka's Identity

Scholars have long struggled to grasp the various nuances of the perception of the figure of Jesus before and after his death.[1] Similar problems are encountered by researchers dealing with the reception of Mateczka. There is no doubt that she was treated with special reverence during her lifetime. The Mariavite priests confessed their sins to her, bowed to her, and sometimes kissed her feet or the ground on which she stood.[2] But these practices need to be put into context, given that in many cases the attitude of the Mariavite priests towards Maria Franciszka was, consciously or not, misrepresented by their opponents.[3] The disclosure of sins was not treated

---

1 It wasn't that long ago that scholars started talking about the next quest for the historical Jesus. See James Crossley and Chris Keith, eds., *The Next Quest for the Historical Jesus* (Grand Rapids, MI: Wm. B. Eerdmans, 2024).
2 Warchoł, *Wybrane*, 41.
3 For instance, Szembek – quoting Koźmiński – claimed in 1904 that the Mariavites believed that Mateczka reached the level of holiness of the first parents in Paradise before the fall. See Warchoł, *Reakcja*, 62. The same year Szembek incorrectly claimed that the Mariavites regarded Maria Franciszka as equal to Mary. Cf. Stobiecki, 'Założycielka', 21. In fact, even Kowalski was fully aware, prior to the schism, that Mateczka was not the same as Jesus' mother. See Kowalski, 'Krótki', 158.

as a confession but rather as a spiritual conference aimed at eradicating all the imperfections associated with the monastic rule. Prostration was the consequence of monastic obedience to the Spiritual Mother and humility.[4] Admittedly, it was believed that, apart from Mary, no one else followed the will of Jesus as much as Mateczka did.[5] She was also viewed as the woman clothed with the sun (Rev 12:1), but this was read symbolically. The sun symbolised the Will of God, which Mateczka was to conscientiously fulfil.[6] In the opinion of the Mariavites, this verse could not be speaking about Mary since the Apocalypse was about future events.[7] In opposition to the Catholic hierarchy, including the pope, Maria Franciszka was not concerned with luxury, fame, and comfort but only with the glory of God.[8] It should come as no surprise, then, that the Mariavites, even before their break with the Catholic Church, began to regard her as a kind of saint, though not in a canonical way.[9] She was viewed as a tabernacle that constantly carried Jesus in her heart.[10] In principle, the attitudes of the Mariavite priests towards Mateczka before 1906 did not seem to violate any canonical precepts, but this depends on interpretation. After the schism, however, opponents were unwilling to explore the Mariavite perspective. They claimed, among other things, that Kozłowska sat on a special portable throne during religious services. These allegations were untrue, as even non-Mariavites attending Mariavite services testified. Nevertheless, this did not stop the process of creating lying stories.[11]

---

4 Similarly, Mateczka's humility led her to bow and kiss the feet of the priests or the ground on which they stood. See Kowalski, 'Krótki', 139. The same practices, having to do with respect for superiors, can be found in the life of Francis. Cf. Thompson, *Francis*, 42.
5 Kozłowska, 'Początek', 26. God did not make such declarations even about the Old Testament prophets. Cf. 'DMHM IV', *MCPS* 18 (1907): 284.
6 Kozłowska, 'Uzupełnienia', 80 a.
7 Kowalski, 'Wykład', 150.
8 Próchniewski, 'Mariae-Vita', *KBNZ* 9 (1933): 67. Mary was the Queen of Heaven and stood at the top of the entire heavenly hierarchy. Even if the pope was Peter's successor, the Mariavites had to prefer to follow Mary, who was above Peter. See 'Niepokalana Marya', *MCPS* 49 (1907): 778.
9 Similarly, Gabriel Sarrazin (1853–1935), a French literary critic, called Towiański a saint and his religious doctrine the doctrine of Christ. Cf. Wacław M. B. Przysiecki, 'Nowy patron Polski', *GSK* 27 (1938): 418–419.
10 The Mariavites justified this by referring to the ancient practice of giving theophoric names. See 'Synowie Królestwa: Żywot i Dzieła św. Jana Złotoustego', *KBNZ* 8 (1929): 61. Clare of Assisi also called women who followed God's will dwellings of the Trinity. Cf. Jerzy Misiurek, *Wielkie mistyczki Kościoła* (Lublin: Wyd. KUL, 1996), 32.
11 'Odpowiedzi Redakcyi', *WDM* 29 (1908): 232. Catholic newspapers, such as the Polak-Katolik, falsely claimed that Mateczka was incensed during Mass. At the same time, the Catholics were incensing the pope. See 'Odpowiedzi Redakcyi', *WDM* 32 (1908): 256.

Undoubtedly, Mateczka is at the centre of the Mariavite identity. For this reason, attacks on her morality were the same as attacks on the decency of the entire Mariavite Union. After the revelations, Maria Franciszka saw herself as a great sinner, but this needs clarification.[12] From the beginning, the Mariavites struggled with the idea that she was both a great saint and a great sinner. As early as 1907, or perhaps even earlier, they began to take the view that the expression 'great sinner' need not be interpreted literally. Her sins were regarded as minor imperfections, magnified to the maximum when confronted with God's perfection.[13] Her confessors (Kowalski, Próchniewski, and Gołębiowski testified that she had not violated any of God's laws in her entire life.[14] These opinions were certainly shaped by their unwavering faith in the Work of Great Mercy but were not unprecedented in the history of the Church. Similar opinions concerning other significant individuals are well known. For example, Palladius of Galatia (d. 430) wrote that John Chrysostom never lied after his baptism and became a Christian par excellence.[15] Cardinal John Henry Newman (1801–1890) expressed the hope that his close friend Ambrose St. John (1815–1875) had not committed even one mortal sin during his entire priestly life.[16] Maria Franciszka believed that Jesus had forgiven her all her sins, which she herself did not regard as mere imperfections, and confirmed her in grace so that she could carry out her mission.[17] Only then could she unite with God in a mystical marriage. But this was not a privilege reserved exclusively for her, though she believed that such absolution had been granted to other people in history.[18]

12 Jesus revealed to Kozłowska that Mary was conceived without sin, but Mateczka was a great sinner. See Kozłowska, 'Początek', 27.

13 'DMHM IV', *MCPS* 18 (1907): 286. Interestingly, in antiquity it was believed that Mary also had some imperfections that were not necessarily understood as sins. Pope Leo I (pontificate 440–461) in his letter to Patriarch of Constantinople, Flavian (in office 446–449) wrote that 'from the Mother the Lord took His nature, but no fault'. Cf. Leo I, 'Letter to Bishop Flavian', in *St. Leo the Great Letters*, trans. Edmund Hunt (New York: The Catholic University of America Press, 1957), 97.

14 In 1903, Kowalski stated that Mateczka had never committed any sin in her life. Cf. Kowalski, 'Krótki', 175. See also Próchniewski, *Żywot*, 139.

15 'Synowie Królestwa: Żywot i Dzieła św. Jana Złotoustego', *KBNZ* 8 (1929): 61.

16 Alan Bray, '*Wedded Friendships*', https://web.archive.org/web/20120207071228/https://www.thetablet.co.uk/article/5030.

17 Kozłowska, 'Wyjątki', 40. Other saints, such as Francis of Assisi, also received such confirmation. See 'DMHM IV', *MCPS* 19 (1907): 302.

18 For example, to Catherine of Siena. Cf. ibid., 301. Mateczka also claimed that Jesus granted absolution from all censures, prohibitions and anathemas in 1907 because he wanted to save all people. However, this did not make them sinless. Cf. Felicja M. F. Kozłowska, 'List 47', in *Ku Królestwu*, 147.

From the perspective of the Mariavites, nevertheless, there was one very important difference. Most saints submitted to strict ascetic practices in order to be forgiven of their sins. Mateczka only had to accept the call to remove all imperfections.[19] It can be argued that Mateczka did not accept this way of reasoning. In her own eyes, she had many private sins and protested vehemently when anyone tried to venerate her or call her a saint.[20] After her death, the objections were understood to stem from humility and zeal for God's glory.[21] After all, prior to his death and resurrection, Jesus also behaved in a humble way and was portrayed as sinless, even though he had received baptism for the remission of sins.[22] Moreover, Towiański also did not want his followers to glorify him, but they did so anyway to emphasise their belief that he had been chosen by God to fulfil a certain mission.[23] It is difficult to clearly determine when exactly the Mariavites came to the conclusion that Maria Franciszka was sinless and how widely this was accepted by the clergy and the faithful.[24] This was undoubtedly supported by the fact that in many cultures the sacrifice must be pure to be accepted by God.[25] Finally, it is important to emphasise that sinlessness is not equivalent to being born without original sin. Even after the death of Mateczka, the Mariavites believed that she was conceived in sin, as were all other human beings, except Mary.[26]

In response to the revelations, Mateczka agreed to become an atoning sacrifice for the sins of the priests.[27] She also sacrificed her life for the good of Płock, Poland, and the whole church.[28] Although such statements seem

---

19 'DMHM IV', *MCPS* 19 (1907): 302.

20 In the early years of Mariavitism, Kowalski painted a portrait of Mateczka and hung it above the altar in the church in Sobótka. In 1918, Mateczka asked Kowalski to burn the portrait because she saw in it a reflection of the golden calf made by Aaron in Ex 32. See Kozłowska, 'Uzupełnienia', 80b.

21 Similarly, those who almost became martyrs in antiquity but survived humbly reprimanded anyone who dared to address them with the title of martyr. Cf. Eusebius, *Ecclesiastical History I*, 439.

22 Henryk Radecki, 'Czy Kult Mateczki to Wypaczenie', *PNS* 26 (2001): 21.

23 Przysiecki, 'Czy Towiański', *GP* 44 (1937): 345.

24 Wojciechowski referred to the period from 1922 to 1937 as the period of bringing out the holiness of Mateczka, stressing that it was a process. Cf. Wojciechowski, 'Mariawityzm', 99.

25 The Mariavites knew, however, that in some cultures war captives or prisoners were also sacrificed and were not completely clean. See 'Przenajświętsza Eucharystya', *MCPS* 9 (1907): 138.

26 Kowalski, 'Wykład', 152. But the consequences of this sin were removed by Jesus. Cf. ibid., 154.

27 Kozłowska, 'Początek', 28.

28 Kowalski, 'Krótki', 301.

controversial, they need not be so at all. Prior to Maria Franciszka's death, sacrificial language was most likely understood by Mariavites according to the examples of the early Christians imitating Jesus in his sacrificial death.[29] Paul wrote in Phil 2:17 of 'being poured out like a drink offering'. Ignatius of Antioch claimed that he desired to be 'poured out as a libation to God while there is still an altar at hand …'.[30] The author of *Martyrdom of Polycarp* stated that Polycarp 'was like an exceptional ram taken from a great flock for a sacrifice, prepared as a whole burnt offering that is acceptable to God'.[31] It was undoubtedly believed that Mateczka died for others, but this was most likely understood through the prism of the Maccabean Martyrs at least.[32] After 1921, the cult of Mateczka increased rapidly. People began to pray to her in public, including in a liturgical context, portraits of her appeared in churches, and a special mass was created.[33] Given how fundamental a figure she was to the Mariavites, this should not come as a surprise. Mateczka's death became a significant factor in bringing about the establishment of the Kingdom of God on earth. This required a re-evaluation of hitherto held theological concepts. For Kowalski, it became obvious that Mateczka was to fulfil in her flesh what was lacking with regard to the sacrifice of Jesus (Col 1:24).[34] The bile that accumulated in her body was recognised as the sins of the Church, which she took upon herself.[35] Later, probably after the schism in the Church of Mariavites in 1935, this gave rise to the idea that she was a great sinner because, like Jesus, she took upon herself the sins of the whole world.[36]

---

29   All Mariavites were called to sacrifice themselves, seeking to imitate Mateczka, just as Paul sought to imitate Jesus for the glory of God and the salvation of the world. Cf. M. C. Kraszewska, 'O miłości dla naszej Najdroższej Mateczki', *KBNZ* 33 (1929): 257.

30   Ignatius, 'Letter to the Romans', in *The Apostolic Fathers I*, 273.

31   'Martyrdom of Polycarp', *The Apostolic Fathers I*, 387.

32   In 4 Maccabees 6:28-29 we read: 'Be merciful to your people, and let our punishment suffice for them. Make my blood their purification and take my life in exchange for theirs.' Some scholars have argued that the Maccabean martyrs inspired early Christians to develop the concept of Jesus' sacrificial death. See Eduard Lohse, *Martyrer und Gottesknecht: Untersuchungen zur Urchristlichen Verkundigung vom Suhntod Jesu Christi* (Gottingen: Vandenhoeck & Ruprecht, 1963), 37–78.

33   Warchoł, *Starokatolicki*, 49.

34   Previously, the verse was read in reference to the whole Church of Mariavites, which should suffer with Christ in order to imitate Him as His Bride. It emphasised that Jesus' sacrifice was sufficient, but that the Church was called to follow her Master. See Kowalski, 'Wykład', 144.

35   Anita Broda, 'Mariawityzm: Historia i teraźniejszość ruchu w setną rocznicę jego powstania', *NP* 52 (2007): 5.

36   Wojciechowski, 'Nie: Dla grzeszności', 2–5.

Around 1930, Kowalski came up with the idea that Mateczka was 'like the son of man' in Rev 1:13. This was conspicuously absent from his earlier commentaries on the Apocalypse.[37] After further research, however, especially in the area of biblical languages, Kowalski noted that the Greek word for 'chest' used in Rev 1:13, ὁ μᾰστός, was rendered in the Vulgate as mamilla, which referred to female breasts elsewhere in the Bible (e.g., Gen 49:25; Jb 3:12, 24:9; Isa 28:9, 32:12, 66:11; Hos 2:4; Lk 11:27, 23:29). He then began to interpret the rest of the text as if it was describing a woman. The hair on his head became the hair on her head (Rev 1:14), likewise the eyes, feet, voice and head. The verse still referred to the Ancient of Days (Dan 7:9) understood as God the Father. But in this new exegesis, the hair and other attributes were taken symbolically as the union of Mateczka's mind, heart, and will with God.[38] In fact, Kowalski was not the first person in the history of Christianity to believe that 'the son of man' could refer to a woman.[39] This new reading allowed the archbishop to set aside one of the most fundamental dogmas of the Christian faith, namely, the second coming of Christ.[40] He believed that the promises concerning the return of the Son of Man (Mk 9:1; Mt 16:28) were fulfilled at the transfiguration (Mk 9:2).[41] Jesus promised Christians that he would be with them until the end of the world (Mt 28:20), which meant that he did not have to descend a second time. He was permanently present in the Blessed Sacrament.[42] Since Jesus had already come as the second Adam and fulfilled his task, humanity should look forward to the coming of the second Eve.[43] Her arrival was

---

37 The 1923 Mariavite translation of the New Testament shows no sign of such an interpretation. Cf. 'Objawienie Błog. Jana Apostoła 1:13', *NTPP*, 788.

38 Jan M. M. Kowalski, 'Apokalipsa w szczegółach: Podobna Synowi Człowieczemu', *KBNZ* 23 (1930): 179.

39 Judith Kovacs and Christopher Rowland, *Revelation: The Apocalypse of Jesus Christ* (Oxford: Blackwell Publishing, 2004), 46: 'Lady Eleanor Davies, one of several women prophets in England in the 1640s and 1650s, identifies the figure of John's call vision (1:13) as a female divine being who will bring peace.'

40 It is worth noting that some Christian readers could have assumed that 'like a son of man' refers to an angel. See Craig R. Koester, *Revelation A New Translation with Introduction and Commentary* (New Haven: Yale University Press, 2014), 252–253. The gender of angels has been ambiguously portrayed in some Christian texts (e.g., Mt 22:30).

41 Jan M. M. Kowalski, 'Królestwo Boże Królestwem Eucharystyi', *KBNZ* 3 (1928): 17.

42 Jan M. M. Kowalski, 'Królestwo Boże jest Królestwem Adoracyi', *KBNZ* 4 (1928): 25.

43 Kalina Wojciechowska, 'Postać podobna Synowi Człowieczemu z kobiecym biustem przepasanym złotym pasem (por. Ap 1,13) – teologiczne konsekwencje zróżnicowania terminów στῆθος oraz μᾰστοί w przekładzie Apokalipsy Arcybiskupa Jana Marii Michała Kowalskiego używanym w Kościołach Mariawitów w Polsce', Cf. *Colloquia Theologica Ottoniana* 2 (2017): 235.

hinted at in Lk 22:43, when an angel, identified by Kowalski as the spirit of Mateczka, gave strength to Jesus before the crucifixion and was ready to 'drink the cup' instead of Jesus (Lk 22:42–43).[44] Such an interpretation was also possible because the Mariavites began to play with the idea of the transmigration of souls.[45] During Kozłowska's lifetime, they emphatically rejected reincarnation, although they were aware that the concept had been adopted, in slightly different forms, by Towiański, Słowacki, Cieszkowski, and Lutosławski.[46] After Mateczka's death, Kowalski slowly began to see too many similarities between her and significant figures known from Christian history.[47] Earlier statements of Maria Franciszka, such as the claim that she was present when God shaped the world, took on a new meaning.[48]

Suddenly, claims that the Mateczka was the co-saviour of the whole world did not sound as heretical as they once did and could be defended on theological grounds. Nevertheless, this idea was put forward in its most acute form among Kowalski's followers only after the split in the Church of Mariavites in 1935. In my opinion, the origin of this idea may have another source, hitherto overlooked by researchers. As has already been pointed out, the cult of Mateczka was closely linked to the Marian cult,

44 Kowalski, 'Kielich Mateczki', *KBNZ* 10 (1931): 73.

45 On the other hand, it was previously believed that Mary was also spiritually present on the Mount of Olives and was not the angel who strengthened Jesus. This shows that the reader should not assume a priori that the Mariavites always believed in the transmigration of souls, even if they claimed that Mateczka was spiritually present at some of the events mentioned in the Bible. Cf. 'Niepokalana Marya', *MCPS* 48 (1909): 765–766.

46 'Bóg w Trójcy Świętej Jedyny', MCPS 36 (1908): 565. Wincenty Lutosławski (1863–1954) founded the religious association Eleusis in 1902 with the aim of reviving Catholic virtues in the Polish people. There were many similarities between them and the Mariavites. Eleusis members were strongly opposed to drinking alcohol, smoking cigarettes, and gambling. They read the works of Mickiewicz through a national and esoteric prism and promoted Catholic spirituality (e.g., frequent communion). They also tried to adapt some spiritual exercises from different religious traditions. This was another 'grassroots' initiative, persecuted by the Prussian authorities and not officially approved by the Catholic hierarchy. See Ignacy Stobiecki, 'ELEUSIS', *PNS* 3 (1997): 12–13. The Mariavites were familiar with their views. Cf. 'Bóg w Trójcy Świętej Jedyny', *MCPS* 29 (1908): 451.

47 In 1931, for example, he concluded that Beatrice, who was the main inspiration for Dante Alighieri's *Vita Nuova*, showed not only 'accidental resemblances to' but also identification with Mateczka. Cf. Jan M. M. Kowalski, 'Wstęp' in Dante Alighieri, *Boska Komedia*, trans. Jan M. M. Kowalski (Płock: KSM 1932), 10.

48 Previously, it was assumed that God symbolically revealed the mysteries of Genesis to Kozłowska. See 'Pismo Święte. Księga Rodzaju. Uwagi do Rozdziału III', *MCPS* 6 (1907): 87.

which in turn was linked to the cult of Jesus.[49] Mary was a key figure for the Mariavites from the beginning. She was the only person described in Scripture as being κεχαριτωμενη (highly favoured) (Lk 1:28).[50] The Mariavites believed that the Wisdom of God permeated the whole being of the Mother of God and that she was completely protected from sin.[51] Only the Holy Trinity was above her.[52] She shared in all the earthly experiences of Jesus, co-suffered with her son and made the act of redemption possible.[53] Such views were also present among Catholic and Orthodox theologians.[54] Pope Leo XIII, who was highly venerated by the Mariavites, wrote in his 1894 encyclical *Iucunda semper expectatione*: 'The recourse we have to Mary in prayer follows upon the office she continuously fills by the side of the throne of God as Mediatrix of Divine grace; being by worthiness and by merit most acceptable to Him, and, therefore, surpassing in power all the angels and saints in Heaven. Now, this merciful office of hers, perhaps, appears in no other form of prayer as manifestly as it does in the Rosary. For in the Rosary all the part that Mary took as our co-Redemptress comes to us ....'[55] She was, of course, subordinate to Jesus, but she could nevertheless be called a co-redemptrix, and thus Mateczka, at least according to some Mariavites, could also be one.[56]

---

49 To this day, the icon of Our Lady of Perpetual Help is placed just behind the monstrance with the Blessed Sacrament in the Churches of Mariavites. Cf. Mames, 'Charyzmat', 8.

50 The Mariavites reject translations such as 'greatly favoured' or even 'full of grace' as insufficient. For them, the Greek term meant that Mary always fully possessed God's grace. Cf. Konrad M. P. Rudnicki, 'Bogurodzica a Trójca Święta w ujęciu mariawickim', *Salvatoris Mater* 3 (2000): 382.

51 'Pismo Święte. Księga Rodzaju. Rozdział II', *MCPS* 4 (1907): 56.

52 Roman M. J. Próchniewski, 'Słowo Boże', *GSK* 24 (1938): 372.

53 'Niepokalana Marya', *MCPS* 2 (1910): 26.

54 According to Orthodox theologians, Mary was not merely a helper in the cause of redemption, like the other saints or angels but was a leading figure in it together with her Son. Cf. Jarosław Charkiewicz, 'Wybrane aspekty kultu Matki Bożej w Prawosławiu', *Elpis* 16 (2014): 28.

55 Leo XIII, 'Iucunda semper expectatione', http://www.vatican.va/content/leo-xiii/en/encyclicals/documents/hf_l-xiii_enc_08091894_iucunda-semper-expectatione. However, it is worth noting that this title has never been officially adopted in the Catholic Church, and the current Pope Francis (pontificate 2013–2025) is opposed to it. See Ines San Martín, 'Pope calls idea of declaring Mary co-redemptrix "foolishness"'; cf. https://cruxnow.com/vatican/2019/12/pope-calls-idea-of-declaring-mary-co-redemptrix-foolishness/.

56 The Mariavites claimed that Mary could be called co-redemptrix only because of Jesus. Cf. 'Niepokalana Marya', *MCPS* 4 (1907): 57.

2. Kowalski's Identity

From the moment he joined the Congregation of Mariavite Priests in 1900, Kowalski played an important role within it. Just two years later, he was spiritually united to Mateczka, not as her son but as her spouse.[57] In 1903, he was elected to be the first Minister General.[58] It was believed that Jesus confirmed the election by calling the newly elected leader 'beloved son' (Mt 3:17).[59] After the death of Leo XIII, Mateczka received a revelation from Jesus that it was Kowalski, at least unofficially, who would become Christ's vicar on earth.[60] This was symbolic language, meaning primarily a choice rather than a literal replacement. After the Mariavite priests terminated their obedience to the bishops in 1906, Mateczka was instructed by Jesus to transfer all authority to the future archbishop.[61] Although Maria Franciszka was the undisputed authority in the Church before her death, the Minister General did not remain completely passive. After all, charismatic leaders, legitimised by revelations, often need an efficient organiser to represent the movement in official dealings with the outside world.[62]

Mateczka's death had a profound effect on Kowalski. From that point onwards, he was to undergo a spiritual rebirth for a period of six years to establish himself in grace.[63] It was most likely during this time that he came to the conclusion that he had a certain religious mission to fulfil, in which there was no room for compromise. To some, it looked as if the idea of the papacy, which the Mariavites wanted to abandon, was trying to slip in through the back door.[64] For the Mariavites, the Commander (*Wódz*), as Kowalski was often called, was God's chosen one, who would lead his

---

57 In the same way, Mateczka was paired with Próchniewski in 1901, and with Feldman and Przysiecki a few years later. See Kowalski, 'Krótki', 167.

58 All Mariavites, except Przyjemski, voted for him in a secret ballot. Cf. ibid., 174.

59 Kozłowska, 'Wyjątki', 48.

60 Kowalski, 'Krótki', 172.

61 Kozłowska, 'Wyjątki', 52.

62 For example, in the circle of Towiański's followers, Towiański was the Master (*Mistrz*), Mickiewicz the brother-bard (*brat-Wieszcz*), and Różycki the brother-in-chief (*brat-Wódz*). See Walicki, 'Millenaryzm', 30.

63 Wojciechowski, 'Mariawityzm', 93.

64 The Mariavites were aware of Słowacki's poem about the Slavic pope and published it in their 1909 Calendar, but without any commentary. Cf. Juliusz Słowacki, 'Papież Słowiański', *KM* (1909): 185–186. According to Anna Dziedzic, Słowacki imagined the Slavic pope to be a person who would break with the old system and officially support the Polish struggle for freedom. It is possible that he did not represent an individual person,but the whole nation, making Poland the Redeemer and the herald of a new order based on freedom and brotherhood. Cf. Tomasz Diatłowicki and Anna Dziedzic, 'Słowacki: Heretyk królom równy. Rozmowa z Anną Dziedzic', https://www.focus.pl/artykul/slowacki-heretyk-krolom-rowny.

people into the Kingdom of God.[65] Apocalyptically, he was understood to be 'a son, a male child, who will rule all the nations with an iron scepter' (Rev 12:5).[66] In itself, this justified obedience to the Commander. Other arguments from the Bible (e.g., Heb 13:17) and the history of Christianity were also invoked.[67] Above all, however, they were monks and tertiaries who understood obedience differently from their secular counterparts.[68] For some religious in the history of Christianity, obedience was more important than the transgression of morality. For example, Abba Saios became a thief at Abba Moue's behest.[69] After 1909, Kowalski combined the role of Minister General with that of bishop and was therefore expected to follow God's will as diligently as Mateczka did.[70] In an attempt to legitimise his decisions, he used arguments from the Bible, the church fathers, Mateczka's statements, her revelations, and his own inspirations. All this was to reassure him that he was acting in accordance with God's will. The biggest problem, which some Mariavites gradually began to become aware of, was that at times the temptations could take on the appearance of God's will.[71] Eventually, they concluded that the Commander had abused their obedience to his inspirations.[72] Even before the schism in 1935,

65 'Jubileusz Najprzewielebniejszego Ojca Arcybiskupa Maryi Michała', *KBNZ* 34 (1928): 266.

66 The verse was also applied to the Church of Mariavites as a whole. See Kowalski, 'Wykład', 150. After the 1935 schism, Kowalski's opponents ridiculed him for this analogy. Cf. 'Wyjątki z 'listów apostolskich: Wysłanych z Felicjanowa do Filipowa', *GP* 24 (1935): 193–194.

67 For example, the Patriarch of Alexandria, John the Merciful (in office 606–616), asked his parishioners to listen to his words/commands/requests because they came directly from God and not from a mere human being. These words referred to a specific situation but can be extended to all commands. See 'Synowie Królestwa: Żywot Św. Jana Jałmużnika', *KBNZ* 38 (1928): 299.

68 It is worth noting that in ancient monastic communities, obedience did not always apply to the bishop. The latter were sometimes ridiculed by the monks because they led a conventional life. See Andrew Thomas, The Holy Fools: A Theological Enquiry (Nottingham: University of Nottingham, unpublished PhD thesis, 2009), 33. Monks (abbas) were also occasionally portrayed as obedient to their disciples or weaker brothers. Authority was not always associated with obedience. Cf. ibid., 33.

69 Other monks lived with the assumption that they had to remain obedient even if they had to participate in sinful activities, including murder. Cf. ibid., 28.

70 According to Ignatius of Antioch, the bishop was not only the successor of the apostles, but also a reflection of God. See Ignatius, 'Letter to the Smyrneans', in *The Apostolic Fathers I*, 303–305.

71 'Ewangelia według św. Mateusza', *MCPS* 14 (1908): 215.

72 The ancient Jew Trypho also protested when someone tried 'only to say that it was God's will. For that is always the sly stock reply of those who cannot answer the question'. Cf. Justin Martyr, *Dialogue with Trypho*, trans. Thomas B. Falls (Washington: The Catholic University of America Press, 2003), 43.

many Mariavites had begun to criticise his actions. They did so secretly, however. Outwardly, they acknowledged that he was an extraordinary thinker, mystic, and theologian who nevertheless tried to put into practice everything he read without worrying about the consequences. His main mistake was not believing in the idea of the Kingdom of God on earth but tried to hasten its arrival.[73]

As the defender of the Work of Great Mercy, Kowalski was compared to the Archangel Michael, who also defended the glory of God. As early as 29 September 1900, during the feast of Archangel Michael, Mateczka was informed by Jesus through a revelation of Kowalski's resemblance to the Archangel.[74] Peterkiewicz saw this primarily as a point of contact with the controversial 'prophet' Eugène Vintras (1807–1875).[75] The latter founded the new religious movement, l'Œuvre de la Miséricorde, whose name resembled the Work of Great Mercy. Indeed, Mickiewicz, from whom – as has been indicated – Kowalski drew inspiration, mentioned Vintras in one of his letters and positively assessed his spirituality.[76] Nevertheless, even if Kowalski ever came into contact with l'Œuvre de la Miséricorde, for which we have no evidence as Rudnicki rightly pointed out, having contact, even direct contact, does not mean he took over its ideas.[77] The similarity between Kowalski and the Archangel Michael was initially only a comparison that had nothing to do with the transmigration of souls.[78] A few

---

73 Stobiecki, 'Dwugłos', 19.

74 Kowalski, 'Krótki', 95.

75 After a vision received from the Archangel Michael, the prophet of Tilly-sur-Seulles took the name Michael. He was characterised by a particular reverence for the Eucharist, and his successor Joseph-Antoine Boullan (1824–1893) was to introduce various sexual excesses and rituals into the movement. Cf. Peterkiewicz, *Third Adam*, 68–71. A certain Catholic author fantasised that Kowalski, whom he described as a Satanist, was Boullan's disciple, and Boullan was also a Satanist. See Witold Sawicki, *Organizacje Tajne w walce z Kościołem* (Krzeszowice: Wyd. Ostoja, 2005), 102.

76 Adam Mickiewicz, *Współudział Adama Mickiewicza w sprawie Andrzeja Towiańskiego: listy i przemówienia, Tom 1* (Paryż [Paris?]: Księgarnia Luxemburgska, 1877), 53–55.

77 Bishop Szulgowicz added that the archbishop, as can be inferred from his writings, correspondence, and other preserved materials, including oral messages, based all his ideas on the works of the church fathers, the writings of the Polish messianists, as well as the Bible and teachings and revelations of Maria Franciszka. He had no connection with occultism. Cf. Zbigniew Łagosz, 'Mariawici a okultyzm: Próba dotarcia do prawdy', in *Prawda i Fałsz o Polskiej chwale i wstydzie*, ed. Włodzimierz K. Pessel i Stanisław Zagórski (Łomża: Wyd. Stopka, 2010), 268.

78 In 1908, the Mariavites called the idea of reincarnation an absurdity. See 'Bóg w Trójcy Świętej Jedyny', *MCPS* 37 (1908): 578. Irenaeus of Lyon thought the same. Cf. Irenaeus, 'Against Heresies', 677–678.

years after Mateczka's death, the issue was re-examined, and the Mariavites began to look more favourably at the question of transmigration. Our primary sources, however, show that the issue was never completely resolved, and the existence of many conflicting opinions does not help in understanding the issue. Moreover, new problems arose in connection with it. First, the Mariavites tried to establish the relationship between spirit and soul. At one point, they adopted a tripartite anthropology in which the human being was thought to consist of body, soul, and spirit (1 Thess 5:23).[79] Elsewhere, however, it was argued that after spirits fell from heaven, they became souls attached to bodies, an argument which seems to juxtapose souls with spirits.[80] The question then arises, does transmigration involve the soul or the spirit, or perhaps both? Second, the Polish word wcielenie is difficult to translate. It can refer to both incarnation and incorporation. In the first sense, the descending spirit or soul exercises authority over the body it inhabits. In the second sense, the spirit or soul is considered to merely coexist in the human body and does not replace or eliminate the personality of the owner.[81] The Mariavites did not delineate clear boundaries between the terms image, example, incarnation, and incorporation, thereby causing many exegetical problems. Even if Mateczka were to be understood as a pre-existent being due to her extraordinary nature, this would not solve the problem of other persons.[82] It is therefore impossible to answer conclusively as to whether Kowalski was regarded merely as an image of the Archangel Michael or as an incarnation of him. In 1929, it was imagined that Kowalski, like Michael, was fighting the forces of Lucifer that opposed Jesus hidden in the Blessed Sacrament.[83] The fact that

---

79 Jan M. M. Kowalski, 'Nowy Hexahemeron, czyli Nowe Pojęcia o Sześciu Dniach Stworzenia', *KBNZ* 41 (1929): 321. This concept, though not always in the same form, was particularly popular among the early Greek and Alexandrian church fathers, such as Clement of Alexandria, Origen, and Gregory of Nyssa. Others, such as Athanasius of Alexandria (c. 296/298–373), strongly rejected it. The Latin church fathers always favoured a twofold division of human nature. Cf. Louis Berkhof, *Systematic Theology* (Grand Rapids, MI: Wm. B. Eerdmans, 1996), 191–192.

80 'Synowie Królestwa: Żywot Błogosławionego Orygenesa Wielkiego Ojca Kościoła', *KBNZ* 39 (1929): 308.

81 Konrad M. P. Rudnicki, 'Myśli o mariawityzmie. O co oskarżają mariawityzm felicjanowski?', *PNS* 62 (2011): 28. Latin has two separate terms, *incarnatio* and *incorporatio*, which in Polish are rendered by the single word *wcielenie*. Rudnicki, 'Bogurodzica', 384.

82 For example, Wiłucka was understood to be an image of Mateczka when she was celebrating mass, but this did not mean that Mateczka literally inhabited her body. Cf. 'Pierwsza Msza św. Matki Przewielebnej i Sióstr', *KBNZ* 15 (1929): 115.

83 Examples of other noble warriors, such as Zawisza Czarny (1379–1428), who fought in defense of the Christian faith, were also cited. See Zenon M. J. Łuszczewski,

the Mariavites understood their present situation in the context of a cosmic battle was not unusual in Christianity.[84] But if we assume that the Mariavite archbishop was regarded as the incarnation of the Archangel Michael in this battle, then we would have to assume that the pope and the Catholic clergy were seen as incarnations of Lucifer and the army of fallen angels. It seems that the author of the articles who mentioned this situation did not necessarily conceive of it in this way.[85]

It is worth dwelling for a moment more on the question of Christian reincarnation. In 1929, some leading Mariavite theologians, having become more familiar with Origen, accepted some of his theories they had previously rejected or disregarded.[86] They realised that, although some of Origen's ideas were eventually condemned by the Church, this did not completely solve the problem of reincarnation.[87] Augustine, for example, seemed to oppose the idea when discussing the meaning of the term 'ages of ages', but his words merely implied that souls do not repeat their previous incarnations, just as ages do not repeat themselves, something that

---

'Proroctw nie lekceważcie: Michał i Aniołowie Jego walczyli ze Smokiem', *KBNZ* 18 (1929): 138–141.

84 Martyrs from the second century onwards were commonly depicted as involved in a cosmic battle, where 'verbal and physical exchanges between the martyrs and their persecutors were portrayed as grand battles between God's emissaries and Satan.' See Candida Moss, *The Other Christ: Imitating Jesus in Ancient Christian Ideologies of Ancient Martyrdom* (Oxford: Oxford University Press, 2010), 88.

85 The Mariavites were portrayed as the offspring of women (Eve, Mateczka) who fought the Serpent (Satan) and his offspring (opponents of the Eucharist). It was symbolic and prophetic language, full of types and images but did not necessarily speak of incarnation or incorporation. See Łuszczewski, 'Michał i Aniołowie Jego', 141.

86 His authority clearly grew, and he became a great church father and a saint. Cf. 'Synowie Królestwa: Żywot Błogosławionego Orygenesa Wielkiego Ojca Kościoła', *KBNZ* 38 (1929): 302. A year earlier, the Mariavites had not awarded him any of these titles. See 'Synowie Królestwa: Święta Eugenia', *KBNZ* 23 (1928): 180. There is a possibility that Origen taught the transmigration of souls; see Jerome, 'Letter no 124 to Avitus', trans. William H. Fremantle, https://www.newadvent.org/fathers/3001124.htm. Others who seem to have succumbed to this view, such as Didymus the Blind (313–398), were influenced by Origen. Cf. John N. D. Kelly, *Early Christian Doctrines* (London: R. & R. Clark, 1968), 344–345.

87 Despite the condemnation of some of Origen's ideas by the Second Council of Constantinople in 553, Rudnicki believed that some versions of the preexistence of souls could be read in harmony with Catholic orthodoxy. He argued that it was difficult to reconstruct what Origen really taught, since some of the allegations cannot be found in his extant writings. He was rejected for allegedly maintaining that rational beings grew cold and descended into human bodies, which only makes sense in Greek where there is a play on words between ψυχοω ('to get cold') and ψυχη ('soul'). See Konrad M. P. Rudnicki, 'Czy dusza ludzka może istnieć poza ciałem', *PNS* 16 (2000): 69.

the Mariavites also rejected.[88] To address this issue, reference was made to certain obscure passages in the Bible (e.g., Mt 11:14).[89] Tempczyk argued that the pre-existence of souls came to the Mariavites directly from the Polish messianists, in particular from Towiański.[90] This may be true, but attempts were made to confirm this teaching by appealing to ancient authorities. Towiański taught that human spirits could be reincarnated in different bodies and even objects. Transmigration was supposed to help them be purified, get rid of any imperfections, and bring them closer to God.[91] According to the Mariavites, these ideas could be derived from the Bible (e.g., from Num 22:21–32; Mk 5:1–13; Mt 8:23–27).[92] The classic example is John the Baptist, who was considered a second Elijah (Mt 17:11), which some Mariavites interpreted as metempsychosis after 1929.[93] The latter term was more precise because it involved incorporation, and the Mariavites believed that the spirit of Elijah could be in two places at once, that is, in the body of John the Baptist and in heaven.[94] After the schism in 1935, the idea of metempsychosis could be found among members of two opposing factions. Bishop Przysiecki of the Old Catholic Mariavite Church, who opposed the archbishop, accepted the idea of reincarnation as taught by Słowacki, but he may also have had incorporation in mind.[95] Some of his church colleagues seemed to reject this possibility altogether.

---

88   Augustine, *The City of God*, trans. Gerald G. Walsh and Grace Monahan (Washington: The Catholic University of America Press, 1952), 282.

89   Jan M. M. Kowalski, 'Mój Ideał. Powieść Obyczajowa', *GP* 28 (1932): 218. Słowacki also believed that reincarnation was rejected because people did not study the Bible in depth. Cf. Wacław M. B. Przysiecki, 'Ku czemu Polska idzie?', *GP* 22 (1936): 170.

90   Tempczyk, 'Nowe przymierze', 94. Others, such as Mickiewicz, also believed in reincarnation and influenced the Mariavites. See 'Notatki z tego, co Brat Adam Mickiewicz mówił', *GP* 3 (1937): 20. The Polish literary critic, essayist and social activist Tadeusz Boy-Żeleński saw Towiański's works in Felicjanów, in Kowalski's library. Cf. Gołębiowski, *W obronie*, 100–101.

91   The Mariavites added confirmation in grace to this list. Mateusz M. F. Szymkiewicz, *Koncepcja utwierdzenia w łasce Bożej w teologii mariawickiej* (Warsaw: Chrześcijańska Akademia Teologiczna, unpublished Master's thesis, 2015), 59–60. It was believed that souls could also experience degradation and consequently dwell in their future lives in lower forms or morally inferior people. This is what happened, for example, to Bolesław the Bold (Boleslaw II) (1042–1082), who took a step backwards and was reincarnated in the Russian Mikhail of Tver (1271–1318). See Przysiecki, 'Ku czemu Polska idzie?', *GP* 22 (1936): 169.

92   The Mariavites also noted that in the Catholic Church inanimate objects are exorcised, which entails that they can be inhabited by evil spirits. Cf. Jan M. M. Kowalski, 'Nowy Hexahemeron', *KBNZ* 42 (1929): 330.

93   Ibid., 331.

94   Jan M. M. Kowalski, 'Nowy Hexahemeron', *KBNZ* 46 (1929): 361.

95   The spirits of the first human beings were able to be incarnated in Moses, Homer, Anthony the Great, and others because they wanted to reach the state of pure, selfless love

They accused people who remained faithful to Kowalski of believing that he was the incarnation of Jesus.[96] Nonetheless, this may have been a deliberate misrepresentation to discredit former co-religionists. During the schism, both sides spared no bitter words for each other and were prepared to do anything just to defend their own interests. After all, it was a struggle for them to survive in a society that was generally hostile to them. In fact, the archbishop's followers seemed to believe that Jesus resided in him as much as in any other Christian after receiving communion.[97] This can at best be compared to the ancient idea of imitating Christ.[98]

Archbishop Kowalski's story has a sad ending. On 25 January 1940, he was arrested by the Gestapo because of, among other reasons, articles in which he had argued that the territories of Gdańsk and East Prussia were an integral part of Poland. In another article, he claimed that Stalin (1878–1953), Mussolini (1663–1945), and Hitler (1889–1945) were three manifestations of Lucifer. He was sent to Dachau concentration camp in Germany in 1942. Until the last moments of his life, Kowalski remained loyal to Mariavitism and Mateczka. He died on 26 May 1942 at the Nazi Hartheim Euthanasia Centre in Alkoven, Ostmark (Austria).[99] According to Mariavite sources, his death confirmed the words Jesus spoke to Mateczka, i.e., that the supervisor of the Order would become a martyr.[100] Despite his tragic death, the archbishop remains a controversial figure for many Mariavites. For some, he is a symbol of schism, whose abuses squandered the chance for the development of Mariavitism. For others, he is a holy martyr without whose work the Work of Great Mercy would have no *raison d'être*. The reforms he introduced after Mateczka's death play a large role in the assessment of this figure. Let us therefore take a look at the changes he inaugurated, starting with marriage.

3. Antecedents of Mariavite Marriage

To begin with, it is necessary to answer the question of why Kowalski waited with marriage until after the death of Maria Franciszka. Although it was a kind of break with her legacy for many, it seems that this introduction

---

that was available before the Fall. Cf. Wacław M. B. Przysiecki, 'Ku czemu Polska idzie?', *GP* 18 (1936): 137–138.

96 'Sprawiedliwości stało się zadość', *GP* 29 (1936): 218.

97 Tomasz M. D. Mames, 'Wokół kwestii współczesnych przemian doktrynalnych i organizacyjnych w felicjanowskim nurcie mariawityzmu', *Studia Laurentiana* 5 (2005): 80.

98 Ignatius wrote that Christians 'should be seen to be eager to imitate the Lord'. Cf. Ignatius, 'Letter to Ephesians' in *The Apostolic Fathers I*, 231.

99 For more details, see Cyrocki, 'Jan Kowalski'.

100 Kozłowska, 'Pierwotny', 119.

of marriage for priests earlier was simply not possible since these unions were supposed to reflect the perfect union of Jesus and Mateczka that was accomplished at the moment of her death. According to the archbishop, this would only work in the end times, when perfect weddings – modelled on the wedding at Cana, where the best wine was served at the end – could be celebrated.[101] The wine symbolised the blood of Jesus, which was inextricably linked to the 1922 reform introducing the Eucharist in both kinds for all Mariavites.[102] Even this seemingly insignificant change, supposedly merely reinstating a once neglected practice, was in fact an essential part of the wider concept of the Kingdom of God. As already mentioned, the Mariavites openly claimed that Mateczka was a spouse of Jesus, even if they were members of the Roman Catholic Church. After 1921, however, she became the Spouse.[103] The idea of a spiritual marriage with Jesus is well known in the history of Christianity. Nuptial symbolism can be found in the earliest Christian writings, such as the Shepherd of Hermes, 2 Clement, the works of Irenaeus and Clement of Alexandria, to name but a few.[104] It was developed by Origen in particular, whom the Mariavites honoured greatly.[105] Nevertheless, because of original sin, human beings could not be perfectly united with God and also with each other.[106] Spiritual marriage required them to finally surrender their own will, which was called 'unio mystica'.[107] For the Mariavites, only Mateczka achieved this state to the highest degree at the moment of death.

101 Kowalski, 'Wykład', 144.
102 Jan M. M. Kowalski, 'O istocie i rozwoju Królestwa Bożego na Ziemi: O odrodzeniu i odnowieniu natury ludzkiej przez Chrzest i Sakrament Ciała i Krwi Pańskiej', *KBNZ* 48 (1928): 377–378.
103 She once had a vision in which Jesus presented her to Mary as His bride. See Kozłowska, 'Uzupełnienia', 80a. During her lifetime, this was most likely interpreted in analogy with the claim by Venantius Fortunatus (530–600/609), Bishop of Poitiers, who stated that virgins enter the court of heaven under the guidance of Mary. See McGinn, *The Growth*, 31. After her death, however, her case could no longer be compared to others, as for some she became the Bride in the highest sense of the word.
104 J. Christopher King, *Origen on the Song of Songs as the Spirit of Scripture: The Bridegroom's Perfect Marriage-Song* (Oxford: Oxford University Press, 2005), 2–3. Hippolytus of Rome in his commentary on the Song of Songs also devoted some space to discussing the relationship between the Bridegroom and the Bride. He understood this mainly as a metaphor for Jesus and the Church, although there are occasional instances where this is taken as a union between Christ and an individual soul. Cf. Andrew Louth, *The Origins of the Christian Mystical Tradition: From Plato to Denys* (Oxford: Oxford University Press, 2007), 54.
105 This idea seems to permeate most of his work. See Crouzel, *Origene*, 166–171.
106 'Pismo Święte: Księga Rodzaju. Uwagi do Rozdziału III', *MCPS* 7 (1907): 101.
107 A similar concept is also found in Islam. Cf. Geo Widengren, *Fenomenologia religii*, trans. Joannna Białek (Krakow: NOMOS, 2008), 528–529.

Although the Mariavites believed that their marriages were based on the perfect union between Jesus and Maria Franciszka, introducing an entirely new quality, some of their constitutive elements can be found in relationships familiar from Christian history. Rudnicki pointed to chapter 11 of the Didache, a brief anonymous early Christian treatise, dated to the first or early second century: 'You are not to condemn any prophet who has been approved and is true, and who acts on behalf of the earthly mystery of the church [μνστήριον κοσμικόν εκκλησίας], even if he does not teach others to do what he himself does, since he has his judgment with God. For even the ancient prophets behaved in this way'.[108] According to him, μνστήριον κοσμικόν εκκλησίας should be juxtaposed with *τὸ μυστήριον* from Eph 5:32 describing the union between Jesus and the Church.[109] In other words, these ancient prophets may have been married but not in the conventional/secular sense.[110] When Kowalski attempted to explain relationships to non-Mariavites, he used examples drawn from the Bible. He invoked the relationships of Sarah and Abraham, Isaac and Rebecca, Jacob and Rachel, or Tobias and Sarah.[111] To show that God's decisions in this matter should be obeyed without hesitation, he referred to the example of Hosea, who was commanded by God to marry a promiscuous woman and have children with her to show Israel's unfaithfulness to the Lord (Hos 1:2). Similarly, Abraham and Jacob were commanded to have more than one wife, and Mary, despite being a virgin, was asked to marry.[112] The Orthodox bishop of Libya compared the marriages of the Mariavites to the relationship between the apostles and their sister-wives mentioned in 1 Cor 9:5.[113] Contrary to what they had previously believed, the Mariavites concluded that the apostles, even after Jesus' ascension, had wives and children.[114] Peter and Philip, for example, begat children, and some ancient writers even believed, on the basis of Phil 4:3, that the apostle Paul had a

---

108 'Didache', in *The Apostolic Fathers I*, 435–437.

109 Konrad M. P. Rudnicki, 'O Mariawitach materialistycznie', *PNS* 9 (1998): 31.

110 Kurt Niederwimmer considered a similar interpretation: '[I]t may happen that the prophet will not arrive alone but accompanied by a Christian woman with whom he lives in a spiritual marriage.' Cf. Kurt Niederwimmer, *The Didache: A Commentary* (Minneapolis: Fortress Press, 1998), 181.

111 *Z podróży*, 15.

112 Kowalski, 'List do Arcybiskupa Edwarda Roppa (21.11.1929)', 41.

113 The Mariavites still maintained that the Greek word γυνή could mean woman in general, but they were now more willing to admit that it was most likely a reference to a normal wife who also acted as a sister in the faith and collaborated with her husband for the glory of God. Cf. *Z podróży*, 74.

114 The Mariavites claimed that Peter's wife's name was Petronilla. See 'Synowie Królestwa: Święta Eugenia', *KBNZ* 12 (1928): 91. According to some legends, however, she

wife.¹¹⁵ John, whom the Mariavites identified as the beloved disciple, did indeed remain celibate throughout his life, but this does not mean that he was better than other married disciples of Jesus.¹¹⁶ Hegesippus (110–180) recounted that relatives of Jesus had families and begat children.¹¹⁷

On the other hand, the Mariavites considered themselves monks, which was significant in that the word μοναχός derives from μόνος meaning solitary, lonely.¹¹⁸ Their opponents called Kowalski the new Luther, who broke with Rome because he wanted to marry a former nun.¹¹⁹ In fact, the matter was much more complicated. John the Faster, Patriarch of Constantinople in years 582–595, recounted that there were many nuns who indulged in sexual activities despite wearing the habit.¹²⁰ But this only shows that some monks and nuns sometimes broke their vows of chastity. Another situation was described by Jerome and concerned a monk named Malchus who was forced to marry another slave after being sold into slavery. Despite this, they decided to live celibate lives, ran away from their owner, and separated to join different monasteries.¹²¹ At the end of their lives, they met again and lived as a monastic couple in what could be called a virgin marriage.¹²² A clas (pl. clasau), was a native Christian church in early medieval Wales, headed by an abbot. This monastic system was organised on a family basis, where a community of clergy, styled as monks, lived with

---

was not Peter's wife but his daughter. Cf. John Schwarz, *A Handbook of the Christian Faith* (Minneapolis: Bethany House Publishers, 1993), 81.

115 Clement, *Stromateis*, 289. Eusebius may have thought that Philip was one of the Twelve. Cf. Eusebius, *Ecclesiastical History I*, 295.

116 'Bóg w Trójcy Świętej Jedyny', *MCPS* 8 (1910): 115.

117 Eusebius, *Ecclesiastical History I*, 237.

118 *Z podróży*, 8.

119 Indeed, such comparisons emerged fairly quickly, but they were initially limited to the fact that they both broke with Rome. See Górecki, *Mariawici*, 275. Surprisingly, the Mariavites also used this analogy, but in a different sense. Cf. Kowalski, 'List do Arcybiskupa Edwarda Roppa (21.11.1929)', 40. In 1524, Luther firmly stated that he did not want a wife because he expected to die as a result of accusations of heresy. He eventually married Katharina von Bora in 1425. Trevor O'Reggio, 'Martin Luther on Marriage and Family', *History Research* 2 (2012): 197–198.

120 John Boswell, *Same-Sex Unions in Premodern Europe* (New York: Vintage, 1994), 363–364.

121 Similarly, Amoun, founder of the famous monastic community in Nitria in the fourth century, lived in a chaste marriage with his wife for 18 years before they separated and he moved to the desert. Cf. Hill, *Christianity*, 250–251. If one considered marriage to be indissoluble, one could argue that Amoun was a married monk.

122 Virginia Burrus, *The Sex Lives of Saints: An Erotics of Ancient Hagiography* (Philadelphia: University of Pennsylvania Press, 2004), 35–38. The Mariavites knew a similar, but only legendary, story in which a woman became a nun but was still married. Cf. 'Synowie Królestwa: Święta Eugenia', *KBNZ* 14 (1928): 107.

their wives.[123] Abbots in Ethiopian monasteries were sometimes married and had children, but it is disputed whether they were monks or secular priests.[124] Barsauma, Metropolitan of Nisibis between 460 and 491, married a woman in 484 called Mamai, who may have been a former nun (daughter of the covenant).[125] It is also worth citing the example of syneisaktism. This practice, which emerged around the second century, allowed men, often clergymen, even bishops, to live together with women in a chaste partnership. Basil of Ancyra (die 362) considered it 'absurd that those who lead a virginal life are stupidly involved in the imitation of a marriage', but other Christians had different opinions on the subject.[126] Christians in Antioch called them subintroductae, meaning 'those brought in covertly'.[127] It is difficult to determine how widespread this custom was, but it was certainly considered by many to be a problem as local synods attempted to resolve it.[128] Even the Mariavites adopted laws prohibiting the practice.[129]

---

123 Even after the Norman Conquest, they rejected celibacy. The problem was that some of their marriages were between forbidden degrees, mainly to stepmothers or brothers-in-law. Membership was hereditary. Cf. Nora K. Chadwick, *The Age of the Saints in the Early Celtic Church* (London: Oxford University Press, 1961): 139–140.

124 Taddesse Tamrat, 'The Abbots of Däbrä-Hayq 1248–1535', *Journal of Ethiopian Studies* 8 (1970): 87–117.

125 A synod convened in 486 under the supervision of Catholicos Acacius (patriarch of the Church of East from 485 to 496) adopted Canon III, which stated that clergy marriages were permitted in the Eastern Church. It was argued that it was better to allow priests to have wives than if they were to burn with lust, which could lead to debauchery and adultery. Bishops were also allowed to marry, so Barsauma's marriage was considered valid. See Philip Wood, *The Chronicle of Seert: Christian Historical Imagination in Late Antique Iraq* (Oxford: Oxford University Press, 2013): 97.

126 Susanna Elm, *'Virgins of God': The Making of Asceticism in Late Antiquity* (Oxford: Oxford University Press, 1994), 50.

127 The controversial bishop of Antioch, Paul of Samosata (200–275), and the presbyters and deacons in his company had such 'spiritual sisters'. They were very devoted to him because he made them rich. Paul's opponents argued that even if he did nothing promiscuous, his behaviour aroused suspicion and others may have begun to follow him, not always ready to resist temptation. It is said that he sent away one of his subintroductae but kept two young and beautiful women who accompanied him on all his pastoral journeys. Cf. Eusebius, *Ecclesiastical History II*, 221–223.

128 Canon 27 of the Synod of Elvira, which was convened in 300, is believed to have been intended to end this practice. It permitted a bishop or other clergyman to live only with a sister or virgin daughter consecrated to God. Cf. 'Elwira (ok. 306)', in *Dokumenty Synodów od 50 do 381 roku*, ed. Arkadiusz Baron, Henryk Pietras SJ (Krakow: Wyd. WAM, 2006), 54.

129 At the time of their ordination, Mariavite bishops were warned that women were not allowed to enter their homes, and when they planned to visit the convent of sisters, they were advised to do so in the company of others so as not to give believers cause for offense. See 'Konsekracya Biskupów', *KM* (1911): 104.

Finally, there was the problem of how to reconcile the First Rule of Francis with the idea of married monks. It is possible that the Mariavites and Mateczka misidentified the First Rule. They thought it was the Rule from 1221, but it could have been the *Regula prima* from 1209.[130] Thompson wrote that, for eleven years, the Franciscan movement 'had no confirmed "rule" but a "form of life" merely "conceded" provisionally by the pontiff'.[131] One of the first scholars to notice this problem was Paul Sabatier, a French Protestant clergyman and historian who published his book on Francis in the same year that Mateczka received her revelations. The Mariavites were not aware of the content of this publication, for it had been placed on the index of banned books. It was only around 1945 that some Mariavites, gathered around Przysiecki, began to read Mateczka's revelations in its light.[132] They noted that the early Franciscans were not divided into branches. Women were equal to men, and married couples were no different from unmarried members.[133] Francis did not consider himself a monk or the founder of a new order.[134] According to Rudnicki, the first Franciscans did not take vows of chastity, poverty, or obedience.[135] It is worth noting that, after the Mariavites returned from Rome in 1903, Mateczka received the message from Jesus that she did not have to renew her vows but only needed to vow to follow God's will. This one vow stood above all others, making them superfluous.[136]

4. The Nature of Mariavite Marriage

The early Mariavites always understood marriage as an integral part of the Kingdom of God.[137] It was not until 1922, however, that Archbishop

---

130 Konrad M. P. Rudnicki, 'Dzieje Reguły świętego Franciszka', *PNS* 24 (2002): 32–35.

131 Thompson, *Francis*, 91.

132 At that time, there was no Mariavite press, so they could not immediately share this information with the wider public. Cf. 'Odpowiedź Redakcji', *PNS* 44 (2007): 21–22.

133 Rudnicki, 'Dzieje Reguły', 34–35. Moreover, the revelations required Mateczka to establish only one community, which was perhaps wrongly divided into three parts – monks, nuns, and laity. See Rudnicki, 'Liczba zgromadzeń', 29–31.

134 Jacques Le Goff, *Święty Franciszek z Asyżu*, trans. Joanna Guze (Warszawa: Wyd. Czytelnik, 2001), 168.

135 Rudnicki, 'Dzieje Reguły', 32. When people honoured Francis and called him a saint, he replied that he was not sure he would not have sons and daughters in the future. Cf. Thompson, *Francis*, 43.

136 Kozłowska, 'Wyjątki', 49.

137 Agreement between spouses was already recognised as one of the key elements of the Kingdom of God in 1914. Cf. 'Małżeństwo', *KM* (1914): 37.

Kowalski introduced marriages between Mariavite priests and nuns, which, as already stated, were qualitatively different phenomena from conventional unions. Opponents derisively referred to them as 'mystical marriages'.[138] From the Mariavite point of view, the problem was not necessarily in the name itself, but in the meaning attached to it.[139] In the language of mysticism, the union of a believer with God is called matrymonium mysticum.[140] The Mariavites wanted to maintain the distinction between human union with God and relationships between people. This created the problem of finding the right term for the relationship between Mariavite priests and nuns. For the sake of convenience, this phenomenon will be referred to as 'Mariavite marriages' in this work. The reader must bear in mind that this term is only used to refer to marriages between priests and nuns.

When the Mariavites were in the Catholic Church, they often criticised their fellow priests for breaking their vows of celibacy and indulging in forbidden sexual activities. They continued this rhetoric even after the schism.[141] Not surprisingly, after 1906, their opponents scrupulously monitored them in this regard. The Mariavites were constantly accused of sexual misconduct, but many of these accusations turned out to be false.[142] There were reports that Mateczka allowed Mariavite priests to violate the rules of celibacy, which the priests vehemently denied.[143] After unification with the Old Catholic Churches, the Mariavites continued to insist that, though celibacy was an ideal, it could not be enforced.[144] Their exegesis of certain biblical verses shows that they were not thinking of setting celibacy aside. For example, the Greek word γυναῖκα in 1 Cor 9:5 was understood by them to refer to a sister, not a wife.[145] They acknowledged that the word had a wide

138 Nowowiejski, *Płock*, 673.

139 Kowalski, 'List do Arcybiskupa Edwarda Roppa (21.11.1929)', 41.

140 This marriage is established by the frequent reception of the Eucharist. After such nuptials, a person's soul is united to God forever. See 'DMHM VI', *MCPS* 30 (1907): 479.

141 'DMHM X', *MCPS* 39 (1907): 623.

142 In 1909, for example, a certain Matylda Męsicka stole money belonging to Mariavite parish. After being caught, she confessed to the crime, but for some reason changed her testimony, accusing the Mariavite priest Pągowski of seducing her and offering money for her silence. Private letters proved beyond doubt that her change in testimony was unfounded. See 'Wrogom Prawdy', *WDM* 65 (1909): 513–516.

143 'Humorystom warszawskim', *WDM* 33 (1909): 258. The Russian newspaper *Nowem Wremieni* accused them of officially abolishing celibacy. The credibility of the article was even questioned by the Orthodox bishop of Chełm, Eulogius Georgiyevsky (1868–1946), who was a member of the Duma and a native Russian. Cf. 'Z Prasy. List Biskupa Eulogiusza', *WDM* 36 (1909): 286–287.

144 'Międzynarodowy Kongres Starokatolicki w Wiedniu', *WDM* 78 (1909): 619.

145 According to the Mariavites, she could be a biological or spiritual sister. Cf. 'Odpowiedzi Redakcyi', *WDM* 7 (1908): 56. Tertullian argued that it could not be inferred

range of meanings, but they argued that it could not be inferred that the disciples had sexual relations with their wives after they became followers of Jesus.[146] The Mariavites held to this on the basis of Luke 18:28–29, where Peter claimed that the disciples left everything they had to follow Jesus.[147] Mateczka was of the same opinion. She knew that the longing for a family was a great temptation but one that had to be overcome.[148] According to the early Mariavites, celibacy was only gradually being replaced in the history of Christianity by the more lenient practice of allowing priests to marry.[149] But some of their arguments were either completely wrong or could be interpreted differently.[150] For example, they referred to canon 33 of the fourth-century Synod of Elvira, which says that bishops, presbyters, deacons, and all clergy serving at the altar should abstain from sexual relations with their wives if they were married and should not conceive children. But canon 65 speaks of married clergy and encourages them to immediately separate from their wives who have committed adultery. The synod presupposed the existence of married clergy but wanted to impose certain

---

from this passage that the apostles had wives. Tertullian, 'On Monogamy', in *Ante-Nicene Fathers*, vol. 4, ed. Alexander Roberts et al., trans. Sydney Thelwall (New York: Christian Literature Publishing Co., 1885), 111.

146 It was also noted that 1 Cor 9:5 does not discuss only γυναῖκα but ἀδελφὴν γυναῖκα, which allegedly reinforced their perspective that this refers to sisters, not wives. See 'List I św. Pawła Ap. do Koryntian 9:5', *NTPP*, 468. In support of this interpretation, they cited Augustine's *Of the Works of Monks*, which reads: 'They were misled by the ambiguity of the Greek word, because both wife and woman are expressed in Greek by the same word. Though indeed the Apostle has so put this that they ought not to have made this mistake; for that he neither says a woman merely, but a sister woman; nor to take (as in marriage), but to take about (as on a journey). Howbeit other interpreters have not been misled by this ambiguity, and they have interpreted woman not wife'. See Augustine, *Of the Works of Monks*, trans. Henry Browne, http://www.newadvent.org/fathers/1314.htm.

147 'Odpowiedzi Redakcyi', *WDM* 7 (1908): 55.

148 Felicja M. F. Kozłowska, 'List to Sister Teresa Sieczko (04.02.1918)', in *Ku Królestwu*, 89–90.

149 'Odpowiedzi Redakcyi', *WDM* 12 (1908): 94–95.

150 They argued that canon 19 of the Apostolic Canons states that only lectors and cantors can be married. In fact, Canon 19 states that 'whoever marries two sisters, or a niece, may not be a clergyman'. Most likely, they had Canon 26 in mind ('As to bachelors who have entered the clergy, we allow only anagnosts (lectors, readers) and psalts (cantors) to marry, if they wish to do so'). But even this did not confirm their opinion since other members of the clergy were allowed to marry but only before ordination. Cf. *The Rudder (Pedalion) of the Metaphorical Ship of the One Holy Catholic and Apostolic Church of the Orthodox Christians, or All the Sacred and Divine Canons*, ed. Nicodemus the Hagiorite and Agapius the Monk, trans. D. Cummings (Chicago: The Orthodox Christian Educational Society, 1957), 30, 38.

restrictions on them.[151] The Mariavites argued that it was Pope Gregory VII who enforced celibacy throughout the Western Church.[152] In fact, the story was more complex. Scholars argue that it was non-Orthodox Christians who were the first to demand compulsory celibacy for their clergy and, in some cases, even for the laity. For example, Encratites, whose founder is said to have been Tatian (120–180), required compulsory celibacy for all Christians and denied salvation to Adam on the grounds that he had sexual intercourse with Eve.[153] At the Council of Nicea (325), Paphnutius, bishop of one of the Upper Thebaid cities, himself a lifelong celibate, successfully defended the rights of married bishops, priests, deacons and subdeacons to sleep with their wives and conceive children.[154] He even called these relationships 'chaste', which the Mariavites also did with regard to their relationships.[155] After a while, the Mariavites changed or broadened their perspective, but this did not mean that they immediately broke with celibacy.[156] It is interesting to note that as early as 1908 they were debating the opinion of the German Benedictine theologian and canonist Dominic Schram (1722–1797), who argued that a priest would have to marry, even against canon law, if instructed to do so directly by God.[157] Mateczka was still advising priests to remain celibate in 1920. But this was understood as

---

151 'Elwira', 55, 59. The Mariavites also appealed to the authority of Jerome, who argued in his *Adversus Jovinianum* that marriage could be a burden on the priest. 'A layman, or any believer, cannot pray unless he abstain from sexual intercourse. Now a priest must always offer sacrifices for the people: he must therefore always pray. And if he must always pray, he must always be released from the duties of marriage'. Cf. Jerome, '*Against Jovinianus*, Book I', trans. William H. Fremantle, http://www.newadvent.org/fathers/30091.htm.

152 'Odpowiedzi Redakcyi', *WDM* 12 (1908): 95. The situation remained unclear for a long time. For example, the Catholic bishop of Iceland, Jon Arason (1484–1550), opposed the Reformation together with his sons. See 'Jon Arason – The Reformation', https://www.sagamuseum.is/overview/#jon-arason.

153 According to Irenaeus of Lyon, the Encratites argued that marriage, intimate relationships, and childbearing were not part of God's original plan but merely one of the consequences of the Fall. Cf. David G. Hunter, *Marriage and Sexuality in Early Christianity* (Minneapolis: Fortress Press, 2018), 20.

154 Kowalski knew his case and later used it to defend Mariavite marriages. See Kowalski, 'List do Arcybiskupa Edwarda Roppa (21.11.1929)', 45.

155 Sokrates Scholastyk, *Historia Kościoła*, trans. S. J. Kazikowski (Warsaw: Wyd. PAX, 1986), 101.

156 They began to give other reasons as to why Jesus lived a celibate life. For example, he wanted to cross national boundaries and could not start a family because of his mission. Cf. Kowalski, 'List do Arcybiskupa Edwarda Roppa (21.11.1929)', 42.

157 This opinion can be found in his work *Institutiones theologiae mysticae*. Cf. 'Odpowiedzi Redakcyi', *WDM* 20 (1908): 159. It was later used to legitimise Mariavite marriages. See Kowalski, 'List do Arcybiskupa Edwarda Roppa (21.11.1929)', 41.

her private opinion and not a command given directly by God. Moreover, there are some problems with the contextualisation of this statement. For example, it is difficult to establish whether it applied in all times.[158]

As indicated, Mateczka was spiritually united with some priests during her lifetime.[159] She was also united, at least temporarily, with Szembek and Pius X.[160] These marriages were compared to the union of Adam and Eve in the context of doing God's will. After the death of Mateczka, the practice continued, and there were cases of spiritual union between two men. For example, Kowalski kissed and exchanged rings with Feldman, calling him Jonathan, which was undoubtedly a reference to David's friend.[161] The kiss may sound scandalous, but it should be compared to what Augustine once said: '[W]hen your lips draw near to those of your brother, do not let your heart withdraw from his'.[162] There is no evidence that there was anything other than friendship between Kowalski and Feldman. Similarly, Anselm of Canterbury (1033–1109) may have written to his friend Lanfranc (1005/1010–1089), whom he called his 'beloved lover': 'Wherever you go my love follows you, and wherever I remain my desire embraces you …. How then could I forget you? He who is imprinted on my heart like a seal on wax – how could he be removed from my memory? Without your saying a word I know that you love me, and without my saying a word, you know that I love you'. But Anselm did not necessarily mean anything more than close friendship.[163] After the schism of 1935, when many

---

158 Konrad M. P. Rudnicki, 'Celibat w Zgromadzeniu Mariawitów', *PNS* 61 (2011): 23.

159 Jesus united the will and heart of Mateczka with those of Kowalski, Próchniewski, Feldman, and Przysiecki. See Kowalski, 'Krótki', 162.

160 Ibid., 186.

161 Jan M. M. Kowalski, 'Świadectwo O. Arcybiskupa Michała', in *Początki Królestwa Bożego na ziemi* (Płock: KSM, 1928), 28. Some scholars see David and Jonathan's relationship as more than friendship and suspect that they may have had a romantic relationship, but this is not certain. Cf. Boswell, *Same-Sex Unions*, 135–137. Even if this were the case, it says nothing about the relationship between Kowalski and Feldman.

162 Augustine had a liturgical context in mind. See Augustine, 'Sermon 227', in Augustine, *Sermons on the Liturgical Seasons*, trans. Mary S. Muldowney R. S. M. (Washington: The Catholic University of America Press, 1959), 198.

163 This comes from Epistle 1.4, quoted in John Boswell, *Christianity, Social Tolerance, and Homosexuality: Gay People in Western Europe from the Beginning of the Christian Era to the Fourteenth Century* (Chicago: The University of Chicago Press, 1980), 218. There has also been some controversy about Newman's relationship with St John. Catholic historians, including the leading authority on Newman, Ian Ker, believe that it is a mistake to treat the language used by the cardinal as meaning something sexual. See Ian Ker, *John Henry Newman: A Biography* (Oxford: Oxford University Press, 2009), 746–750. Bernard of Clairvaux (1090–1153) could also claim in his sermon that the 'bed' of the Song of Songs means a monastery where souls can rest in Christ. McGinn, *The Growth*, 205.

members of Mariavite clergy tried to distance themselves from the idea of Mariavite marriages, Kowalski tried to legitimise them by appealing to Mateczka's authority. He carelessly used the word 'carnal' to describe Maria Franciszka's relationship with Mariavite priests. Having realised the implications of the term, he attempted unsuccessfully to withdraw from circulation all copies of *Wiadomości Maryawickie* in which the unfortunate word appeared and to replace them with a new version of the same issue without that troublesome term.[164] This inadequate handling of the problem led to further speculation and accusations. In fact, however, there are good reasons to assume that Mateczka remained chaste and expected Mariavite priests to emulate her in this regard throughout her life. First, it should be noted that, when Kowalski attempted to introduce Mariavite marriages, he was initially met with fervent opposition from his closest associates. If Mateczka had openly broken her vow of celibacy and advised others to do the same, it would be difficult to explain their reactions.[165] Second, the Mariavites claimed that Mariavite marriages were only possible because those involved were prepared by a lifelong celibate.[166] Kowalski even stated that he could not have been so close to Mateczka if he had committed any sexual sin. There was, however, one sin of Kowalski's that Mateczka was aware of. It was related to the issue of sensuality and involved some of Mariavite sisters. The nature of this sin remains unknown, but Maria Franciszka assured the Minister General that he had not sinned greatly.[167] Some clues related to this mystery can be found in the novel *Mój ideał* (My Ideal), which was partly based on Kowalski's life. At one point, the main character, tempted by sensuality, lay with a woman for whom he had certain feelings. She was clothed, and no sexual intercourse took place, but the whole event was described as a great fall.[168] It is likely that Kowalski, taking Mt 5:28 as his guide, may have regarded any inappropriate contact between a man and a woman as a mortal sin.

---

164 Własta, 'Odpowiedź ws. małżeństw mistycznych', https://www.ekumenizm.pl/religia/inne/odpowiedz-ws-malzenstw-mistycznych/.

165 This can be compared to the question of whether Jesus kept kosher. And if he did not, why was it so keenly debated after his death? Cf. Daniel Boyarin, *The Jewish Gospels: The Story of the Jewish Christ* (New York: The New Press, 2012), 102–129.

166 *Z podróży*, 15.

167 Kowalski, 'Świadectwo', 26. Mateczka claimed that the sin stemmed from the fact that Kowalski allegedly denied the dogma of the Immaculate Conception in conversations with the Old Catholics. See 'Odpowiedź Redakcyi na list b. Arcybiskupa', *GP* 15 (1935): 120.

168 Kowalski, 'Mój ideał', *GP* 17 (1932): 130.

After the death of Mateczka, the Minister General spent more time with Mariavite sisters in spiritual conferences. After a while, he began to feel an inexpressible love for those he considered to be religiously advanced. This manifested itself in occasional kisses on the head, cheeks, or temples.[169] These kisses, also known from Scripture (e.g., Rom 16:16; 1 Cor 16:20), could lead to dangerous situations. Athenagoras of Athens (133–190) warned that 'it is necessary to be careful of the kiss, or the salutation, because if our thoughts are the least stirred by it, it places us outside eternal life'.[170] Similarly, Tertullian (155–220) recommended caution in this regard, noting that pagans did not approve of their Christian wives attending Christian gatherings where kisses were exchanged with their religious brothers.[171] Neither Kowalski nor Klichowska, who was very close to Mateczka, saw anything sinful in these kisses.[172] The practice of kissing was opposed by Antonina M. Izabela Wiłucka (1890–1946) and Próchniewski who tried intensely to put an end to it.[173] Wiłucka believed that she was devoted solely to Jesus and would not betray him.[174] Kowalski, at least initially, accepted their arguments, but then something unexpected happened.

169 Kowalski, 'Świadectwo', 13. The link between kisses and spiritual development can be found in the Apostolic Tradition (also known as the Egyptian Church Order), a work attributed to Hippolytus and dating from the third century. There we read that the catechumens were not allowed to give each other the kiss of peace because their kisses were not yet pure. Since they were newly baptised, they were still considered newborns of the faith. Cf. Henryk Paprocki, 'Hipolita Rzymskiego "Tradycja Apostolska": wstęp, przekład, komentarz', *Studia Theologica Varsaviensia* 14 (1976): 157.

170 Quoted in Michael P. Penn, *Kissing Christians, Ritual and Community in the Late Ancient Church* (Philadelphia, PA: University of Pennsylvania Press, 2005), 107.

171 Derek Cooper, *Sinners and Saints: The Real Story of Early Christianity* (Grand Rapids, MI: Kregel Academic, 2018), 65. Wayne Meeks noted that a full kiss on the lips was the custom between close relatives in Roman society. Christians used this practice to indicate that they formed a spiritual family and were children of God. Cf. Wayne A. Meeks, 'Social and Ecclesial Life of the Earliest Christians', in *The Cambridge History of Christianity*, vol. 1, *Origins to Constantine*, ed. Margaret M. Mitchell, Frances M. Young (Cambridge: Cambridge University Press, 2008), 170.

172 Only later did Klichowska become jealous of Kowalski. The latter read her a passage from the Bible in which Aaron and Miriam disobeyed Moses because of his Ethiopian wife. In this analogy, Aaron referred to Próchniewski, Miriam to Klichowska, and Moses and Zipporah to Kowalski and Wiłucka. See Zofia M. H. Klichowska, 'Świadectwo Siostry Honoraty', in *Początki Królestwa*, 71.

173 Kowalski, 'Świadectwo', 17.

174 Antonina M. I. Wiłucka-Kowalska, 'Świadectwo Przew: Matki Izabeli', in *Początki Królestwa*, 46. A similar logic can be found among some second-century Christians who claimed to be betrothed only to Jesus. Clement attempted to address their objections by arguing that the Church cannot marry anyone else, positing Jesus as the bridegroom, though each [male] Christian could individually 'marry the woman he wishes according to the law'. Cf. Clement, *Stromateis*, 301.

Unaware of the whole situation, Feldman became seriously ill and almost died. During his illness, he experienced a vision of Mateczka who told him to trust in the archbishop's understanding.[175] For Kowalski, this was a sign that legitimised his actions. While reading the Bible, he came across a passage in Hos 11:4, which he translated as 'Więzami Adamowymi powiążę ich, związkami miłości'. This can be translated into English as 'I unite them with cords of Adam, bonds of love'.[176] He also came across other verses which he interpreted in his own way. For example, he interpreted the apostle Peter's vision to stop considering impure what God had made pure to be referring to marriage.[177] The Minister General also recalled that Mateczka saw couples in heaven in one of her visions.[178] When Paul was taken up to the third heaven, he was able to see similar mysteries but did not reveal their contents to anyone (2 Cor 12:4). As already mentioned, the third heaven could only be opened in the end times, after Mateczka's death and was to inaugurate the Kingdom in which heaven would be mirrored on earth.[179] Kowalski believed that until then people were not prepared to hear about marriages that were not based on physical lust.[180]

The first marriages took place in a private room on 3 October 1922. Kowalski married Wiłucka, and Feldman married Rafaela. The ceremony was preceded by three days of fasting and prayer.[181] It was believed that the

---

175 Klemens M. F. Feldman, 'Świadectwo P. Ojca Filipa', in *Początki Królestwa*, 36–37.

176 A footnote was added later to clarify that the passage refers to Mariavite marriages. See footnotes, 'Księga Ozeasza Proroka 11:4', *PŚST II*, 395.

177 Wiłucka-Kowalska, 'Świadectwo', 58. Furthermore, Song 3:7 was understood to refer to the thirty clerical marriages, as Kowalski translated מִטָּתוֹ as 'bed'. See 'Księga Pieśni nad pieśniami 3:7', *PŚST II*, 125.

178 Wiłucka-Kowalska, 'Świadectwo', 57. Perhaps this idea was later modified: during a conversation with the Serbian Orthodox Patriarch Dimitrije (in office 1920–1930) Kowalski argued that people in heaven do not marry and conceive offspring, while they do in the Kingdom on earth. Cf. *Z podróży*, 9. Tertullian believed that there would be no marriages on the day of the resurrection because people would be in the same state as angels are. See Tertullian, 'To his Wife, Book 1', in *Ante-Nicene Fathers*, vol. 4, 65. Similarly, the Mariavites once claimed that there would be no marriage or procreation after the physical resurrection of the dead. Cf. 'Ewangelia według św. Marka', *MCPS* 37 (1910): 580. Surprisingly, Kowalski used Mateczka's vision here to legitimise marriages in the last period of his life in the concentration camp. See Franciszek Korszyński, *Jasne promienie w Dachau* (Poznań: Wyd. Pallottinum, 1957), 28–29.

179 Kowalski, 'Wykład', 138.

180 Kowalski also pointed out that Jesus appeared for forty days after his resurrection to speak about the unspecified mysteries of the Kingdom of God (Acts 1: 3). See Wiłucka-Kowalska, 'Świadectwo', 58.

181 This was a typical procedure for ancient Christians awaiting the revelation of God's will. See Hermes, *Shepherd of Hermas*, in *The Apostolic Fathers II*, 193.

unions were authorised by Mateczka that same night through a vision.[182] Neither Kowalski nor the others knew the nature of the unions initially.[183] It should be noted that not all of them ended in pregnancy or sexual intimacy. For example, one of the priests who participated in them and whose identity was kept secret turned out to be homosexual and there was no sexual activity in his marriage.[184] One thing was certain from the outset, they were to be different from traditional marriages. They had different goals and focused solely on following the will of God. For this reason, priests were not allowed to marry secular women but only nuns.[185] Kowalski wanted to restore the ideal original marriage in which there would be no room for sin and pagan marriages would not serve as the model. Rather, their model would be the relationship between the Lamb and the Church (Rev 21:9).[186] Adam's love for Eve was not motivated by passion, given that the first couple felt no shame even when they were naked.[187] In this sense, but not biologically, these marriages were regarded as virgin.[188] Of course, opponents of the Mariavites did not want to admit that the word 'virginity'

---

182 Kowalski, 'Świadectwo', 31–32. Kowalski was not the only person to whom Mateczka appeared in dreams or visions. See Józef M. L. Miłkowski, 'Z pamiętnika o Matce Maryi Franciszce', *GP* 35 (1937): 276. There are similar cases in the history of Christianity. For example, the martyr Potamiaena, who died in 205 during the persecution under Septimius Severus (reign 193–211), appeared in dreams to many Alexandrians after her death, leading them to faith in Christ. Eusebius Pamphilus, *Ecclesiastical History II*, trans. John E. L. Oulton (London: William Heinemann, 1932), 27.

183 Wiłucka compared it to the marriage of Mary and Joseph, perhaps expecting a virgin union in the biological sense for some time. See Wiłucka-Kowalska, 'Świadectwo', 46.

184 'Problem homoseksualizmu a świadomość mariawicka', *PNS* 50 (2008): 13.

185 *Główne Zasady Wiary i Ustrój Kościoła Maryawickiego* (Płock: Wyd. O. O. Maryawitów, 1927), 3.

186 The idea that ancient Christianity incorporated pagan institutions, including marriage, and symbolically Christianised them was present in Russian philosophy at the time. Cf. Jerzy Klinger, 'Drugi List świętego Piotra Apostoła', in Jerzy Klinger, *O istocie prawosławia* (Warsaw: Wyd. PAX, 1983), 67. Kowalski knew that the early Christians used pagan philosophy and concepts. See Kowalski, 'List do Arcybiskupa Edwarda Roppa (21.11.1929)', 46.

187 John Chrysostom argued that they felt no shame because sin and disobedience had not yet entered the scene. Cf. Andrew Louth, ed., *Ancient Christian Commentary on Scripture, Genesis 1-11* (Illinois: Inter Varsity Press, 2001), 72.

188 Kowalski rejected the view that the Fall was linked to sexual intercourse in Eden. Eve gave birth to Cain after the Fall (Gen 4:1), but this does not exclude the possibility that intercourse occurred earlier. See Jan M. M. Kowalski, 'O istocie i rozwoju Królestwa Bożego na Ziemi. Istota Upadku pierwszych ludzi, czyli grzechu pierworodnego', *KBNZ* 46 (1928): 362. Similarly, in his *Literary Commentary on Genesis*, Augustine 'concluded that God had originally created human beings to procreate in a physical, sexual manner. But unlike sexual relations in the present, sexual intercourse in paradise (which had never actually occurred) would have been conducted in an entirely rational manner as a result of a

could carry other connotations. Peterkiewicz wrote that Kowalski perhaps imagined virginal intercourse along the lines of a ghost passing through the walls.[189] One can only wonder if he would have assessed the theology of the famous Orthodox theologian, Sergei Bulgakov (1871–1944), in the same way. The latter argued that there was no contradiction between marriage, procreation, and virginity, and that if it had not been for the Fall, this discrepancy would not be present today.[190] For Origen, too, the term virgin was not only biological in meaning but also a matter of morals and doctrine.[191] This is also why, for the Mariavites, virginity did not necessarily entail the lack of sexual relations.[192] Chastity was associated with non-egoistic love, oriented towards the spouse and God.[193] The case of Sister Melania, who married Father Jan, epitomised the focus on the spiritual rather than the physical side of marriage.[194] Because there was no room in these unions for carnal lust, which could lead to selfishness and sin, it was the archbishop who united couples.[195] In his letter to Polycarp, Ignatius

---

decision of the will. It would not have been driven by the irrational impulses that now characterize human sexual desire'. Cf. Hunter, *Marriage*, 30–31.

189 Peterkiewicz, *Third Adam*, 87.

190 Сергей Н. Булгаков, *Свет Невечерний. Созерцания и умозрения* (Moscow: Put, 1917), 297: 'Заповедь размножения не связана с грехопадением, она дана до него и не с тем, конечно, чтобы нарушить целомудренную чистоту супругов, но чтобы осуществить в них и чрез них полноту жизни. Между девством и браком принципиально нет противоречия, и, если бы не совершилось грехопадение, Адам и Ева были бы первыми девственными супругами на земле'.

191 Henri Crouzel, *Origene* (Paris: Lethielleux, 1985), 189: 'La virginité, et aussi la chasteté sous toutes ses formes, suppose des conditions morales. La virginité des mœurs doit être vécue dans la virginité de la foi.'

192 Jan M. M. Kowalski, 'O istocie i rozwoju Królestwa Bożego na Ziemi: Potrzebna czystość pierwotna', *KBNZ* 46 (1928): 361. Kowalski was aware that there may have been an ecclesiastical office of virgins (παρθηνος) during the time of Ignatius of Antioch who were also called widows (χήρας). Cf. Kowalski, *List pasterski o Nowem Świętych Dziewic Kapłaństwie*, 82. Macrina was also referred to as a virgin widow, but in a different sense. See Elm, *Virgins*, 45.

193 Jan M. M. Kowalski, 'O istocie i rozwoju Królestwa Bożego na Ziemi: Stan małżeński pierwszych ludzi', *KBNZ* 47 (1928): 369.

194 Peterkiewicz, *Third Adam*, 88–89. Posthumous marriage (ghost marriage) is known in many cultures, especially in China. See David K. Jordan, *Gods, Ghosts and Ancestors* (Los Angeles: University of California Press, 1972).

195 Mariavite nuns did not have to agree with their spouse's choice and could refuse, but this was understood as a burden on their path to spiritual development. Cf. *Katechizm Życia Zakonnego* (Płock: Wyd. O. O. Maryawitów, 1927), 66–67. On the other hand, after reform, it was not possible to remain an unmarried priest in the Church of Mariavites. See *Z podróży*, 9. Some priests wanted to choose their own wives, which was interpreted as a sin of impurity. See Antoni M. F. Tułaba, *Wspomnienia bp. Antoniego M. Feliksa Tułaby* (Felicjanów: KKM, unpublished 1924), 66.

of Antioch wrote that men and women should unite with the consent of the bishop so that their marriage (ὁ γάμος) would be in accordance with the Lord (κατα κύριον) and not out of passion (κατ' επιθυμίαν).[196] If the Mariavites wished to establish the Kingdom of God on earth, which would only happen after the inauguration of authentic marriage, they would have to be prepared to sacrifice their own will, even when it came to choosing a spouse. After all, they were to sanctify the whole community that would eventually follow them.[197]

5. Reactions and Accusations of Immorality

The marriages were hidden from the Polish public and even from Mariavite parishioners because Kowalski feared that his ideas might not be understood without proper theological training.[198] When the affair finally came to light, it drew many insults and unfavourable articles against the Mariavites.[199] They were accused of all sorts of indecent acts, even though the case only involved marriages between priests and nuns.[200] In fact, the first change after Mateczka's death was an ordinance that any Mariavite priest who conducted services for money or in a state of moral sin, especially if it concerned sexuality, was to be deposed.[201] Previously, the Mariavites had also openly condemned pornography and nudity in public life.[202] The use of hostile rhetoric in response to incomprehensible practices in various churches is well attested in the history of Christianity.[203] The reactions of Mariavite parishioners varied, but only a few chose to leave the Church. Their only fear was that this change would give their opponents gain another tool

---

196 Ignatius, 'Letter to Polycarp', in *The Apostolic Fathers I*, 316–317. Kowalski knew this fragment. Cf. Kowalski, 'List (08.12.1929)', 72.

197 *Z podróży*, 8.

198 People were first informed about them in 1924 in a pastoral letter. See Jan M. M. Kowalski, 'O wprowadzeniu małżeństw duchownych', *MMN* 1 (1924): 6–7. Clement of Alexandria also believed that most Christians were not able to grasp the Christian gnosis immediately. See Clement, *Stromateis*, 32–33. Similarly, the early Mormons kept polygamy a secret because they knew it was unacceptable to monogamous nineteenth-century American society. Cf. Richard S. Van Wagoner, 'Sarah Pratt: The Shaping of an Apostate', *Dialogue: A Journal of Mormon Thought* 19 (1986): 71.

199 Rybak, *Mariawityzm*, 53–54.

200 Grelewski, *Wyznania*, 98–99. For the Mariavite defence, see 'Jezuitom i Masonom słów parę odpowiedzi', *MMN* 2 (1924): 2–3.

201 'Wieczory Mesyaniczne. Nasi Mesyaniści', *KBNZ* 14 (1928): 109–110.

202 Kozłowska, Próchniewski, 'Dzieło Miłosierdzia III', *MCPS* 21 (1910): 334.

203 Jennifer W. Knust, *Abandoned to Lust: Sexual Slander and Ancient Christianity*. Gender, Theory, and Religion Series (New York: Columbia University Press, 2006).

to ridicule them.²⁰⁴ The opinions of the clergy were also mixed. Priests Jan M. Ignacy Modrzejewski, Józef M. Wawrzyniec Pągowski, Ludwik M. Alfons Ryttel, Roman M. Cyryl Żmudzki, Antoni M. Serafin Bołłoczko, and Tomasz M. Gabriel Krakiewicz demanded that the General Chapter be convened in January 1923 to discuss the idea, believing that it could lead to anarchy and even disbelief.²⁰⁵ After some time, Bołłoczko and Żmudzki decided to remain obedient to Kowalski and accepted his reforms.²⁰⁶ Ryttel, Modrzejewski, and Krakiewicz returned to the Roman Catholic Church, costing the Mariavites several parishioners, three churches, and one chapel.²⁰⁷ Pągowski organised the independent Old Catholic Church, taking the church and many people from Zgierz with him.²⁰⁸ Moreover, Father Edward M. Serafin Marks, who declared when he left Mariavitism in 1913 that he would not claim any rights to the properties acquired in his name, suddenly changed his mind and demanded their return.²⁰⁹ Some secular and Catholic officials demanded the liquidation of the Church of Mariavites for allegedly promoting immorality.²¹⁰ Ultimately, this was one of the reasons why the Old Catholics suspended relations with the Mariavites.²¹¹

After a while, there were rumours that the Mariavites had introduced free love and polygamy.²¹² This may have been related to their millenarian beliefs, as such beliefs were already associated with carnal indulgences in antiquity.²¹³ Surprisingly, Towiański, Mickiewicz, and Słowacki also

204 Warchoł, *Starokatolicki*, 57.

205 Mames, *Mysteria*, 39.

206 Such a shift in views on reform related to the sphere of sexuality can also be found in Mormonism, where Brigham Young went from being a staunch opponent of polygamy to an apologist for it. See John G. Turner, *Brigham Young: Pioneer, Prophet* (Cambridge: Belknap Press of Harvard University, 2012), 91.

207 Warchoł, *Starokatolicki*, 72–73.

208 Mames, *Mysteria*, 40.

209 According to Gołębiowski, his decision was influenced by Bishop Wincenty Tymieniecki (1871–1934). Cf. Gołębiowski, 'Testament', 20.

210 Warchoł, *Starokatolicki*, 59.

211 Jan M. M. Kowalski, 'Wyjaśnienie niektórych wątpliwości odnośnie do zawieranych przez duchowieństwo Maryawickie ślubów małżeńskich', *MMN* 2 (1924): 4. The main reason, however, was the declaration that the Eucharist consecrated by godless priests was invalid. Cf. Kowalski, 'Przede wszystkiem', 3.

212 Nowowiejski, Płock, 673. In antiquity, there were rumours, unsupported by any evidence, that some Christians participated in orgies in which husbands and wives were passed from one partner to another. See Anthony Le Donne, *The Wife of Jesus: Ancient Texts and Modern Scandals* (London: Oneworld, 2013), 176.

213 For example, Nepos, a bishop in Egypt, believed in a literal millennial kingdom on earth dedicated to bodily indulgences. Dionysius of Alexandria (pontificate 248–264) took the opposite side, which eventually prevailed in the Church of Egypt. Cf. Eusebius, *Ecclesiastical History II*, 191–197.

had to face similar accusations.[214] Since the Mariavites made marriage a central element of the Kingdom, accusations of sexual immorality were to be expected. In many cases, these were built on the false premise that the Kingdom must not be associated with carnal pleasures.[215] According to Wacław M. Innocent Gołębiowski (1913–1985), Prime Bishop of the Old Catholic Mariavite Church from 1965 to 1972, polygamy may indeed have existed for a time in a Mariavite monastery.[216] It is not certain, however, what he meant by this.[217] It is possible that he wanted to draw attention to the fact that some husbands cheated on their wives, but in that case it would not have been polygamy but adultery.[218] As Sławomir Gołębiowski rightly pointed out, the essence of marriage is determined by a contract between a man and a woman concerning cohabitation recognised by the relevant state institutions, not by physical cohabitation.[219] In fact, the history of Christianity has witnessed more drastic scenes played out in monasteries. One example is the story of a young married woman whose father-in-law was an abba in a monastery 18 miles from Alexandria. One day he tried to have sex with her, and when she refused, he killed her in

---

214 'Bronzownicy: P. Boya-Żeleńskiego Najdroższy Męczennik', *GP* 46 (1931): 361–364.

215 There were Christians in antiquity who denied the authorship of the Revelation of John simply because it promoted the millennial Kingdom on earth. They attributed authorship to Cerinthus (c. 50–100) who was believed to be 'the lover of the body and altogether carnal'. See Eusebius, *Ecclesiastical History II*, 197. The Mariavites knew that Pope Dionysius of Alexandria held that another John could have written the Apocalypse. Cf. 'Bóg w Trójcy Świętej Jedyny', *MCPS* 43 (1909): 676.

216 Mazur, *Mariawityzm*, 96.

217 Polygamy has been understood differently in the history of Christianity. Tertullian believed that it made no difference whether someone had two wives consecutively (or at the same time. See Tertullian, 'On Monogamy', in *Ante-Nicene Fathers*, vol. 4, 105. Socrates of Constantinople (c. 380–after 439) wrote that the Roman emperor Valentinian I had two wives and allowed his subjects to practise plural marriage. But there is no trace of such a provision in any surviving Roman law. Valentinian I (ruled 364–375) divorced his first wife before marrying his mistress, which apparently amounted to bigamy for Socrates. Cf. Scholastyk, *Historia*, 381–382.

218 Especially after the internal split in the Church of Mariavites in 1935, some marriages fell apart because one side supported Kowalski and the other opposed him. It was difficult to settle the whole situation at the civil office due to hostility and mutual accusations. See Jan M. M. Kowalski, 'List pierwszy do R. M. J. Próchniewskiego (27.06.1935)', *WM* 3 (1935): 2. Kowalski accused Feldman of marrying another after illegally separating from his first wife. But this cannot be verified as both sides wanted to portray their opponents in the worst possible light. See Jan M. M. Kowalski, 'List drugi do R. M. J. Próchniewskiego', *WM* 5 (1935): 2.

219 Gołębiowski, *W obronie*, 175.

a brutal way.[220] Mieczysław Skrudlik, who lived in the Płock monastery for a time, also claimed to have heard from several Mariavite nuns that Kowalski was involved in polygamous relationships.[221] Skrudlik was not trustworthy, however, because he had been sentenced to prison for spying for the Soviet Union.[222] Moreover, he used fictional literary works to create narratives against the Mariavites. For example, some of his stories were inspired by Boccaccio's *Decameron* with Mariavite names simply inserted into the plot.[223] A former Mariavite priest, Pągowski, similarly maintained that Kowalski slept with many sisters in one bed.[224] But he did not specify whether he meant sexual intercourse or just sleeping.[225] As with Skrudlik, Pągowski's testimony should be approached with caution.[226] Both relied mainly on unverified rumours spread by former Mariavites, who most likely were not direct witnesses or misunderstood what they heard. Similarly, the former Catholics were sometimes responsible for publications in which Catholic nuns were portrayed as sex slaves with certain sadomasochistic tendencies.[227] Nonetheless, such books are generally dismissed as fantasies because the Catholic Church has the means to defend its reputation and the Mariavites do not.

---

220 There was controversy later on the question of where to bury her body, as some monks did not want to bury her among the fathers. Abba Daniel settled the issue by calling her his spiritual mother (amma), who died defending chastity even though she was married. See John Wortley, ed. and trans., *The Anonymous Sayings of the Desert Fathers: A Select Edition and Complete English Translation* (Cambridge: Cambridge University Press, 2013), 437–439.

221 Mieczysław Skrudlik, *Z tajemnic 'klasztoru' płockiego* (Warsaw: Drukarnia 'Ars', 1928), 20.

222 Sławomir Gołębiowski and Krzysztof Mazur, 'Naukowość, czy Naukawość?' *PNS* 56 (2009): 32–33.

223 'Przez moje okno', *KBNZ* 37 (1928): 292.

224 Warchoł, *Starokatolicki*, 73.

225 For example, a religious pilgrim described in The Shepherd of Hermas kissed, danced, and slept among naked Christian virgins, but it all ended in prayer, without any sexual contact. Hermas, Shepherd of Hermas, in *The Apostolic Fathers II*, 415–417.

226 He accused Kowalski of collaboration with the Germans, Russians, Bolsheviks, and financial embezzlement. In 1935, he sought to be appointed as one of the commissioners overseeing the Church of Mariavites on behalf of the state. His allegations were not taken seriously even in court. Cf. Gołębiowski, *W poszukiwaniu prawdy …*, 61–63. He also tried to take over the Mariavite church in Dąbrowa Górnicza in 1928. See 'Z kroniki parafjalnej', *GP* 16 (1936): 124–125.

227 Jenkins, *Mystics*, 29. Most infamous was Charles Chiniquy (1809–1899), a former Catholic priest who claimed that lewd Catholic priests sexually abused female parishioners and that the Catholic Church was pagan. Cf. Charles P. Chiniquy, *Fifty Years in the Church of Rome* (New York: Fleming H. Revell, 1886), 118–128.

Most contemporary Mariavites deny that polygamy was ever introduced into the monastery, but there is no doubt that it was discussed as a historical event.[228] An article was even written on the subject, but since it was censored, its content remains unknown.[229] Tempczyk believed that polygamy may have existed in Mariavitism in the form of religious unions that were not acceptable by secular law.[230] This perspective may be confirmed by accounts by an unknown author using the pseudonym A. K., who claimed that the Mariavites did not first register these marriages in the civil office.[231] Also, rumours that the Mariavites had united Emil Zegadłowicz (1888–1941), the controversial Polish poet and novelist, and his secretary while he was still married to his first wife, supported the charge of polygamy.[232] There are, however, some problems with this point of view. First, when it comes to Zegadłowicz's marriage to his secretary, there is no evidence that this ever took place.[233] Second, and most importantly, the Mariavites

228 They claimed that Muhammad had been dishonoured because of the practice of polygamy. Cf. 'Przenajświętsza Eucharystya' (c. 570–632), *MCPS* 41 (1908): 665. Tertullian also analysed this issue, although he was a staunch supporter of monogamy. See Hunter, *Marriage*, 45. In many ways, Kowalski's approach to sexuality was revolutionary. He made no distinction between children born in legal unions and out of wedlock and also wondered what conditions sexual relations could be allowed under before marriage. See Rudnicki, 'O rozłamie', 26.

229 The article was published on 23 July 1931, but the pages are blank. Cf. 'Problemat wielożeństwa' *GP* 29 (1931): 225 – 227. Polygamy is not something completely unheard of in Christianity. According to Shmuel Safrai, polygamy was still part of traditional Jewish teaching and practice in the first century when Jesus lived. Cf. Shmuel Safrai, M. Stern, David Flusser, and W. C. van Unnik, 'Home and Family', in Shmuel Safrai et al., eds., *The Jewish People in the First Century, vol. 2: Historical Geography, Political History, Social, Cultural and Religious Life and Institutions* (Leiden: Brill, 1988), 728–792. Vladimir the Great, venerated as a saint in many churches, had several wives when he converted to Christianity and remained in polygamous relationships until his death. See Konrad M. P. Rudnicki, 'Pomówmy o 'nowościach' arcybiskupa Michała', *PNS* 25 (2002): 27. John of Leiden (1509–1536) allegedly tried to establish a polygamous theocracy in Münster. See Jenkins, *Mystics*, 26. Even today, Mswati III, King of Eswatini, despite being a Christian, has as many as fifteen wives. Cf. Aislinn Laing, 'King of Swaziland chooses teenager as 15th wife', https://www.telegraph.co.uk/news/worldnews/africaandindianocean/swaziland/10315849/King-of-Swaziland-chooses-teenager-as-15th-wife.html. After the schism in 1935, the Synod of the Old Catholic Mariavite Church distanced itself from Kowalski's opinion in this regard but did not state whether these ideas had been realised. See 'Pierwsze posiedzenie Synodu', *GP* 4 (1935): 29–30.

230 As an example, she cited some Mormon groups that recognise polygamy as a valid religious marriage though illegal under civil law. See Katarzyna Tempczyk, 'Głos w dyskusji o przypadkach wielożeństwa w małżeństwach 'mistycznych', *PNS* 64 (2011): 23.

231 A. K., *Smutny koniec marjawityzmu* (Płock: Druk Tow Wydawniczego 'Dziennik Płocki', 1923), 22.

232 Ignacy Stobiecki, 'Emil Zegadłowicz mariawitą?!', *PNS* 16 (2000): 17–18.

233 Ibid., 18.

followed the law and regulated all relationships as soon as they became public.[234] It should be noted that they were never officially charged with promoting or practising polygamy. The state administration never rejected the Mariavite metrical books on the grounds that they violated marriage law by accepting bigamous unions.[235] This is why the allegations that the Mariavites practised or promoted polygamy are highly questionable.

6. Children Born without Original Sin

As already stated, Kowalski and others were initially unaware of the nature of Mariavite marriages. Kowalski did not fully understand the notion of the Kingdom and could not sufficiently explain all the elements associated with it to the ordinary churchgoers.[236] The problem arose with the appearance of the first pregnancy, which could no longer be concealed. This caused great consternation, requiring a theological explanation.[237] Following the logic that the spouses were focused solely on doing God's will, Kowalski began to express the hope that their children would be born without original sin. They were to form a new population that would live in the coming Kingdom.[238] It was imagined that they would be filled with the Holy Spirit even before they were born, like John the Baptist (Lk 1:15).[239] This followed naturally from Kowalski's conviction that they were 'born not of natural descent, nor of human decision or of a husband's will, but born of God' (Jn 1:13). Consequently, these children were expected to be holy and pure.[240] As in other cases, Kowalski did not rely solely on his own assumptions but also tried to find legitimacy for his ideas in Catholic publications. He was particularly inspired by August Rohling's books *Die Zukunft der Menschheit als Gattung* and *Erklärung der Apokalypse*, in which Rohling considered the possibility that children would be born without sin in the Kingdom of God.[241] Similarly, Kowalski believed that in

---

234 Gołębiowski and Mazur, 'Naukowość', 36–37.

235 Gołębiowski, *W obronie*, 177.

236 'Ewangelia według św. Mateusza', *MCPS* 29 (1909): 458.

237 Krzysztof Mazur and Jarosław M. J. Opala, 'Mariawityzm w Mińsku Mazowieckim', *Rocznik Mińskomazowiecki* 27 (2019): 74.

238 These were the people of whom the Polish messianist Krasiński wrote and who were to inhabit the new world. Cf. 'W sprawie małżeństw Biskupów i Kapłanów Maryawickich', *MMN* 1 (1924): 10.

239 Kowalski, 'Wyjaśnienie', 5.

240 'W sprawie małżeństw', 9.

241 He relied on Scripture and the church fathers and even gained the approval of Pope Pius X. Cf. *Z podróży*, 9. See also Kowalski, 'List do Arcybiskupa Edwarda Roppa (21.11.1929)', 46.

the Kingdom there would be no need to be born again (Jn 3:3) because all would be perfectly united with God.[242]

Since it was believed that children would be born without original sin, it could be concluded that they would not need baptism. The Mariavites took a different view despite the allegations made by their opponents.[243] Kowalski argued that, in the case of children, baptism and other sacraments were administered for the sole purpose of multiplying the gifts of grace from the Holy Spirit.[244] All this was also closely related to the Mariavites' understanding of the nature of original sin. From their perspective, it was deeply intertwined with selfishness.[245] The first humans sinned because they replaced pure virgin love with selfish desires. Consequently, they were deprived of their immortal nature and lost their likeness to the Trinity. Mariavite marriages sought to restore the original priorities, which meant putting God first in everything. In doing so, they drew inspiration from the examples of Thecla, who preferred to die rather than marry a pagan, and Lucia of Syracuse (283–304), who was prepared to gouge out her eyes to make herself less attractive, avoid rape, and remain a virgin.[246] In the opinion of the Mariavites, God had to take priority even above children (Mt 10:37).[247] This led to the shocking conclusion that parents did not have full rights to their offspring, given that they were conceived by the will of God.[248] It was decided that the children would be brought up in a monastery. Plato promoted a similar idea in his *Republic*, which the Mariavites were familiar with.[249] Some Christian groups also followed this path. The Shakers, for example, raised their children together, but the Shakers' practice of lifelong celibacy made their children (born before they

---

242 Kowalski, 'Stan małżeński pierwszych ludzi', 370.
243 Contrary to what the opponents of the Mariavites claimed. See Feldman, 'Zraniona bestya', 15.
244 Kowalski, 'Wyjaśnienie', 5.
245 'W sprawie małżeństw', 8.
246 She reportedly said that if she had been forced to have sex against her will, her virginity would have counted double in a spiritual sense. Cf. 'Z życia maryawickiego', *WDM* 6 (1907): 45.
247 'Życie pierwszych chrześcijan', *WDM* 8 (1913): 114–116.
248 Warchoł, *Starokatolicki*, 56.
249 The ideal community made up of real citizens (philosopher-kings and soldier-guards) was to abolish private property, and even women and children were to be shared. Stanley Rosen, *Plato's Republic: A Study* (New Haven: Yale University Press, 2005), 28. The Mariavites criticized the Polish translation of this work by Stanisław Lisiecki (1872–1960). Cf. 'Z Bibliografji polskiej: Przekład 'Rzeczpospolitej' Platona przez Stanisława Lisieckiego', *GP* 36 (1931): 282–285.

became Shakers) virtual orphans.[250] The Mariavites never rejected the idea of children being raised by biological parents, but they hoped that, with the coming of the Kingdom, all people would be one big family.[251]

Being brought up together in the monastery by Mariavite nuns was intended to help children grow physically, and most importantly, spiritually.[252] Although it was believed that they were born without original sin, this did not preclude spiritual growth and confirmation in grace after some time.[253] Kowalski shared the well-known opinion among Orthodox theologians that the primordial parents, though sinless, still had the potential for spiritual growth. Ultimately, however, they sinned, squandering the potential for perfection and immortality.[254] The children were given to the monastery voluntarily, and their biological parents could easily identify them and spend time with them.[255] This had some practical advantages. When parents were overwhelmed with pastoral duties, they did not have to worry about the children. If one spouse died, the other did not have to enter into a new marriage to provide for the children.[256] Their opponents, however, were not convinced by these arguments and accused the Mariavites of Bolshevism and communism.[257] In fact, they were inspired by the model provided by the early Christians and presented in Acts 4:32.[258] Nevertheless, they never thought of abolishing private property, believing that certain matters would be sorted out directly by God when the Kingdom

---

250 Metin M. Coşgel, 'The Family in Utopia: Celibacy, Communal Child Rearing, and Continuity in a Religious Commune', *Journal of Family History* 25 (2000): 494.

251 In fact, only children born of Mariavite marriages and perhaps orphans were brought up together. With respect to other children, the Mariavites continued the 1910 practice that parents would raise their own offspring. See 'Ewangelia według św. Marka', *MCPS* 20 (1910): 311.

252 *Z podróży*, 8.

253 Różyk, *'Objawienia' Marii Franciszki Kozłowskiej*, 144.

254 '[I]t was possible for God Himself to have made man perfect from the first, but man could not receive this [perfection], being as yet an infant'. Cf. Irenaeus, 'Against Heresies', 874–875.

255 Jan M. P. Adamiec, 'Życie blisko Nieba – wspomnienia', *MPKSM* (2018): 24.

256 *Z podróży*, 8.

257 Ibid., 77.

258 It is worth quoting Dale Allison here since the Mariavites may have shared some of the sentiments he attributes to Jesus. Dale C. Allison, *Jesus of Nazareth: Millenarian Prophet* (Minneapolis: Fortress Press, 1998), 210: 'Jesus' free attitude toward property may also have had an element of proleptic eschatology. For Genesis 3 makes it plain that, before they succumbed to temptation, Adam and Eve did not have to toil in the cursed ground and eat bread by the sweat of their faces.... Nor did they need clothing. Business and money, then, were not part of their world. One wonders whether Jesus' call to live without anxiety for food and clothing ... originally harked back to the primeval state.'

arrived.²⁵⁹ Kowalski suspected that not everyone, particularly those who valued worldly goods too much, would be happy when this came about.²⁶⁰

7. The Ordination of Women

One of the arguments in favour of Mariavite marriages was to provide priests with assistance in their pastoral work. Theoretically, these unions were between equal partners, to reflect the equality that existed between Adam and Eve.²⁶¹ The priesthood of women was a logical extension of this reform, although it was not planned from the outset.²⁶² As already stated, marriages were only contracted between monks and nuns who were traditionally considered to transcend gender and sexual roles.²⁶³ Abba Abraham believed that, to protect himself from sinful thoughts, an authentic monk does not look at a woman as a female.²⁶⁴ This resonated with some opinions from ancient Christian writings. The Second Epistle of Clement states 'that a brother who sees a sister should think nothing about her being female and she should think nothing about his being male'.²⁶⁵ According to the Gospel of Thomas, Jesus said that 'when you make the two one, and when you make the inside like the outside, and the outside like the inside, and the above like the below, in order that you make the male and the female one and the same, so that the male be not male nor the female'.²⁶⁶ Commenting

---

259 'Artykuły polityczne', *GP* 42 (1930): 249. It is worth noting that even the early Christians were not fully in favour of common property. Mary, for example, had her own private home (Acts 12:12).

260 Jan M. M. Kowalski, 'Królestwo Boże to święty komunizm', *KBNZ* 27 (1928): 209.

261 Linda L. Belleville, *Two Views on Women in Ministry*, ed. James R. Beck (Michigan: Zondervan, 2005), 19–105. The Mariavites noted that ancient Christians called their wives sisters in faith because they were all equal. Cf. 'Synowie Królestwa: Święta Eufrozya', *KBNZ* 28 (1928): 220.

262 Kowalski, 'List do Arcybiskupa Edwarda Roppa (21.11.1929)', 40. If Epiphanius of Salamis was right, some churches in the second century introduced the priesthood of women on the basis of the view that both sexes are equal and 'there is neither male nor female' (Gal 3:28). See Kevin Madigan and Carolyn Osiek, eds., *Ordained Women in the Early Church: A Documentary History* (Baltimore: The John Hopkins University Press, 2005), 165.

263 Blurring gender differences was part of the Mariavite Kingdom. Cf. 'DMHM XIV', *MCPS* 5 (1909): 79.

264 Thomas Merton, ed. and trans., *The Wisdom of the Desert: Sayings from the Desert Fathers of the Fourth Century* (New York: New Directions Publishing Corporation, 1960), 68–69.

265 'Second Epistle of Clement', in *The Apostolic Fathers*, vol. I, 183–184.

266 'The Coptic Gospel of Thomas', in Bart D. Ehrman, ed. and trans., *Lost Scriptures: Books That Did Not Make it into the New Testament* (Oxford: Oxford University Press, 2003), 22. This text, unearthed in 1945, could not, of course, have inspired the first Mariavites. Cf. Bart D. Ehrman, *Lost Christianities: The Battles for Scripture and the Faiths We Never Knew*

on this passage, Simon Gathercole noted that the dissolution of duality was to lead to the coming of the Kingdom of God in which men and women were to achieve genderless status.[267] Some Mariavites may have had similar ideas.[268] The gender of monks and nuns is concealed beneath their robes. For example, stories about female hermits, particularly Mary of Egypt, suggest that their gender was often unknown to pilgrims.[269] In Poland, there was the notorious case of Agnieszka Mikuliczówna (1648–1710) who disguised herself as a man and spent a year in a Carmelite nunnery, unnoticed.[270] Becoming a sexless ascetic helped these women achieve an independent status in a society where they were seen as an anomaly.[271] The Mariavites, however, did not want their nuns to lose their own gender. Rather, they desired their full equality with men. This is why, from the beginning of their independent existence, they paid close attention to the process of women's emancipation in the world.[272] They also followed the news regarding the ordination or nomination of women to leadership positions in various churches.[273] In their view, the attitude of the Catholic

---

(Oxford: Oxford University Press, 2003), 51–55. But they were familiar with the works of Clement of Alexandria who was aware of similar traditions. See Clement, *Stromateis*, 314.

267 Simon Gathercole, *The Gospel of Thomas: Introduction and Commentary* (Leiden: Brill, 2014), 308–311.

268 Wojciechowski, 'Mariawityzm', 32.

269 April D. DeConick, *Holy Misogyny: Why the Sex and Gender Conflicts in the Early Church Still Matter* (New York: The Continuum International, 2011), 116. The Mariavites believed that Eugenia of Rome put on men's clothes to get into a male monastery. Her bishop was aware of her gender but did not reject her – partly because of a prophetic dream he had. See 'Synowie Królestwa: Święta Eugenia', *KBNZ* 7 (1928): 53–54.

270 When she was caught, she tried to justify her behaviour by citing the example of Euphrosyne of Alexandria. Cf. Małgorzata Borkowska, *Życie codzienne polskich klasztorów żeńskich w XVII–XVIII wieku* (Warsaw: Państwowy Instytut Wydawniczy, 1996), 14. Euphrosyne of Alexandria was a holy woman in fifth-century Egypt who adopted male attire and lived in a local monastery as an ascetic. Similarly, 'Castissima tonsured her hair, gave up women's clothing, took on the name Emerald, and passed herself off as a eunuch monk in order to live in a monastery rather than a nunnery. She fasted to the point that she was mistaken as a man by her own father when he visited the monastery where she had cloistered herself.' Cf. DeConick, *Holy Misogyny*, 117.

271 Hill, *Christianity*, 255.

272 'Prawa kobiet w różnych krajach', *GSK* 4 (1938): 64.

273 In 1909, for example, it was reported that a woman, Miss Smith, had been elected as the first female pastor of Southport Congregational Church in England. See 'Wiadomości bieżące', *WDM* 9 (1909): 68. Most likely, the first woman to be ordained in the UK by the Scottish Universalist Convention was Caroline Soule (1824–1903). Cf. Russell E. Miller, *The Larger Hope: The First Century of the Universalist Church in America, 1770–1870, vol. 1* (Boston: Unitarian Universalist Association, 1979), 557. The Congregationalist Church in England and Wales ordained its first woman minister, Constance Coltman (1889–1969) in 1917. She is believed to be the first ordained pastor in England, as Soule was ordained

Church hierarchy towards women was disappointing for them. According to the Mariavites, the Catholic bishops believed that women were incapable of knowing the mysteries of the faith because they were not as intellectually developed as men.[274] Kowalski lamented that the clergy did not understand the Apocalypse because they were unable to comprehend even the writings of the Polish messianists and the role of women depicted in them. In fact, the Polish bards may have been supporters of the ordination of women.[275] Towiański believed that in the new age, which the Mariavites understood as the Kingdom, women would replace priests.[276]

The first ordination of women in the Church of Mariavites took place on 28 March 1929. Twelve women were first ordained deaconesses and then, on the same day, priestesses. Wiłucka, along with Feldman and Przysiecki, was appointed bishop.[277] Prior to the consecration, Mariavite sisters were carefully observed by Kowalski, who assessed whether they were worthy and ready to become priestesses. None of them responded negatively to the call.[278] The day of the ordination and the number of candidates were

in Scotland and in another Christian church. See Margaret Adolphus, 'Coltman, Constance Mary', in *A Historical Dictionary of British Women*, ed. Cathy Hartley (London: Europa Publications, 2003), 122. The first woman to be ordained in 1853 as a mainstream Protestant minister in the United States was Antoinette Louisa Brown (1825–1921). Cf. Borys Przedpełski, 'Kapłaństwo kobiet w Kościele Mariawitów', *NP* 38 (1993): 25.

274 Kowalski, 'Mój ideał', *GP* 8 (1932): 59. In support of this claim, they quoted section 83 of the Apostolic Constitution *Unigenitus*, in which Pope Clement XI (pontificate 1700–1721) condemned the arguments of Paschasius Quesnel (1634–1719), including the one stating that 'it is an illusion to persuade oneself that knowledge of the mysteries of religion should not be communicated to women by the reading of Sacred Scriptures. Not from the simplicity of women, but from the proud knowledge of men has arisen the abuse of the Scriptures and have heresies been born'. See Clement XI, 'Unigenitus', https://www.papalencyclicals.net/clem11/c11unige.htm.

275 Mickiewicz always preached the equality of men and women. See Adam Mickiewicz, 'Skład Zasad 11', https://pl.wikisource.org/wiki/Skład_zasad. This was written in Rome on 29 March 1848.

276 Stanisław Pigoń (1885–1968), professor of the history of Polish literature, claimed that Mickiewicz saw the problem of women's emancipation and believed that it should begin in the Church. This was in line with his theory of the reincarnation of spirits, as he imagined that disembodied spirits were sexless and could take different forms. See Przysiecki, 'Czy Towiański', *GP* 42 (1937): 329–330.

277 The names of the women who were ordained, in addition to Wiłucka, are M. Celestyna Kraszewska, M. Dilekta Rostawicka, M. Honorata Klichowska, M. Rafaela Komorowska, M. Cherubina Marynowska, M. Melania Kubicka, M. Eufemia Nykówna, M. Nadzieja Sasinówna, M. Dezyderia Spodarówna, M. Emma Piotrowska, M. Miłość Wnukówna. Cf. 'Wiekopomna Uroczystość poświęcenia Sióstr na kapłanki oraz konsekracja Matki Izabeli i Ojców Filipa i Bartłomieja na Biskupów', *KBNZ* 14 (1929): 105–111.

278 Damiana M. B. Szulgowicz, Hanna M. R. Woińska, Krzysztof Mazur, 'O trudnych dziejach mariawityzmu, w których przyszło mariawitom realizować Orędzie Dzieła Wielkiego Miłosierdzia', in *MD II*, 250.

no coincidence. It took place on Maundy Thursday, when it was believed that Jesus introduced the priesthood by celebrating the first Eucharist with the twelve apostles. This corresponded to the number of newly appointed priestesses.[279] The latter celebrated their first Mass after their installation, but it was only a joint celebration with Kowalski. During the ceremony, Kowalski stated that, up to that point in Christian history, only men had been ordained priests.[280] The first independent Mass (primitiae) celebrated by female priests took place on 31 March 1929, the first day of Easter.[281]

Following the introduction of women as priests, some Catholics demanded the Church of Mariavites be outlawed.[282] In response, the Mariavites claimed that they were not disruptive to society and, most importantly, did not contradict any principles of Christian faith or morals.[283] The archbishop attempted to justify his position by referring to Rev 21:5, where the one 'who was seated on the throne' promised to make everything new. promised to make all things new. He presented his opponents with cases of ordained female deacons (deaconesses) and other significant women known from Christian history. Drawing on the Greek text of Rom 16:1 ('διάκονον τῆς ἐκκλησίας τῆς ἐν Κεγχρεαῖς') he alluded to Phoebe, a deacon and Paul's co-worker in Christ.[284] He then cited the example of Junia (Rom 16:7), whom he said was called outstanding among the apostles.[285] He noted that Euodia and Syntyche (Phil 4:2–3) were called by Paul to preach the Gospel in unity.[286] The widows of 1 Tim 5:1–2 were seen as deaconesses.[287] Kowalski was also aware that Thecla was known in the Eastern Churches as 'equal to the apostles'; Mariamne, sister of the apostle

---

279 Marcin Karas, 'Święcenie kobiet na kapłanki w felicjanowskiej wspólnocie mariawickiej', *NP* 46 (2001): 9.

280 'Wiekopomna', 106.

281 'Pierwsza Msza św. Matki', 114.

282 'Z życia religijnego Kościołów. Inkwizycja Papieska się gniewa', *KBNZ* 13 (1929): 103.

283 Jan M. M. Kowalski, 'List do Arcybiskupa Edwarda Roppa (24.11.1929)', in *Wymiana*, 57–58.

284 In a 1921 translation, he called Phoebe only a sister in ministry and did not use the words deacon or deaconess. Cf. 'List św. Pawła Apostoła do Rzymian 16:1-2', *NTPP*, 443–444.

285 Kowalski, *List pasterski o Nowem Świętych Dziewic Kapłaństwie*, 82.

286 Some scholars suspect that these women may have been incorporated into the ranks of ἐπίσκοποι. See Carolyn Osiek, *Philippians & Philemon* (Nashville: Abingdon New Testament Commentaries, 2000), 110–113.

287 Kowalski, *List pasterski o Nowem Świętych Dziewic Kapłaństwie*, 82. Clement also regarded them as deaconesses. Cf. Clement, *Stromateis*, 289. Similarly, they are viewed as such in the Codex Theodosianus from the fifth century. See Madigan and Osiek, *Ordained Women in the Early Church*, 119.

Philip, was said to have assisted her brother and the apostle Bartholomew in their missionary work; and Mary Magdalene was said to have preached the Gospel in Italy, informing Emperor Claudius (reigned 41–54) of the resurrection, and later to have collaborated with the apostle John.[288] Kowalski was familiar with the fact that women in antiquity received holy orders as deaconesses through the laying on of hands (χειροτονία).[289] Similarly, *the Constitution of the Holy Apostles* mentioned the ordination of deaconesses.[290] According to Kowalski, they could place the chalice with the Eucharist on the altar and distribute the bread and wine, especially in convents where some abbesses were ordained.[291] At the same time, he was convinced that the history of Christianity did not recognise the office of a female priest.[292] When I visited Felicjanów in 2019, I was told that Kowalski could not always fully understand his own teachings, and the fact that women could be ordained in an earlier period, which only confirmed his intuitions. Rudnicki attempted to defend Kowalski's decision by referring to the case of Pope Gelasius I (pontificate 492–496) that prohibited the bishops of southern Italy and Sicily from allowing women to serve at the altar.[293] He also referred to the testimony of Atto, Bishop of Vercelli in the tenth century, who mentioned in a letter to the priest Ambrose that 'not only men but also women presided over the churches [*sed etiam feminae praeerat ecclesiis*] because of their great usefulness', until the Council of

---

288 Kowalski, *List pasterski o Nowem Świętych Dziewic Kapłaństwie*, 82.

289 Ibid., 82. His view is confirmed by Canon 15 of the Ecumenical Council of Chalcedon (451), which discusses the ordination of deaconesses. The Greek word used there, χειροτονία, means 'laying on of hands'. In the same way, the Polish translation of the canon suggests ordination. 'Sobór Chalcedoński (451)', in *Dokumenty Soborów Powszechnych*, ed. Baron and Pietras, 239.

290 Cf. 'Constitution of the Holy Apostles': 'Ordain also a deaconess who is faithful and holy, for the ministrations towards women. For sometimes he cannot send a deacon, who is a man, to the women, on account of unbelievers. Thou shalt therefore send a woman, a deaconess, on account of the imaginations of the bad.' 'Constitution of the Holy Apostles', in *Fathers of the Third and Fourth Centuries: Lactantius, Venantius, Asterius, Victorinus, Dionysius: Apostolic Teaching and Constitutions, Homily, and Liturgies*, ed. Philip Schaff et al., trans. James Donaldson (Edinburgh: T. & T. Clark, 1885), 639.

291 Kowalski, *List pasterski o Nowem Świętych Dziewic Kapłaństwie*, 83.

292 He clearly had orthodox Christianity in mind and was not discussing cases of 'heretics'. Cf. Elm, *Virgins*, 31.

293 Rudnicki, 'Pomówmy o 'nowościach', 26. However, the text is difficult to interpret. Women are encouraged (*firmentur*) to serve at the sacred altars (*ministrare sacris altaribus*) and to perform all other tasks (*cunctaque*) that are assigned only to the service of men (*non nisi virorum famulatui sexum*) and for which they [women] are inadequate (*cui non competunt*). Scholars dispute what may have been meant by *ministrare sacris altaribus*. See Madigan and Osiek, *Ordained Women in the Early Church*, 186.

Laodicea (363–364) put an end to this practice.²⁹⁴ Furthermore, Rudnicki pointed to inscriptions containing the ambiguous word πρεσβυτέρα.²⁹⁵ The title is commonly used, even today, in Orthodox countries to designate a priest's wife, but it may once have referred to deaconesses or possibly women priests.²⁹⁶ Rudnicki was particularly interested in the case of the presbytera Leta, whose tombstone, made by her husband, did not indicate his ecclesiastical status.²⁹⁷ During my visit to Felicjanów, we have discussed an image of a mysterious woman named Cerula from the fifth century, who may have been a bishop, was discussed. For the Mariavites, this was further evidence that confirmed Kowalski's intuitions.²⁹⁸ Scholars are still debating whether the practice of ordaining women continued into the Middle Ages.²⁹⁹ Kowalski knew that some prominent Christians had opposed women as priests.³⁰⁰ He felt obliged to respond to some of their objections. For example, according to 1 Cor 14:34, women should remain

---

294 Rudnicki, 'Pomówmy o 'nowościach', 26. According to Joannes Zonaras, a Byzantine theologian from the thirteenth century, this canon forbids the appointment of women to guard other women from disturbing the order in the church (among other things, showing them where to sit or stand) and forbids them from being called presbytides (elderly women). This office used to be useful in the church but lost its value later because of greed. See *The Rudder*, 556.

295 Rudnicki, 'Pomówmy o 'nowościach', 25.

296 Francisco Torres (1509–1584), a Spanish Jesuit, stated that deaconesses were called presbytides because they were recruited from among 'older women', i.e., those over sixty years of age. Cf. *The Rudder*, 557. In ancient Judaism, women who served as heads of synagogues were called πρεσβυτέρα. See Bernadette J. Brooten, 'Female Leadership in the Ancient Synagogue', in: *From Dura to Sepphoris: Studies in Jewish Art and Society in Late Antiquity*, Journal of Roman Archeology Supplementary Series 40, ed. by L. I. Levine and Z. Weiss (Portsmouth: Journal of Roman Archaeology, 2000), 215–218.

297 Details of the tombstone can be found in Madigan and Osiek, *Ordained Women in the Early Church*, 193–194.

298 Olivia Rudgard, 'Early church found place for female bishops, experts claim', https://www.telegraph.co.uk/news/2018/03/31/early-church-found-place-female-bishops-experts-claim/.

299 Gary Macy, *The Hidden History of Women's Ordination: Female Clergy in the Medieval West* (Oxford: Oxford University Press, 2008). The Mariavites also referred to the legend of a female Pope Joan. It did not matter whether she existed or not, but the very fact that some theologians took her seriously and did not necessarily see her as a big problem confirmed, according to the Mariavites, that the priesthood of women was not contrary to the decency and faith of the Catholic Church. Cf. 'Czy mogła być kobieta papieżem?', *KBNZ* 6 (1930): 45–46.

300 For instance, John Chrysostom, 'On the Priesthood, Book 3', in *Nicene and Post-Nicene Fathers*, First Series, vol. 9, ed. Philip Schaff (New York: Christian Literature Publishing, 1889), 69. This work was translated and published in a Mariavite newspaper after the introduction of women's ordination. Cf. 'O Kapłaństwie: Świętego Jana Chryzostoma', *KBNZ* 16 (1932): 121–122.

silent in churches, but Kowalski read such verses in light of Mateczka's indication that only Jesus' words are immutable. The opinions of the inspired apostles and other ancient Christians were significant but had to be contextualised.[301] The situation in Corinth was read in juxtaposition with other verses, in particular 1 Cor 11:5, where women were allowed to pray and prophesy, clearly in a liturgical context.[302] Attitudes towards women were much different in antiquity than in modern times.[303] For example, a man was considered the head (κεφαλή) of a woman (1 Cor 11:3).[304] According to Kowalski, it was men in antiquity were responsible for women not being allowed to perform all liturgical functions.[305]

For Kowalski, historical arguments were not enough – at most, they could be a starting point for consideration. Of much greater importance were theological reasons. Kowalski refused to accept that Mary and Mateczka could have been deprived of the priesthood.[306] Maria Franciszka offered bread and blood at Mass, through the hands of male priests, for the Divine Mercy and the rebirth of the Church and the whole world.[307] in giving birth to Jesus, Mary participated in the transubstantiation. Therefore, according to the principle qui potest malus, potest et minus, she could also preside at the Eucharist.[308] According to Gregory Thaumaturgus (213–270),

---

301 Szulgowicz, Woińska, and Mazur, 'O trudnych', 248. Finally, Paul also stated that 'every man who prays or prophesies with his head covered dishonors his head' (1 Cor 11:4), but Catholic bishops pray in churches wearing mitres. See Jan M. M. Kowalski, 'List do Arcybiskupa Edwarda Roppa (12.12.1929)', in *Wymiana*, 91.

302 Kowalski indicated that women could teach (διδάσκω) elsewhere, such as in private homes. Cf. ibid., 88. But some ancient authors argued that there was no clear indication that Jesus allowed women to preach, even those who accompanied him. See *Constitution of the Holy Apostles*, 634.

303 Galen (130–210) believed that women did not have enough warm seed in them to achieve equal status with men. Peter Brown, *Ciało i społeczeństwo: Mężczyźni, kobiety i abstynencja seksualna we wczesnym chrześcijaństwie*, trans. Ireneusz Kania (Kraków: Homini, 2006), 28–29 [Better to quote the original English version].

304 Lucy Peppiatt made some noteworthy observations about the meaning of κεφαλή, which does not necessarily presuppose power relations, only chronology. See Lucy Peppiatt, *Women and Worship at Corinth: Paul's Rhetorical Arguments in 1 Corinthians* (Eugene, OR: Wipf and Stock, 2015), 88.

305 Kowalski, 'List (12.12.1929)', 89–90.

306 Of course, he acknowledged that they were not ordained in the conventional way, but he also believed that they held the priesthood to a higher standard than others. Cf. Kowalski, 'Krótki', 173.

307 Kowalski, 'List (24.11.1929)', 57.

308 Jan M. M. Kowalski, 'O Kapłaństwie. Czy N. Marya Panna, Matka Boża, była kapłanką', *KBNZ* 9 (1929): 65.

she lived a more excellent life than others.[309] Since she was known as the Lady (Queen) of the Apostles, there is a chance that she could have literally offered the Eucharist, even if there is no historical evidence for this.[310] The Mariavites were convinced that, because she was full of grace (κεχαριτωμένη), she was the only person to offer Jesus perfectly.[311] There is another theological argument that pushes the issue even further. According to Orthodox theologians, the moment of epiclesis (the invocation of the Holy Spirit) is the time when the bread and wine are fully transformed into the true Body and Blood of Christ.[312] According to the Mariavites, Mary's presence in the upper room was fundamental because it was through her prayers that the Holy Spirit descended.[313] In other words, without her help, the liturgical act could not have taken place.[314]

It is worth reflecting on the motivation for the ordination of women. One of the purposes of women as priests was to compensate God for all the male priests who did not celebrate Mass with a pure intention. Women were not meant to replace male priests but to complement them.[315] Initially, they were sent to help parish priests manage churches and chapels but soon began to run parishes on their own.[316] It soon became apparent that female priests performed their tasks very well.[317] Kowalski was not surprised by this turn of events, by the way, for women often understood the myster-

---

[309] 'Gregory Thaumaturgus', in *Ante-Nicene Fathers vol. 6. Fathers of the Third Century*, ed. Philip Schaff, Alexander Roberts, and James Donaldson (Grand Rapids, MI: William B. Eerdmans Publishing Co., 1988), 109.

[310] Kowalski, 'List (12.12.1929)', 92.

[311] Próchniewski, *Żywot*, 20. The Mariavites knew that Jesus sacrificed himself, but they also believed that Mary participated in this act. Similarly, Mary sacrificed herself, but Jesus also participated in this act. See 'Niepokalana Marya', *MCPS* 17 (1910): 266.

[312] Michael Pomazansky, *Orthodox Dogmatic Theology*, trans. Seraphim Rose (Platina: Saint Herman of Alaska Brotherhood, 1984), 279. The importance of epiclesis was well known in the Polish Orthodox Church. Cf. Jerzy Klinger, *Geneza sporu o epiklezę. Eschatologiczny a memorialny aspekt Eucharystii w kanonie pierwszych wieków* (Warszawa: Chrześcijańska Akademia Teologiczna, 1969). However, the date of the article's publication is too late to affect the early Mariavites.

[313] They based it on an interpretation of Song 4:9, where the heart was supposed to refer to the Holy Spirit. See footnotes in 'Księga Pieśni nad pieśniami 4:9', *PŚST II*, 126.

[314] 'Przenajświętsza Eucharystya', *MCPS* 32 (1907): 505. Even after the schism, the two Churches of Mariavites agreed on this. Cf. Roman M. J. Próchniewski, 'Słowo Boże', *GSK* 22 (1939): 340.

[315] For example, women confessed only to women and children up to the age of 14. Men and adolescents, except in exceptional circumstances, revealed their sins to male priests. Kowalski, 'List (12.12.1929)', 90–94.

[316] Szulgowicz, Woińska, and Mazur, 'O trudnych', 251.

[317] Archbishop Rafael Wojciechowski spoke very highly of women priests and acknowledged that they often serve better than men. Wojciechowski, 'Mariawityzm', 34.

ies of God better than men.[318] It was women who first learned of Jesus' resurrection and passed this knowledge on to others (Mt 28:10; Lk 24:9). In the later history of Christianity, they were eagerly consulted because of their spiritual talents.[319] Moreover, women were regarded as an antidote to an intellectual form of religion in which there was not enough room for emotion. Finally, the Mariavites believed that God gave the woman clothed in the sun (Rev 12:1) in the last days to usher in the Kingdom. Thus, it was through women, and not male priests, that God decided to transform the world.[320] Since the Eucharist was at the centre of the Kingdom, it is no coincidence that the first sermons preached by women dealt exclusively with this subject.[321]

How did the faithful react to this change? The majority of them, if the sources are to be believed, reacted positively to the ordination.[322] They saw this as the fulfilment of the revelations given to Mateczka, maintaining that the Mariavites were the beloved people, both women and men, who would conquer the whole world. As early as 1909, it was noted that women were chronologically listed first, but it was originally understood that the female branch of the Congregation was established before the male one.[323] Between 1929 and 17 January 1935, 137 women were ordained.[324] This also shows that the practice was widely accepted, but it also gave rise to a serious problem. There were too many priests and too few parishes. Archpriestess Wiłucka, who, for unknown reasons, was not called archbishop, together with her husband and with the help of Feldman and Przysiecki, ordained two more women as bishops, Wiktoria M. Celestyna Kraszewska and M. Dilekta Rostawicka, on the first day of Easter 1931, establishing an independent female hierarchy.[325] It seems, therefore, that either this problem was overlooked or it was hoped that God would soon help resolve the issue.

---

318 For example, the Samaritans in Jn 4 or the woman who wet Jesus' feet with her tears in Lk 7:38. Kowalski, *List pasterski o Nowem Świętych Dziewic Kapłaństwie*, 83.
319 For example, Hildegard of Bingen or Theresa of Avila. Cf. ibid., 83.
320 'Cześć papiestu', *GP* 19 (1931): 145–146.
321 'Pierwsze kazania nowowyświęconych kapłanek', *KBNZ* 16 (1929): 121.
322 Wacław M. B. Przysiecki, 'Co mówi nasz lud Maryawicki o wyświęceniu Sióstr na kapłanki i dyakonise', *KBNZ* 20 (1929): 155. According to Mariavite sources, the churches were full, and even Catholic girls wanted their confessions to be heard by Mariavite female priests. See 'Z objazdu parafii mariawickich przez Przełożonych i Siostry Kapłanki', *KBNZ* 20 (1929): 159–160. It was also considered interesting internationally. See 'Prasa egipska o Marjawitach', *GP* 44 (1937): 351–352.
323 'Odpowiedzi Redakcyi', *WDM* 22 (1909): 175.
324 Warchoł, *Starokatolicki*, 63.
325 Ibid., 63.

8. The Priesthood of the Laity

Although Kowalski announced the abolition of the priesthood as early as 2 August 1930, there were no immediate plans to implement this reform.[326] In fact, it can be argued that the introduction of the new priesthood had been anticipated since at least 1918.[327] It was believed that Jesus removed the authority of all the priests that year and began to rule over the souls of believers himself.[328] All of this had clear apocalyptic overtones since Mateczka was given fine linen at the same time to prepare for the wedding with the Lamb (Rev 19:7–8).[329] The Mariavite marriages discussed above were intended to imitate this wedding. In 1930, Kowalski concluded that it was high time to introduce another reform. After all, the office of priest was needed only until the full manifestation of the Kingdom, and this was fast approaching.[330] For this reason, the prerogatives of priests had already been significantly curtailed by 1918. They were needed for two reasons: first, for the administration of the sacraments, above all the Eucharist,[331] and, second, for the proper explanation of the Bible to lay people who were not yet able to fully grasp God's mysteries.[332] Kowalski looked forward to a time when all Mariavites would rely entirely on God and need no additional help from those more spiritually developed.[333] This did not preclude the need for overseers, who would, however, act differently from the familiar secular and ecclesiastical authorities.[334] Kowalski decided to introduce

---

326 It is worth noting that this was welcomed by other clergy. Feldman, for example, saw it as an opportunity to further spread devotion to the Blessed Sacrament. See Klemens M. F. Feldman, 'Dziennik z podróży do Ameryki', *KBNZ* 10 (1931): 79.

327 Kowalski linked the abolition of the priesthood to the cessation of the Eucharist announced by Mateczka in 1918. Cf. Jan M. M. Kowalski, 'O zniesieniu stanu duchownych (02.08.1930)', *KBNZ* 32 (1930): 24–250.

328 Kozłowska, 'Notatki', 78.

329 Kowalski, 'Wykład', 155–156.

330 Similarly, Mickiewicz assumed that spiritually advanced beings had a duty to lead the less advanced until the latter reached a higher level. See Adam Mickiewicz, *Les Slaves: Cours professe au College de France* (Paris: Au comptoir des imprimeurs réunis, 1914), 10

331 Kowalski, 'O zniesieniu stanu duchownych', 250.

332 From the beginning, the Mariavites were aware of difficult Bible verses that could be misinterpreted. See 'Bóg w Trójcy Świętej Jedyny', *MCPS* 23 (1909): 356. Only frequent communion, which was the foundation of the Kingdom, could ensure proper exegesis. Cf. Jan M. M. Kowalski, 'O istocie i rozwoju Królestwa Bożego na ziemi: Komunia święta jest potrzebna do zrozumienia Królestwa Bożego', *KBNZ* 53 (1928): 418.

333 Similarly, Mateczka was at one point forbidden to read ascetic and hagiographic literature and to rely solely on Jesus. See Kozłowska, 'Początek', 26.

334 Kowalski, 'List pasterski (21.04.1927)', 243. It is possible that he changed his mind on this issue several times. At the time of the publication of this letter, he did not anticipate the advent of the priesthood of the laity.

the reforms gradually. In April 1930, he announced that the faithful should confess their sins only to Christ in order to free themselves from the influence of the priests.[335] In May of that same year, he abolished clerical titles to emphasise that all citizens of the future Kingdom would be equal and would not need teachers.[336]

In fact, the laity in the Church of Mariavites were understood from the beginning to be chosen to fulfil God's mission. Mateczka was told by Jesus that Satan would not be able to tempt them.[337] They were regarded as 'a chosen people, a royal priesthood, a holy nation, God's special possession' (1 Pet 2:9).[338] No wonder, then, that Kowalski expected all Mariavites to reach the highest level of spirituality so that they could dwell in the Kingdom on earth. These ideas were further reinforced when the Mariavites adopted the Polish messianic perspective on reincarnation. It was believed that all individuals had to work on their spiritual progress through successive incarnations until they finally reached a stage where all hierarchy and authority became redundant.[339] The issue, as suggested earlier in this work, was more complex, but the idea of progression was certainly incorporated into Kowalski's theological schema.[340] The final stage was synonymous with the coming of the Kingdom, which will be revealed in the end times, as the Apocalypse indicates. Until this final stage arrived and the Mariavites reached the status of holiness, it was believed that the hierarchy would be needed.[341] Obedience to the more spiritually advanced, led by Kowalski,

---

335 Jan M. M. Kowalski, 'List pasterski o Spowiedzi przed Chrystusem (13.04.1930)', *KBNZ* 16 (1930): 121–123. Previously, confession before a priest was thought to be useful but not an integral part of the sacrament of penance. Cf. Szulgowicz, 'Ideologia', 155. Moreover, even the Polish messianists believed that there would be no place for confession in the Kingdom. Cf. Przysiecki, 'Czy Towiański', *GP* 42 (1937): 329.

336 Jan M. M. Kowalski, 'O zniesieniu tytułów (18.05.1930)', *KBNZ* 21 (1930): 161–162. Previously, the Mariavites believed that titles were acceptable as long as they were not abused. See 'Odpowiedzi Redakcyi', *WDM* 7 (1908): 56. The Polish messianists, gathered around Towiański, called themselves brothers and sisters, apart from their leader, who was temporarily referred to as father or master. See 'Adam Mickiewicz o losach Sprawy Bożej na ziemi', *GP* 32 (1937): 253. A similar ambiguity is known from the history of Christianity. For example, when one monk was informed of his father's death, he replied: 'Stop blaspheming; my Father is immortal!' Cf. Evagrius, 'Praktikos', in *Evagrius of Pontus: The Greek Ascetic Corpus*, ed. and trans. Robert E. Sinkewicz (Oxford: Oxford University Press, 2003), 113. However, Evagrius had no problem calling his spiritual superiors father. See Evagrius, 'To Monks in Monasteries and Communities', in *Evagrius*, 127–128.

337 Kozłowska, 'Wyjątki', 47.
338 'Organizacya parafii mariawickich', *WDM* 70 (1909): 553–554.
339 Walicki, 'Mesjanistyczne', 93–94.
340 Kozłowska, Próchniewski, 'Dzieło Miłosierdzia. Wstęp', *MCPS* 18 (1909): 287.
341 *W Obronie*, 5.

was supposed to help in the effective fight against selfishness and victory over sin.[342] Their authority had certain limitations, however, and Kowalski, at least initially, was fully aware of them.[343]

It is, therefore, a complete misunderstanding to accuse Kowalski of desacralisation, Protestantisation, or decatholicisation.[344] His reforms can be understood only if one takes the wider theological picture into account. The fact that people in the Kingdom did not need priests was a logical consequence of the egalitarian nature of that place where all would walk in the light of God's glory (Rev 21:23–24).[345] It was believed that, in the Kingdom, direct contact between man and God, lost after the Fall, would be restored and no intermediaries would be needed.[346] This was not an entirely novel concept. Something similar, though certainly not identical, may have existed in early Christianity but was neglected after the Edict of Milan. According to the Jesuit priest Henryk Pietras (1954–), after 313 Christianity adopted many models taken directly from pagan cults, which fundamentally changed the essence of the office of the priest and effectively set aside the concept of the priesthood of the laity.[347] It was through the prism of these events that apostolic succession came to be understood. In ancient Christianity, it meant defending the purity of the faith and was not necessarily linked to the authority of local bishops.[348] It is doubtful, however, whether Kowalski was guided by this kind of historical reconstruction. In his view, the laity and the clergy simply had different roles to fulfil.[349] He maintained that people were ordained as early as New Testament times and were distinguished from others.[350] Kowalski placed more emphasis on the fact that the Mariavites were living in the end times,

---

342 In fact, the Mariavites believed that egoism was the main consequence of original sin. Cf. 'Pismo Święte. Księga Rodzaju. Uwagi do Rozdziału III', *MCPS* 7 (1907): 101.

343 The Rule justified obedience as long as it did not lead to sin. See Felicja M. F. Kozłowska, 'List do Siostry Alina,' in *Ku Królestwu*, 109. Kowalski believed that people should listen to Mariavite clergy only if they preach the Gospel. Cf. Kowalski, 'List pasterski (31.12.1909)', *MCPS* 4 (1910): 63.

344 Konrad M. P. Rudnicki, 'Opinie prasowe o mariawitach', *PNS* 16 (2000): 23.

345 Konrad M. P. Rudnicki, 'Co z sukcesją apostolską', *PNS* 26 (2002): 14.

346 Szulgowicz, 'Ideologia', 146.

347 Rudnicki, 'Pomówmy o 'nowościach', 26.

348 Rudnicki, 'Co z sukcesją apostolską', 13–14. This was in line with Einar Molland's ideas presented in the article 'Irenaeus of Lugdunum and the Apostolic Succession', *JEH* 1 (1950): 12–28.

349 Jan M. M. Kowalski, 'List pasterski (31.12.1909)', *MCPS* 4 (1910): 63.

350 For example, the situation described in Acts 14:23, in which Paul and Barnabas elected/appointed (χειροτονήσαντες) elders, was understood by Kowalski as an example of ordination. There was no equality between clergy and laity because the former had authority (ἐξουσία). See Jan M. M. Kowalski, 'O 120.000 złotych nagrody', *GP* 12 (1931): 91.

in which everything would become new (Rev 21:5) and people would become spiritually pure.[351] Surprisingly, members of the Circle of God's Cause believed that, if they purified themselves spiritually, God would take the priesthood away from the godless priests and give it to them so that they could consecrate the Eucharist for themselves.[352] This was another idea of the Polish messianists that were adopted in Mariavitism.[353]

It was only after an internal schism in the Church of Mariavites in 1935 that the idea became a reality and some people were appointed, but not ordained, as the people's priests.[354] This was interpreted through the prism of the 1918 revelations, maintaining that all priests were deprived of their authority over the people. Those who showed fidelity to Kowalski and to God were to be rewarded with the priesthood for their fidelity.[355] In fact, the situation was more necessitated by a well-founded fear that Kowalski's followers might lose all churches and the apostolic succession handed down by legally ordained bishops.[356] The Płock Mariavites responded that it was not Kowalski but only the Eucharist that merited their fidelity since it was only through the latter that 'a new heaven and a new earth, where righteousness dwells' (2 Pet 3:13) could be established.[357] In fact, the popular priesthood never fully replaced the hierarchical clergy in the Catholic Mariavite Church (CMC), where it was introduced.[358] The people's priesthood does not impose any ordination but only requires the approval of

---

351 Any Mariavite family that wished to participate in the people's priesthood had to be holy, which required them to fulfil certain conditions, such as love for their neighbour; abstinence from all stimulants, including vodka; wearing modest clothing; or knowledge of the Scriptures. Cf. Jan M. M. Kowalski, 'List pasterski o kapłaństwie powszechnym (10.08.1930)', *KBNZ* 34 (1930): 265–266.

352 Przysiecki, 'Czy Towiański', *GP* 41 (1937): 321.

353 The people had to take the fulfilment of the Kingdom into their own hands because the clergy had failed. See 'Ewangelia według św. Mateusza', *MCPS* 29 (1909): 460.

354 It is worth noting that the prerogatives of people's priests are the same as those of conventionally ordained presbyters. The Catholic Mariavite Church does not recognise an office of the people's deaconate. Cf. Tomasz M. D. Mames, 'Diakonat ludowy: Refleksje na marginesie emancypacji liturgicznej kobiet w Kościołach katolickich', *Studia Religiologica* 40 (2007): 104.

355 Jan M. M. Kowalski, 'List pasterski (07.11.1935)', *PNS* 35 (2004): 16. Kowalski believed that, in order to become saints, the Mariavites had to obey the commandments of God and the Church as well as obey him and other superiors. See Jan M. M. Kowalski, 'Królestwo Boże jest Zgromadzeniem Świętych', *KBNZ* 15 (1928): 113.

356 Kowalski, 'List pasterski (07.11.1935)', 15–19.

357 Roman M. J. Próchniewski, 'Słowo Boże', *GSK* 41 (1938): 645–647.

358 As early as June 1935, Stanisław M. T. Siedlecki was ordained a bishop by three female bishops. See Zofia M. H. Próchniewska, Helena M. M. Kubicka, Stanisława M. D. Spodarówna, 'List pasterski (09.06.1030)', *WM* 1 (1935): 3.

the Church's superiors. Priests are appointed or delegated.[359] They do not need any liturgical vestments, possibly a surplice and a stole. The people's Mass includes an invocation to the Holy Spirit, confession before Christ, consecration of the Eucharist, epiclesis, communion and thanksgiving. It lasts about 15 minutes.[360] Even an altar is not necessary and can be replaced by a hand.[361] Kowalski was not afraid to allow people to celebrate Mass in their homes without supervision. He was aware that in the early days of Christianity there were no churches and people were forced to do likewise.[362] Furthermore, based on the testimony of Cyprian of Carthage, he knew that Christians in the third century kept the consecrated Eucharist in their homes in case of unexpected persecution, which involved the possibility of martyrdom.[363] It is also interesting to note that Bishop Eustathius of Sebaste (300–377) encouraged people who did not go to church to hold services in their homes, but his statement is unclear.[364]

To conclude this chapter, it is worth emphasising once again that the idea of the priesthood of the laity was closely linked to the idea of a new humanity that would dwell in the Kingdom.[365] It must not be forgotten that the Mariavites did not initially envisage the creation of a new Church. They were a group of monks and nuns gathered in a secret congregation who encouraged the laity to become more religious.[366] Later, because of the changing situation, they followed the opinion of John Chrysostom, who argued that monasteries were needed as a separate category as long as the whole world was not Christian.[367] They would most likely have agreed with Martin Luther when he stated that there were no differences between monks and laypeople, but they would also have encouraged the latter to

359 Jan M. M. Kowalski, 'Uzasadnienie Kapłaństwa Powszechnego: Czy Kapłaństwo Powszechne potrzebuje ceremonji święceń', *WM* 3 (1935): 5–6.

360 They may use liturgical vestments if they are celebrating Mass or leading prayers for a group of people. See Wojciechowski, *Pisma*, 140.

361 Wojciechowski, 'Mariawityzm', 69.

362 Jan M. M. Kowalski, Antonina M. I. Wiłucka-Kowalska, 'List pasterski (12.05.1030)', *WM* 1 (1935): 2.

363 Anonymous, "Przenajświętsza Eucharystya', *MCPS* 35 (1909): 557.

364 Scholastyk, *Historia Kościoła*, 259.

365 These ideas were discussed and shared by the Old Catholics as early as 1909, so one might suspect that they first referred to the conventional call to live a moral Christian life. Cf. 'Rok 1909', 113–114.

366 For example, they tried to focus people's attention on adoration of the Blessed Sacrament. See 'DMHM XI', *MCPS* 51 (1907): 814.

367 Georges V. Florovsky, 'Le Corps du Christ vivant. Une interprétation orthodoxe de l'Eglise', in *La sainte Eglise universelle: Confrontation œcuménique*, ed. Georges V. Florovsky et al. (Neuchatel: Delachaux et Niestlé S.A., 1948), 56.

follow the former.³⁶⁸ For the Mariavites, the apostles were already authentic monks, which meant Christians par excellence.³⁶⁹ The later Christians still had religious fervour, but by the end of the third century it had gradually begun to fade.³⁷⁰ Kowalski hoped that it could be restored by people who were not formally educated but were prepared to sacrifice everything they had, including their own egos.³⁷¹ As already noted, for the Mariavites, egoism was a direct consequence of original sin.³⁷² They believed that the time had come to unleash the spiritual potential that had long been hidden in simple people.³⁷³ This corresponded to the messianic role of Poland, a Slavic people to whom a priestly hierarchy was alien, as faith alone was sufficient.³⁷⁴ The Slavs, according to Mickiewicz, were the least tainted with sin and still had vivid memories of their spiritual homeland, even though they adopted Christianity later than the Franks or Germans.³⁷⁵ They were characterised by love and freedom, necessary features of the Kingdom.³⁷⁶ As representatives of those people, the Mariavites, needed to sanctify themselves in order to save others.³⁷⁷ They needed theosis, which was achievable through the frequent reception of the Eucharist.³⁷⁸ The words uttered by Athanasius of Alexandria that Jesus 'was God, and then

---

368 Greg Peters, *Reforming the Monastery: Protestant Theologies of the Religious Life* (Eugene, OR: Wipf and Stock, 2014), 35.

369 *W Obronie*, 62. But even they did not follow God's will perfectly. Cf. Jan M. M. Kowalski, 'Królestwo Boże Królestwem Ducha Świętego', KBNZ 1 (1927): 2.

370 Kozłowska, Próchniewski, 'Dzieło Miłosierdzia. Wstęp', *MCPS* 12 (1909): 190. According to Nicholas Afanasiev, there were no observers in Christian churches until the fourth century, only participants. See Nicholas Afanasiev, *Trapeza Gospodnia* (Paris: YMCA Press, 1952), 53. From time to time, enthusiasm returned among members of the monasteries who tried to implement the Kingdom but without success. See Kowalski, 'Królestwo Boże Królestwem Ducha', 2.

371 Jesus' disciples also lacked formal education. See Jan M. M. Kowalski, 'Uzasadnienie Kapłaństwa Powszechnego. Czy ludzie prości mogą być Kapłanami', *WM* 3 (1935): 6–7. Cf. Słowacki maintained that sacrifice was the sine qua non of spiritual progress. See Walicki, 'Mesjanistyczne', 97.

372 According to Mickiewicz, only a person devoid of egoism could communicate with God through revelation. Cf. Adam Mickiewicz, *Dzieła, tom X* (Warsaw: Spółdzielnia Wydawnicza 'Czytelnik', 1955), 409–410.

373 Walicki, 'Mesjanistyczne', 89–91.

374 'Les Slaves ne possèdent à l'origine aucune mythologie, et par conséquent – pas de sacerdoce, ni de hiérarchie, ni d'esprit de conquête'. Cf. Tomasz Szymański, 'Les cours parisiens d'Adam Mickiewicz et l'idée de religion universelle', *Slavia Meridionalis* 17 (2017): 5.

375 'Maryawityzm Mickiewicza', *WDM* 22 (1909): 171.

376 'Przeznaczenie Szczepu Słowiańskiego', *GP* 32 (1935): 255–256.

377 'Religia Odrodzenia', *KM* (1914): 19.

378 'Przenajświętsza Eucharystya', *MCPS* 42 (1908): 667.

became man, and that to deify us' became the foundation of the Mariavite idea of the Kingdom.[379] It was believed that on a renewed earth, people would finally be able to attain likeness to God, not just the image of God.[380] When the lay Mariavites became priests, their marriages were immediately elevated to the status of marriages as discussed earlier, ensuring that their children were born with the assistance of the Holy Spirit.[381] After all, there was no room for original sin in the Kingdom.[382]

---

379 Athanasius of Alexandria, 'Against the Arians', trans. John H. Newman, https://www.newadvent.org/fathers/28161.htm. Mickiewicz proved to be of a similar opinion when he claimed that the Word had become flesh in Jesus Christ, but for Towiański the flesh became the Word (or a Word). Cf. Przysiecki, 'Czy Towiański', *GP* 44 (1937): 346.

380 Kowalski, 'Królestwo Boże Królestwem Ducha', 2.

381 'Wieczory Mesyaniczne. Nasi Mesyaniści', *KBNZ* 12 (1928): 94.

382 Kowalski, 'List pasterski (21.04.1927)', 241–242.

Chapter 6

The Aftermath of the Reforms

The final chapter discusses the schism in the Church of Mariavites that took place in 1935. Depending on one's perspective, this was either the end of the plans to bring the Kingdom of God on earth and the fulfilment of the Apocalypse or the next step on the road towards it. In this chapter we will deal with what Kowalski's opponents did to his reforms and ideas about the Kingdom. They will also see that he and his followers certainly did not abandon their aims and introduced the final element of the Kingdom concerning the nature of the Trinity. An analysis of the idea of the Kingdom and the related apocalyptic parts is presented at the end of this chapter.

1. The Schism

There are various reasons for the split in the Church of Mariavites. Most of the Mariavite clergy feared that their church and Mateczka's mission of would eventually be outlawed if they followed Kowalski's reforms. It should be made clear that they never received support from the secular authorities. On the contrary, when the geopolitical situation changed and some of the lands of Congress Poland were occupied by the Austro-Hungarian Empire, the Mariavite churches were closed. They were reopened only after the Provisional Council of State, the first government of the Kingdom of Poland, came to power.[1] The Mariavites, however, were allowed to operate only in areas previously occupied by Russia, which shows the attitude of the state towards this denomination.[2] And this was the situation before Maria Franciszka's death. What were the reasons behind this? As shown in the first chapter, a symbiosis between the Catholic Church and the Polish state developed over the years. When Poland signed the concordat in 1925, it became easier to attack the Mariavites for offending Catholic

1   Gołębiowski, 'Wpływ prawa', 54–55.
2   When a large Old Catholic parish in Katowice wanted to be under the jurisdiction of a Mariavite bishop, it was forbidden to do so. Cf. 'Zniesienie parafii Staro-kat. w stolicy Śląska', *GSK* 31 (1938): 493.

sensibilities, even if they only discussed historical issues, in particular the evolving role of the pope.[3] The schism in the Church of Mariavites changed little in this regard. Even after the events of 1935, both Mariavite Churches criticised the privileged role of the Catholic Church in society.[4] The Catholics used their influence to bring the Mariavites to court and have them delegitimised.[5] The trial against Kowalski and his alleged lewd acts began in the autumn of 1928.[6] In fact, it was a trial not only against Kowalski but against the entire Church of Mariavites.[7] They were unfairly portrayed as the only monks in history who were guilty of sexual abuse.[8] Many rules were violated during the trial. It was open to the public, filmed, and shown in cinemas. Although witnesses changed their testimony and their stories were not consistent, the justice system chose, for unknown reasons, to ignore this.[9] Moreover, foreign Catholic newspapers began to publish negative articles about the Mariavites in order to influence the Polish government and to set Polish society against Kowalski.[10] For foreign non-Catholic Christians, these events were a great enigma. They could not understand where this almost fanatical dislike of the Mariavites among the Catholics came from.[11] The Mariavites compared Kowalski to Jesus, who was unable to defend himself even though he was innocent.[12] From their perspective, he was being persecuted and it could have ended in his martyrdom.[13] Eventually, Kowalski was sentenced in 1928 to two years

3   Stobiecki, 'Dwugłos', 20.
4   'Polska a Watykan. Na marginesie konkordatu', *GP* 19 (1935): 149–150.
5   Akcja Katolicka (Catholic Action) was considered the most committed. Cf. 'Z życia Maryawickiego', *KBNZ* 49 (1928): 390. The influence of the Catholic hierarchy on the affairs of the country can be seen from the fact that, during the debate on the constitution in 1931, the Catholic bishops sent their comments on changes to the document. See 'Kto godzi na suwerenność Państwa Polskiego', *GP* 30 (1931): 233–235.
6   Gołębiowski, *W poszukiwaniu prawdy…*, 52.
7   Kowalski's potential imprisonment may have affected the existence of the Church. Cf. Stobiecki, 'Dwugłos', 20.
8   In fact, the Mariavites knew and wrote about Catholic institutions that were accused of similar crimes. For example, the German government closed some Catholic institutions in Bavaria for immoral relations between monks and students. See 'Z głosów prasy starokatolickiej', *GSK* 1 (1938): 14.
9   Gołębiowski and Mazur, 'Naukowość, czy Naukawość?', 33–34.
10 Józef Gawlina, *Wspomnienia* (Katowice: Wyd. Księgarnia św. Jacka, 2004), 56–57. For example, a Dutch newspaper suggested that the Mariavites were trying to unite with the Old Catholic churches just to improve their reputation. See 'Prasa zagraniczna o Maryawitach w Polsce', *KBNZ* 37 (1928): 291.
11 'Kronika marjawicka', *GP* 47 (1937): 376.
12 'Dlaczego Brat Arcybiskup został skazany', *GP* 43 (1931): 337–338.
13 'Najdroższy Męczennik', *GP* 43 (1931): 338.

and eight months in prison by the Regional Court in Płock with the right of appeal.[14] After all possibilities of appeal had been exhausted, the official sentence was passed in 1931. but Kowalski was not imprisoned until 9 July 1936, and he left the Rawicz prison on 9 January 1938.[15]

In addition to the well-founded fears that the Church of Mariavites might be liquidated, there were also some private animosities that contributed to the split. Kowalski and Próchniewski had their minor disagreements already during Mateczka's lifetime.[16] According to Kowalski's supporters, Feldman changed his attitude towards Kowalski around 1930, when he was in the United States.[17] Mateczka wanted all changes in the church to be approved by the four pillars, namely, Kowalski, Feldman, Próchniewski, and Przysiecki, who symbolically represented the four corners of the altar (Ex 27:2) and the four living creatures (Rev 4:6).[18] But Kowalski ruled the Church autocratically, which was not always accepted.[19] The other bishops therefore decided to remove him from office. The problem was that this could not be done legally, since the 1907 Statutes stated that the position of the Minister General was for life or as long as the Minister was able to hold office.[20] In 1934, all Mariavite clergy and people declared their allegiance to Kowalski.[21] At the same time, at the General Chapter convened in October 1934, some reforms were suggested to him. The bishops demanded that Kowalski stop appointing women as parish priests because the weddings they performed were not recognised by the secular authorities.[22] Kowalski rejected these proposals.

On 29 January 1935, opponents of the Minister General, later known as the Płock Mariavites or members of the Old Catholic Mariavite Church (OCMC), convened the General Chapter which removed Kowalski from

14 'Kronika tygodniowa', *KBNZ* 43 (1928): 344.
15 Gołębiowski, *W poszukiwaniu prawdy*, 70–71.
16 Kowalski, 'Krótki', 173.
17 Wojciechowski, 'Mariawityzm', 53.
18 'Księga Wyjścia 27:2', *PŚST I*, 108. Similarly, the ninth-century Metropolitan Nitrophan compared the four patriarchs (of Rome, Antioch, Alexandria, and Jerusalem) to the four rivers of Eden. Cf. Paprocki, *Focjusz*, 63.
19 Totalitarianism is a commonly observed feature of millenarian groups. See Martha F. Lee, 'Apocalypse and Community: Rethinking the Origins of Millennialism', in *Millennial Visions: Essays on Twentieth-Century Millenarianism*, ed. Martha F. Lee (Westport: Praeger, 2000), 65.
20 The latter was quite ambiguous and could be interpreted in many ways. See Felicja M. F. Kozłowska, 'Ustawy Zgromadzenia Kapłanów Maryawitów Nieustającej Adoracyi Ubłagania', *MCPS* 3 (1907): 45.
21 Mazur, *Mariawityzm*, 101.
22 Przedpełski, 'Kapłaństwo kobiet', 28.

his leadership position.²³ The supporters of the archbishop, later known as the Felicjanów Mariavites or members of the CMC, claimed that the Chapter was an illegal assembly that seriously violated certain basic principles.²⁴ Female bishops and priests loyal to Kowalski were not allowed to actively participate in the discussions.²⁵ His opponents feared that if the two sides started to argue, some secrets would come to light, further damaging the reputation of the church.²⁶ This was a self-preservation tactic, also used by other Churches.²⁷ For example, in 1909, a scandal broke out at the Jasna Góra Monastery when a Pauline monk, Damazy Macoch (1874–1916), stole from the monastery, desecrated an icon of the Black Madonna, was involved in the murder of his own cousin, and had an affair with his penitent Helena Krzyżanowska. He was presented to the Polish public as a Russian agent whose mission was to discredit the Catholic Church.²⁸ The Catholic Church did everything in its power to defend its own reputation, including bypassing some uncomfortable aspects of the case. Macoch was held responsible for everything. Similarly, Kowalski became the scapegoat (Lev 16:21–22) for the Church's offence, regardless of his guilt or innocence.²⁹ Eventually, in March 1935, Kowalski was forced to relinquish his position as supervisor and was transferred to Felicjanów.³⁰ On 13

---

23 It was extended to nuns and lay people. Cf. Rudnicki, 'O rozłamie', 28.

24 For example, with regard to the convening date. See Rudnicki, 'O co oskarżają', 27.

25 Many of them, including Kowalski, were not even allowed to be present at the event. Cf. 'Rzekoma prawomocność Kapituły Zbuntowanych', *Świątynia Miłosierdzia i Miłości* 3 (1935): 21.

26 Rudnicki, 'O rozłamie', 28–29.

27 It should be remembered that the attitude of the Poles towards the Mariavites was very negative and can be compared to the attitude of the ancient Romans towards the first Christians when the latter were accused of practising incest, adultery, or worshipping genitals. Cf. Marcus Minucius Felix, *The Octavius*, trans. G. W. Clarke (New York: Newman Press, 1974), 64–65. It is quite possible that this analogy was also noted by the Mariavites; see 'Synowie Królestwa: Święta Eugenia', *KBNZ* 21 (1928): 161. They did not want such opinions to influence their parishioners.

28 The trial had some similarities with the Kowalski trial; for example, several issues were not discussed, newspapers published the sentence before the final verdict was made, parts of the acts were missing, etc. Cf. Tadeusz Dyniewski, *Zbrodnia, zdrada, kara: Pitaval śląski* (Katowice: KAW, 1986). This time, however, the Catholic Church was attacked, so Polish society proved more forgiving.

29 The Płock Mariavites argued that, just as Macoch did not represent the entire Catholic Church, Kowalski did not reflect the entire Church of Mariavites. See 'Prosto z mostu. Symbole', *GP* 4 (1935): 32.

30 Kowalski, 'List pasterski (07.11.1935)', 16. One of his supporters had a dream in which Mateczka and Jesus left the Temple and went with Kowalski to Felicjanów. Cf. Helena Grzegrzółka, 'Pan Jezus opuszcza Świątynię i przechodzi do Felicjanowa', *WM* 6 (1935): 5.

March 1935, Kowalski's loyal priestesses celebrated the last Mass in the Temple.[31] Kowalski was supported by nine female bishops, 50 priestesses, 60 nuns, 10 priests and 7,000 faithful. His opponents could count on five male bishops, 48 priests, three female bishops, 100 priestesses, 300 nuns, and about 40,000 people.[32] The problem for his opponents was certainly that Mateczka's last will ceded the rights to the Temple and other Mariavite buildings to Kowalski as long as they were used for religious purposes.[33] In this situation, fights over churches were inevitable.[34] They lasted for a long time and gave rise to many shameful moments.[35] Both sides occasionally used force, as in the case of Grzmiąca, for example.[36] They were also keen to appeal to the secular authorities, even if it was the Gestapo.[37] Physical attacks were accompanied by verbal attacks, deliberate misrepresentation of the other side, and fear of confronting their own weaknesses and faults.[38] As for the latter, the Mariavites were not saints despite their efforts, but their condition and behaviour were not as overtly immoral as that of the French monasteries of the seventeenth century or some ancient Egyptian monks.[39]

Both sides interpreted the events of 1935 symbolically and biblically. The Płock Mariavites compared themselves to the ancient Hebrews wandering through the desert to the Promised Land, which symbolised the Kingdom. The period between the exodus and the settlement in Israel was

31 'Ostatnia Msza Święta w Świątyni', *WM* 2 (1935): 8.
32 Krzysztof Mazur, *Ruch mariawicki w Polsce w latach 1893–1980: Geneza, rozwój i stan obecny* (Warszawa, 1988), 421.
33 Felicja M. F. Kozłowska, 'Testament Mateczki', *DWM*, 313–314.
34 Henryk M. F. Jarzymowski, 'Odpowiedź na fałszywe informacje podane prasie przez Kowalskiego', *GP* 36 (1937): 286–288.
35 When Poland was occupied by the Nazis, some female clergy members from Felicjanów denounced Feldman as a Jew in order to get the Temple back. They probably did not realise the consequences that this could have had. Feldman turned out to be German and was forced to move to Germany. After the war, Kowalski's supporters, ashamed of the incident, decided to relinquish their rights to the Temple. See Rudnicki, 'O rozłamie', 29.
36 'Kronika Maryawicka', *GP* 15 (1935): 120–121.
37 Dariusz Bruncz, 'Rozłam mariawityzmu w pigułce-niepojednana przeszłość kościoła w Grzmiącej', https://www.ekumenizm.pl/specjalne/rozlam-mariawityzmu-w-pigulce-niepojednana-przeszlosc-kosciola-w-grzmiacej/. For cases in which conflicts were brought before secular judicial bodies, see 'Kronika marjawicka', *GSK* 2 (1939): 30.
38 There were also cases where both sides have prayed for each other and sought reconciliation. Cf. Warchoł, *Starokatolicki*, 112–113.
39 Drunkenness, brawls, and sexual relations occurred in French monasteries. See 'Port-Royal: Próba reformy Kościoła w XVII w', *KM* (1910): 21–22. And when it comes to cases of ancient monks, we have the opinion of Abba Eulogius, who claimed that monks embraced naked women, violated male youths, and even 'anointed them with human excrement'. See Wortley, *The Anonymous*, 629.

difficult and full of erroneous theological decisions.[40] Kowalski was juxtaposed with Moses, who did not enter the Promised Land but saw it from afar.[41] This proves conclusively that the idea of the Kingdom was preserved in the OCMC.[42] Mateczka was still viewed as the one who inaugurated the new era heralded by the Polish messianists.[43] The Płock Mariavites also saw themselves as the young girl who fell asleep (Mt 9:24), mistakenly thought to be dead but was in fact only sick, and eventually she recovered. The illness in the Church of Mariavites subsided after the dismissal of the Minister General.[44] All those who followed Kowalski were thought to have left Mariavitism.[45] Obviously, Felicjanów saw it differently, claiming that the actions of the Płock side only exposed how shallow they were spiritually.[46] Kowalski viewed events through an apocalyptic prism. According to him, the CMC was about to experience a rebellion similar to that initiated by the fallen angels and Lucifer against the will of God in heaven.[47] These radically different perspectives led to a situation in which both sides discouraged any contact with each other.[48] There were, however, situations in which believers from both sides changed their minds and joined the opposing faction.[49] The schism was undoubtedly a huge tragedy for the Church. As a result, up to 30 percent of the people left Mariavitism altogether.[50]

2. What about the Reforms?

The Płock Mariavites used the rhetoric of returning to the state of the church at the time of Mateczka's death.[51] Some scholars even claim that they achieved this goal.[52] In my opinion, such an assessment is completely wrong. First, some of Kowalski's reforms were preserved,[53] and, second,

---

40   Augustyn Gostyński, 'Na co reforma', *GP* 5 (1936): 38.
41   Wacław M. B. Przysiecki, 'Obrońca Marjawityzmu', *GP* 24 (1935): 189.
42   Zenon M. J. Łuszczewski, 'Jeszcze o reformie', *GP* 14 (1935): 110.
43   'Pamięci naszej Mistrzyni', *GP* 26 (1935): 205–206.
44   Roman M. J. Próchniewski, 'Słowo Boże', *GSK* 40 (1938): 630–631.
45   Włodzimierz Wójtecki, 'W zdrowym ciele zdrowy duch', *GSK* 30 (1939): 477.
46   They claimed that Mateczka had already predicted the revolt in 1914. Cf. 'Rozmowa z naszą Najdroższą Mateczką w 1914r.', *WM* 4 (1935): 6.
47   Stanisław M. T. Siedlecki, 'List pasterski (10.06.1935)', *WM* 1 (1935): 4.
48   Anonymous, "Wyjątki z 'listów apostolskich', 195.
49   Polikarp, 'Kronika marjawicka: Z Cegłowa', *GSK* 19 (1939): 303.
50   Pasek, 'Geneza', 58.
51   Łuszczewski, 'Jeszcze o reformie', 109.
52   Broda, 'Mariawityzm', 6.
53   For example, communion under two forms and confession before the Blessed Sacrament. Cf. Pasek, 'Geneza', 58.

due to social and mental changes, it was simply impossible to return to where they once were. When Kowalski was the Minister General, the monastic element dominated the church's structure. It was time to rethink the whole situation. The OCMC adopted the synodal system, which was an innovation. This alone shows that the rhetoric of return was not taken seriously even by the Mariavites. The synod consisted of all the bishops and six priests, who decided all matters concerning the church. For example, they had the prerogative to appoint and dismiss parish priests, taking this right away from lay parishioners.[54] The discredited office of archbishop was replaced by that of prime bishop.[55] The Płock Mariavites slowly moved away from a monastic organisation in which the Rule governed everything.[56] In 1936, seven new priests were admitted to the church, although they were not monks.[57] Mariavite priests retained the habit and novitiate but began to look more and more like their secular Catholic counterparts. In fact, Feldman was the last Minister General in the OCMC.[58] The Congregation lost the confrontation with the church. This must have affected the idea of the Kingdom and other reforms.

As the church began to adopt a synodal system, there was more room for debate and the flow of different opinions. As far as marriages were concerned, some argued that they should be preserved, but wives could no longer consider themselves nuns. Many agreed and took off their habits. Others, however, continued to wear them.[59] In 1937, the General Chapter decided that marriages were in accordance with God's will, but the new situation required them to suspend their practice for an unknown period of time in order to restore traditional monastic patterns. Only those who chose to follow the Third Rule of Francis were allowed to marry lay women.[60] There were also calls for celibacy for all newly ordained priests and seminarians,

---

54 'Sprawozdanie z posiedzeń Synodu', *GP* 35 (1936): 266.

55 Klemens M. F. Feldman et al. 'List pasterski Biskupów i całego duchowieństwa Kościoła Maryawitów do Ludu Maryawickiego', *Jednodniówka Marjawicka* 1 (1935): 2.

56 They distinguished between the Rule, which applied to the Congregation, and the statutes of the Church. Cf. 'Z prasy pseudomarjawickiej', *GP* 19 (1935): 151.

57 'Z życia Marjawickiego', *GP* 23 (1936): 183.

58 Konrad M. P. Rudnicki, 'Z Dziejów Zgromadzenia. Pierwsza kapituła', *PNS* 9 (1998): 19. Paradoxically, Kowalski correctly guessed that his successor would be Feldman. See Jan M. M. Kowalski, *Świadectwo*, 28.

59 Mazur, Opala, 'Mariawityzm w Mińsku', 77.

60 'Sprawozdanie z Kapituły Generalnej biskupów i kapłanów Marjawitów odbytej w dniach 17, 18, 19, i 20 sierpnia 1937 roku przy Świątyni Miłosierdzia w Płocku', *GP* 38 (1937): 304. In 1938, one married priest wanted to follow the First Rule, but the Synod forbade him to do so because he was married. See 'Kronika Marjawicka. Sprawozdanie Synodu', *GSK* 38 (1938): 606.

but this could have led to fewer men wanting to take on the clerical role. In time, it was decided in Płock that all priests could marry, but only lay women, which completely changed the meaning and purpose of previous unions.[61] Mariavite marriages were completely suspended in Felicjanów, with the possibility of reactivating them in the same form when the time was right.[62] To show the complexity of the issue, it is worth mentioning the peculiar case of Józef M. Polikarp Zaborek (1924–2010). He was an Old Catholic Mariavite priest who married a nun, Wiktoria M. Dilekta Mucha. For the sake of the marriage, his spouse voluntarily stopped seeing herself as a nun. In 1976, they joined the Catholic Mariavite Church, where Zaborek continued his pastoral work. Wiktoria was formally recognised as a nun again in 1979 since such unions were accepted in Felicjanów.[63]

The problem of the ordination of women was also complex. The male clergy in Płock may have been suspicious of the female clergy because many of them appeared to be blindly obedient to Kowalski.[64] Even Mariavite nuns who supported Feldman admitted that most of those who remained faithful to Kowalski were women.[65] The Synod never questioned the validity of female ordination.[66] They accepted the teaching that Mary's prayer in the Upper Room was necessary for the sending of the Holy Spirit, without which the Eucharist would not be possible.[67] They were aware of the existence of the office of deaconess in the Armenian Church.[68] On 2 May 1935, the Synod decided that already ordained priestesses should regard their ordination as a private charism in the Congregation and could not perform pastoral duties. Only a man could be appointed as a parish priest.[69] On 24 February 1938, however, the Synod abolished the priesthood of women, and female priests voluntarily agreed not to celebrate Mass.[70] The Mariavites decided to wait for changes in other churches on

---

61 Rudnicki, 'O co oskarżają', 29.
62 Wojciechowski, 'Mariawityzm', 41.
63 Konrad M. P. Rudnicki, 'O bracie kapłanie Marii Polikarpie Zaborku', *PNS* 59 (2010): 13.
64 'Przełom styczniowy w Marjawityzmie', *Jednodniówka Marjawicka* 1 (1935): 4.
65 Przedpełski, 'Kapłaństwo kobiet', 32.
66 *Główne Zasady*, 9.
67 Próchniewski, 'Słowo Boże', *GSK* 22 (1939): 340.
68 Maria J. Wielopolska, 'Jak się Amor niechcący przysłużył teologii', *GP* 52 (1932): 413.
69 'Uchwały Synodu St.-Katolickiego Kościoła Marjawitów', *GSK* 9 (1938): 129. There is some evidence that women were ordained in Płock even after 1935. See Konrad M. P. Rudnicki, 'Mariawityzm a Unia Utrechcka', *PNS* 21 (2001): 19–29.
70 'Uchwały Synodu', 129.

this issue.[71] In fact, in the 1970s, in exceptional situations where male priests were not available, ordained women were allowed to consecrate the Eucharist or celebrate the last rites.[72] The CMC neither stopped ordaining women nor limited their functions.[73] On the question of the sanctity of Mateczka, the Płock Mariavites tried to work out a solution that would not expose them to exaggerated criticism from other churches. In order not to offend the Catholics, they sought to abolish all forms of public worship of her. At the same time, they continued private devotions. For example, when pilgrims went to the Temple, they sang devotional songs about Maria Franciszka, a special votive Mass was held in her honour, and the tradition of individual prayers to Mateczka continued. But all this was mainly of a private nature.[74]

The members of the OCMC sought to distance themselves decisively from the archbishop, who was compared in a negative sense to the pope.[75] It was claimed that he wanted to replace papal infallibility with his own.[76] The bishops of the OCMC refused to accept the role of the falling stars (Rev 6:13), which, according to them, symbolised the Catholic hierarchy, which had accepted the dogma of papal infallibilty in 1870.[77] Satan falling like lightning from heaven (Lk 10:18) became the figure of the former Minister General.[78] This is further evidence that the Płock Mariavites maintained an apocalyptic orientation since they continually understood the opening of the sixth seal (Rev 6:13) as the next step on the road to the Kingdom.[79] They also tried to justify their rebellion against Kowalski by appealing to the authority of Mateczka, who stated in 1909 that Satan would strike

71   Wacław M. B. Przysiecki, 'Odpowiedź miesięcznikowi 'Sumienie Społeczne', *GSK* 28 (1938): 438.
72   Rudnicki, 'O co oskarżają', 30.
73   In 1955, for example, they had 36 priests, 26 of whom were women. Cf. Kazimierz Urban, 'Z 'peryferii' polskiej nierzymskokatolickiej mapy wyznaniowej połowy lat 50 ubiegłego wieku', in *W kręgu sacrum i pogranicza*, ed. Ewa Matuszczyk and Maciej Krzywosz (Białystok: Wydział Historyczno-Socjologiczny Uniwersytetu w Białymstoku, 2004), 290.
74   Rudnicki, 'O co oskarżają', 30.
75   Roman M. J. Próchniewski, 'Do Braci i Sióstr Marjawitów', *GP* 4 (1936): 26.
76   'Z życia parafij maryawickich', *GP* 17 (1935): 137. He demanded that his view be accepted uncritically. See Roman M. A. Gostyński, 'Głosy rozsądku i porozumienia', *Jednodniówka Marjawicka* 1 (1935): 5–6.
77   Kowalski, 'Nowy Hexahemeron', *KBNZ* 46 (1929): 363. Similarly, the sun, moon and stars in Lk 21:25 represented bishops and priests. Cf. Roman M. J. Próchniewski, 'Słowo Boże', *GSK* 42 (1938): 662.
78   Wacław M. B. Przysiecki, 'Z życia Marjawickiego', *GP* 5 (1936): 38.
79   Jan M. M. Kowalski, 'Otworzenie 7 Pieczęci Apokaliptycznych', *KBNZ* 9 (1930): 65–67.

Mariavite priests with impure temptations.[80] Similarly, Mickiewicz broke off relations with Towiański, without questioning his spiritual talents, when the latter demanded slavish submission to his authority.[81] Criticism of Kowalski was not always presented openly. The Płock Mariavites wrote in their newspapers that sect leaders were characterised by a lack of humility and strange reforms. For example, the Russian Doukhobors, Skoptsy, and Khlysts were concerned with pseudo-mysticism, free love, communism, and strange apocalyptic beliefs.[82] There was also a sect in Scandinavia whose leader, Sikowara, predicted the end of the world and called himself the second incarnation of Jesus, although he had many wives. Members of the sect were allowed to indulge in sexual orgies.[83] It was not necessary to mention the name of the former Minister General for the analogies to become apparent. His wife Izabela Wiłucka-Kowalska also came under attack and was compared to the infamous Jezebel of 1 Kings.[84] On the other hand, the role of both was exalted in the CMC. It was believed there that, without Kowalski, the Work of Great Mercy and the Kingdom could not have come to fruition.[85] Kowalski could not have been responsible for all the things he was accused of because he was free of all sinful sexual inclinations and evil thoughts.[86] He may have sinned at one point, but he had been spiritually resurrected later.[87] His wife, who also fought to defend the Work of Great Mercy, was symbolically taken to be Mateczka's younger sister.[88] Finally, it should be mentioned that the Płock Mariavites restored the titles of the clergy, the seven sacraments, the schedule of Easter Masses and abandoned the concept of the Book of Life, without losing sight of the theology of the end times and the coming of the Kingdom.[89]

3. The Trinity

The Mariavites were accused of holding heterodox views on the Trinity as early as 1906. They were accused of claiming the existence of five divine

---

80 Felicja M. F. Kozłowska, 'List 14', in *Ku Królestwu*, 64.
81 'Adam Mickiewicz o losach Sprawy Bożej', 254.
82 'Nadużywanie Pisma Świętego', *GP* 28 (1935): 221–222.
83 'W kulturalnej Szwecji szerzy się sekciarstwo', *GSK* 34 (1939): 552.
84 'Jezabel w Marjawityzmie', *Jednodniówka Marjawicka* 1 (1935): 2–4.
85 'Michael', *KBNZ* 2 (1936): 6.
86 Wojciechowski, 'Mariawityzm', 59.
87 Ibid., 59.
88 Mames, 'Wokół kwestii', 80–81.
89 Pasek, 'Geneza', 58.

persons instead of three, but this turned out to be completely untrue.[90] In later years they had to deal with a peculiar group of women who believed that Gołębiowski was the incarnation (or incorporation) of God the Father, Kowalski that of Jesus, Próchniewski that of the Holy Spirit, and Mateczka that of the Theotokos. To hasten the coming of the Kingdom, they were prepared to go quite far and crucify Kowalski to recreate the sacrificial death of Jesus.[91] The beliefs of these women faced constant reprimands from Mariavite hierarchy. The archbishop did not allow them to attend church. It is said that, after Wiłucka was elevated to the position of bishop, she managed to convince them that the worship of ordinary men was a serious theological error.[92] Nevertheless, the group survives to the present day, and its members claim to represent authentic Mariavitism.[93]

Why did Kowalski claim that Mateczka was indissolubly united with the Holy Spirit? As late as 1923, it was believed that she did not have the Holy Spirit's constant assistance.[94] First, the perfect resemblance to Mary may have led to Kozłowska's theosis. It is worth pointing out that, according to Orthodox theologians, the teachings on Mary were inextricably linked to the notion of theosis and had been developed even before the Council of Nicea.[95] Second, the influence of the Polish messianists is evident. Mickiewicz expected the appearance of an ideal person who would combine the zeal of the first apostles, the dedication of the martyrs, the simplicity of the monks, and the bravery of the French soldiers.[96] This individual was to be a virgin, undisturbed by rationalism, alien to industrialisation,

---

90 Even the Catholic clergy admitted that such criticism was unjustified. See 'Sprostowanie', *WDM* 1 (1907): 7.

91 Tempczyk, 'Nowe przymierze', 86.

92 'Z objazdu parafii mariawickich przez Przełożonych i Siostry Kapłanki', *KBNZ* 19 (1929): 151.

93 After the schism, they were expelled by the Płock Mariavites from the church in Łódź. Cf. Henryk M. F. Jarzymowski, 'Z życia Marjawickiego', *GP* 18 (1936): 142. On their existence in modern times, see Rudnicki, 'O co oskarżają', 25.

94 Kowalski, 'Słowo wstępne na Wykład Apokalipsy', 766.

95 Jerzy Klinger, 'Zarys prawosławnej Mariologii', in Klinger, *O istocie*, 215–224. According to Origen, when John was asked to take Mary home (Jn 19:26-27), he spiritually became her son and therefore Jesus (Ga 2:20). Cf. Origen, *Commentary on the Gospel of John*, trans. Ronald E. Heine (Washington: The Catholic University of America Press, 1989), 38. According to the Mariavites, John was the symbol of the children of God. See Próchniewski, 'Słowo Boże', *GSK* 24 (1938): 372.

96 Adam Mickiewicz, *L'église et le messie II* (Paris: Comptoir des Imprimeurs-Unis, 1845), 247: 'Tel a été l'homme-Dieu, tel doit être l'homme chargé de continuer son œuvre dans l'époque actuelle. Cet homme devra avoir le zèle des apôtres, le dévouement des martyrs, la simplicité des moines, l'audace des hommes de 93, la valeur ferme, inébranlable et foudroyante des soldats de la grande armée, et le génie de leur chef.'

and unencumbered by the historical past.[97] She or he would symbolise both the individual and the Polish nation as a whole. When Polish poets representing Romanticism spoke of the Messiah filled with the Holy Spirit, who would save the whole world, they often used the pronoun she, a fact that did not escape the attention of the Mariavites.[98] Even if the poets had Poland in mind, Mateczka was the personification of the country for the Mariavites in the full sense of the word, as both were understood as those who would never kneel before Lucifer (Satan).[99] Third, the archbishop's in-depth theological reflections played a major role. He used various models to understand the nature of Mateczka. Initially she was 'only' a great saint, but over time she came to be understood as the Bride of the Lamb and 'like a son of man' (Rev 1:13), who came to earth to bring ultimate salvation in the end times. At this point, she was certainly imagined as a pre-existent being, but her relation to the Trinity remained ambiguous for some time. Around 1929, the Mariavites adopted the theory of the transmigration of souls.[100] This helped Kowalski distinguish between the divine Son of God and the spirit of Jesus.[101] In other words, the Son of God, whose hypostasis was eternal, possessed both a created spirit (soul) and a created body.[102] Neither Mary nor Mateczka were gods, but the highest and purest spirits created in the beginning, along with the spirit of Jesus.[103] Problems began when other spirits lower in the angelic hierarchy refused to pay homage to the spirits of Jesus, Mary and Mateczka, and a revolt broke out.[104] Consequently, all spirits had to be incarnated (or incorporated)

---

97 Szymański, *Les cours parisiens*, 5: 'Selon Mickiewicz, les Slaves, ignorant les sciences et les arts, ayant conservé leur pureté originelle, étaient le mieux disposés à accueillir le christianisme.' The Mariavites were aware of Mickiewicz's ideas. Cf. 'Maryawityzm Mickiewicza', *WDM* 24 (1909): 186–187.

98 Jan P. Skupiński, 'Obraz Ducha Świętego z Felicjanowa', *PNS* 40 (2006): 27.

99 'Wieczory Mesjaniczne. Misterium', *KBNZ* 7 (1928): 54.

100 It survived in both churches after the schism but was gradually marginalised in later years. See Przysiecki, 'Ku czemu Polska idzie?', *GP* 10 (1936): 73–74.

101 Some scholars believe that the Mariavites then broke with the orthodox interpretation of the Catholic faith with regard to the Trinity. Cf. Tempczyk, 'Nowe przymierze', 94–95. It should be remembered, however, that they were only discussing certain ideas but did not recognise them as new dogmas. A year later, in 1930, they still held to the orthodox understanding of the Trinity found in the writings of Basil of Caesarea. Cf. 'Brednie Pana Profesora', *GP* 24 (1930): 105.

102 Kowalski, 'Apokalipsa w szczegółach. Pierwszy i ostatni', *KBNZ* 24 (1930): 185.

103 Kowalski would certainly have agreed in 1929 with the opinions of the Mariavites expressed in 1907 that Mary was created but perfectly united with the Trinity, transformed into the image of God with ever-increasing glory (2 Cor 3:18). See 'Niepokalana Marya', *MCPS* 4 (1907): 56–61.

104 Kowalski, 'Nowy Hexahemeron', *KBNZ* 43 (1929): 337–338.

temporarily in different bodies as a punishment, allowing them to eventually return to their original state, which was symbolically described in Genesis. Their progress was only achievable through sacrifice.[105] The spirit of Jesus was greater than the spirits of Mary and Mateczka only because it was perfectly united, through the hypostatic union, with the divinity of the Son. On the one hand, this explanation shows that, in 1929, the Mariavites did not maintain that the spirits of Mary or Mateczka were hypostatically united with the Divinity of the Father or the Holy Spirit. On the other hand, however, it illustrates the theological development of Kowalski's thought as he continued to try to establish the identity of Mateczka and used various models of interpretation.

According to Peterkiewicz, the archbishop borrowed the idea that Mateczka was the dwelling place of the Holy Spirit from the work of Dmitry Merezhkovsky, who found traces of the Trinity in the Mother-Spirit of ancient Egyptian or Eleusinian Mysteries.[106] It is true that Kowalski translated the works of this Russian author, but he did so only in 1938 when the idea had already formed.[107] Previously, he looked to Christian sources for inspiration, for example citing passages such as Jn 14:16–17.[108] His interpretation was largely based on the discovery that the words ruah in Hebrew and ruha in Aramaic could be feminine.[109] This was consistent with the Gospel to the Hebrews, where the Holy Spirit is presented as the mother of Jesus.[110] The Syriac Christian Aphrahat (280–345) was another witness that the Holy Spirit was understood by some ancient Christians as feminine.[111] Kowalski also referred to the fact that it was commonly

---

105 Many of the details of this narrative were taken from the Polish messianists. See Diatłowicki, *Słowacki*.

106 Peterkiewicz, *Third Adam*, 60–61.

107 Gołębiowski, *W obronie*, 174.

108 Wojciechowski, 'List Pasterski (8.09.1969)', 211.

109 Wojciechowski, *Pisma Wybrane*, 211. In some situations, however, they can function as masculine. See Joseph Jacobs, Ludwig Blau, 'Holy Spirit', in *Jewish Encyclopedia*, ed. Isidore Singer, 448, http://www.jewishencyclopedia.com/articles/7833-holy-spirit.

110 Origen juxtaposed this with Mt 12:50, arguing that every woman is 'the mother of Christ' when she follows the will of God. See Origen, *Commentary*, 116–117. Most scholars believe that the Gospel of the Hebrews was written in the first half of the second century in Greek rather than Aramaic or Hebrew. It may therefore have inherited some older concepts. Cf. Ehrman, *Lost Scriptures*, 15.

111 Surprisingly, even the Syriac word for logos, *melta*, is feminine. Cf. Susan A. Harvey, 'Feminine Imagery for the Divine: The Holy Spirit, the Odes of Solomon, and Early Syriac Tradition', *St. Vladimir's Theological Quarterly* 37 (1993): 117. The Holy Spirit was also represented as a woman in Gnostic traditions. See DeConick, *Holy Misogyny*, 102. The transition from the feminine to the masculine gender for the Holy Spirit took place in Syriac Christianity around the fifth century due to a number of factors, most notably the influence

believed that the Holy Spirit dwelt in significant people in Christian history, such as prophets. There were even Catholic theologians who seriously considered the possibility of the Holy Spirit uniting with human nature in the same way that Jesus did.[112] In fact, Mateczka never claimed to be the Holy Spirit in the sense presented by Kowalski, but, like Jesus (Mk 13:32), she did not have to reveal everything. Some of her statements, such as 'The whole Bible talks about me', may have pointed in this direction.[113] The archbishop also claimed that when he sometimes referred to Maria Franciszka as 'my God', she did not protest.[114]

A new idiosyncratic understanding of the Trinity came to the archbishop during his imprisonment from 1936 to 1938.[115] His supporters maintain that the mystery was supernaturally revealed to him and did not arise from his studies.[116] The impact of the latter aspect should not be underestimated, however. Before the archbishop was imprisoned, the Płock side published an article on members of the Ethiopian Orthodox Church who called Mary the creator of the world. Such lofty language could certainly have affected Kowalski.[117] It should be reiterated that it is uncertain whether the CMC superior had incarnation or incorporation in mind when establishing a new perspective of the Trinity.[118] He began with the Catholic assumption, expressed at the Fourth Lateran Council (1215), that the whole Trinity is

---

of Greek theological terminology. See Sebastian P. Brock, 'The Holy Spirit as Feminine in Early Syriac Literature', in Janet M. Soskice, ed., *After Eve* (London: Marshall-Pickering, 1990), 73–88.

112 Skupiński, 'Obraz', 29.

113 Mames, 'Wokół kwestii', 75.

114 Tempczyk, 'Nowe przymierze', 114.

115 It is worth noting that the Płock Mariavites denied having anything to do with Kowalski's imprisonment. See 'Odpowiedzi Redakcji', *GP* 29 (1936): 224. His wife, Izabela, became the leading authority in the CMC during his absence. Cf. Wojciechowski, 'Mariawityzm', 70.

116 Kowalski became a type of Moses, to whom Goodness was shown (Ex 33:19). Goodness, capitalised in the Mariavite translation of the Bible, was interpreted as the mystery of the Trinity. Cf. Wojciechowski, *Pisma*, 130.

117 He had access to OCMC newspapers and read them. See 'Religja w Abisynji', *GP* 25 (1935): 199.

118 Undoubtedly, later CMC theologians accepted this as the incarnation, although it may have been a long process during which many different interpretations emerged. The 2004 CMC Missal contains a prayer after the Eucharist which states: 'The Holiest Mary, true God and true Woman ...'. See *Dodatek do Mszału: Nowe mariawickie formularze mszalne* (Felicjanów: KKM, 2004), 8–9. The 1967 CMC Little Breviary (prayer book) calls Mary our Father, Mother, and God, but only in one song. *Brewiarzyk Mariawicki* (Felicjanów: KKM, 1967), 427. With regard to Mateczka, there are more songs in the Little Breviary linking her to the Holy Spirit, but there are also places where this connection is not emphasised. Cf. Mames, 'Wokół kwestii', 80.

at work in all aspects of salvation, including the incarnation.[119] By way of illustration, he refers to the three visitors who appeared to Abraham near the trees of Mamre (Gen 18:1).[120] Kowalski then cites a number of passages of Scripture that indicate, in his view, that Mary's body may have been the dwelling place of God the Father. For example, God was identified with a mother comforting her child in Isa 66:13. Mal 3:1 was understood not only to foreshadow the coming of John the Baptist ('my messenger, who will prepare'), but also the incarnation/incorporation of the Father ('the Lord you are seeking') and the Son ('the messenger of the covenant').[121] Finally, the archbishop cites authorities from church history, such as Irenaeus (second century), Epiphanius (fourth century), Thomas Aquinas (thirteenth century), and Marian apparitions, such as that of Lourdes (nineteenth century).[122] When Mary stated at Lourdes that she was the Immaculate Conception, Kowalski argued that only someone perfectly united to God could have uttered such words.[123] Surprisingly, he did not refer to the Odes of Solomon, a text composed sometime in the first three centuries, most likely because he did not know it. Ode 19 depicts God the Father with breasts that were milked by the Holy Spirit.[124] According to Rudnicki, Mary, who was above all cherubim and seraphim, could be one of the uncreated energies of God known in Orthodox theology. There are good liturgical and theological reasons to link her with the Wisdom of God (Prov 8:22–36).[125] The latter is not only the energy of one of the hypostases but is related to all three. Accordingly, there are three types of icons depicting Hagia Sophia (Wisdom), each combined with a different hypostasis. Oddly enough, the icon connecting wisdom with the hypostasis of the Father depicts Mary wearing an omophorion, a vestment worn by a bishop. It can be argued that this icon not only associates Mary with the

---

119 Skupiński, 'Obraz', 25.

120 Józef M. R. Wojciechowski, 'List Pasterski. Słowo Wyjaśniające wydarzenia w Kościele w 1935 r. (8.09.1969)', in Wojciechowski, *Pisma*, 211.

121 Wojciechowski, *Pisma*, 12–128.

122 Irenaeus' testimony is used by some Catholics to support the idea of Marian Co-redemption. Cf. Michael L. J. Haynes, *Mary, the Motherly Co-Redemptrix* (Morrisville, NC: Lulu, 2019), 24–25. The book received an imprimatur from Mark Davies, Catholic Bishop of Shrewsbury.

123 At La Salette, Mary said she gave people six days of work and one day for herself. See Józef M. R. Wojciechowski, 'List pasterski o Niepokalanym Poczęciu Maryi i niepojętej wielkości Jej Dzieła (08.09.1985)', in Wojciechowski, *Pisma*, 175–178.

124 James H. Charlesworth, ed. and trans., *The Earliest Christian Textbook: The Odes of Solomon* (Cambridge: James Clarke & Co, 2009), 55.

125 According to Rudnicki, this also explains why the Theotokos is placed in the apse of Orthodox churches dedicated to Hagia Sophia. Cf. Rudnicki, 'Bogurodzica', 383–384.

office of bishop but should also be taken as a representation of the Father offering the Son.[126] This is why the Orthodox theologian Vladimir Lossky could conclude that 'the hypostatic Wisdom of the Father "built Himself a house" in the most pure flesh of the Virgin'.[127] Kowalski was therefore not the first person to link Mary to God the Father.

There were two main problems with this new teaching. First, the question why no one had articulated it in this way before in the history of Christianity, despite the existence of a certain premise, needed an answer. The CMC Mariavites believed that the new understanding of the Trinity could only be fully understood in the end times. It was an eschatological and apocalyptic teaching, and even Rev 1:4 was considered a prophecy of the coming of the Holy Spirit in Mateczka.[128] The second problem was to put this teaching into practice, to integrate it into the liturgy and spiritual life. Because it was difficult to understand, it is questionable whether Kowalski and his followers were fully aware of all its logical implications. For example, since all persons of the Trinity are incarnate, the whole Trinity was viewed as present in the Eucharist.[129] Not all liturgical prayers, particularly the Eucharistic anaphora, reflected this new understanding.[130] Furthermore, if Maria Franciszka had been viewed as the incarnation of the Holy Spirit, her writings would have been elevated to the status of Scripture.[131] It can therefore be argued that Kowalski was either misunderstood or did not sufficiently explain his ideas.

This new teaching was not well received in Płock. Feldman required all former followers of Kowalski who wished to unite with the OCMC to reject the teaching that Mary was an incarnation of God the Father, Mateczka of the Holy Spirit, and Kowalski of Jesus.[132] In addition, after the schism, there were rumours that Kowalski was understood by his followers

---

126 Ibid., 384.
127 Vladimir Lossky, *The Mystical Theology of the Eastern Church* (Cambridge: James Clarke and Co., 1973), 139.
128 Mames, 'Wokół kwestii', 75; Wojciechowski, 'List Pasterski (8.09.1969)', 211.
129 Ibid., 210.
130 Mames, 'Wokół kwestii', 77–78.
131 Mames notes that the late twentieth century CMC Missal forms recognise *the Work of Great Mercy* as part of Scripture, but this was preceded by a long process of acceptance. See Mames, 'Wokół kwestii', 79. CMC is not the only Christian church where the canon of Scripture is open to modification; cf. Bruk A. Asale, 'The *Ethiopian Orthodox* Tewahedo Church *Canon* of the Scriptures: Neither *Open* nor Closed', *The Bible Translator* 67 (2016): 202–222.
132 Klemens M. F. Feldman, 'Kronika marjawicka. Łowicz', *GSK* 27 (1939): 430.

to be an incarnation (or incorporation) of Jesus.[133] Since these accusations came from the pen of the archbishop's opponents, they should be read with caution. Similarly, Towiański was accused of claiming to be an incarnation of Christ, which turned out to be a misunderstanding.[134] First, Kowalski's supporters regarded him as a defender of the Work of Great Mercy and addressed him in elevated terms.[135] Second, Kowalski openly admitted that his goal, like that of all Christians, was theosis.[136] In fact, he was viewed as the second Adam, but this only meant that the time of the Kingdom of God had come, and he was the first person to fully comprehend this.[137] On the other hand, his resemblance to the Archangel Michael, fighting to defend the honour of Mary and Maria Franciszka, was maintained, which could indicate an incarnation (or incorporation) related to the idea of the transmigration of souls.[138] It is worth noting that some Protestants identified the archangel with the pre-incarnate Christ.[139] In contrast – apart perhaps from the previously mentioned heterodox women's group, the Mariavites did not share such sentiments.[140] The first prayers to Kowalski after his death were introduced in the CMC only spontaneously and were not imposed on the faithful on the authority of superiors in the Church.[141]

---

133 Wawrzyniec M. F. Rostworowski, 'List Brata Biskupa do Redaktora "Głosu Prawdy,"' *GP* 23 (1935): 183. It was widely believed that he had put himself in the position of God. See 'Na przełomie', *GP* 32 (1937): 250.

134 Wacław M. B. Przysiecki, 'Czy Towiański', *GP* 43 (1937): 338.

135 Similarly elevated language is used to refer to the Pope of Alexandria. His official title is 'the Most Blessed, Most Divine, and All-Holy, Pope and Patriarch of the Great City of Alexandria …, Father of fathers, Shepherd of shepherds, Thirteenth Apostle and Judge of All the Earth'. Cf. Otto F. A. Meinardus, *Two Thousand Years of Coptic Christianity* (Cairo: The American University in Cairo Press, 1999), 127.

136 Antoni M. F. Tułaba, 'Znad Niemna: List otwarty do Braci Biskupów i Kapłanów', *WM* 3 (1935): 8. This was also due to his role as bishop. After all, Ignatius of Antioch claimed that the local Christians 'are clearly obliged to look upon the bishop as the Lord himself'. See Ignatius, 'Letter to Ephesians', in *The Apostolic Fathers I*, 225.

137 Tempczyk, 'Nowe przymierze', 41.

138 There seems to have been a fundamental difference between the manifestation of the Archangel Michael in the person of Kowalski and the manifestations of God the Father and the Holy Spirit in the persons of Mary and Mateczka. Cf. 'Michael', *KBNZ* 2 (1936): 7. Kowalski was also matched with Isaac, David, Solomon and Dante. Rostworowski, 'List', 182.

139 John A. Lees, 'Michael', *The International Standard Bible Encyclopedia*, https://www.internationalstandardbible.com/M/michael.html.

140 Rudnicki, 'O co oskarżają', 25.

141 These prayers were officially incorporated into the Breviary in 1967. See Wojciechowski, 'List Pasterski (8.09.1969)', 212.

4. The Kingdom of God

The Mariavites can be classified as millenarists according to the classic model presented by Norman Cohn. Cohn characterised millenarian movements as groups believing in a salvation that is collective, earthly, close in time, complete, and attainable through supernatural help.[142] The Mariavites met all these criteria. Admittedly, some scholars add revolutionary tendencies to this list, but not all are convinced of this.[143] However, even if we took this factor into account, the Mariavites still would qualify as millenarists. The fact of the matter is that they were not revolutionaries in the social sense, but, following Słowacki, they accepted the theory that a revolution could take place at the spiritual level when people representing the lower social strata unleashed their religious potential.[144] It can be argued that the evolutionary messianism represented by Cieszkowski did not ideally define them either, as they eagerly awaited divine intervention and the fulfilment of prophecies.[145]

Before Mateczka's death, the idea of the Kingdom was conventionally understood by the Mariavites. The mystic was familiar with the concept of the Kingdom and imagined it as a place dominated by humility, poverty, openness to suffering, and simplicity.[146] During her lifetime, the Kingdom was mainly understood as the Church's mission to reform people's lives and morals.[147] It did, however, have a distinctly apocalyptic flavour, as the Mariavites believed that they were living in the end times.[148] Although they

---

142 Norman Cohn, 'Medieval Millenarism: Its Bearing on the Comparative Study of Millenarian Movements', in *Millennial Dreams in Action: Essays in Comparative Study*, ed. Sylvia C. Thrupp (Hague: Mouton & Co, 1962), 31–32.

143 Walicki pointed out that many millenarian sects, such as Jehovah's Witnesses and Adventists, are not revolutionary in nature. See Walicki, 'Millenaryzm', 31. On the other hand, Wilson argued that authentic millenarianism is always revolutionary. Cf. Bryan A. Wilson, 'Millennialism in Comparative Perspective', *Comparative Studies in Society and History* 6 (1963): 97. For further discussion of related typologies of millenarianism, see Catherine Wessinger, 'Millennialism in Cross-Cultural Perspective' in Catherine Wessinger, ed., *The Oxford Handbook of Millennialism* (Oxford: Oxford University Press, 2011), 3–24.

144 In this sense, every revolution was preceded by a moral transformation. Cf. Wacław M. B. Przysiecki, 'Lud w ideologii Słowackiego', *GP* 20 (1937): 153–154.

145 Cieszkowski's philosophy did not assume a historical breakthrough characterised by a catastrophic event but a gradual, evolutionary idea of social progress. See Walicki, 'Millenaryzm', 32.

146 Kozłowska, 'Uzupełnienia', 58.

147 'Najprzewielebniejszy', 98.

148 After the schism, both sides maintained the belief that they were living in the end times. Płock argued that the church of the end times must be the Church of Divine Mercy. See Janusz M. S. Bucholc, 'W promieniach Miłosierdzia Bożego', *GP* 4 (1936): 29.

referred to the Kingdom in their writings, they did not spend much time during this period reflecting on the nature of the Kingdom and what needed to be done to realise it, beyond spreading the Christian message. Quite quickly, however, they came to the conviction that only after the coming of the Kingdom could the book of Revelation be completely fulfilled.[149] Its primary role was to reveal what was hidden before the coming of the end times.[150] The Mariavites believed that the work of redemption could only be fulfilled in the eschatological time described in the Apocalypse when Jesus would become the sole leader of the Church.[151] Therefore, the Eucharist was at the centre of the Kingdom.[152] In fact, it was believed that the Kingdom was hidden in the Blessed Sacrament from the very beginning. It had its roots in biblical times and gradually extended its influence through Holy Communion.[153] The Mariavites noted the important place the Eucharist played in the teachings of the church fathers and the Polish messianists.[154] The Kingdom was to be modelled on the early apostolic community, dedicated to 'breaking bread and praying' (Acts 2:42), where believers were to constitute one family and one holy community.[155]

For the Mariavites, the end of the world, as has already been partly hinted at, meant above all a transformation of the social order. They were familiar with and studied the book *Millions Now Living Will Never Die* by Joseph Franklin Rutherford (1869–1942), which had become quite popular among the Jehovah's Witnesses.[156] The Mariavites found several statements in it that were accurate from their point of view. They agreed with the conviction that earth would not be actually destroyed (2 Pet 3:6) and that the new age had already begun. But there were also some points that did not appeal to them. Rutherford maintained that the second world order, tantamount to the second epoch, had ended in 1914. The Mariavites argued that this took place when Jesus began to rule the world from the Temple

---

149 'Odpowiedzi Redakcyi', *WDM* 22 (1909): 174–175.
150 'Bóg w Trójcy Świętej Jedyny', *MCPS* 14 (1909): 211–212.
151 'Pismo Święte. Nowy Testament', *MCPS* 30 (1907): 470.
152 Kowalski, 'Królestwo Boże Królestwem Eucharystyi', *KBNZ* 2 (1927): 10.
153 'Ewangelia według św. Marka', *MCPS* 47 (1910): 741.
154 Jan M. M. Kowalski, 'O istocie i rozwoju Królestwa Bożego na ziemi: Wielcy Nasi Wieszczowie z Komunii św. Czerpali Swe Światło', *KBNZ* 5 (1929): 33.
155 Kowalski, 'Królestwo Boże Królestwem Eucharystyi', *KBNZ* 2 (1927): 9.
156 He was responsible for the doctrinal development of the Jehovah's Witnesses. Cf. James A. Beckford 'The Embryonic State of a Religious Sect's Development: The Jehovah's Witnesses', in *Sociological Yearbook of Religion in Britain* 5, ed. Michael Hill (London: SCM Press, 1972), 11–12.

in 1918.[157] They read many passages from the Bible metaphorically, such as those referring to the second coming of Jesus. The clouds mentioned in Rev 1:7 symbolised Jesus' disciples being filled with the Holy Spirit. The burning fire of 2 Thess 1:7 may have pointed to military action during the First World War. It was believed that Jesus 'returned' on 15 August 1918, when he revealed to Mateczka that he himself would reign over the whole world and the souls of human beings, hidden in the Eucharist laid on the altar in the Temple of Mercy and Charity in Płock.[158] The Mariavites were also familiar with the theories of Friedrich Nietzsche (1844–1900), especially about the Übermensch (super-human or beyond-man) and the possibility of going beyond conventionally understood good and evil. From their perspective, the German philosopher did not fully understand the significance of his own ideas. To reach the level of the Übermensch, people were not expected to free themselves from the precepts of the Gospel but to adhere to them completely.[159] In the opinion of the Mariavites, Europeans had reached a level of satisfaction with their own progress and their self-confidence would eventually collapse.[160]

Following Joachim de Fiore, the Mariavites divided human history into three epochs. The first belonged to the Father, the second to the Son, and the third to the Holy Spirit.[161] Cieszkowski believed that the third epoch would begin in the nineteenth century.[162] Kowalski also enumerated three Christian churches, the first being Peter's for the Jews, the second Paul's for the Gentiles, and the third John's which was based on devotion to the Blessed Sacrament and would unite the previous ones.[163] The same conception, though sometimes in altered form, could be found among the Polish messianists.[164] This was another belief that both Churches of Mariavites retained after the schism.[165] It may have been related to the tri-division of

---

157 'Proroctw nie lekceważcie. 1 Tess. 5,20: Miljony ludzi z obecnie żyjących nigdy nie umrą!', *KBNZ* 44 (1928): 348.

158 'Proroctw nie lekceważcie: O powtórnym przyjściu Pana Jezusa w ogniu', *KBNZ* 18 (1928): 137–138.

159 'Luźne myśli o współczesnej kulturze', *KM* (1913): 59.

160 Ibid., 54–60.

161 Wacław M. B. Przysiecki, 'Słowo Boże', *GP* 22 (1937): 171.

162 Cieszkowski, *Ojcze Nasz*, 20.

163 Kowalski, 'Apokalipsa w szczegółach: Trzy Kościoły: Piotrowy, Pawłowy i Janowy', *KBNZ* 15 (1930): 113–114.

164 Mickiewicz, for example, believed that there were three churches corresponding to three epochs – the Synagogue, the Catholic Church, and the Church of the Holy Spirit. See 'Notatki z tego, co Brat Adam Mickiewicz mówił', *GP* 1 (1937): 5–6.

165 'Triumf dobra na ziemi', *GP* 29 (1935): 229–231.

salvation announced by Mateczka in 1911.[166] In addition to the division of human history into three epochs, the Mariavites also referred to the sevenfold divisions contained in the prophecies of Hildegard of Bingen (1098–1179). The seventh epoch signified the seventh day of rest, or Kingdom, when God's people would receive all prophetic gifts and security in the face of cosmic cataclysm (Joel 2:28–32; 3:1–5).[167] The seven seals of the Apocalypse represented seven periods in the history of the Church. Each period lasted 300 years, and the first began in the year 70 with the destruction of the Jerusalem Temple. The first period (70–370; represented symbolically in Rev 6:1–2) was a time of martyrdom and victory over Arianism. It corresponded to the years 1906–1914 in Mariavitism, when the Mariavites fought for the victory of the Blessed Sacrament. The second period (370–670; Rev 6:3–4) was a time of struggle against the barbarians and the coming of Islam. In Mariavitism, it coincided with the years 1914–1921, until the sacrificial death of Mateczka.[168] The third period (670–970; Rev 6:5–6) was a time of pride and struggles for supremacy between the popes of Old and New Rome. During this phase, Poland, initially Christianised by the Eastern Church, came under the influence of the Western Church after the baptism of Mieszko I (reigned 960–992) in 966. This corresponded to the years 1921–1928 in Mariavitism, when it was revealed that the Eucharist had ceased to be valid in the Catholic Church.[169] The fourth period (970–1270; Rev 6:7–8) was the time of the Crusades. In Mariavitism it coincided with the years 1928–1935, when another world war was expected to be initiated by the forces of communism and religious crusaders against Russia.[170] It is worth adding that this periodisation appeared in 1930, and Kowalski could only guess at what would come next. The fifth period (1270–1570; Rev 6:9–11) was the time of the Inquisition and the fall of Constantinople. This corresponded to the years 1935–1942 in Mariavitism, but no description of this time was given.[171] The sixth period (1570–1870; Rev 6:12–17) was the time of the introduction of the blasphemous dogma of papal infallibility and the undermining of the meaning of the Blessed Sacrament. According to the Mariavites, the words 'the kings of the earth, the princes, the generals, the rich, the mighty,

---

166 First, through Exodus; second, through Redemption; and third, through Mercy. See Kozłowska, 'Notatki', 70.
167 'Proroctw nie lekceważcie', *KBNZ* 12 (1928): 90.
168 Jan M. M. Kowalski, 'Otworzenie 7 Pieczęci Apokaliptycznych', *KBNZ* 9 (1930): 65–67.
169 Ibid., 73–74.
170 Ibid., 81–82.
171 Ibid., 89–90.

and everyone else, who hid in caves and among the rocks of the mountains' (Rev 6:15) pointed to the church fathers and the Polish Romantic poets who taught the principles of the faith untainted by the 1870 dogma. This would correspond to the years 1942–1949, but this period also lacked description.[172] The last seal would open in 2170 and correspond to the years 1949–1956 in Mariavitism, but no further information is given about this period. According to Towiański, the number seven was significant because it was the sum of the number three, symbolising heaven, and the number four, symbolising humanity. Seven was the number of salvation.[173] The church consisting only of pure believers, which Augustine spoke of in Sermon 248, was expected to come on the seventh day. For the Mariavites, this was synonymous with the Kingdom they expected.[174] But it would last not just a thousand years, but forever.[175]

Mariavites' understanding of the idea of the Kingdom of God was, undeniably, hugely influenced by Polish Romantics. It is difficult to determine when exactly they became familiar with Romanticist ideas.[176] They certainly weren't the first to recognise Polish poets as authentic prophets of God in the end times.[177] Both the Mariavites and Polish messianists had many elements in common – above all, the belief in the imminent inauguration of the Kingdom of God.[178] Both were branded heretics and traitors, viewed Rome and the Catholic Church with suspicion, and linked Poland's rebirth with the idea of salvific transformation.[179] The Mariavites complained

---

172 Ibid., 97–98.
173 'Adam Mickiewicz o losach Sprawy Bożej na ziemi', *GP* 32 (1937): 253.
174 'Na przełomie', *GP* 32 (1937): 250.
175 Kowalski, 'List pasterski (21.04.1927)', 221.
176 Since Cieszkowski's *Ojcze Nasz* was on the Index Librorum Prohibitorum, it was not known to the Mariavites before 1906 at the earliest. Cf. Roman M. J. Próchniewski, 'Symbol pojednania', *GSK* 3 (1939): 33–34. Articles on Mickiewicz's 'Mariavitism' were published as early as 1909: e.g., 'Maryawityzm Mickiewicza', *WDM* 22 (1909): 169–171. Przysiecki, however, claimed that the Mariavites only began to study their works more diligently thirty years after the founding of the Congregation. See Przysiecki, 'Czy Towiański', *GP* 36 (1937): 281.
177 Fortunat Strowski (1866–1952), a historian of French literature, had similar ideas. See 'Wieczory Mesyaniczne. Nasi Mesyaniści', *KBNZ* 12 (1928): 95.
178 'Wieczory Mesyaniczne. Co to jest Mesyanizm Polski', *KBNZ* 35 (1928): 277. Belief in the coming of the Kingdom was shared by Hoene-Wroński, Towiański, Bronisław Ferdynand Trentowski (1808–1869), and also by French philosophers Jules Michelet (1798–1874) and Egdar Quinet (1803–1875). See 'Synowie Królestwa: Mistrz Andrzej Towiański i jego uczniowie', *KBNZ* 14 (1930): 107.
179 Wacław M. B. Przysiecki, 'Ku czemu Polska idzie?', *GP* 27 (1936): 201. Mickiewicz reported that Polish Catholic priests in France called them heretics. See Wacław M. B. Przysiecki, 'Zmartwychwstanie idei', *GP* 44 (1936): 338. The Catholic newspaper

that the Polish intelligentsia did not appreciate the achievements of Polish Romantic thinkers and did not want to implement their ideas.[180] Mateczka's disciples even saw themselves as continuing Towiański's Koło Sprawy Bożej (Circle of God's Cause).[181] Despite their love for Poland, seen as both a patriotic and religious duty, neither the Polish messianists nor the Mariavites were nationalists.[182] It is highly probable that the Mariavites understand nation not in terms of ethnicity but in terms of 'associations of kindred individual souls'.[183] There was no room for national particularism in the Kingdom. In addition to the 144,000 from all the tribes of Israel (Rev 7:4), it was to be inhabited by countless masses from every nation in the world.[184] Cieszkowski wrote that Poland had been chosen as an apostle to other nations as a reward for its constant sacrifices, sufferings, and efforts.[185] It was in this sense that the Mariavites understood Słowacki's view that the whole world must become Poland.[186] They compared the Poles to the first Jewish followers of Jesus, who eventually transcended national boundaries and spread God's message throughout the world.[187] There was always a danger that Poland would not understand its mission and would remain loyal to the papacy, but the Mariavites ruled out such a possibility, believing that the time of the fulfilment of the Apocalypse had come.[188] They maintained that the woman depicted in Rev 12:13 was a type of the new Poland, opposing the Catholic hierarchy depicted as a serpent

---

Osservatore Romano also called Mickiewicz a blasphemer who died of cholera because of his sins. Cf. 'Organ papieża o Mickiewiczu', *KBNZ* 6 (1930): 47.

180 'Rozpaczliwy stan naszej inteligencji', *GP* 35 (1931): 276.

181 Members of the Circle often received the Eucharist, adored the Blessed Sacrament, and wore medallions depicting Our Lady of Perpetual Help. Cf. 'Adam Mickiewicz o losach Sprawy Bożej na ziemi', *GP* 32 (1937): 253. According to the Mariavites, Towiański played the same role in relation to the Work of Great Mercy as John the Baptist did in relation to the redemptive act of Jesus. See Przysiecki, 'Czy Towiański', *GP* 36 (1937): 281.

182 'Miłość Ojczyzny', *GP* 47 (1936): 361. Kłoczowski argued that Polish Messianists represented a mixture of patriotism and universalism. See Adrianyi and Kłoczowski, 'Catholic Nationalism', 278–279.

183 Walicki, 'Polish', 5.

184 'Bóg w Trójcy Świętej Jedyny', *MCPS* 43 (1909): 677.

185 Kowalski, 'Słowo wstępne na Wykład Apokalipsy', 739.

186 Kowalski, 'Wola Boża', 3. Krasiński also believed that Poland would become the Messiah who would save all other nations. Cf. Jan M. M. Kowalski, 'Dla Chwały Bożej', *MMN* 2 (1924): 2. According to Walicki, this concept emphasised Poland's servile role towards other nations. See Walicki, 'Mesjanistyczne', 103.

187 'Ewangelia według św. Mateusza', *MCPS* 20 (1908): 311.

188 'Przenajświętsza Eucharystya', *MCPS* 49 (1908): 780.

(Rev 12:15), which persecuted the Mariavites.[189] Because of the salvific role of the Polish nation, the Mariavites paid close attention to politics. They saw Józef Piłsudski (1867–1935), a father of the Second Polish Republic, as a providential figure who noted that Tadeusz Kościuszko (1746–1817) and Mickiewicz were great Polish patriots.[190] For example, some Mariavites believed that the Eucharist in the Catholic Church ceased on 11 August 1924. They added 1335 days to this date (Dan 12:11-2), which gave them 8 April 1928 and associated this day with the political and ideological victory of Piłsudski.[191] He was seen as the instrument by which God would resurrect Poland politically and establish the Kingdom in the not-too-distant future.[192] Neither the pope nor the Catholic clergy were needed for this since true religious knowledge came from the Gospels, the Symbols of Faith, the church fathers, and the prophets of Polish Romanticism and often stood in opposition to the decisions of the popes.[193]

In concluding these reflections, it is worth mentioning briefly how the Mariavites envisioned the Kingdom. For them, it was a place of the perfect union of body and spirit.[194] All its members were to be filled with the Holy Spirit so that they could understand the will of God and judge whether the commands of their superiors were in accordance with it.[195] It was expected to be a Kingdom of love and peace in which punishments would cease to exist.[196] It was believed that it would be a Kingdom of mercy even for hardened sinners, as long as they accepted God's love.[197] Potential

---

189 'Proroctw nie lekceważcie. 1 Tess. 5,20: Bestya wypuszcza z gęby swej rzekę', *KBNZ* 37 (1928): 290.

190 Józef Piłsudski, 'O patrjotyzmie', *GP* 25 (1937): 197. He decided to bury Słowacki at Wawel despite the protests of the Catholic hierarchy. Cf. Diatłowicki, *Słowacki*.

191 'Proroctw nie lekceważcie: Wypełnienie się proroctwa Daniela w tych dniach', *KBNZ* 13 (1928): 99.

192 Wacław M. B. Przysiecki, 'Rządy Opatrzości', *GP* 30 (1935): 237–238. Even after the schism, both sides consistently supported Piłsudski, seeing him as a guarantor of the realisation of the Kingdom. See 'Pierwsze posiedzenie', 29. They did all this despite the fact that it did not improve the situation of the Church of Mariavites in the country. Cf. Mazur, *Mariawityzm*, 90–91.

193 Kowalski, 'Słowo wstępne na Wykład Apokalipsy', 746. The Mariavites claimed that Polish Romantic thinkers often opposed the Catholic Church. For example, Towiański openly criticised the dogma of papal infallibility, calling it a sin against the Holy Spirit. Cf. 'Proroctw nie lekceważcie. 1 Tess. 5,20: Znieważenie stolicy', *KBNZ* 33 (1928): 259.

194 'Bóg w Trójcy Świętej Jedyny', *MCPS* 25 (1910): 386.

195 Kowalski, 'Królestwo Boże Królestwem Ducha', 1.

196 Jan M. M. Kowalski, 'Królestwo Boże ma dwie tablice Prawa Bożego', *KBNZ* 12 (1928): 90.

197 Jan M. M. Kowalski, 'Królestwo Boże rządzi się samym Miłosierdziem', *KBNZ* 13 (1928): 97.

criminals and offenders were to be punished only with love.[198] There was one common language – Polish, which was the language of Mateczka, the Queen of the Kingdom, the Bride of Jesus. The Mariavites emphasised that they were not guided by unbridled nationalism and did not want to force people to adopt the Polish language and customs. They believed that everyone would adopt this language voluntarily, guided by their love for Poland and its salvific role.[199] Surprisingly, the Mariavites were very interested in developing Esperanto to help them communicate with the world.[200] Since every earthly kingdom needs a capital, the Temple in Płock was selected for the Kingdom of God. It was chosen because of the greatest number of pure hearts that adored Jesus in Płock.[201] The Kingdom also had its own registry, known as the Book of Life, kept in the Płock Temple under the monstrance, separately for the Mariavites and non-Mariavites.[202] According to Kowalski, as citizens of the Kingdom, the Mariavites would never die, but this idea needs clarification. First, not all people who considered themselves Mariavites were in fact so, and it was not the role of the archbishop to decide who was a genuine believer. As has already been pointed out, excommunication did not exist in the Church of Mariavites.[203] All people who devoutly and frequently received the Eucharist were authentic Mariavites and therefore inhabitants of a Kingdom that tolerated nothing impure.[204] Through this practice (Jn 6:54), people were already developing a Eucharistic, spiritual body (1 Cor 15:39–46) on earth that was not visible, like Jesus hidden in the Blessed Sacrament. It was believed that the old body would be shaken off at death and the indestructible body would be released.[205] If people clothed themselves with the new self (Eph

---

198 Jan M. M. Kowalski, 'Królestwo Boże znosi wszelkie kary cielesne na przestępców', *KBNZ* 20 (1928): 153.

199 Jan M. M. Kowalski 'Królestwo Boże będzie miało jeden wspólny język', *KBNZ* 11 (1928): 81.

200 Katarzyna Tempczyk, 'Mariawityzm a esperanto', *PNS* 28 (2003): 11–17.

201 Jan M. M. Kowalski, 'Królestwo Boże ma swoją stolicę na ziemi', *KBNZ* 5 (1928): 33.

202 Jan M. M. Kowalski, 'Królestwo Boże ma swoje księgi rejestracyjne', *KBNZ* 6 (1928): 41.

203 It was understood that the people whose names were removed from the Book of Life had cut themselves off because they did not want to reform their lives and enter the Kingdom. Kowalski always encouraged them to repent. See Jan M. M. Kowalski, 'List pasterski (08.03.1928)', *KBNZ* 13 (1928): 98. He claimed that the living had judged themselves. Kowalski, 'List pasterski (21.04.1927)', 222.

204 Szulgowicz, 'Ideologia', 191.

205 The resurrection of the earthly bodies left behind was possible but certainly not a sine qua non for the Kingdom of God on earth. Ibid., 174.

4:24) already on earth, they were not expected to be found naked at death and did not have to wait for the final resurrection.[206] They would be with Jesus eternally in the Kingdom (Rev 20:3), called the third heaven (2 Cor 12:2-4) and established in the Temple of Mercy and Charity in Płock.[207] Just as for the world as a whole, the end did not mean the literal destruction of the planet but transformation, so the end also meant transformation for the individual.[208] This was not the first metamorphosis in their lives since they understood the first resurrection mentioned in Rev 20:6 as a metaphorical resurrection from religious indifference.[209] The Mariavites did not expect further reincarnation to achieve perfect union with Christ since they often participated in the Eucharist and developed a spiritual body.[210] In this sense, they hoped to be holy people.[211] Augustine's sermon 248, in which he distinguished between two churches, had a particular impact on the Mariavites. The first church was made up of both good and bad people, whom the Bible represented as good and bad fish (Mt 13:48). The second was represented by the catch of fish that took place only after the resurrection and attracted only good fish (Jn 21:6).[212] There was no place for impurity and sinners in the Kingdom.[213] All its citizens would be established in grace, and Satan would have no power over them because he would be cast into the Abyss forever (Rev 20:3).[214]

---

206 Jan M. M. Kowalski, 'O 120.000 złotych nagrody', *GP* 17 (1931): 129–130.

207 Jan M. M. Kowalski, 'Królestwo Boże na Ziemi obcuje ze Świętymi w Niebie', *KBNZ* 21 (1928): 161.

208 'Ewangelia według św. Mateusza', *MCPS* 29 (1909): 459.

209 Jan M. M. Kowalski, 'Królestwo Boże jest pierwszym zmartwychwstaniem', *KBNZ* 17 (1928): 129.

210 Kowalski, 'Nowy Hexahemeron', *KBNZ* 44 (1929): 349.

211 A similar thought can be found in the writings of Lactantius (250–325): 'Then, those who will be living in bodies will not die, but will generate an infinite multitude during those same thousand years, and their offspring will be holy and dear to God.' Cf. Lactantius, *The Divine Institutes, I–VII*, ed. Mary F. McDonald O. P. (Washington: The Catholic University, 1964), 530.

212 This idea was shared by both OCMC and CMC after 1935. See Przysiecki, 'Słowo Boże', *GP* 24 (1937): 186–187.

213 Kowalski, 'Królestwo Boże Królestwem Eucharystyi', *KBNZ* 2 (1927): 10.

214 Jan M. M. Kowalski, 'Królestwo Boże na Ziemi nigdy upaść nie może', *KBNZ* 22 (1928): 169. Confirmation in grace was only possible through the Eucharist. See Jan M. M. Kowalski, 'O istocie i rozwoju Królestwa Bożego na Ziemi. Utwierdzenie w łasce przez Komunię Św', *KBNZ* 8 (1931): 57.

Conclusions

As indicated at the very beginning of this book, an analysis of the Mariavites in their historical and cultural context has never been undertaken academically and critically by English-speaking scholars. This was the main reason for the present work. Academics who have written extensively on the Mariavites in Polish and with whom I have been able to discuss the contents of this book have been positively surprised by it. To date, only a few scholars have dealt with the early Mariavite reception of the book of Revelation, even though it was a central reference point for them. As far as English-language publications are concerned, such a study had yet not been undertaken. This knowledge gap has its positive aspects. Of course, it is always good to be the first and to pave the way for subsequent researchers. But there are also some negative aspects. Most notably, the researcher is not able to compare his or her findings with others. This means that the work can only be regarded as the beginning of a discussion.

Due to the limited amount of space, not all aspects of Mariavite apocalyptic thought have been discussed. Nonetheless, I hope that, given the limits of the work, I have succeeded in achieving the goals I set at the beginning. A balance between the relevant historical context and the main thread of the work has been attempted. All the landmarks in the relatively short history of the Mariavites in the Roman Catholic Church have been outlined since their absence would make it impossible to properly contextualise Mariavite apparently idiosyncratic interpretations of Revelation (e.g., Mateczka is both 'like a son of man' (1:13) and the woman clothed with the sun (12:1); the Mariavites represent the new Jerusalem (21:2)). I also felt that the political situation that gave rise to Mariavitism should be thoroughly discussed and that the reader should be able to grasp the complex web of connections between politics and religion in Poland. It would be extremely difficult to understand all the changes and the whole concept of the Kingdom of God (e.g., Mateczka as the spouse of Christ, the marriages of priests and nuns giving birth to children without original sin, the equality of all sexes epitomised by the priesthood of women and the abolition of boundaries between priests and laity) without an awareness of this context.

After introducing the reader to the history of Mariavitism, I analysed the reforms introduced by Kowalski, in particular those established on the basis of his exegesis of the Apocalypse. Polish society at the time considered them scandalous and controversial. One example was the elevation of Mariavite women to the priesthood at a time when they were not allowed to hold secular positions in the Polish state administration. Despite the tumultuous nature of these changes, however, it seems that most – if not all – of them had some antecedents in the wider history of Christianity that, at least partially, can help us understand why such innovations took place. Kowalski's more immediate aim was to introduce a new quality, as he anticipated the arrival of a new age, but he also sought to embed it in the exegesis of earlier Christians. In the broad history of Christianity, we can find examples of married monks and nuns, the ordination of women, and even ideas that 'like a son of man' (Rev 1:13) may be a reference to a woman.

Contrary to the views of critics and some scholars, I aimed to show that Kowalski was a consistent thinker who developed a coherent, though not always clear, theological system. His Catholic opponents tried to attribute 'evil' things to him, such as following in Luther's footsteps and violating the sacramental aspect of the Catholic Church, especially by introducing the priesthood of the laity. But such opinions have been shown to be wholly or at least partially wrong, if one considers their theological explanation. The archbishop sought to return to the original state in which all Christians would perfectly fulfil the will of God. This would mean that they would not need any intermediaries, but Kowalski did not completely rule out this possibility, believing that even the Kingdom might need some hierarchical organisation. Nevertheless, he expected God to make all things new (Rev 21:5).

Kowalski was also accused of violating Mateczka's legacy. She advocated the celibacy of priests, while he introduced the marriage of Mariavite priests and nuns. She opposed any sign of exalting her, but he made her the 'embodiment' of the Holy Spirit and one 'like a son of man' (Rev 1:13). She never mentioned the priesthood of women, but he had no problem making this change. Claims that he deliberately wanted to rebel against her seem to be unfounded, however. Until his death, Kowalski firmly believed that he had remained faithful to Kozłowska and her teachings. The reforms were not introduced haphazardly. They were understood to require adequate time for implementation, and some of them were not ready to be put into practice when Mateczka was on earth and was not ideally connected to Christ. According to Kowalski, the book of Revelation would reveal its meaning gradually.

The full history of Mariavites is still to be written in English. This is why it was important to outline in the first two chapters of this work all the relevant moments of their history. In the Polish literature, the subject has been given more extensive study, but there are still many aspects that need fresh analysis in light of new textual evidence that occasionally arrives for researchers interested in this issue. Moreover, it seems that there are still texts in the Polish, Russian, and Vatican archives that have never been consulted. There are further complexities that need to be properly investigated. For example, there are accusations of forgery that have never been cleared up, so it would be beneficial to consult the originals, provided they exist. Many English-speaking readers derive their knowledge from Peterkiewicz's work, which turned out not to be a proper historical investigation but a fantasy with some historically accurate passages in the background. It would be useful to warn potential future readers that it does not convey reliable information and to offset its impact with an authoritative description. Finally, the Mariavites still exist and, although they are not very numerous, they still have much to say about both Revelation and the Kingdom of God. A full history of the Mariavites would require the inclusion and consideration of this more recent data.

Bibliography

Mariavite sources

'Pismo Święte'. *MCPS* 1 (1907): 6–8.
'DM'. *MCPS* 1 (1907): 12–16.
'Pismo Święte: Księga Rodzaju. Rozdział I'. *MCPS* 2 (1907): 23–27.
'Pismo Święte: Księga Rodzaju. Rozdział II'. *MCPS* 4 (1907): 53–56.
'Niepokalana Marya: Matka Boga'. *MCPS* 4 (1907): 57–61.
'Pismo Święte: Księga Rodzaju. Uwagi do Rozdziału III'. *MCPS* 6 (1907): 84–89.
'DMHM. Wstęp', *MCPS* 6 (1907): 93–96. https://doi.org/10.1051/lhb/1907020
'Pismo Święte. Księga Rodzaju. Uwagi do Rozdziału III'. *MCPS* 7 (1907): 99–102.
'DMHM II'. *MCPS* 10 (1907): 157–160. https://doi.org/10.1002/mmnd.47919071006
'Przenajświętsza Eucharystya'. *MCPS* 9 (1907): 137–142.
'Pismo Święte. Księga Rodzaju. Uwagi do Rozdziału IV'. *MCPS* 10 (1907): 149–153.
'Przenajświętsza Eucharystya'. *MCPS* 10 (1907): 153–157.
'DMHM II'. *MCPS* 11 (1907): 173–176. https://doi.org/10.1136/ewjm.176.1.11
'DMHM II'. *MCPS* 12 (1907): 189–192.
'DMHM II'. *MCPS* 13 (1907): 205–208. https://doi.org/10.1090/S0002-9904-1907-01447-7
'DMHM III'. *MCPS* 14 (1907): 221–224. https://doi.org/10.1002/lipi.19070140905
'DMHM III'. *MCPS* 16 (1907): 250–253. https://doi.org/10.3928/1542-8877-19850401-09
'DMHM III'. *MCPS* 17 (1907): 270–272. https://doi.org/10.1086/206298
'DMHM IV'. *MCPS* 18 (1907): 284–288. https://doi.org/10.1177/001452460701800610
'DMHM IV'. *MCPS* 19 (1907): 300–304. https://doi.org/10.3928/1542-8877-19880401-29
'DMHM IV'. *MCPS* 20 (1907): 317–320. https://doi.org/10.2307/1322455
'DMHM IV'. *MCPS* 21 (1907): 332–336.
'DMHM IV'. *MCPS* 22 (1907): 348–352.
'DMHM IV'. *MCPS* 23 (1907): 363–368. https://doi.org/10.1080/00369220708733766
'DMHM V'. *MCPS* 24 (1907): 380–384. https://doi.org/10.3928/0090-4481-19950701-11
'Nowy Testament. Wstęp'. *MCPS* 25 (1907): 389–392. https://doi.org/10.1159/000286582
'DMHM VI'. *MCPS* 28 (1907): 443–448.
'DMHM VI'. *MCPS* 29 (1907): 460–464. https://doi.org/10.2307/1776777
'Pismo Święte: Nowy Testament'. *MCPS* 30 (1907): 469–471.
'DMHM VI'. *MCPS* 30 (1907): 476–480.
'DMHM VII'. *MCPS* 31 (1907): 492–496.
'Przenajświętsza Eucharystya'. *MCPS* 32 (1907): 505–506. https://doi.org/10.5479/si.00963801.1542.505

'DMHM VIII'. *MCPS* 32 (1907): 506–512.
'DMHM VIII'. *MCPS* 33 (1907): 524–528.
'DMHM VIII'. *MCPS* 35 (1907): 553–560.
'DMHM VIII'. *MCPS* 36 (1907): 571–576.
'DMHM IX'. *MCPS* 37 (1907): 588–592.
'DMHM IX'. *MCPS* 38 (1907): 603–608. https://doi.org/10.1049/jiee-1.1907.0034
'DMHM IX'. *MCPS* 39 (1907): 620–624.
'DMHM IX'. *MCPS* 40 (1907): 636–640.
'DMHM X'. *MCPS* 42 (1907): 668–672. https://doi.org/10.1007/BF02231514
'Ewangelia według św. Mateusza'. *MCPS* 43 (1907): 677–680.
'DMHM X'. *MCPS* 43 (1907): 685–688.
'DMHM X'. *MCPS* 44 (1907): 700–704.
'Niepokalana Marya. Matka Boga'. *MCPS* 48 (1907): 761–764.
'DMHM X'. *MCPS* 49 (1907): 781–784.
'Niepokalana Marya: Matka Boga'. *MCPS* 50 (1907): 793–796.
'DMHM XI'. *MCPS* 50 (1907): 796–800.
'DMHM XI'. *MCPS* 51 (1907): 812–816.
'DMHM XI'. *MCPS* 52 (1907): 827–832.
'Sprostowanie'. *WDM* 1 (1907): 6–8.
'Wiadomości bieżące'. *WDM* 4 (1907): 26–29.
'Wiadomości bieżące'. *WDM* 5 (1907): 35–37.
'Z życia maryawickiego'. *WDM* 5 (1907): 37.
'Sprostowanie'. *WDM* 5 (1907): 37–40.
'Z życia maryawickiego'. *WDM* 6 (1907): 45.
'Sprostowanie'. *WDM* 7 (1907): 53–56. https://doi.org/10.1002/zaac.19070560105
'Sprostowanie'. *WDM* 8 (1907): 61–64. https://doi.org/10.1038/scientificamerican07271907-61asupp
'Sprostowanie'. *WDM* 10 (1907): 77–80. https://doi.org/10.1038/077080d0
'Sprostowanie'. *WDM* 11 (1907): 86–88. https://doi.org/10.18174/njas.v11i2.17551
'Sprostowanie'. *WDM* 12 (1907): 94–96. https://doi.org/10.1029/TE012i002p00094
'Sprostowanie'. *WDM* 31 (1907): 247–248.
'Z życia maryawickiego'. *WDM* 34 (1907): 268–269.
'Sprostowanie fałszywych wiadomości o Maryawitach'. *WDM* 34 (1907): 269–272.
'Sprostowanie'. *WDM* 35 (1907): 278–280. https://doi.org/10.1175/1520-0493(1907)35<278b:TWOTM>2.0.CO;2
'Sprostowanie'. *WDM* 36 (1907): 286–288.
'Z życia maryawickiego'. *WDM* 51 (1907): 405.
'Z niedalekiej przeszłości'. *KM* (1908): 21–40.
'Pierwsze zebranie ogólne księży Maryawitów'. *KM* (1908): 71–76.
'DMHM XI'. *MCPS* 1 (1908): 12–16. https://doi.org/10.1086/435102
'DMHM X'. *MCPS* 3 (1908): 45–48.
'DMHM XI'. *MCPS* 5 (1908): 77–80.
'DMHM XI'. *MCPS* 8 (1908): 125–128.
'Ewangelia według św: Mateusza'. *MCPS* 13 (1908): 197–199.
'Przenajświętsza Eucharystya'. *MCPS* 13 (1908): 200–204.
'Ewangelia według św: Mateusza'. *MCPS* 14 (1908): 213–216.
'Ewangelia według św: Mateusza'. *MCPS* 20 (1908): 309–312.
'Ewangelia według św: Mateusza'. *MCPS* 23 (1908): 357–360.

'Przenajświętsza Eucharystya'. *MCPS* 24 (1908): 377–380.
'Bóg w Trójcy Świętej Jedyny'. *MCPS* 29 (1908): 449–452.
'Ewangelia według św. Mateusza'. *MCPS* 32 (1908): 501–504.
'Bóg w Trójcy Świętej Jedyny'. *MCPS* 36 (1908): 561–565.
'Bóg w Trójcy Świętej Jedyny'. *MCPS* 37 (1908): 577–579.
'Przenajświętsza Eucharystya'. *MCPS* 41 (1908): 649–653.
'Przenajświętsza Eucharystya'. *MCPS* 42 (1908): 665–668.
'DMHM XIII'. *MCPS* 43 (1908): 684–688.
'Przenajświętsza Eucharystya'. *MCPS* 46 (1908): 729–732.
'Przenajświętsza Eucharystya'. *MCPS* 47 (1908): 745–747. https://doi.org/10.1002/mmnd.48019080616
'Przenajświętsza Eucharystya'. *MCPS* 49 (1908): 778–781. https://doi.org/10.2307/907822
'DMHM XIII'. *MCPS* 49 (1908): 782–784.
'DMHM XIII'. *MCPS* 51 (1908): 813–816.
'Odpowiedzi Redakcyi'. *WDM* 1 (1908): 5–8.
'Odpowiedzi Redakcyi'. *WDM* 4 (1908): 30–32.
'Odpowiedzi Redakcyi'. *WDM* 7 (1908): 54–56.
'Odpowiedzi Redakcyi'. *WDM* 9 (1908): 70–72.
'Odpowiedzi Redakcyi'. *WDM* 12 (1908): 94–96. https://doi.org/10.5962/bhl.part.5606
'Odpowiedzi Redakcyi'. *WDM* 13 (1908): 102–104.
'Odpowiedzi Redakcyi'. *WDM* 14 (1908): 110–112.
'Msza Polska'. *WDM* 15 (1908): 113–115. https://doi.org/10.5962/bhl.part.5651
'Odpowiedzi Redakcyi'. *WDM* 20 (1908): 159–160. https://doi.org/10.1056/NEJM190807301590519
'Odpowiedzi Redakcyi'. *WDM* 21 (1908): 166–168. https://doi.org/10.1016/S0033-3506(08)80065-0
'Odpowiedzi Redakcyi'. *WDM* 25 (1908): 198–200. https://doi.org/10.1086/103785
'Odpowiedzi Redakcyi'. *WDM* 29 (1908): 231–232.
'Odpowiedzi Redakcyi'. *WDM* 32 (1908): 255–256.
'Odpowiedzi Redakcyi'. *WDM* 38 (1908): 303–304.
'Przyjdź Królestwo Twoje …'. *KM* (1909): 15–18.
'Fakta mówią'. *KM* (1909): 21–185. https://doi.org/10.1159/000294184
'DMHM XIV'. *MCPS* 5 (1909): 78–80.
'DMHM XIII'. *MCPS* 7 (1909): 109–112.
'Bóg w Trójcy Świętej Jedyny'. *MCPS* 14 (1909): 209–212.
'Bóg w Trójcy Świętej Jedyny'. *MCPS* 18 (1909): 273–277.
'Bóg w Trójcy Świętej Jedyny'. *MCPS* 19 (1909): 285–287.
'Bóg w Trójcy Świętej Jedyny'. *MCPS* 23 (1909): 353–356.
'Ewangelia według św. Mateusza'. *MCPS* 29 (1909): 454–459.
'Bóg w Trójcy Świętej Jedyny'. *MCPS* 30 (1909): 465–469.
'Przenajświętsza Eucharystya'. *MCPS* 35 (1909): 554–557.
'Bóg w Trójcy Świętej Jedyny'. *MCPS* 43 (1909): 673–677.
'Dzieło Miłosierdzia: Kronika Maryawicka'. *MCPS* 46 (1909): 733–736.
'Niepokalana Marya: Matka Boga'. *MCPS* 48 (1909): 764–766.
'Delegaci Związku Maryawickiego w Petersburgu'. *WDM* 4 (1909): 25–28. https://doi.org/10.2475/ajs.s4-28.166.405
'Z krainy obłudy i kłamstwa'. *WDM* 6 (1909): 47–48.

'Wiadomości bieżące'. *WDM* 9 (1909): 68–70. https://doi.org/10.1038/scientificamerican07311909-70asupp
'Odpowiedzi Redakcyi'. *WDM* 9 (1909): 72.
'Maryawityzm Mickiewicza'. *WDM* 20 (1909): 153–155.
'Do Maryawityzmu przechodzi sama ciemna masa'. *WDM* 20 (1909): 158–159. https://doi.org/10.3928/0090-4481-19910301-10
'Maryawityzm Mickiewicza'. *WDM* 22 (1909): 169–171.
'Odpowiedzi Redakcyi'. *WDM* 22 (1909): 174–175. https://doi.org/10.1016/S0140-6736(01)64241-7
'Maryawityzm Mickiewicza'. *WDM* 24 (1909): 185–187.
'Z krainy obłudy i kłamstwa'. *WDM* 25 (1909): 200.
'Humorystom warszawskim'. *WDM* 33 (1909): 257–259.
'Z Prasy. List Biskupa Eulogiusza'. *WDM* 36 (1909): 286–287.
'Wrogom Prawdy'. *WDM* 65 (1909): 513–516.
'Organizacya parafii mariawickich'. *WDM* 66 (1909): 521–522.
'Organizacya parafii mariawickich'. *WDM* 68 (1909): 537–539.
'Z życia maryawickiego'. *WDM* 69 (1909): 550–551. https://doi.org/10.1177/002205740906902012
'Organizacya parafii mariawickich'. *WDM* 70 (1909): 553–554. https://doi.org/10.1177/002205740907002034
'Prawowite bezprawie'. *WDM* 72 (1909): 569–571.
'Międzynarodowy Kongres Starokatolicki w Wiedniu'. *WDM* 77 (1909): 609–611.
'Międzynarodowy Kongres Starokatolicki w Wiedniu'. *WDM* 78 (1909): 617–620.
'Konsekracja Biskupa Naszego w Utrechcie'. *WDM* 81 (1909): 641–645.
'Z życia maryawickiego'. *WDM* 83 (1909): 663–664.
'Port Royal. Próba reform Kościoła w XVII w'. *KM* (1910): 19–68.
'Historya Kościoła w Holandyi'. *KM* (1910): 68–88.
'Rok 1909'. *KM* (1910): 99–114. https://doi.org/10.3406/ccmaa.1910.8832
'Najprzewielebniejszy Ojciec Jan Marya Michał Kowalski'. *KM* (1910): 88–98.
'Niepokalana Marya. Matka Boga'. *MCPS* 2 (1910): 25–28.
'Dzieło Miłosierdzia. Kronika Maryawicka'. *MCPS* 6 (1910): 94–96.
'Bóg w Trójcy Świętej Jedyny'. *MCPS* 8 (1910): 113–117.
'Niepokalana Marya. Matka Boga'. *MCPS* 17 (1910): 265–268.
'Ewangelia według św. Marka'. *MCPS* 20 (1910): 308–313.
'Niepokalana Marya. Matka Boga'. *MCPS* 24 (1910): 377–380.
'Bóg w Trójcy Świętej Jedyny'. *MCPS* 25 (1910): 385–388.
'Ewangelia według św. Marka'. *MCPS* 25 (1910): 389–392.
'Bóg w Trójcy Świętej Jedyny'. *MCPS* 27 (1910): 417–420.
'Bóg w Trójcy Świętej Jedyny'. *MCPS* 29 (1910): 449–452.
'Ewangelia według św. Marka'. *MCPS* 30 (1910): 469–472.
'Bóg w Trójcy Świętej Jedyny'. *MCPS* 34 (1910): 529–532.
'Ewangelia według św. Marka'. *MCPS* 37 (1910): 580–581.
'Ewangelia według św. Marka'. *MCPS* 47 (1910): 740–742.
'Z życia maryawickiego'. *WDM* 7 (1910): 53–55. https://doi.org/10.1001/jama.1910.04330010055036
W Obronie Zasad Ewangelii. Łódź: Wyd. OO. Maryawitów, 1910.
'Kościół Maryawicki w roku 1910'. *KM* (1911): 19–66.
'Życie wewnętrzne Kościoła Maryawickiego'. *KM* (1911): 67–84.

'Konsekracya Biskupów'. *KM* (1911): 85–114.
'Wyjaśnienie'. *WDM* 18 (1911): 137–139. https://doi.org/10.2307/2974390
'Założenie kamienia węgielnego i poświecenie fundamentów pod kościół katedralny Maryawitów w Płocku'. *KM* (1912): 21–31.
'Kościół Maryawicki w roku 1912'. *KM* (1913): 35–52.
'Luźne myśli o współczesnej kulturze'. *KM* (1913): 53–60.
'Z życia Kościołów Starokatolickich'. *KM* (1913): 63–69.
'Powszechne budzenie się Katolicyzmu'. *KM* (1913): 91–96.
'Odpowiedzi Redakcyi'. *WDM* 7 (1913): 112.
'Życie pierwszych chrześcijan'. *WDM* 8 (1913): 114–116.
'Religia Odrodzenia'. *KM* (1914): 18–23.
'Małżeństwo'. *KM* (1914): 37.
'Kościół Maryawicki w roku 1913'. *KM* (1914): 53–64.
'Leszno'. *KM* (1914): 65–78. https://doi.org/10.1007/BF02216619
'Wilno'. *KM* (1914): 87–89. https://doi.org/10.1029/2008EO090010
'Porządek Pism Starego Testamentu'. Page III in *PŚST* I. Płock: KSM, 1923.
'W sprawie małżeństw Biskupów i Kapłanów Maryawickich'. *MMN* 1 (1924): 7–10.
'Jezuitom i Masonom słów parę odpowiedzi'. *MMN* 2 (1924): 2–4.
'Wstęp do Trzeciej i Czwartej Księgi Ezdrasza'. Page 482 in *PŚST* II. Płock: KSM, 1925.
Z podróży do ziemi świętej. Płock: Wyd. OO. Maryawitów, 1927.
'Proroctw nie lekceważcie'. Cel proroctw'. *KBNZ* 3 (1928): 18–19.
'Synowie Królestwa' Święta Eugenia'. *KBNZ* 7 (1928): 51–54.
'Wieczory Mesjaniczne. Misterium'. *KBNZ* 7 (1928): 54–55.
'Proroctw nie lekceważcie'. *KBNZ* 12 (1928): 90.
'Synowie Królestwa' Święta Eugenia'. *KBNZ* 12 (1928): 90–94.
'Wieczory Mesyaniczne. Nasi Mesyaniści'. *KBNZ* 12 (1928): 94–95.
'Proroctw nie lekceważcie: Wypełnienie się proroctwa Daniela w tych dniach'. *KBNZ* 13 (1928): 98–99.
'Synowie Królestwa: Święta Eugenia'. *KBNZ* 14 (1928): 107–109. https://doi.org/10.2307/3602633/
'Wieczory Mesyaniczne: Nasi Mesyaniści'. *KBNZ* 14 (1928): 109–111.
'Proroctw nie lekceważcie: O powtórnym przyjściu Pana Jezusa w ogniu'. *KBNZ* 18 (1928): 137–138.
'Synowie Królestwa: Święta Eugenia'. *KBNZ* 21 (1928): 164–166.
'Synowie Królestwa: Święta Eugenia'. *KBNZ* 23 (1928): 179–181. https://doi.org/10.1086/361019
'Synowie Królestwa: Święta Eufrozya'. *KBNZ* 28 (1928): 219–222.
'Proroctw nie lekceważcie: 1 Tess. 5, 20. Znieważenie stolicy'. *KBNZ* 33 (1928): 258–260.
'Jubileusz Najprzewielebniejszego Ojca Arcybiskupa Maryi Michała'. *KBNZ* 34 (1928): 266.
'Wieczory Mesyaniczne. Co to jest Mesyanizm Polski'. *KBNZ* 35 (1928): 277–278.
'Proroctw nie lekceważcie: 1 Tess. 5, 20. Bestya wypuszcza z gęby swej rzekę'. *KBNZ* 37 (1928): 290–291.
'Prasa zagraniczna o Maryawitach w Polsce'. *KBNZ* 37 (1928): 291.
'Przez moje okno'. *KBNZ* 37 (1928): 291–292.
'Synowie Królestwa: Żywot Św. Jana Jałmużnika'. *KBNZ* 38 (1928): 299–300.

'Kronika tygodniowa'. *KBNZ* 43 (1928): 344. https://doi.org/10.2307/2914158
'Proroctw nie lekceważcie: 1 Tess. 5, 20. Miljony ludzi z obecnie żyjących nigdy nie umrą!' *KBNZ* 44 (1928): 346–349.
'Z życia maryawickiego'. *KBNZ* 49 (1928): 390–391.
'Synowie Królestwa: Żywot i Dzieła św. Jana Złotoustego'. *KBNZ* 8 (1929): 60–62.
'Z życia religijnego Kościołów: Inkwizycja Papieska się gniewa'. *KBNZ* 13 (1929): 103.
'Wiekopomna Uroczystość poświęcenia Sióstr na kapłanki oraz konsekracja Matki Izabeli i Ojców Filipa i Bartłomieja na Biskupów'. *KBNZ* 14 (1929): 105–111.
'Pierwsza Msza św: Matki Przewielebnej i Sióstr'. *KBNZ* 15 (1929): 114–119.
'Pierwsze kazania nowowyświęconych kapłanek'. *KBNZ* 16 (1929): 121–122.
'Z objazdu parafii mariawickich przez Przełożonych i Siostry Kapłanki'. *KBNZ* 19 (1929): 150–151.
'Z objazdu parafii mariawickich przez Przełożonych i Siostry Kapłanki'. *KBNZ* 20 (1929): 159–160. https://doi.org/10.1007/BF01805231
'Synowie Królestwa: Żywot św. Abrama Pustelnika'. *KBNZ* 35 (1929): 279.
'Błąd papiestwa'. *KBNZ* 38 (1929): 300–302.
'Synowie Królestwa: Żywot Błogosławionego Orygenesa Wielkiego Ojca Kościoła'. *KBNZ* 38 (1929): 302–303.
'Synowie Królestwa: Żywot Błogosławionego Orygenesa Wielkiego Ojca Kościoła'. *KBNZ* 39 (1929): 307–310.
'Uczył Kuba Marcina'. *GP* 14 (1930): 29.
'Brednie Pana Profesora'. *GP* 24 (1930): 105–106.
'Artykuły polityczne'. *GP* 42 (1930): 249.
'Błąd papiestwa'. *KBNZ* 2 (1930): 13–15.
'Z prasy przeciwmaryawickiej: Niesłuszne oskarżenie'. *KBNZ* 5 (1930): 37–38.
'Czy mogła być kobieta papieżem?' *KBNZ* 6 (1930): 45–46.
'Organ papieża o Mickiewiczu'. *KBNZ* 6 (1930): 47.
'Synowie Królestwa' Mistrz Andrzej Towiański i jego uczniowie'. *KBNZ* 14 (1930): 107.
'Cuda Teresy Neuman'. *GP* 5 (1931): 33–35.
'Cześć papiestu'. *GP* 19 (1931): 145–147. https://doi.org/10.1038/scientificamerican0731-19
'Problemat wielożeństwa'. *GP* 29 (1931): 225–227.
'Kto godzi na suwerenność Państwa Polskiego'. *GP* 30 (1931): 233–235.
'Rozpaczliwy stan naszej inteligencji'. *GP* 35 (1931): 275–277.
'Z Bibliografji polskiej: Przekład 'Rzeczpospolitej' Platona przez Stanisława Lisieckiego'. *GP* 36 (1931): 282–285.
'Dlaczego Brat Arcybiskup został skazany'. *GP* 43 (1931): 337–338.
'Najdroższy Męczennik'. *GP* 43 (1931): 338–339.
'Bronzownicy' P. Boya–Żeleńskiego Najdroższy Męczennik'. *GP* 46 (1931): 361–364.
'Synowie Królestwa' Juljusz Słowacki a Kościół Rzymski'. *KBNZ* 52 (1931): 413–414. https://doi.org/10.1029/EO052i005p00413-02
'Prorocy Polscy'. *GP* 16 (1932): 126. https://doi.org/10.3928/1542-8877-19850201-15
'Kowalski czy Kucharski'. *GP* 35 (1932): 276–277.
'Dysputa z panem Inspektorem'. *GP* 38 (1932): 297–298.
'O Kapłaństwie' świętego Jana Chryzostoma'. *KBNZ* 16 (1932): 121–122.

'Synowie Królestwa: Kwiatki świętego Franciszka z Asyżu'. *KBNZ* 16 (1932): 126–127.
'Pierwsze posiedzenie Synodu'. *GP* 4 (1935): 29–30.
'Prosto z mostu. Symbole'. *GP* 4 (1935): 32–33.
'Odpowiedź Redakcyi na list b. Arcybiskupa'. *GP* 15 (1935): 118–120.
'Kronika Maryawicka'. *GP* 15 (1935): 120–121. https://doi.org/10.1086/481589
'Z życia parafij maryawickich'. *GP* 17 (1935): 136–137. https://doi.org/10.1038/136137b0
'Polska a Watykan: Na marginesie konkordatu'. *GP* 19 (1935): 149–150.
'Z prasy pseudomarjawickiej'. *GP* 19 (1935): 150–152.
'Wyjątki z 'listów apostolskich' wysłanych z Felicjanowa do Filipowa'. *GP* 24 (1935): 193–195.
'Religja w Abisynji'. *GP* 25 (1935): 199.
'Pamięci naszej Mistrzyni'. *GP* 26 (1935): 205–206.
'Nadużywanie Pisma Świętego'. *GP* 28 (1935): 221–222.
'Triumf dobra na ziemi'. *GP* 29 (1935): 229–231.
'Przeznaczenie Szczepu Słowiańskiego'. *GP* 32 (1935): 254–256.
'Jezabel w Marjawityzmie'. *Jednodniówka Marjawicka* 1 (1935): 2–4.
'Przełom styczniowy w Marjawityzmie'. *Jednodniówka Marjawicka* 1 (1935): 4–5.
'Rzekoma prawomocność Kapituły Zbuntowanych'. *Świątynia Miłosierdzia i Miłości* 3 (1935): 20–22.
'Ostatnia Msza Święta w Świątyni'. *WM* 2 (1935): 8.
'Rozmowa z naszą Najdroższą Mateczką w 1914r'. *WM* 4 (1935): 6.
'Z kroniki parafjalnej'. *GP* 16 (1936): 124–126. https://doi.org/10.1093/ptj/16.3.126c
'Akt wiary czy demonstracja polityczna'. *GP* 22 (1936): 170–172.
'Z życia marjawickiego'. *GP* 23 (1936): 183. https://doi.org/10.3928/0147-7447-20000301-03
'Odpowiedzi Redakcji'. *GP* 29 (1936): 224. https://doi.org/10.1093/jee/29.1.224
'Sprawiedliwości stało się zadość'. *GP* 29 (1936): 218.
'Sprawozdanie z posiedzeń Synodu'. *GP* 35 (1936): 266–268.
'Miłość Ojczyzny'. *GP* 47 (1936): 361–362.
'Michael'. *KBNZ* 2 (1936): 6–7.
'Notatki z tego, co Brat Adam Mickiewicz mówił na ogólnych zgromadzeniach do Siódemek, albo w prywatnych rozmowach'. *GP* 1 (1937): 3–6.
'Notatki z tego, co Brat Adam Mickiewicz mówił na ogólnych zgromadzeniach do Siódemek, albo w prywatnych rozmowach'. *GP* 3 (1937): 19–22.
'Notatki z tego, co Brat Adam Mickiewicz mówił na ogólnych zgromadzeniach do Siódemek, albo w prywatnych rozmowach'. *GP* 6 (1937): 43–46.
'Notatki z tego, co Brat Adam Mickiewicz mówił na ogólnych zgromadzeniach do Siódemek, albo w prywatnych rozmowach'. *GP* 7 (1937): 51–52.
'Na przełomie'. *GP* 32 (1937): 250–251. https://doi.org/10.2113/gsecongeo.32.8.1069
'Adam Mickiewicz o losach Sprawy Bożej na ziemi'. *GP* 32 (1937): 252–254.
'Sprawozdanie z Kapituły Generalnej biskupów i kapłanów Marjawitów odbytej w dniach 17, 18, 19, i 20 sierpnia 1937 roku przy Świątyni Miłosierdzia w Płocku'. *GP* 38 (1937): 304.
'Prasa egipska o Marjawitach'. *GP* 44 (1937): 351–352. https://doi.org/10.1080/00029890.1937.11987991
'Kronika Marjawicka'. *GP* 47 (1937): 375–376.

'Jubileusz 50–lecia istnienia Zgromadzenia Sióstr Mariawitek Nieustającej Adoracji Ubłagania 8.IX.1887–8.IX.1937'. *KBNZ* 15 (1937): 1–6.
'Z głosów prasy starokatolickiej'. *GSK* 1 (1938): 14.
'Prawa kobiet w różnych krajach'. *GSK* 4 (1938): 64.
'Uchwały Synodu St.-Katolickiego Kościoła Marjawitów'. *GSK* 9 (1938): 129.
'Zniesienie parafii Staro–kat. w stolicy Śląska'. *GSK* 31 (1938): 492–493.
'Święty Franciszek–Matka Marja Franciszka'. *GSK* 34 (1938): 529–531.
'Kronika Marjawicka. Sprawozdanie Synodu'. *GSK* 38 (1938): 606.
'Kronika Marjawicka'. *GSK* 2 (1939): 30.
'Zgon papieża Piusa XI'. *GSK* 8 (1939): 125.
'W kulturalnej Szwecji szerzy się sekciarstwo'. *GSK* 34 (1939): 552.
'Skarga włościan na duchowieństwo rzymskokatolickie w Polsce (17.05.1905)'. *Proces wydzielania się Związku Mariawitów Nieustającej Adoracji Ubłagania z doktrynalnych i organizacyjnych ram Kościoła rzymskokatolickiego*. Edited by Edward Warchoł. Pp. 111–115. Radom: Wyd. Diecezjalne, 2006.
'Dekret Świętej Rzymskiej i Powszechnej Inkwizycji (05.12.1906)'. *Proces wydzielania się Związku Mariawitów Nieustającej Adoracji Ubłagania z doktrynalnych i organizacyjnych ram Kościoła rzymskokatolickiego*. Edited by Edward Warchoł. Pp. 152–153. Radom: Wyd. Diecezjalne, 2006.
'Odpowiedź Redakcji'. *PNS* 44 (2007): 21–22. https://doi.org/10.18356/2fefea9f-en
'Problem homoseksualizmu a świadomość mariawicka'. *PNS* 50 (2008): 12–14.
'Ksiądz Lucjan Balter'. *PNS* 58 (2010): 25–26.
'Nasi Mejsaniści'. *MD* II. Edited by Damiana M. B. Szulgowicz and Hanna M. R. Woińska. Pp. 175–192. Felicjanów: KKM, 2013.
Adamiec, Jan M. P. 'Życie blisko Nieba–wspomnienia'. *MPKSM* 8 (2018): 23–27.
Brewiarzyk Mariawicki. Felicjanów: KKM, 1967.
Bucholc, Janusz M. S. 'W promieniach Miłosierdzia Bożego'. *GP* 4 (1936): 28–29.
Czarnohorski, Juliusz M. O. 'Z misji Marjawickiego Kościoła na Węgrzech'. *GSK* 32 (1939): 509–510.
Dębowska, Elżbieta M. T. 'Mariae-vita: Wspomnienia Siostry Elżbiety'. *Święta Maria Franciszka Kozłowska i Jej Zgromadzenie zakonne we wspomnieniach i pamiętnikach*. Edited by Damiana M. B. Szulgowicz and Hanna M. R. Woińska. Pp. 153–208. Felicjanów: KKM, 2007.
Dodatek do Mszału. Nowe mariawickie formularze mszalne. Felicjanów: KKM, 2004.
Feldman, Klemens M. F. 'Zraniona bestya'. *MMN* 5 (1924): 15–16.
Feldman, Klemens M. F. 'Świadectwo P. Ojca Filipa'. *Początki Królestwa Bożego na ziemi*. Płock: KSM, 1928. Pp. 34–38.
Feldman, Klemens M. F. 'Dziennik z podróży do Ameryki'. *KBNZ* 10 (1931): 79.
Feldman, Klemens M. F. 'Dziennik z podróży do Ameryki'. *KBNZ* 52 (1931): 414–416.
Feldman, Klemens M. F., ed. 'List pasterski Biskupów i całego duchowieństwa Kościoła Maryawitów do Ludu Maryawickiego'. *Jednodniówka Marjawicka* 1 (1935): 1–2.
Feldman, Klemens M. F. 'Kronika marjawicka. Łowicz'. *GSK* 27 (1939): 429–430.
Ginter, Władysław S. 'Błogosławiona Maria Franciszka Kozłowska: (Szkic do portretu psychologicznego postaci) cz. I'. *NP* 182 (2000): 7–13.
Ginter, Władysław S. 'Mariawici płoccy w czasie okupacji niemieckiej w latach 1939–1942'/ *NP* 51 (2006): 36–39.
Główne Zasady Wiary i Ustrój Kościoła Maryawickiego. Płock: Wyd. O. O. Maryawitów, 1927.

Gołębiowski, Sławomir. *Św. Maria Franciszka Feliksa Kozłowska 1862–1921: Życie i Dzieło*. Płock: KSM, 2002.
Gołębiowski, Sławomir. 'Wpływ prawa państwowego na kształtowanie organizacji mariawickich'. *PNS* 41 (2006): 52–59.
Gołębiowski, Sławomir. 'Testament księdza Pągowskiego'. *PNS* 50 (2008): 19–23.
Gołębiowski, Sławomir. 'Mariavites credunt–Mariawici wierzą'. *PNS* 53 (2009): 21–26.
Gołębiowski, Sławomir. 'Glosy mariawickie'. *PNS* 54 (2009): 15–18.
Gołębiowski, Sławomir, and Krzysztof Mazur. 'Naukowość, czy Naukawość?' *PNS* 56 (2009): 31–38.
Gołębiowski, Sławomir. 'Moje votum separatum'. *PNS* 59 (2010): 19–25.
Gołębiowski, Sławomir. 'Kto dokonał zmian w tekście objawień Marii Franciszki Kozłowskiej przesłanych do Rzymu?' *MD* I. Edited by Damiana M. B. Szulgowicz and Hanna M. R. Woińska. Pp. 255–269. Felicjanów: KKM, 2012.
Gołębiowski, Sławomir. 'O rzetelność i prawdę'. *PNS* 65 (2012): 23–25.
Gołębiowski, Sławomir. *W poszukiwaniu prawdy... Sądowe Procesy Arcybiskupa Jana M. Michała Kowalskiego*. Felicjanów: KKM, 2014.
Gołębiowski, Sławomir. *W obronie własnej tożsamości*. Płock: KSM, 2024.
Gostyński, Roman M. A. 'Głosy rozsądku i porozumienia'. *Jednodniówka Marjawicka* 1 (1935): 5–6.
Gostyński, Roman M. A. 'Na co reforma'. *GP* 5 (1936): 38.
Grzegrzółka, Helena. 'Pan Jezus opuszcza Świątynię i przechodzi do Felicjanowa'. *WM* 6 (1935): 5.
Jabłoński, Michał M. L., and Bronisław Dembowski, eds. *Dwustronna refleksja na temat podstawowych pism Matki Marii Franciszki Kozłowskiej dotyczących Dzieła Wielkiego Miłosierdzia*. Łódź–Włocławek: Wyd. ELWIT, 2006.
Jabłoński Michał M. L., and Bronisław Dembowski, eds. *Ze źródeł kwestii mariawickiej: nieznane dokumenty z lat 1903–1906*. Płock: Płocki Instytut Wydawniczy, 2011.
Jarzymowski, Henryk M. F. 'Z życia marjawickiego'. *GP* 18 (1936): 141–142.
Jarzymowski, Henryk M. F. 'Odpowiedź na fałszywe informacje podane prasie przez Kowalskiego'. *GP* 36 (1937): 286–288.
Katechizm Życia Zakonnego. Płock: Wyd. O. O. Maryawitów, 1927.
Klichowska, Zofia M. H. 'Świadectwo Siostry Honoraty'. *Początki Królestwa Bożego na ziemi*. Pp. 66–96. Płock: KSM, 1928.
Kowalski, Jan M. M. 'Stanowisko Kapłanów Maryawitów względem hierarchii katolickiej i wyznań chrześcijańskich'. *MCPS* 9 (1909): 140–144.
Kowalski, Jan M. M. 'List pasterski (31.12.1909)'. *MCPS* 3 (1910): 44–48.
Kowalski, Jan M. M. 'List pasterski (31.12.1909)'. *MCPS* 4 (1910): 58–64.
Kowalski, Jan M. M. 'Słowo Wstępne od Biskupa Mariawitów (17.12.1921)'. *NTPP*. Pp. 1–4. Płock: KSM, 1921.
Kowalski, Jan M. M. 'Słowo Wstępne na Wykład Apokalipsy (10.02.1923)'. *NTPP*. Pp. 699–785. Płock: KSM, 1921.
Kowalski, Jan M. M. 'Krótki Życiorys Mateczki'. *DWM*. Pp. 81–316. Płock: SKKM, 1922.
Kowalski, Jan M. M. 'Wola Boża'. *MMN* 1 (1924): 1–3.
Kowalski, Jan M. M. 'O wprowadzeniu małżeństw duchownych'. *MMN* 1 (1924): 6–7.
Kowalski, Jan M. M. 'Dla Chwały Bożej'. *MMN* 2 (1924): 1–2.

Kowalski, Jan M. M. 'Wyjaśnienie niektórych wątpliwości odnośnie do zawieranych przez duchowieństwo Maryawickie ślubów małżeńskich'. *MMN* 2 (1924): 4–6.
Kowalski, Jan M. M. 'Wezwanie wszystkich aby się zapisali do Księgi Żywota'. *MMN* 4 (1924): 16.
Kowalski, Jan M. M. 'Przede wszystkiem jedność z Panem Jezusem w Boskiej Eucharystyi'. *MMN* 6 (1924): 1–12.
Kowalski, Jan M. M. 'Dary papieży dla Polski. Co rzymski Kościół dał Polsce'. *MMN* 11 (1925): 1–11.
Kowalski, Jan M. M. 'Królestwo Boże Królestwem Ducha Świętego'. *KBNZ* 1 (1927): 1–2.
Kowalski, Jan M. M. 'List pasterski (24.12.1927)'. *KBNZ* 1 (1927): 2–5.
Kowalski, Jan M. M. 'Królestwo Boże Królestwem Eucharystyi'. *KBNZ* 2 (1927): 9–10.
Kowalski, Jan M. M. 'Świadectwo O. Arcybiskupa Michała'. *Początki Królestwa Bożego na ziemi*. Pp. 7–33. Płock: KSM, 1928.
Kowalski, Jan M. M. 'Królestwo Boże Królestwem Eucharystyi'. *KBNZ* 3 (1928): 17–18.
Kowalski, Jan M. M. 'Królestwo Boże jest Królestwem Adoracyi'. *KBNZ* 4 (1928): 25.
Kowalski, Jan M. M. 'Królestwo Boże ma swoją stolicę na ziemi'. *KBNZ* 5 (1928): 33–34.
Kowalski, Jan M. M. 'Królestwo Boże ma swoje księgi rejestracyjne'. *KBNZ* 6 (1928): 41–42.
Kowalski, Jan M. M. 'Królestwo Boże będzie miało jeden wspólny język'. *KBNZ* 11 (1928): 81.
Kowalski, Jan M. M. 'Królestwo Boże ma dwie tablice Prawa Bożego'. *KBNZ* 12 (1928): 89–90.
Kowalski, Jan M. M. 'Królestwo Boże rządzi się samym Miłosierdziem'. *KBNZ* 13 (1928): 97.
Kowalski, Jan M. M. 'List pasterski (08.03.1928)'. *KBNZ* 13 (1928): 97–98. https://doi.org/10.1086/bullnattax41786027
Kowalski, Jan M. M. 'Królestwo Boże jest Zgromadzeniem Świętych'. *KBNZ* 15 (1928): 113.
Kowalski, Jan M. M. 'Królestwo Boże jest pierwszym zmartwychwstaniem'. *KBNZ* 17 (1928): 129.
Kowalski, Jan M. M. 'Królestwo Boże znosi wszelkie kary cielesne na przestępców'. *KBNZ* 20 (1928): 153–154.
Kowalski, Jan M. M. 'List pasterski o Zapisie do Ksiąg Królestwa Bożego (22.04.1928)'. *KBNZ* 20 (1928): 154–156.
Kowalski, Jan M. M. 'Królestwo Boże na Ziemi obcuje ze Świętymi w Niebie'. *KBNZ* 21 (1928): 161.
Kowalski, Jan M. M. 'Królestwo Boże na Ziemi nigdy upaść nie może'. *KBNZ* 22 (1928): 169.
Kowalski, Jan M. M. 'Królestwo Boże to święty komunizm'. *KBNZ* 27 (1928): 209–210.
Kowalski, Jan M. M. 'O istocie i rozwoju Królestwa Bożego na Ziemi: Potrzebna czystość pierwotna'. *KBNZ* 46 (1928): 361.
Kowalski, Jan M. M. 'O istocie i rozwoju Królestwa Bożego na Ziemi: Istota Upadku pierwszych ludzi, czyli grzechu pierworodnego'. *KBNZ* 46 (1928): 362.

Kowalski, Jan M. M. 'O istocie i rozwoju Królestwa Bożego na Ziemi: Stan małżeński pierwszych ludzi'. *KBNZ* 47 (1928): 369–370.

Kowalski, Jan M. M. 'O istocie i rozwoju Królestwa Bożego na Ziemi: O odrodzeniu i odnowieniu natury ludzkiej przez Chrzest i Sakrament Ciała i Krwi Pańskiej'. *KBNZ* 48 (1928): 377–378.

Kowalski, Jan M. M. 'O istocie i rozwoju Królestwa Bożego na ziemi: Komunia święta jest potrzebna do zrozumienia Królestwa Bożego'. KBNZ 53 (1928): 417–419.

Kowalski, Jan M. M. 'O istocie i rozwoju Królestwa Bożego na ziemi: Wielcy Nasi Wieszczowie z Komunii św. Czerpali Swe Światło'. *KBNZ* 5 (1929): 33–34.

Kowalski, Jan M. M. 'O Istocie Rozwoju Królestwa Bożego na Ziemi: Utwierdzenie w łasce przez Komunię Św'. *KBNZ* 8 (1929): 57–58.

Kowalski, Jan M. M. 'O Kapłaństwie. Czy N. Marya Panna, Matka Boża, była kapłanką'. *KBNZ* 9 (1929): 65–66.

Kowalski, Jan M. M. 'List pasterski o Nowem Świętych Dziewic Kapłaństwie (21.02.1929)'. *KBNZ* 11 (1929): 81–83.

Kowalski, Jan M. M. 'List pasterski o Związaniu Szatana (19.07.1929)'. *KBNZ* 31 (1929): 241–244.

Kowalski, Jan M. M. 'Nowy Hexahemeron, czyli Nowe Pojęcia o Sześciu Dniach Stworzenia'. *KBNZ* 41 (1929): 321–322. https://doi.org/10.5026/jgeography.41.321

Kowalski, Jan M. M. 'Nowy Hexahemeron'. *KBNZ* 42 (1929): 329–331. https://doi.org/10.1292/jvms1888.42.329

Kowalski, Jan M. M. 'Nowy Hexahemeron'. *KBNZ* 43 (1929): 337–338.

Kowalski, Jan M. M. 'Nowy Hexahemeron'. *KBNZ* 44 (1929): 348–350.

Kowalski, Jan M. M. 'Nowy Hexahemeron'. *KBNZ* 46 (1929): 361–363.

Kowalski, Jan M. M. 'Błyskawice, głosy i gromy'. *KBNZ* 8 (1930): 57–58.

Kowalski, Jan M. M. 'Otworzenie 7 Pieczęci Apokaliptycznych'. *KBNZ* 9 (1930): 65–67.

Kowalski, Jan M. M. 'Otworzenie 7 Pieczęci Apokaliptycznych'. *KBNZ* 10 (1930): 73–74.

Kowalski, Jan M. M. 'Otworzenie 7 Pieczęci Apokaliptycznych'. *KBNZ* 11 (1930): 81–82. https://doi.org/10.1175/1520-0477-11.4.81

Kowalski, Jan M. M. 'Otworzenie 7 Pieczęci Apokaliptycznych'. *KBNZ* 12 (1930): 89–90.

Kowalski, Jan M. M. 'Otworzenie 7 Pieczęci Apokaliptycznych'. *KBNZ* 13 (1930): 97–98.

Kowalski, Jan M. M. 'Apokalipsa w szczegółach: Trzy Kościoły: Piotrowy, Pawłowy i Janowy'. *KBNZ* 15 (1930): 113–114.

Kowalski, Jan M. M. 'List pasterski o Spowiedzi przed Chrystusem (13.04.1930)'. *KBNZ* 16 (1930): 121–123.

Kowalski, Jan M. M. 'O zniesieniu tytułów (18.05.1930)'. *KBNZ* 21 (1930): 161–162.

Kowalski, Jan M. M. 'Apokalipsa w szczegółach: 'Podobna Synowi Człowieczemu'. *KBNZ* 23 (1930): 178–179.

Kowalski, Jan M. M. 'Apokalipsa w szczegółach. Pierwszy i ostatni'. *KBNZ* 24 (1930): 185–186.

Kowalski, Jan M. M. 'O zniesieniu stanu duchownych (02.08.1930)'. *KBNZ* 32 (1930): 249–251.

Kowalski, Jan M. M. 'List pasterski o kapłaństwie powszechnym (10.08.1930)'. *KBNZ* 34 (1930): 265–266.

Kowalski, Jan M. M. 'List pasterski o Wykreśleniu z Księgi Żywota i z liczby członków Kościoła Maryawickiego (18.04.1931)'. *KBNZ* 16 (1931): 121.

Kowalski, Jan M. M. 'O 120.000 złotych nagrody'. *GP* 8 (1931): 58–60.

Kowalski, Jan M. M. 'O 120.000 złotych nagrody'. *GP* 12 (1931): 91–92. https://doi.org/10.1080/0005772X.1931.11093043

Kowalski, Jan M. M. 'O 120.000 złotych nagrody'. *GP* 17 (1931): 129–131.

Kowalski, Jan M. M. 'Kielich Mateczki'. *KBNZ* 10 (1931): 73–74.

Kowalski, Jan M. M. 'Mój ideał: Powieść Obyczajowa'. *GP* 8 (1932): 58–60.

Kowalski, Jan M. M. 'Mój ideał: Powieść Obyczajowa'. *GP* 17 (1932): 129–131.

Kowalski, Jan M. M. 'Mój ideał: Powieść Obyczajowa'. *GP* 28 (1932): 217–220.

Kowalski, Jan M. M. and Antonina M. I. Wiłucka-Kowalska, 'List pasterski (12.05.1030)'. *WM* 1 (1935): 2–3.

Kowalski, Jan M. M. 'List pierwszy do R. M. J. Próchniewskiego (27.06.1935)'. *WM* 3 (1935): 1–5.

Kowalski, Jan M. M. 'Uzasadnienie Kapłaństwa Powszechnego: Czy Kapłaństwo Powszechne potrzebuje ceremonji święceń'. *WM* 3 (1935): 5–6.

Kowalski, Jan M. M. 'Uzasadnienie Kapłaństwa Powszechnego. Czy ludzie prości mogą być Kapłanami'. *WM* 3 (1935): 6–7.

Kowalski, Jan M. M. 'List drugi do R. M. J. Próchniewskiego (29.07.1935)'. *WM* 5 (1935): 1–8.

Kowalski, Jan M. M. 'Okólnik ks: Jana Kowalskiego (13.04.1906)'. *Wyznania Wiary i główne zasady doktrynalne. Katolicyzm.* Edited by Marcin Karas. P. 172. Krakow: MEDIA-PRESS, 2000.

Kowalski, Jan M. M. 'List do Arcybiskupa Edwarda Roppa (31.10.1929)'. *Wymiana prywatnych listów między Biskupami Maryawickimi i Rzymskokatolickimi.* Edited by Edward Warchoł. Pp. 21–24. Sandomierz: Wyd. Diecezjalne, 2003.

Kowalski, Jan M. M. 'List do Arcybiskupa Edwarda Roppa (17.11.1929)'. *Wymiana prywatnych listów między Biskupami Maryawickimi i Rzymskokatolickimi.* Edited by Edward Warchoł. Pp. 27–34. Sandomierz: Wyd. Diecezjalne, 2003.

Kowalski, Jan M. M. 'List do Arcybiskupa Edwarda Roppa (21.11.1929)'. *Wymiana prywatnych listów między Biskupami Maryawickimi i Rzymskokatolickimi.* Edited by Edward Warchoł. Pp. 38–47. Sandomierz: Wyd. Diecezjalne, 2003.

Kowalski, Jan M. M. 'List do Arcybiskupa Edwarda Roppa (24.11.1929)'. *Wymiana prywatnych listów między Biskupami Maryawickimi i Rzymskokatolickimi.* Edited by Edward Warchoł. Pp. 50–59. Sandomierz: Wyd. Diecezjalne, 2003.

Kowalski, Jan M. M. 'List do Arcybiskupa Edwarda Roppa (08.12.1929)'. *Wymiana prywatnych listów między Biskupami Maryawickimi i Rzymskokatolickimi.* Edited by Edward Warchoł. Sandomierz: Pp. 63–72. Wyd. Diecezjalne, 2003.

Kowalski, Jan M. M. 'List do Arcybiskupa Edwarda Roppa (12.12.1929)'. *Wymiana prywatnych listów między Biskupami Maryawickimi i Rzymskokatolickimi.* Edited by Edward Warchoł. Pp. 87–96. Sandomierz: Wyd. Diecezjalne, 2003.

Kowalski, Jan M. M. 'List pasterski (07.11.1935)'. *PNS* 35 (2004): 15–19.

Kowalski, Jan M. M. 'Odezwa ks. Jana Kowalskiego do księży i wiernych świeckich–mariawitów (1906)'. *Proces wydzielania się Związku Mariawitów Nieustającej Adoracji Ubłagania z doktrynalnych i organizacyjnych ram Kościoła rzymskokatolickiego.* Pp. 124–125. Edited by Edward Warchoł. Radom: Wyd. Diecezjalne, 2006.

Kowalski, Jan M. M. 'List pasterski o Nowym Przekładzie Pisma Św. (23.08.1923)'. in *Ku Królestwu Bożemu*. Edited by Damiana M. B. Szulgowicz and Hanna M. R. Woińska. Pp. 193–205. Felicjanów: KKM, 2009.

Kowalski, Jan M. M. 'O ustaniu Ofiary Mszy Świętej w Kościele Rzymskim. Objawienie Boże (11.08.1924)'. *Ku Królestwu Bożemu*. Edited by Damiana M. B. Szulgowicz and Hanna M. R. Woińska. Pp. 216–217. Felicjanów: KKM, 2009.

Kowalski, Jan M. M. 'List pasterski o Królestwie Bożem na ziemi (21.04.1927)'. *Ku Królestwu Bożemu*. Edited by Damiana M. B. Szulgowicz and Hanna M. R. Woińska. Pp. 220–245. Felicjanów: KKM, 2009.

Kowalski, Jan M. M. 'Wykład na Apokalipsę (12.04.1923)'. *MD* I. Edited by Damiana M. B. Szulgowicz and Hanna M. R. Woińska. Pp. 121–170. Felicjanów: KKM, 2012.

Kozłowska, Anna M. H. 'Mariae-vita, Z opowiadań Babci i innych Sióstr Zakonnych'. *Święta Maria Franciszka Kozłowska i Jej Zgromadzenie zakonne we wspomnieniach i pamiętnikach*. Edited by Damiana M. B. Szulgowicz and Hanna M. R. Woińska. Pp. 15–149. Felicjanów: KKM, 2007.

Kozłowska, Felicja M. F. 'Ustawy Zgromadzenia Kapłanów Maryawitów Nieustającej Adoracyi Ubłagania'. MCPS 3 (1907): 45–47.

Kozłowska, Felicja M. F., and Roman M. J. Próchniewski. 'Dzieło Miłosierdzia: Życie Duchowne. Wstęp'. MCPS 12 (1909): 189–192.

Kozłowska, Felicja M. F., and Roman M. J. Próchniewski. 'Dzieło Miłosierdzia: Życie Duchowne. Wstęp'. MCPS 18 (1909): 285–288.

Kozłowska, Felicja M. F., and Roman M. J. Próchniewski. 'Dzieło Miłosierdzia. Życie Duchowne. Wstęp'. MCPS 21 (1909): 328–332.

Kozłowska, Felicja M. F., and Roman M. J. Próchniewski. 'Dzieło Miłosierdzia: Życie Duchowne. Rozdział II'. MCPS 33 (1909): 525–528.

Kozłowska, Felicja M. F., and Roman M. J. Próchniewski. 'Dzieło Miłosierdzia: Życie Duchowne. Rozdział III'. MCPS 21 (1910): 333–336.

Kozłowska, Felicja M. F., and Roman M. J. Próchniewski. 'Dzieło Miłosierdzia: Życie Duchowne. Rozdział IV'. MCPS 30 (1910): 477–480.

Kozłowska, Felicja M. F. 'Początek Zawiązku Zgromadzenia Kapłanów (1902)'. *DWM*. Pp. 5–33. Płock: KSM, 1922.

Kozłowska, Felicja M. F. 'Wyjątki z Objawień w roku 1899 i 1900'. *DWM*. Pp. 34–53. Płock: KSM, 1922.

Kozłowska, Felicja M. F. 'Uzupełnienia Objawień Mateczki z 'Maryawity'. *DWM*. Pp. 54–68. Płock: KSM, 1922.

Kozłowska, Felicja M. F. 'Notatki Rekolekcyjne z r. 1911'. *DWM*. Pp. 69–76. Płock: KSM, 1922.

Kozłowska, Felicja M. F. 'Pierwotny tekst Objawień Mateczki (1894)'. *DWM*. Pp. 113–135. Płock: KSM, 1922.

Kozłowska, Felicja M. F. 'Testament Mateczki (1920)'. *DWM*. Pp. 312–316. Płock: KSM, 1922.

Kozłowska, Felicja M. F. 'List drugi (1893)'. PNS 7 (1998): 15–24.

Kozłowska, Anna M. H. 'Mariae-vita, Z opowiadań Babci i innych Sióstr Zakonnych'. *Święta Maria Franciszka Kozłowska i Jej Zgromadzenie zakonne we wspomnieniach i pamiętnikach*. Edited by Damiana M. B. Szulgowicz and Hanna M. R. Woińska. Pp. 15–149. Felicjanów: KKM, 2007.

Kozłowska, Felicja M. F. 'List 1'. *Ku Królestwu Bożemu*. Edited by Damiana M. B. Szulgowicz and Hanna M. R. Woińska. Pp. 53–54. Felicjanów: KKM, 2009.

Kozłowska, Felicja M. F. 'List 3'. *Ku Królestwu Bożemu*. Edited by Damiana M. B. Szulgowicz and Hanna M. R. Woińska. P. 55. Felicjanów: KKM, 2009.

Kozłowska, Felicja M. F. 'List do O. Jana Przyjemskiego (19.11.1904)'. *Ku Królestwu Bożemu*. Edited by Damiana M. B. Szulgowicz and Hanna M. R. Woińska. P. 57. Felicjanów: KKM, 2009.

Kozłowska, Felicja M. F. 'List do O. Jana Przyjemskiego (1905)'. *Ku Królestwu Bożemu*. Edited by Damiana M. B. Szulgowicz and Hanna M. R. Woińska. Pp. 58–59. Felicjanów: KKM, 2009.

Kozłowska, Felicja M. F. 'List do O. Jana Przyjemskiego (1904)'. *Ku Królestwu Bożemu*. Edited by Damiana M. B. Szulgowicz and Hanna M. R. Woińska. Pp. 63–64. Felicjanów: KKM, 2009.

Kozłowska, Felicja M. F. 'List 14'. *Ku Królestwu Bożemu*. Edited by Damiana M. B. Szulgowicz and Hanna M. R. Woińska. P. 64. Felicjanów: KKM, 2009.

Kozłowska, Felicja M. F. 'List do Siostry Teresy Sieczko (04.02.1918)'. *Ku Królestwu Bożemu*. Edited by Damiana M. B. Szulgowicz and Hanna M. R. Woińska. Pp. 89–90. Felicjanów: KKM, 2009.

Kozłowska, Felicja M. F. 'Notatki, jakie Mateczka sobie poczyniła, mając mieć konferencję do Sióstr'. *Ku Królestwu Bożemu*. Edited by Damiana M. B. Szulgowicz and Hanna M. R. Woińska. Pp. 83–86. Felicjanów: KKM, 2009.

Kozłowska, Felicja M. F. 'List 47'. *Ku Królestwu Bożemu*. Edited by Damiana M. B. Szulgowicz and Hanna M. R. Woińska. Pp. 90–91. Felicjanów: KKM, 2009.

Kozłowska, Felicja M. F. 'List do Siostry Aliny'. *Ku Królestwu Bożemu*. Edited by Damiana M. B. Szulgowicz and Hanna M. R. Woińska. P. 109. Felicjanów: KKM, 2009.

Kozłowska, Feliksa M. F. 'List do Papieża (09.06.1904)'. Translated by Henryk Seweryniak, PNS 58 (2010): 16–17.

Kozłowska, Felicja M. F. 'Protokół przesłuchania Matki Marii Franciszki Kozłowskiej dnia 28 V 1903 roku'. *MD* I. Edited by Damiana M. B. Szulgowicz and Hanna M. R. Woińska. Pp. 13–30. Felicjanów: KKM, 2012.

Kraszewska, M. C. 'O miłości dla naszej Najdroższej Mateczki'. *KBNZ* 33 (1929): 257.

Legański, Wacław. 'List do Redakcyi'. *WDM* 16 (1908): 125–126.

Łuszczewski, Zenon M. J. 'Proroctw nie lekceważcie' – 'Michał i Aniołowie Jego walczyli ze Smokiem'. *KBNZ* 18 (1929): 138–141.

Łuszczewski, Zenon M. J. 'Jeszcze o reformie'. *GP* 14 (1935): 109–110.

Mames, Tomasz M. D. 'Objawienia świętej Marii Franciszki Kozłowskiej jako instrumentarium egzegetyczne perykop Pisma Świętego'. *Księgi Święte a Słowo Boże*. Edited by Łukasz Kamykowski and Zdzisław J. Kijas. Pp. 111–135. Krakow: Papieska Akademia Teologiczna, 2005.

Mames, Tomasz M. D. 'Wokół kwestii współczesnych przemian doktrynalnych i organizacyjnych w felicjanowskim nurcie mariawityzmu'. *Studia Laurentiana* 5 (2005): 71–85.

Mames, Tomasz M. D. 'Charyzmat Eucharystyczny i Maryjny Duchowości Mariawickiej'. *PNS* 41 (2006): 2–10.

Mames, Tomasz M. D. 'O objawieniach Mateczki sto lat za późno'. https://www.ekumenizm.pl/ekumenizm/o-objawieniach-mateczki-sto-lat-za-pozno/

Mames, Tomasz M. D. 'Diakonat ludowy. Refleksje na marginesie emancypacji liturgicznej kobiet w Kościołach katolickich'. *Studia Religiologica* 40 (2007): 99–106.

Mames, Tomasz M. D. 'Pismo Święte–Jego autorytet i interpretacja w Kościele (1)'. *MPKSM* 4–7 (2008): 15–17.

Mames, Tomasz M. D. 'Pismo Święte–Jego autorytet i interpretacja w Kościele (2)'. *MPKSM* 11–12 (2008): 14–16.

Mames, Tomasz M. D. *Mysteria Mysticorum. Szkice z duchowości i historii Mariawitów*. Krakow: NOMOS, 2009.

Mames, Tomasz M. D. 'Związek Młodzieży Mariawickiej "Templariusze" (1932–1935)'. *Sborník příspěvků mezinárodní vědecké konference Evropské pedagogické forum 2*. Pp. 336–347. Hradec Králové: Magnanimitas, 2012.

Mames, Tomasz M. D. 'Mariawici i Mariawityzm doby I Wojny Światowej: Przykład Austriackiej Okupacji Terenów Królestwa Polskiego'. *Prowincja Galicyjska Wokół I Wojny Światowej*. Edited by Tomasz Pudłocki and Arkadiusz S. Więcha. Pp. 81–94. Przemyśl: Wyd. Towarzystwo Przyjaciół Nauk, 2014.

Mames, Tomasz M. D. *Oświata Mariawitów w latach 1906–1935*. Warszawa: Wyd. DiG, 2015.

Mames, Tomasz M. D. *Eucharystia Kościoła Starokatolickiego Mariawitów*. Warsaw: Wydawnictwo Naukowe Chrześcijańskiej Akademii Teologicznej w Warszawie, 2022.

Mames, Tomasz M. D. '*Kształtowania* się *ustroju* niezależnego od *Rzymu Kościoła mariawitów (1887–1914). Zagadnienia kanoniczno-prawne*'. *Rocznik Przemyski Historia* 58 (2022): 3–36. https://doi.org/10.4467/24497347RPH.22.017.16642

Mames, Tomasz M. D. '*Przyczynek do metaanalizy opowieści o mariawitach Jerzego Pietrkiewicza*', *Studia Teologiczno-Historyczne Śląska Opolskiego* 44 (2025): 105–130. https://doi.org/10.25167/sth.5588

Miłkowski, Józef M. L. 'Z pamiętnika o Matce Maryi Franciszce'. *GP* 35 (1937): 275–276.

Nowy Testament po polsku czyli Święta Pana naszego Jezusa Chrystusa Ewangelia. Płock: SKKM, 1921.

Pismo Święte Starego Testamentu czyli Zakon Mojżeszowy i Prorocy, t. 1. Płock: SKKM, 1923.

Pismo Święte Starego Testamentu czyli Zakon Mojżeszowy i Prorocy, t. 2. Płock: SKKM, 1925.

Polikarp. 'Kronika marjawicka. Z Cegłowa'. *GSK* 19 (1939): 302–303.

Polkowski, Zenon M. M. 'Poczet Biskupów Mariawickich'. *MPKSM* 8–12 (2010): 31–33.

Próchniewska, Zofia M. H., Helena M. M. Kubicka, Stanisława M. D. Spodarówna. 'List pasterski (09.06.1030)'. *WM* 1 (1935): 3.

Próchniewski, Roman M. J. 'Przeniesienie Stolicy Apostolskiej'. *MMN* 4 (1924): 1–6.

Próchniewski, Roman M. J. 'Mariae-vita. Pamiętniki Brata Biskupa Jakóba'. *KBNZ* 10 (1931): 74–75.

Próchniewski, Roman M. J. 'Mariae-vita'. *KBNZ* 52 (1931): 411–412.

Próchniewski, Roman M. J. 'Mariae-vita'. *KBNZ* 16 (1932): 123–124.

Próchniewski, Roman M. J. 'Mariae-vita'. *KBNZ* 4 (1933): 27–28.

Próchniewski, Roman M. J. 'Mariae-vita'. *KBNZ* 9 (1933): 66–67.

Próchniewski, Roman M. J. 'Do Braci i Sióstr Marjawitów'. *GP* 4 (1936): 26–27.

Próchniewski, Roman M. J. 'Na marginesie totalizmu katolickiego'. *GSK* 1 (1938): 5–7.
Próchniewski, Roman M. J. 'Słowo Boże'. *GSK* 7 (1938): 99–100.
Próchniewski, Roman M. J. 'Słowo Boże'. *GSK* 24 (1938): 372–373.
Próchniewski, Roman M. J. 'Kongresy Eucharystyczne'. *GSK* 25 (1938): 385–387.
Próchniewski, Roman M. J. 'Słowo Boże'. *GSK* 40 (1938): 629–631.
Próchniewski, Roman M. J. 'Słowo Boże'. *GSK* 41 (1938): 645–647.
Próchniewski, Roman M. J. 'Słowo Boże'. *GSK* 22 (1939): 339–341.
Próchniewski, Roman M. J. 'Słowo Boże'. *GSK* 42 (1938): 661–663.
Próchniewski, Roman M. J. 'Symbol pojednania'. *GSK* 3 (1939): 33–35.
Próchniewski, Roman M. J. Żywot Przeczystej Pani i objawione jej Dzieło Miłosierdzia. Płock: KSM, 2003. Unpublished manuscript.
Przyjemski, Kazimierz M. J. 'Mariae-vita, Z Pamiętników Ojca Jana, Pierwszego Kapłana Mariawity'. *Święta Maria Franciszka Kozłowska i Jej Zgromadzenie zakonne we wspomnieniach i pamiętnikach*. Edited by Damiana M. B. Szulgowicz and Hanna M. R. Woińska. Pp. 211–308 Felicjanów: KKM, 2007.
Przysiecki, Wacław M. B. 'Co mówi nasz lud Maryawicki o wyświęceniu Sióstr na kapłanki i dyakonise'. *KBNZ* 20 (1929): 155–156.
Przysiecki, Wacław M. B. 'Obrońca Marjawityzmu'. *GP* 24 (1935): 189–190.
Przysiecki, Wacław M. B. 'Rządy Opatrzości'. *GP* 30 (1935): 237–238.
Przysiecki, Wacław M. B. 'Z życia Marjawickiego'. *GP* 5 (1936): 37–38.
Przysiecki, Wacław M. B. 'Ku czemu Polska idzie?' *GP* 10 (1936): 73–74.
Przysiecki, Wacław M. B. 'Ku czemu Polska idzie?' *GP* 18 (1936): 137–138.
Przysiecki, Wacław M. B. 'Ku czemu Polska idzie?' *GP* 22 (1936): 169–170.
Przysiecki, Wacław M. B. 'Ku czemu Polska idzie?' *GP* 27 (1936): 201–202.
Przysiecki, Wacław M. B. 'Zmartwychstanie idei'. *GP* 44 (1936): 337–338.
Przysiecki, Wacław M. B. 'Lud w ideologii Słowackiego'. *GP* 20 (1937): 153–154.
Przysiecki, Wacław M. B. 'Słowo Boże'. *GP* 22 (1937): 170–171.
Przysiecki, Wacław M. B. 'Słowo Boże'. *GP* 24 (1937): 186–187.
Przysiecki, Wacław M. B. 'Czy Towiański był fałszywym prorokiem'. *GP* 33 (1937): 257–258.
Przysiecki, Wacław M. B. 'Czy Towiański był fałszywym prorokiem'. *GP* 36 (1937): 281–282.
Przysiecki, Wacław M. B. 'Czy Towiański był fałszywym prorokiem'. *GP* 41 (1937): 321–322.
Przysiecki, Wacław M. B. 'Czy Towiański był fałszywym prorokiem'. *GP* 42 (1937): 329–330.
Przysiecki, Wacław M. B. 'Czy Towiański był fałszywym prorokiem'. *GP* 43 (1937): 337–338.
Przysiecki, Wacław M. B. 'Czy Towiański był fałszywym prorokiem'. *GP* 44 (1937): 345–346.
Przysiecki, Wacław M. B. 'Nowy patron Polski'. *GSK* 27 (1938): 417–419.
Przysiecki, Wacław M. B. 'Odpowiedź miesięcznikowi Sumienie Społeczne'. *GSK* 28 (1938): 437–439.
Przysiecki, Wacław M. B. 'Kronika marjawicka: Wzmożenie uczuć religijnych'. *GSK* 7 (1939): 108–109.
Przysiecki, Wacław M. B. 'Misja Polski'. *GSK* 27 (1939): 417–419.
Radecki, Henryk. 'Czy Kult Mateczki to Wypaczenie'. *PNS* 26 (2001): 21–22.

Romenko, Tatiana. 'Proces usuwania Mariawitów z Kościoła rzymskiego'. *PNS* 33 (2004): 19–24.
Romenko, Tatiana. 'Mariawici wierzą' – czym jest ten tekst?' *PNS* 52 (2009): 24–29.
Romenko, Tatiana. 'Dwugłos o ustaniu ofiary. Co jest zapisane w objawieniach Mateczki?' *PNS* 65 (2012): 14–19.
Rostworowski, Wawrzyniec M. F. 'List Brata Biskupa do Redaktora 'Głosu Prawdy'. *GP* 23 (1935): 182–183.
Rudnicki, Konrad M. P. 'Teksty objawień bł. Marii Franciszki'. *RTChAT* 1–2 (1974): 455–465.
Rudnicki, Konrad M. P. 'Pierwotny tekst objawień Mateczki'. *RTChAT* 2 (1979): 195–231.
Rudnicki, Konrad M. P. 'Od Redakcji'. *PNS* 2 (1997): 12.
Rudnicki, Konrad M. P. 'Z Dziejów Zgromadzenia. Pierwsza kapituła'. *PNS* 9 (1998): 18–23.
Rudnicki, Konrad M. P. 'O Mariawitach materialistycznie'. *PNS* 9 (1998): 28–31.
Rudnicki, Konrad M. P. 'Bogurodzica a Trójca Święta w ujęciu mariawickim'. *Salvatoris Mater* 3 (2000): 380–386.
Rudnicki, Konrad M. P. 'Czy dusza ludzka może istnieć poza ciałem'. *PNS* 16 (2000): 6–9.
Rudnicki, Konrad M. P. Opinie prasowe o mariawitach'. *PNS* 16 (2000): 23–24.
Rudnicki, Konrad M. P. 'Współczesne objawienia'. *PNS* 20 (2001): 11–24.
Rudnicki, Konrad M. P. 'Mariawityzm a Unia Utrechcka'. *PNS* 21 (2001): 19–29.
Rudnicki, Konrad M. P. 'Komentarz'. *PNS* 24 (2002): 28–29. https://doi.org/10.1097/01.COT.0000285545.52988.30
Rudnicki, Konrad M. P. 'Dzieje Reguły świętego Franciszka'. *PNS* 24 (2002): 29–36.
Rudnicki, Konrad M. P. 'Uwagi o ustawach Związku Katolickiego Nieustającej Adoracji Ubłagania'. *PNS* 24 (2002): 43–48.
Rudnicki, Konrad M. P. 'Pomówmy o "nowościach" arcybiskupa Michała'. *PNS* 25 (2002): 22–32.
Rudnicki, Konrad M. P. 'Co z sukcesją apostolską'. *PNS* 26 (2002): 22–25.
Rudnicki, Konrad M. P. 'Porównanie różnych Objawień Miłosierdzia Bożego'. *Teologia Miłosierdzia Bożego*. Edited by Konrad M. P. Rudnicki and Zdzisław M. W. Jaworski. Pp. 180–194. Płock: KSM, 2003.
Rudnicki, Konrad M. P. 'Czy mariawityzm może istnieć Zgromadzenia Mariawitów'. *PNS* 37 (2005): 21–26.
Rudnicki, Konrad M. P. 'Niezwykła książka o mariawityzmie'. *PNS* 43 (2006): 18–23.
Rudnicki, Konrad M. P. *Moja droga do religii*. Krakow: F. H. U. Elwit, 2008.
Rudnicki, Konrad M. P. 'Fałszerstwo tekstu 'Początek zawiązku zgromadzenia kapłanów'. *PNS* 51 (2008): 26–31.
Rudnicki, Konrad M. P. 'Tablica Chronologiczna Rozwoju Dzieła Miłosierdzia wewnątrz Kościoła Rzymskokatolickiego'. PNS 54 (2009): 22–31.
Rudnicki, Konrad M. P. 'O Pani Tempczyk i Panu Peterkiewiczu'. *PNS* 55 (2009): 19–20.
Rudnicki, Konrad M. P. 'O bracie kapłanie Marii Polikarpie Zaborku'. *PNS* 59 (2010): 12–19.
Rudnicki, Konrad M. P. 'Myśli o mariawityzmie I. O rozłamie w roku 1935'. *PNS* 60 (2010): 25–31.
Rudnicki, Konrad M. P. 'Celibat w Zgromadzeniu Mariawitów'. *PNS* 61 (2011): 21–24.

Rudnicki, Konrad M. P. 'Myśli o mariawityzmie. O co oskarżają mariawityzm felicjanowski?' *PNS* 62 (2011): 24–31.
Rudnicki, Konrad M. P. 'Liczba zgromadzeń w mariawityzmie'. *PNS* 67 (2012): 27–31.
Rybak, Stanisław. *Mariawityzm, studium historyczne*. Warsaw: Wyd. Lege, 1992.
Siedlecki, Stanisław M. T. 'List pasterski (10.06.1935)'. *WM* 1 (1935): 3–5. https://doi.org/10.3109/10520293509115999
Skupiński, Jan P., and Konrad M. P. Rudnicki. 'Mariawityzm – rzymski katolicyzm. To, co łączy – to, co dzieli'. https://www.ekumenizm.pl/publicystyka/mariawityzm-rzymski-katolicyzm-to-co-laczy-to-co-dzieli-rozmowa-z-ks-prof-konradem-m-rudnickim/
Skupiński, Jan P. 'Obraz Ducha Świętego z Felicjanowa'. *PNS* 40 (2006): 27.
Sobala, Dorota. 'Mariawici spowiednikami w Kościele Rzymskokatolickim'. *PNS* 42 (2006): 5–6.
Stanisław, B. 'Z powodu kanonizacji Andrzeja Boboli'. *GSK* 24 (1938): 369–371.
Stobiecki, Ignacy. 'ELEUSIS'. *PNS* 3 (1997): 10–14.
Stobiecki, Ignacy. 'Próba oceny'. *PNS* 9 (1998): 23–28.
Stobiecki, Ignacy. 'Stanisławowi Janowi Rostworowskiemu ku rozwadze'. *PNS* 12 (1999): 24–32.
Stobiecki, Ignacy. 'Emil Zegadłowicz mariawitą?!' *PNS* 16 (2000): 17–19.
Stobiecki, Ignacy. 'Ważne wyjaśnienie'. *PNS* 18 (2000): 35–38. https://doi.org/10.1023/A:1026580627850
Stobiecki, Ignacy. 'Mateczka a ekumenizm'. *PNS* 22 (2001): 3–5.
Stobiecki, Ignacy. 'Dlaczego Rzym rozwiązał Zgromadzenie Mariawitów'. *PNS* 23 (2001): 31–35.
Stobiecki, Ignacy. 'Dwugłos o arcybiskupie Janie M. Michale Kowalskim'. *PNS* 25 (2002): 13–23.
Stobiecki, Ignacy. 'Prostaczka rozważania z siostrami betankami w tle'. *PNS* 47 (2007): 7–11.
Stobiecki, Ignacy. 'Założycielka przed rzymskim sądem'. *PNS* 51 (2008): 13–25.
Stobiecki, Ignacy. 'Tajemnicza siostra W…?!' *PNS* 62 (2011): 18–20.
Szulgowicz, Damiana M. B. 'Ideologia Mariawityzmu w Listach pasterskich i Odezwach arcybiskupa Jana Marii Michała Kowalskiego'. *Z dziejów Królestwa*. Edited by Józef M. R. Wojciechowski, Damiana M. B. Szulgowicz, Hanna M. R. Woińska. Pp. 111–245. Felicjanów: KKM, 1972.
Szulgowicz, Damiana M. B., and Hanna M. R. Woińska, eds. *Ku Królestwu Bożemu*. Felicjanów: KKM, 2009.
Szulgowicz, Damiana M. B., Hanna M. R. Woińska, Krzysztof Mazur, 'O trudnych dziejach mariawityzmu, w których przyszło mariawitom realizować Orędzie Dzieła Wielkiego Miłosierdzia'. *MD* II. Edited by Damiana M. B. Szulgowicz and Hanna M. R. Woińska. Pp. 231–278. Felicjanów: KKM, 2013.
Szymkiewicz, Mateusz M. F. Koncepcja utwierdzenia w łasce Bożej w teologii mariawickiej. Warsaw: Chrześcijańska Akademia Teologiczna, Unpublished Master's Thesis, 2015.
Tułaba, Antoni M. F. Wspomnienia bp. Antoniego M. Feliksa Tułaby. Felicjanów: KKM, Unpublished, 1924.
Tułaba, Antoni M. F. 'Znad Niemna. List otwarty do Braci Biskupów i Kapłanów'. *WM* 3 (1935): 8.
Wieczorkowski, Stanisław. 'Glosy do recenzji'. *PNS* 28 (2003): 21–25.

Wielopolska, Maria J. 'Jak się Amor niechcący przysłużył teologii'. *GP* 52 (1932): 412–415.
Wiłucka–Kowalska, Antonina M. I. 'Świadectwo Przew. Matki Izabeli'. *Początki Królestwa Bożego na ziemi*. Pp. 38–66. Płock: KSM, 1928.
Wojciechowski, Józef M. R. 'Mariawityzm–rys historyczny i odrębność nauki'. *Z dziejów Królestwa*. Edited by Józef M. R. Wojciechowski, Damiana M. B. Szulgowicz, Hanna M. R. Woińska. Pp. 9–110. Felicjanów: KKM, 1972.
Wojciechowski, Józef M. R. 'Nie–dla 'grzeszności' Mateczki'. *PNS* 8 (1998): 1–6.
Wojciechowski, Józef M. R. 'Wyznanie wiary (1988)'. *Wyznania Wiary i główne zasady doktrynalne. Katolicyzm*. Edited by Marcin Karas. Pp. 195–201. Krakow: MEDIA-PRESS, 2000.
Wojciechowski, Józef M. R. *Pisma Wybrane, Dzieło Bożego Ratunku, Mariawicki znak czasu*. Felicjanów: KKM, 2003.
Wojciechowski, Józef M. R. 'List pasterski o Niepokalanym Poczęciu Maryi i niepojętej wielkości Jej Dzieła (08.09.1985)'. Józef M. R. Wojciechowski, *Pisma Wybrane, Dzieło Bożego Ratunku, Mariawicki znak czasu*. Pp. 172–182. Felicjanów: KKM, 2003.
Wojciechowski, Józef M. R. 'List Pasterski. Słowo Wyjaśniające wydarzenia w Kościele w 1935 r. (8.09.1969)'. Józef M. R. Wojciechowski, *Pisma Wybrane, Dzieło Bożego Ratunku, Mariawicki znak czasu*. Pp. 200–214. Felicjanów: KKM, 2003.
Wójtecki, Włodzimierz. 'W zdrowym ciele zdrowy duch'. *GSK* 30 (1939): 477–478.
Żaglewski, Stefan M. R. 'Co sądzili inni o budowie naszej Świątyni'. *PNS* 47 (2007): 18–20.
Żaglewski, Stefan M. R. *Świątynia Miłosierdzia i Miłości w Płocku–święte miejsce mariawitów*. Płock: Wyd. KSM, 2014.

Other sources

Adolphus, Margaret. 'Coltman, Constance Mary'. *A Historical Dictionary of British Women*. Edited by Cathy Hartley. P. 122. London: Europa Publications, 2003.
Adrianyi, Gabriel, and Jerzy Kłoczowski, 'Catholic Nationalism in Great Hungary and Poland'. *World Christianities c. 1815–1914. The Cambridge History of Christianity*. Vol. 8 Edited by Sheridan Gilley and Brian Stanley. Pp. 260–281. Cambridge: Cambridge University Press, 2006.
Afanasiev, Nicholas. *Trapeza Gospodnia*. Paris: YMCA Press, 1952.
Akin, Jimmy. 'La Salette: Sorting Fact from Fiction'. catholic.com. https://www.catholic.com/magazine/print-edition/la-salette-sorting-fact-from-fiction
A. K. *Smutny koniec marjawityzmu*. Płock: Druk Tow. Wydawniczego 'Dziennik Płocki'. 1923.
Alighieri, Dante. *Boska Komedia*. Translated by Jan M. M. Kowalski. Płock: KSM 1932.
Allison, Dale C. *Jesus of Nazareth: Millenarian Prophet*. Minneapolis: Fortress Press, 1998.
Appolis, Emile. 'Une Église des derniers temps: l'Église Mariavite'. *Archives de sociologie des religions* 10 (1965): 51–67. https://doi.org/10.3406/assr.1965.2572
Asale, Bruk A. 'The Ethiopian Orthodox Tewahedo Church Canon of the Scriptures: Neither Open nor Closed'. *The Bible Translator* 67 (2016): 202–222. https://doi.org/10.1177/2051677016651486

Athanasius of Alexandria. 'Against the Arians'. Translated by John H. Newman. https://www.newadvent.org/fathers/28161.htm

Augustine. *Of the Works of Monks*. Translated by Henry Browne. http://www.newadvent.org/fathers/1314.htm

Augustine. *The City of God*. Edited and translated by Gerald G. Walsh and Grace Monahan. Washington: The Catholic University of America Press, 1952.

Augustine. *Sermons on the Liturgical Seasons*. Edited and translated by Mary S. Muldowney R.S.M. Washington: The Catholic University of America Press, 1959.

Auty, Robert. 'The Bible in East-Central Europe'. *The West from the Reformation to the Present Day. The Cambridge History of the Bible*. Vol. 3. Edited by Stanley L. Greenslade. Pp. 129–134. Cambridge: Cambridge University Press, 2008.

Auzépy, Marie-France. *La Vie d'Etienne le Jeune par Étienne le Diacre: Introduction, édition et Traduction*. New York, NY: Routledge, 2016.

Banaszak, Marian. *Historia Kościoła Katolickiego 3: Czasy nowożytne 1578–1914*. Warszawa: Akademia Teologia Katolickiej, 1991.

Bar, Joachim R. 'Z dziejów nowych form organizacyjnych stanów doskonałości w Polsce'. *Prawo Kanoniczne* 3–4 (1965): 189–213. https://doi.org/10.21697/pk.1965.8.3-4.06

Beckford James A. 'The Embryonic State of a Religious Sect's Development: The Jehovah's Witnesses'. *Sociological Yearbook of Religion in Britain* 5, Edited by Michael Hill. Pp. 11–32. London: SCM Press, 1972.

Behr, John. *Irenaeus of Lyon, Identifying Christianity*. Oxford: Oxford University Press, 2013. https://doi.org/10.1093/acprof:oso/9780199214624.001.0001

Belleville, Linda L. *Two Views on Women in Ministry*. Edited by James R. Beck. Grand Rapids, MI: Zondervan, 2005.

Бердяев, Николай А. *Истоки и смысл русского коммунизма*. Paris: YMCA Press, 1955.

Berkhof, Louis. *Systematic Theology*. Grand Rapids, MI: Wm. B. Eerdmans, 1996.

Bermon, Emmanuel. *Le cogito dans la pensée de saint Augustin*. Paris: Librairie Philosophique Vrin, 2001.

Boniface VIII. 'Unam sanctam'. https://www.papalencyclicals.net/Bon08/B8unam.htm

Borkowska, Małgorzata. *Życie codzienne polskich klasztorów żeńskich w XVII–XVIII wieku*. Warsaw: Państwowy Instytut Wydawniczy, 1996.

Boswell, John. *Christianity, Social Tolerance, and Homosexuality: Gay People in Western Europe from the Beginning of the Christian Era to the Fourteenth Century*. Chicago: The University of Chicago Press, 1980.

Boswell, John. *Same-Sex Unions in Premodern Europe*. New York: Vintage, 1994.

Boyarin, Daniel. *The Jewish Gospels: The Story of the Jewish Christ*. New York, NY: The New Press, 2012.

Bradley, Owen. 'Maistre's Theory of Sacrifice'. *Joseph de Maistre's Life, Thought, and Influence*. Edited by Richard A. Lebrun. Pp. 65–83. Montreal, McGill-Queen's University Press, 2001.

Bray, Alan. 'Wedded Friendships'. https://web.archive.org/web/20120207071228/https://www.thetablet.co.uk/article/5030

The Brill Dictionary of Gregory of Nyssa. Edited by Lucas F. Mateo-Seco and Giulio Maspero. Leiden: Brill, 2010.

Brock, Sebastian P. 'The Holy Spirit as Feminine in Early Syriac Literature'. *After Eve*. Edited by Janet M. Soskice. Pp. 73–88. London: Marshall-Pickering, 1990.

Broda, Anita. 'Mariawityzm–historia i teraźniejszość ruchu w setną rocznicę jego powstania'. *NP* 52 (2007): 3–13.

Brooten, Bernadette J. 'Female Leadership in the Ancient Synagogue'. *From Dura to Sepphoris: Studies in Jewish Art and Society in Late Antiquity*. Journal of Roman Archeology Supplementary Series 40. Edited by Lee I. Levine and Zeev Weiss, Portsmouth: Journal of Roman Archaeology (2000): 215–221.

Brown, Peter. *Ciało i społeczeństwo: Mężczyźni, kobiety i abstynencja seksualna we wczesnym chrześcijaństwie*. Translated by Ireneusz Kania. Krakow: Homini, 2006.

Bruncz, Dariusz. 'Rozłam mariawityzmu w pigułce–niepojednana przeszłość kościoła w Grzmiącej'. https://www.ekumenizm.pl/specjalne/rozlam-mariawityzmu-w-pigulce-niepojednana-przeszlosc-kosciola-w-grzmiacej/

Bruncz, Dariusz. '100 lat temu urodził się abp M. Rafael Wojciechowski'. https://www.ekumenizm.pl/koscioly/katolickie/100-temu-urodzil-sie-abp-m-rafael-wojciechowski/

Булгаков, Сергей Н. *Свет Невечерний. Созерцания и умозрения*. Moscow: Put, 1917.

Bułgakow, Siergiej. *Prawosławie. Zarys nauki Kościoła prawosławnego*. Translated by Henryk Paprocki. Białystok–Warsaw: Orthdruk, 1992.

Burrus, Virginia. *The Sex Lives of Saints: An Erotics of Ancient Hagiography*. Philadelphia: University of Pennsylvania Press, 2004.

Callahan, William J. 'Spain and Portugal: The Challenge to the Church'. *World Christianities c. 1815–1914. The Cambridge History of Christianity*. Vol. 8. Edited by Sheridan Gilley and Brian Stanley. Pages 381–394 in Cambridge: Cambridge University Press, 2006.

Chadwick, Nora K. *The Age of the Saints in the Early Celtic Church*. London: Oxford University Press, 1961.

Chadwick, Owen. *A History of the Popes, 1830–1914*. New York: Oxford University Press, 2002.

Chantraine, Pierre. *Dictionnaire étymologique de la langue grecque*. Paris: Klincksieck, 1999.

'Chapter IV of The Twenty-Third Session: On the Ecclesiastical hierarchy, and on Ordination'. *The Canons and Decrees of the Sacred and Oecumenical Council of Trent*. Edited and translated by James Waterworth. London: Dolman, 1848.

Charkiewicz, Jarosław. 'Wybrane aspekty kultu Matki Bożej w Prawosławiu'. *Elpis* 16 (2014): 23–31. https://doi.org/10.15290/elpis.2014.16.04

Charlesworth, James H. ed. and trans. *The Earliest Christian Textbook: The Odes of Solomon*. Cambridge: James Clarke & Co, 2009.

Chernetsov, Sevir B. 'On the Reasons of Empress Taytu's Anger which Come Down upon Afawarq Gabra Iyasus in 1894'. *Proceedings of the XVth International Conference of Ethiopian Studies*. Edited by Siegbert Uhlig. Pp. 218–223 Wiesbaden: Harrassowitz Verlag, 2006.

Chiniquy, Charles P. *Fifty Years in the Church of Rome*. New York: Fleming H. Revell, 1886.

Chrostowski, Waldemar. 'The Suffering, Chosenness and Mission of the Polish Nation'. *Occasional Papers on Religion in Eastern Europe* 11 (1991): 1–14.

Cieszkowski, August. *Ojcze Nasz*. Poznań: Fiszer i Majewski, 1922.

Claeys, Thierry. 'Les Investissements Français en Russie de 1857 à 1914: Conseils, Expertises et Stratégies'. *Quaestio Rossica* 4 (2015): 163–172. https://doi.org/10.15826/qr.2015.4.131

Cleenewerck, Laurent. *His Broken Body: Understanding and Healing the Schism between the Roman Catholic and Eastern Orthodox Churches*. Washington: Euclid University Consortium Press, 2007.

Clement XI. 'Unigenitus'. https://www.papalencyclicals.net/clem11/c11unige.htm

Clement of Alexandria. *Stromateis, Books 1–3*. Fathers of the Church 85. Translated by John Ferguson. Washington: The Catholic University of America Press, 1991.

Cohn, Norman. 'Medieval Millenarism: Its Bearing on the Comparative Study of Millenarian Movements'. *Millennial Dreams in Action. Essays in Comparative Study*. Edited by Sylvia C. Thrupp. Pp. 31–43. Hague: Mouton & Co, 1962.

Coltri, Marzia A. 'Women and NRMs: Location and Identity'. *Female Leaders in New Religious Movements*. Pp. 11–28. Edited by Christian Giudice, Inga B. Tøllefsen. Cham: Palgrave Macmillan, 2017.

Cooper, Derek. *Sinners and Saints: The Real Story of Early Christianity*. Grand Rapids, MI: Kregel Academic, 2018.

Coşgel, Metin M. 'The Family in Utopia: Celibacy, Communal Child Rearing, and Continuity in a Religious Commune'. *Journal of Family History* 25 (2000): 491–503. https://doi.org/10.1177/036319900002500403

Crossley, Ceri. *French Historians and Romanticism: Thierry, Guizot, the Saint-Simonians, Quinet, Michelet*. London: Routledge, 1993.

Crossley, James G. 'History from the Margins: The Death of John the Baptist'. *Writing History, Constructing Religion*. Pp. 147–162. Edited by James G. Crossley and Christian Karner. Aldershot: Ashgate, 2005.

Crossley, James G. *Jesus and the Chaos of History, Redirecting the Life of the Historical Jesus*. Oxford: Oxford University Press, 2015.

Crossley, James G., and Chris Keith, eds. *The Next Quest for the Historical Jesus*. Grand Rapids, MI: Wm. B. Eerdmans, 2024.

Crouzel, Henri. *Origene*. Paris: Lethielleux, 1985.

Cyprian of Carthage. *Letters (1–81)*. Translated by Rose B. Donna, C.S.J. Washington: The Catholic University of America Press, 1964.

Cyril. *Cyril of Alexandria, Selected Letters*. Edited and translated by Lionel R. Wickham. Oxford: Clarendon Press, 1983.

Cyrocki, Damian. *Relacje anglikańsko–prawosławne od początku XIX w. do roku 1938 w perspektywie ważności święceń kapłańskich*. Krakow: Jagiellonian University, Unpublished Bachelor's thesis 2001.

Cyrocki, Damian. 'Jan Kowalski'. *Critical Dictionary of Apocalyptic and Millenarian Movements*. Edited by James Crossley and Alastair Lockhart. 27 May 2021. Retrieved from www.cdamm.org/articles/jan-kowalski

Cyrocki, Damian. 'Adam Mickiewicz'. *Critical Dictionary of Apocalyptic and Millenarian Movements*. Edited by James Crossley and Alastair Lockhart. 24 March 2023. Retrieved from www.cdamm.org/articles/adam-mickiewicz

Cyrocki, Damian. 'Juliusz Słowacki'. *Critical Dictionary of Apocalyptic and Millenarian Movements*. Edited by James Crossley and Alastair Lockhart. 24 March 2023. Retrieved from www.cdamm.org/articles/juliusz-słowacki

Czaczkowska, Ewa K. *Mistyczki. Historie kobiet wybranych*. Krakow: Wyd. Znak, 2019.

Darczewska, Krystyna. 'Elementy mesjanistyczne w polskich kościołach narodowych'. *Studia Religioznawcze* 19 (1984): 73–103.

Davies, Norman. *Europe: A History.* London: Pimlico, 1997.

Davies, Norman. *God's Playground: A History of Poland.* Vol. II: *From 1795 to the Present.* New York: Columbia University Press, 2005.

DeConick, April D. *Holy Misogyny: Why the Sex and Gender Conflicts in the Early Church Still Matter.* New York: The Continuum International, 2011.

Diatłowicki, Tomasz and Anna Dziedzic. 'Słowacki. Heretyk królom równy. Rozmowa z Anną Dziedzic'. focus.pl. https://www.focus.pl/artykul/slowacki-heretyk-krolom-rowny

Dixon, Megan. 'Repositioning Pushkin and the Poems of the Polish Uprising'. *Polish Encounters: Russian Identity.* Edited by David L. Ransel and Bozena Shallcross. Pp. 49–73. Bloomington: Indiana University Press, 2005.

Dokumenty Soborów Powszechnych. Edited by Arkadiusz Baron and Henryk Pietras SJ. Kraków: Wyd. WAM, 2003.

Dokumenty Synodów od 50 do 381 roku. Edited by Arkadiusz Baron and Henryk Pietras SJ. Krakow: Wyd. WAM, 2006.

Dougherty, Joseph. *From Altar-Throne to Table: The Campaign for Frequent Holy Communion in the Catholic Church.* Maryland: Scarecrow Press, 2010.

Dunn, James D. G. *Unity and Diversity in the New Testament: An Inquiry into the Character of Earliest Christianity.* London: SCM Press, 1977.

Dvornik, Francis. *The Photian Schism.* Cambridge: Cambridge University Press, 1948.

Dwojnych, Andrzej and Rafał Łętocha. *W stronę Królestwa Bożego na ziemi: Myśl społeczno-polityczna mariawitów polskich.* Krakow: Wydawnictwo Uniwersytetu Jagiellońskiego, 2021.

Dyniewski, Tadeusz. *Zbrodnia, zdrada, kara: pitaval śląski.* Katowice: KAW, 1986.

Ehrman, Bart D. *Lost Christianities: The Battles for Scripture and the Faiths We Never Knew.* Oxford: Oxford University Press, 2003.

Ehrman, Bart D., ed. and trans. *Lost Scriptures: Books That Did Not Make it into the New Testament.* Oxford: Oxford University Press, 2003.

Ehrman, Bart D., ed. and trans. *The Apostolic Fathers.* Vol. I. Cambridge: Harvard University Press, 2003.

Ehrman, Bart D., ed. and trans. *The Apostolic Fathers.* Vol. II. Harvard: Harvard University Press, 2003.

Ehrman, Bart D. *Forgery and Counterforgery: The Use of Literary Deceit in Early Christian Polemics.* Oxford: Oxford University Press, 2013.

Ehrman, Bart D. *When Jesus became God: The Exaltation of a Jewish Preacher.* New York: Harper Collins, 2014.

Ehrman, Bart D. *The Triumph of Christianity: How a Forbidden Religion Swept the World.* New York: Simon & Schuster, 2018.

Eliade, Mircea. *Sacrum a profanum.* Warsaw: Wyd. Aletheia, 2008.

Elm, Susanna. *'Virgins of God': The Making of Asceticism in Late Antiquity.* Oxford: Oxford University Press, 1994.

'Encyclical of the Eastern Patriarchs, 1848, A Reply to the Epistle of Pope Pius IX to the Easterns'. https://sourcebooks.fordham.edu/mod/1848orthodoxencyclical.asp

Eusebius Pamphilus. *Ecclesiastical History I.* Translated by Kirsopp Lake. London: William Heinemann, 1926.

Eusebius Pamphilus. *Ecclesiastical History II*. Translated by John E. L. Oulton. London: William Heinemann, 1932.
Evagrius. *Evagrius of Pontus: The Greek Ascetic Corpus*. Edited and translated by Robert E. Sinkewicz. Oxford: Oxford University Press, 2003.
Felix, Marcus Minucius. *The Octavius*. Translated by G. W. Clarke. New York: Newman Press, 1974.
Fidura, Jerzy. '100-lecie istnienia Starokatolickiego Kościoła Mariawitów (1906–2006)'. *Studia Ełckie* 8 (2006): 101–111.
Florovsky, Georges V. 'Le Corps du Christ vivant. Une interprétation orthodoxe de l'Eglise'. *La sainte Eglise universelle, Confrontation œcuménique*. Edited by Georges V. Florovsky. Pp. 10–57 Neuchatel: Delachaux et Niestlé S.A, 1948.
Freeze, Gregory L. *The Russian Levites: Parish Clergy in the Eighteenth Century*. Cambridge: Harvard University Press, 1977.
Freeze, Gregory L. 'Russian Orthodoxy: Church, people and politics in Imperial Russia'. *Imperial Russia 1689–1917. The Cambridge History of Russia*. Vol. 2. Edited by Dominic Lieven. Pp. 284–305. Cambridge: Cambridge University Press, 2006.
Gajewski, Jan K. *Gdzie Dyabeł nie może, tam babę pośle*. Sandomierz: Drukarnia W. Byrzyński, 1909.
Gajewski, Stanisław. *Izydor Kajetan Wysłouch 1867–1937*. Lublin: Wyd. KUL, 1995.
Gambero, Luigi. *Mary and the Fathers of the Church: The Blessed Virgin Mary in the Patristic Thought*. San Francisco: Ignatius Press, 1999.
Gathercole, Simon. *The Gospel of Thomas: Introduction and Commentary*. Leiden: Brill, 2014.
Gawlina, Józef. *Wspomnienia*. Katowice: Wyd. Księgarnia św. Jacka, 2004.
Ghalli, M. B. 'Oriental Orthodox Churches'. *The Coptic Encyclopedia*. Vol. 6. Edited by Aziz S. Atiya. Pp. 1845–1846. New York, NY: Macmillan Publishing Company, 2011.
Gibson, Ralph. *A Social History of French Catholicism, 1789–1914*. New York, NY: Routledge, 1989.
Górecki, Artur. *Próby odnowienia życia religijnego w Królestwie Polskim po powstaniu styczniowym–wybrane aspekty*. Toruń: Europejskie Centrum Edukacyjne, 2010.
Górecki, Artur. *Mariawici i mariawityzm–narodziny i pierwsze lata istnienia*. Warsaw: Wyd. DiG, 2011.
Graff, Agnieszka. *Świat bez kobiet. Płeć w polskim życiu publicznym*. Warsaw: Wyd. W.A.B., 2001.
Gralewski, Stefan. *Wyznania protestanckie i sekty religijne w Polsce współczesnej*. Lublin: Diecezjalny Zakład Graficzno-Drukarski w Sandomierzu, 1937.
Gregory XV. 'Cum Primum'. http://www.papalencyclicals.net/Greg16/g16cumpr.htm
Gregory XVI. 'Mirari Vos'. https://www.papalencyclicals.net/greg16/g16mirar.htm
Gregory, Andrew. '1 Clement: An Introduction'. *The Writings of the Apostolic Fathers*. Edited by Paul Foster. Pp. 21–31. New York: T&T Clark, 2007.
Gręźlikowski, Janusz. 'Przechowywanie i kult Eucharystii w ustawodawstwie synodalnym Polski przedrozbiorowej'. *Prawo Kanoniczne: kwartalnik prawno-historyczny* 55 (2012): 99–158. https://doi.org/10.21697/pk.2012.55.1.04
Grossman, James D. 'Philosophers, Decadents, and Mystics: James's Russian Readers in the 1890s'. *William James in Russian Culture*. Edited by Joan D. Grossman and Ruth Rischin. Pp. 95–111. Oxford: Lexington Books, 2003.

Gruszczyńska, Kazimiera. *Historia Zgromadzenia Sióstr Franciszkanek od Cierpiących*. Krakow: Wyd. Avalon, 2019.

Gruziel, Dominik. At the Crossroads of New Catholicism and the 'Woman Question': Polish Roman Catholic Laywomen's Social Activism on Behalf of Women in the Three Zones of Partitioned Poland, 1878–1918. Budapest: Central European University, Unpublished PhD Thesis, 2012.

Harvey, Susan A. 'Feminine Imagery for the Divine: The Holy Spirit, the Odes of Solomon, and Early Syriac Tradition'. *St. Vladimir's Theological Quarterly* 37 (1993): 111–139.

Haynes, Michael L. J. *Mary, the Motherly Co-Redemptrix*. Morrisville, NC: Lulu, 2019.

Heimann, Mary. 'Catholic Revivalism in Worship and Devotion'. *World Christianities c. 1815–1914. The Cambridge History of Christianity*. Vol. 8. Edited by Sheridan Gilley and Brian Stanley. Pp. 70–83 in Cambridge: Cambridge University Press, 2006.

Heinberg, Richard. *Memories and Visions of Paradise: Exploring the Universal Myth of a Lost Golden Age*. Los Angeles: Jeremy P. Tarcher, 1989.

Hill, Jonathan. *Christianity. The First 400 Years*. Oxford: Lion Books, 2013.

'Historia Zgromadzenia'. https://sluzki.pl/index.php?option=com_content&view=article&id=82&Itemid=186&lang=pl

Holmes, Michael W. ed. and trans. *The Apostolic Fathers. Greek Texts and English Translations*. Grand Rapids, MI: Baker Academic, 2007.

Howell, Martha and Walter Prevenier. *From Reliable Sources: An Introduction to Historical Methods*. Ithaca: Cornell University Press, 2001.

Hunter, David G. *Marriage and Sexuality in Early Christianity*. Minneapolis: Fortress Press, 2018.

Incigneri, Brian J. *The Gospel to The Romans: The Setting and Rhetoric of Mark's Gospel*. Leiden: Brill, 2003.

Jacobs, Joseph, Ludwig Blau. 'Holy Spirit'. http://www.jewishencyclopedia.com/articles/7833-holy-spirit

Jaczewski, Franciszek. 'List biskupa Jaczewskiego do proboszcza parafii w Grębkowie'. *Proces wydzielania się Związku Mariawitów Nieustającej Adoracji Ubłagania z doktrynalnych i organizacyjnych ram Kościoła rzymskokatolickiego*. P. 203. Edited by Edward Warchoł. Radom: Wyd. Diecezjalne, 2006.

James, William. *The Varieties of Religious Experience: A Study in Human Nature*. London: Longman, 1902.

Jaroszyński, Piotr. 'Mickiewicz Adam'. http://www.ptta.pl/pef/pdf/m/mickiewicza.pdf

Jedin, Hubert, and John Dolan, eds. *History of the Church: The Church in the Industrial Age*. London: Burns & Oates, 1981.

Jenkins, Philip. *Mystics and Messiahs: Cults and New Religions in American History*. Oxford: Oxford University Press, 2000.

Jerome. 'Against Jovinianus'. Translated by William H. Fremantle. http://www.newadvent.org/fathers/30091.htm

Jerome. 'Letter no 124 to Avitus'. Translated by William H. Fremantle. https://www.newadvent.org/fathers/3001124.htm

'Jon Arason–The Reformation'. https://www.sagamuseum.is/overview/#jon-arason

Jordan, David K. *Gods, Ghosts and Ancestors*. Los Angeles: University of California Press, 1972.

Justin Martyr. 'The First Apology'. in *Writings of Saint Justin Martyr*. Edited and translated by Thomas D. Falls. Pp. 33–111 Washington: The Catholic University of America Press, 1948.

Justin Martyr. *Dialogue with Trypho*. Edited and translated by Thomas B. Falls. Washington: The Catholic University of America Press, 2003.

Kansy, Andrzej. 'Przegląd prasy mariawitów na ziemiach polskich (1907–2017)'. *Studia Medioznawcze* 73 (2018): 41–53. https://doi.org/10.33077/uw.24511617.ms.2018.0.261

Kansy, Andrzej. *Funkcje prasy wyznaniowej: Studium na przykładzie mariawitów*. Płock: Wyd. Naukowe Mazowieckiej Uczelni Publicznej w Płocku, 2020.

Karas, Marcin. 'Kapłaństwo kobiet w felicjanowskim odłamie mariawityzmu na tle jego założeń teologicznych'. *Przegląd religioznawczy* 4 (2000): 83–108.

Karas, Marcin. 'O pewnym 'reformatorze' mariawityzmu'. *PNS* 18 (2000): 30–33.

Karas, Marcin. 'Święcenie kobiet na kapłanki w felicjanowskiej wspólnocie mariawickiej'. *NP* 46 (2001): 9.

Kelly, John N. D. *Early Christian Doctrines*. London: R. & R. Clark, 1968.

Ker, Ian. *John Henry Newman: A Biography*. Oxford: Oxford University Press, 2009.

King, J. Christopher. *Origen on the Song of Songs as the Spirit of Scripture, The Bridegroom's Perfect Marriage-Song*. Oxford: Oxford University Press, 2005.

Klinger, Jerzy. *Geneza sporu o epiklezę: Eschatologiczny a memorialny aspekt Eucharystii w kanonie pierwszych wieków*. Warsaw: Chrześcijańska Akademia Teologiczna, 1969.

Klinger, Jerzy. 'Drugi List świętego Piotra Apostoła'. Jerzy Klinger, *O istocie prawosławia*. Pp. 52–71. Warsaw: Wyd. PAX, 1983.

Klinger, Jerzy. 'Zarys prawosławnej Mariologii'. Jerzy Klinger, *O istocie prawosławia*. Pp. 209–247. Warsaw: Wyd. PAX, 1983.

Knust, Jennifer W. *Abandoned to Lust: Sexual Slander and Ancient Christianity: Gender, Theory, and Religion Series*. New York: Columbia University Press, 2006.

Koester, Craig R. *Revelation A New Translation with Introduction and Commentary*. New Haven: Yale University Press, 2014.

Koropeckyj, Roman R. *Adam Mickiewicz: The Life of a Romantic*. New York: Cornell University Press, 2008.

Korszyński, Franciszek. *Jasne promienie w Dachau*. Poznań: Wyd. Pallottinum, 1957.

Kovacs, Judith, and Christopher Rowland. *Revelation: The Apocalypse of Jesus Christ*. Oxford: Blackwell Publishing, 2004.

Kowalczykowa, Alina. *Słowacki*. Warsaw: Wydawnictwo Naukowe PWN, 1994.

Koźmiński, Honorat. *Prawda o 'Maryawitach'*. Warsaw: 1906.

Krasiński, Zygmunt. *Pisma filozoficzne i polityczne*. Warsaw: Wyd. Spółdzielnia wydawnicza Czytelnik, 1999.

Lactantius, *The Divine Institutes, I–VII*. Edited and translated by Mary F. McDonald O. P. Washington: The Catholic University, 1964.

Laing, Aislinn. 'King of Swaziland chooses teenager as 15th wife'. https://www.telegraph.co.uk/news/worldnews/africaandindianocean/swaziland/10315849/King-of-Swaziland-chooses-teenager-as-15th-wife.html

Lampe, Peter. *From Paul to Valentinus: Christians at Rome in the First Two Centuries*. Translated by Marshall D. Steinhauser. Minneapolis: Fortress Press, 2003.

Le Donne, Anthony. *Historical Jesus: What Can we Know and How Can We Know It*. Cambridge: Wm. B. Eerdmans, 2011.

Le Donne, Anthony. *The Wife of Jesus: Ancient Texts and Modern Scandals.* London: Oneworld, 2013.
Lee, Martha F. ed. *Millennial Visions: Essays on Twentieth-century Millenarianism.* Westport: Praeger, 2000.
Lees, John A. 'Michael'. https://www.internationalstandardbible.com/M/michael.html
Le Goff, Jacques. *Święty Franciszek z Asyżu.* Translated by Joanna Guze. Warsaw: Wyd. Czytelnik, 2001.
Leo I. *St. Leo the Great Letters.* Edited and translated by Edmund Hunt. New York: The Catholic University of America Press, 1957.
Leo XIII. 'Iucunda semper expectatione'. http://www.vatican.va/content/leo-xiii/en/encyclicals/documents/hf_l-xiii_enc_08091894_iucunda-semper-expectatione
Leo XIII. 'Mirae caritatis'. http://www.vatican.va/content/leo-xiii/en/encyclicals/documents/hf_l-xiii_enc_28051902_mirae-caritatis.html
Liniewicz, Łukasz. Mariavitism: Mystical, Social, National. A Polish Religious Answer to the Challenges of Modernity. Tilburg: Tilburg University, Unpublished Master's Thesis, 2013.
Lisak, Agnieszka. *Miłość, kobieta, małżeństwo w XIX wieku.* Warsaw: Bellona, 2009.
Lohse, Eduard. *Martyrer und Gottesknecht; Untersuchungen zur Urchristlichen Verkundigung vom Suhntod Jesu Christi.* Gottingen: Vandenhoeck & Ruprecht, 1963.
Lossky, Vladimir. *The Mystical Theology of the Eastern Church.* Cambridge: James Clarke and Co., 1973.
Louth, Andrew, ed. *Ancient Christian Commentary on Scripture, Genesis 1-11.* Illinois: Inter Varsity Press, 2001.
Louth, Andrew. *The Origins of the Christian Mystical Tradition: From Plato to Denys.* Oxford: Oxford University Press, 2007.
Łagosz, Zbigniew. 'Mariawici a okultyzm–próba dotarcia do prawdy'. *Prawda i Fałsz o Polskiej chwale i wstydzie.* Pp. 253–267. Edited by Włodzimierz K. Pessel i Stanisław Zagórski. Łomża: Wyd. Stopka, 2010.
McMillan, James. 'Catholic Christianity in France from the Restoration to the Separation of Church and State, 1815–1905'. *World Christianities c. 1815–1914. The Cambridge History of Christianity.* Vol. 8. Edited by Sheridan Gilley and Brian Stanley. Pp. 217–232. Cambridge: Cambridge University Press, 2006.
Macy, Gary. *The Hidden History of Women's Ordination: Female Clergy in the Medieval West.* Oxford: Oxford University Press, 2008.
Madigan, Kevin, and Carolyn Osiek, eds. *Ordained Women in the Early Church. A Documentary History.* Baltimore: The John Hopkins University Press, 2005.
Mazur, Krzysztof. *Ruch mariawicki w Polsce w latach 1893–1980. Geneza, rozwój i stan obecny.* Warszawa, 1988.
Mazur, Krzysztof. *Mariawityzm w Polsce.* Krakow: NOMOS, 1991.
Mazur, Krzysztof. 'O łykaniu obrazków–glossa trzecia'. *PNS* 24 (2002): 26–27.
Mazur, Krzysztof. 'Mariawici piszą'. *PNS* 40 (2006): 16.
Mazur, Krzysztof. 'Tworzenie zrębów mariawickiej struktury eklezjalnej'. *PNS* 41 (2006): 47.
Mazur, Krzysztof. 'Dwie figury'. *PNS* 42 (2006): 8.
Mazur, Krzysztof. 'Refleksje po lekturze książki ks. Edwarda Warchoła 'Reakcja biskupa Jerzego Szembeka na formowanie się ideologii religijnej i kształtowanie się struktury organizacyjnej mariawitów'. *PNS* 52 (2009): 30–39.

Mazur, Krzysztof. 'Rozterki Ojca Zenona M. Szymona Kwieka, próba rekonstrukcji'. *PNS* 57 (2010): 18–28.

Mazur, Krzysztof. 'Marii Franciszki Kozłowskiej zmagania z nieteologiczną rzeczywistością'. *MD I*. Edited by Damiana M. B. Szulgowicz and Hanna M. R. Woińska. Pp. 185–254. Felicjanów: KKM, 20012.

Mazur, Krzysztof, and Jarosław M. J. Opala. 'Mariawityzm w Mińsku Mazowieckim'. *Rocznik Mińskomazowiecki* 27 (2019): 74.

McGinn, Bernard. *The Presence of God: A History of Western Christian Mysticism*. Vol. II: *The Growth of Mysticism*. New York: The Crossroad Publishing Company, 1994.

McGrath, Alister E. *Christian History: An Introduction*. West Sussex: Wiley-Blackwell, 2013.

McGuckin, John A. *The Orthodox Church*. Oxford: Blackwell Publishing, 2008.

McLynn, Neil B. *Ambrose of Milan: Church and Court in a Christian Capital*. Berkeley: University of California Press, 1994.

McMillan, James. 'Catholic Christianity in France from the Restoration to the separation of church and state, 1815–1905'. *World Christianities c. 1815–1914. The Cambridge History of Christianity*. Vol. 8. Edited by Sheridan Gilley and Brian Stanley. Pp. 217–232 in Cambridge: Cambridge University Press, 2006.

Meeks, Wayne A. 'Social and Ecclesial Life of the Earliest Christians'. *Origins to Constantine. The Cambridge History of Christianity*. Vol. 1. Edited by Margaret M. Mitchell, Frances M. Young. Pp. 145–176. Cambridge: Cambridge University Press, 2008.

Meinardus, Otto F. A. *Two Thousand Years of Coptic Christianity*. Cairo: The American University in Cairo Press, 1999.

Merton, Thomas, ed. and trans. *The Wisdom of the Desert: Sayings from the Desert Fathers of the Fourth Century*. New York: New Directions Publishing Corporation, 1960.

Mędrzecki, Włodzimierz. 'Konwenans wiejski i nowe wzorce zachowań kobiet na wsi w Królestwie Polskim na przełomie XIX i XX wieku'. *Kobieta i kultura życia codziennego: Wiek XIX i XX. Zbiór studiów*. Edited by Anna Żarnowska and Andrzej Szwarc. Pp. 71–87. Warsaw: Wyd. DiG, 1997.

Mickiewicz, Adam. *L'église et le messie I*. Paris: Comptoir des Imprimeurs-Unis, 1845.

Mickiewicz, Adam. *L' église et le messie II*. Paris: Comptoir des Imprimeurs-Unis, 1845.

Mickiewicz, Adam. *Współudział Adama Mickiewicza w sprawie Andrzeja Towiańskiego: Listy i przemówienia, Tom 1*. Paris: Księgarnia Luxemburgska, 1877.

Mickiewicz, Adam. *Les Slaves: Cours professe au College de France*. Paris: Au Comptoir des imprimeurs réunis, 1914.

Mickiewicz, Adam. *Dzieła, tom X*. Warsaw: Spółdzielnia Wydawnicza 'Czytelnik', 1955.

Mickiewicz, Adam. 'Skład Zasad 11'. https://pl.wikisource.org/wiki/Skład_zasad

Miller, Russell E. *The Larger Hope: The First Century of the Universalist Church in America, 1770–1870*. Vol. 1. Boston: Unitarian Universalist Association, 1979.

Mironowicz, Antoni. 'Swoi czy Obcy. Prawosławni w dawnej Rzeczpospolitej'. in *Latopisy Akademii Supraskiej 8. Cerkiew a asymilacja–Swój i Obcy*. Edited by Marzena Kuczyńska. Pp. 207–224. Białystok: Oikonomos, 2017.

Misiurek, Jerzy. *Wielkie mistyczki Kościoła*. Lublin: Wyd. KUL, 1996.

'Moc'. https://dictionary.cambridge.org/pl/dictionary/polish-english/moc

Molland, Einar. 'Irenaeus of Lugdunum and the Apostolic Succession'. *The Journal of Ecclesiastical History* 1 (1950): 12–28. https://doi.org/10.1017/S0022046900072146

Moss, Candida. *The Other Christ: Imitating Jesus in Ancient Christian Ideologies of Ancient Martyrdom.* Oxford: Oxford University Press, 2010.

Moxnes, Halvor. *Jesus and the Rise of Nationalism: A New Quest for the Nineteenth-Century Quest for Historical Jesus.* London: I. B. Tauris, 2012.

Naumow, Aleksander. 'Powroty do prawosławia' *Latopisy Akademii Supraskiej 8. Cerkiew a asymilacja–Swój i Obcy.* Edited by Marzena Kuczyńska. Pp. 243–256. Białystok: Oikonomos, 2017.

Νεκτάριος Αιγίνης. *Μελέτη ιστορική περί των αιτίων του Σχίσματος.* Αθήνα: Παναγόπουλος Νεκτάριος, 1998.

Niederwimmer, Kurt. *The Didache: A Commentary.* Hermeneia. Minneapolis: Fortress Press, 1998.

Noble, Thomas. 'The Papacy in the Eighth and Ninth Centuries'. *The New Cambridge Medieval History.* Vol. 2. Edited by Rosamond McKitterick. Pp. 563–586. Cambridge: Cambridge University Press, 1995.

Nowowiejski, Antoni J. *Płock: monografja historyczna napisana podczas wojny wszechświatowej, poprawiona i uzupełniona w roku 1930.* Płock: B-Cia Detrychowie, 1931.

Olszewski, Daniel. *Przemiany społeczno-religijne w Królestwie Polskim w pierwszej połowie XIX wieku, Analiza środowiska diecezjalnego.* Lublin: Wyd. KUL 1984.

O'Reggio, Trevor. 'Martin Luther on Marriage and Family'. *History Research* 2 (2012): 195–218.

Origen, *Contra Celsum.* Translated by Henry Chadwick. Cambridge: Cambridge University Press, 1953.

Origen, *Commentary on the Gospel of John.* Translated by Ronald E. Heine. Washington: The Catholic University of America Press, 1989.

Osiek, Carolyn. *Philippians & Philemon.* Nashville: Abingdon New Testament Commentaries, 2000.

Paprocki, Henryk. 'Hipolita Rzymskiego 'Tradycja Apostolska': wstęp, przekład, komentarz'. *Studia Theologica Varsaviensia* 14 (1976): 145–169.

Paprocki, Henryk. *Focjusz.* Krakow: Wyd. WAM, 2004.

Partnerski, Materiał. 'Michał Piotr Radziwiłł. Mecenas i konserwatysta z artystyczną duszą'. Super Express. https://www.se.pl/wiadomosci/polska/michal-piotr-radziwill-mecenas-i-konserwatysta-z-artystyczna-dusza-aa-NEHp-CNc1-6Eyi.html

Pasek, Zbigniew. 'Geneza Mariawityzmu i Przyczyny Jego Podziału'. *Studia Religiologica* 24 (1991): 41–61.

Pastuszko, Marian. *Najświętsza Eucharystia według Kodeksu Prawa Kanonicznego Jana Pawła II.* Kielce: Wyd. Jedność, 1997.

Pease, Neal. *Rome's Most Faithful Daughter: The Catholic Church and Independent Poland, 1914–1939.* Athens: Ohio University Press, 2009.

Penn, Michael P. *Kissing Christians: Ritual and Community in the Late Ancient Church.* Philadelphia, Pa: University of Pennsylvania Press, 2005.

Peppiatt, Lucy. *Women and Worship at Corinth: Paul's Rhetorical Arguments in 1 Corinthians.* Eugene, OR: Wipf and Stock, 2015.

Peterkiewicz, Jerzy. *Third Adam.* Oxford: Oxford University Press, 1975.

Peters, Greg. *Reforming the Monastery: Protestant Theologies of the Religious Life.* Eugene, OR: Wipf and Stock, 2014.

Piłsudski, Józef. 'O patrjotyzmie'. *GP* 25 (1937): 197.
Pius IX. 'Singulari quadam'. https://www.papalencyclicals.net/Pius09/p9singul.htm
Pius X. 'E supremi apostolatus'. http://www.vatican.va/content/pius-x/en/encyclicals/documents/hf_p-x_enc_04101903_e-supremi.html
Pius X. 'Tribus circiter'. *Proces wydzielania się Związku Mariawitów Nieustającej Adoracji Ubłagania z doktrynalnych i organizacyjnych ram Kościoła rzymskokatolickiego*. Edited by Edward Warchoł. Pp. 145–150. Radom: Wyd. Diecezjalne, 2006.
Pomazansky, Michael. *Orthodox Dogmatic Theology*. Translated by Seraphim Rose. Platina: Saint Herman of Alaska Brotherhood, 1984.
Porter, Brian. *When Nationalism Began to Hate: Imagining Modern Politics in Nineteenth-Century Poland*. Oxford: Oxford University Press, 2000.
Porter, Brian. *Catholicism, Ethno-Catholics, and the Catholic Church in Modern Poland*. Washington, DC: The National Council for Eurasian and East European Research, 2006.
Przedpełski, Borys. 'Kapłaństwo kobiet w Kościele Mariawitów'. *NP* 38 (1993): 25–34.
Przedpełski, Borys. 'Powstanie i rozwój Zgromadzenia Sióstr Mariawitek Nieustającej Adoracji Ubłagania w latach 1887–1921'. *MD II*. Edited by Damiana M. B. Szulgowicz and Hanna M. R. Woińska. Pp. 13–52. Felicjanów: KKM, 2013.
Radzikowski, Leszek. 'Motywy mariawickie w pamiętnikach Leszka Radzikowskiego'. *PNS* 16 (2000): 14.
Radziwiłł, Michał P. *Ostateczne Czasy*. Warsaw: Wyd. Księgarni Nakładowej M. Szczepkowskiego, 1905.
Ramet, Sabrina P. *The Catholic Church in Polish History: From 966 to the Present*. New York: Palgrave Macmillan, 2017.
Raymond of Capua. *Life of Saint Catharine of Siena*. Translated by the Ladies of the Sacred Heart. New York, NY: P. J. Kenedy & Sons, 1862.
Refutation of all Heresies. Translated by M. David Litwa. Atlanta: SBL Press, 2016.
Riedl, Matthias. 'Longing for the Third Age: Revolutionary Joachism, Communism, and National Socialism'. *A Companion to Joachim of Fiore*. Edited by Matthias Riedl. Pp. 267–318. Leiden: Brill, 2018.
Roberts, Alexander and James Donaldson, A. Cleveland Coxe, Allen Menzies, Ernest Cushing Richardson, Bernhard Pick, eds. *Ante-Nicene Fathers: Volume 4*. New York: Christian Literature Publishing Co., 1885.
Rodríguez, Rafael. 'The Embarrassing Truth about. Pages 132–151 in *Jesus, Criteria, and the Demise of Authenticity*. Edited by Chris Keith and Anthony Le Donne. Pp. 132–151. London: T&T Clark, 2012.
Rosen, Stanley. *Plato's Republic, A Study*. New Heaven: Yale University Press, 2005.
Rostworowski, Stanisław J. 'Socjologiczna metoda ujęcia Mariawityzmu'. *Nasza Przeszłość* 88 (1997): 399–413. https://doi.org/10.52204/np.1997.88.399-413
Rozanow, Wasilij. *Ciemne oblicze. Metafizyka chrześcijaństwa*. Translated by Henryk Paprocki. Warszawa: ENETEIA, 2006.
Różyk, Wojciech. '*Objawienia*' *Marii Franciszki Kozłowskiej według rękopisu z archiwum watykańskiego: studium teologiczne*. Świdnica: Świdnicka kuria biskupia, 2006.
Rudgard, Olivia. 'Early church found place for female bishops, experts claim'. https://www.telegraph.co.uk/news/2018/03/31/early-church-found-place-female-bishops-experts-claim/

Russell, Ronald. 'The Idle in 2 Thess. 3.6-12: An Eschatological or a Social Problem?' *NTS* 34 (1988): 105–119. https://doi.org/10.1017/S0028688500022244

'Saint Peter Mogila'. oca.org. https://www.oca.org/orthodoxy/the-orthodox-faith/church-history/seventeenth-century/saint-peter-mogilas

Sabatier, Paul. *Życie świętego Franciszka z Asyżu*. Translated by Paweł Hulka-Laskowski. Cieszyn: Wyd. B. Kotula, 1927.

Safrai, Shmuel, M. Stern, David Flusser, and W.C. van Unnik. *The Jewish People in the First Century vol. 2, Historical Geography, Political History, Social, Cultural and Religious Life and Institutions*. Leida: Brill, 1988.

Saliba, John A. *Understanding New Religious Movements*. Oxford: Altamira Press, 2003.

Sanak, Marcin. 'Kult eucharystyczny w Polsce XVII i XVIII wieku'. liturgia.pl. https://www.liturgia.pl/Kult-eucharystyczny-w-Polsce-XVII-i-XVIII-wieku/

San Martín, Ines. 'Pope calls idea of declaring Mary co-redemptrix "foolishness"'. cruxnow.com. https://cruxnow.com/vatican/2019/12/pope-calls-idea-of-declaring-mary-co-redemptrix-foolishness/

Schaff, Philip, ed. *The Apostolic Fathers with Justin Martyr and Irenaeus*. Edinburgh: T. & T. Clark, 1867.

Schaff, Philip, ed. *Fathers of the Third and Fourth Centuries: Lactantius, Venantius, Asterius, Victorinus, Dionysius, Apostolic Teaching and Constitutions, Homily, and Liturgies*. Edinburgh: T. & T. Clark, 1885.

Schaff, Philip, ed. *Nicene and Post-Nicene Fathers*. First Series, Vol. 9. New York: Christian Literature Publishing, 1889.

Schaff, Philip, ed. *Saint Chrysostom: Homilies on the Acts of the Apostles and the Epistle to the Romans*. Edinburgh: T. & T. Clark, 1925.

Schaff, Philip, ed. *The Seven Ecumenical Councils*. Grand Rapids, MI: Eerdmans, 1952.

Schaff, Philip, ed. *Jerome: The Principal Works of St. Jerome*. Grand Rapids, MI: Eerdmans, 1954.

Schaff, Philip, ed. *Ante-Nicene Fathers vol. 6. Fathers of the Third Century*. Grand Rapids, MI: William B. Eerdmans Publishing Co., 1988.

Scholastyk, Sokrates. *Historia Kościoła*. Translated by S. J. Kazikowski. Warsaw: Wyd. PAX, 1986.

Schwarz, John. *A Handbook of the Christian Faith*. Minneapolis: Bethany House Publishers, 1993.

Seweryniak, Henryk. 'Sprawa manipulacji w tekście "Początku zawiązku …" w świetle archiwaliów przechowywanych w Kongregacji Nauki Wiary'. *PNS* 53 (2009): 18–20.

Seweryniak, Henryk. *Święte Oficjum a mariawici*. Płock: Płocki Instytut Wydawniczy, 2014.

Sikora, Adam. *Posłannicy słowa: Hoene-Wroński, Towiański, Mickiewicz*. Warsaw: Państwowe Wydawnictwo Naukowe, 1967.

Silvas, Anna M. *Macrina the Younger: Philosopher of God*. Turnhout: Brepols, 2008.

Skinner, Barbara. 'The Irreparable Church Schism: Russian Orthodox Identity and Its Historical Encounter with Catholicism'. *Polish Encounters, Russian Identity*. Edited by David L. Ransel and Bozena Shallcross. Pp. 20–37. Bloomington: Indiana University Press, 2005.

Skrudlik, Mieczysław. *Z tajemnic 'klasztoru' płockiego*. Warsaw: Drukarnia 'Ars', 1928.

Słowacki, Juliusz. *Dzieła Juliusza Słowackiego tom I*. Edited by Bronisław Gubrynowicz. Lwów: Księgarnia W. Gubrynowicza, 1909.

Słowacki, Juliusz. 'Papież Słowiański'. *KM* (1909): 185–186.

Snyder, Timothy. 'Ukrainians and Poles'. *Imperial Russia 1689–1917. The Cambridge History of Russia*. Vol. 2. Edited by Dominic Lieven. Pp. 165–183. Cambridge: Cambridge University Press, 2006.

Sobiech, Janusz. 'Początki ruchu wolnych chrześcijan w Polsce do 1918 roku'. *RTChAT* 59 (2017): 299–324.

Starzyńska–Kościuszko, Ewa. 'Polish Romantic Messianism'. *Organon* 48 (2016): 51–71.

Staszyński, Edmund. *Polityka oświatowa caratu w Królestwie Polskim*. Warsaw: Państwowe Zakłady Wydawnictw Szkolnych, 1968.

Stopniak, Franciszek. *Kościół na Lubelszyźnie i Podlasiu na przełomie XIX i XX wieku*. Warsaw: Akademia Teologii Katolickiej, 1975.

Stoszewski, Dominik. *Dawne kościoły płockie*. Płock: Druk. K. Miecznikowski, 1912.

Szech, Antoni. *W sprawie mankietnictwa*. Krakow 1906.

Szołdrski, Władysław. 'Les Rédemptoristes polonais dans l'empire Russe de 1905 à 1910'. Spicilegium Historicum: Congregationis Ssmi Redemptoris 53 (2005): 389–485.

Szyjewski, Andrzej. *Etnologia religii*. Krakow: NOMOS, 2008.

Szymański, Tomasz. 'Les cours parisiens d'Adam Mickiewicz et l'idée de religion universelle'. *Slavia Meridionalis* 17 (2017): 1–29. https://doi.org/10.11649/sm.1339

Tabbernee, William. 'Material Evidence for Early Christian Groups During the First Two Centuries C. E'. *Annali di Storia dell'Esegesi* 30 (2013): 287–301.

Tamrat, Taddesse. 'The Abbots of Däbrä-Hayq 1248–1535'. *Journal of Ethiopian Studies* 8 (1970): 87–117.

Tatarkiewicz, Władysław. *Historia filozofii tom 2: Filozofia nowożytna do roku 1830*. Warsaw: Wyd. Naukowe PWN, 2007.

Tazbir, Janusz. 'Specyfika polskiej tolerancji'. *Naród. Kościół. Kultura: Szkice z historii Polski 2*. Pp. 57–70. Edited by Adam Chruczewski. Lublin: Wyd. KUL, 1986.

Tazbir, Janusz. *Polskie przedmurze chrześcijańskiej Europy: Mity a rzeczywistość historyczna*. Warsaw: Wyd. Książkowe Twój Styl, 2004.

Tempczyk, Katarzyna. 'Mariawityzm a esperanto'. *PNS* 28 (2003): 11–17.

Tempczyk, Katarzyna. 'Głos w dyskusji o przypadkach wielożeństwa w małżeństwach 'mistycznych''. *PNS* 64 (2011): 23.

Tempczyk, Katarzyna. *'Nowe przymierze uczynił Pan z nami...' Teologia Kościoła Katolickiego Mariawitów*. Warsaw: Ex Libris, 2011.

'The Fourteen Theses of the Old Catholic Union Conference at Bonn A. D. 1874'. https://www.ccel.org/ccel/schaff/creeds2.vii.i.html

The Rudder (Pedalion) of the Metaphorical Ship of the One Holy Catholic and Apostolic Church of the Orthodox Christians, or All the Sacred and Divine Canons. Edited by Nicodemus the Hagiorite and Agapius the Monk. Edited and translated by D. Cummings. Chicago: The Orthodox Christian Educational Society, 1957.

Thomas, Andrew. *The Holy Fools: A Theological Enquiry*. Nottingham: University of Nottingham, Unpublished PhD Thesis, 2009.

Thompson, Augustine. *Francis of Assisi: A New Biography*. Ithaca: Cornell University Press, 2012.

Tilliette, Xavier. *Untersuchungen über die intellektuelle Anschauung von Kant bis Hegel*. Stuttgart–Bad Cannstatt: Frommann-Holzboog, 2015.
Turner, John G. *Brigham Young: Pioneer, Prophet*. Cambridge: Belknap Press of Harvard University, 2012.
Urban, Kazimierz. 'Z "peryferii" polskiej nierzymskokatolickiej mapy wyznaniowej połowy lat 50 ubiegłego wieku'. *W kręgu sacrum i pogranicza*. Edited by Ewa Matuszczyk and Maciej Krzywosz. Pp. 153–176. Białystok: Wydział Historyczno-Socjologiczny Uniwersytetu w Białymstoku, 2004.
Van Wagoner, Richard S. 'Sarah Pratt: The Shaping of an Apostate'. *Dialogue: A Journal of Mormon Thought* 19 (1986): 69–99. https://doi.org/10.2307/45225431
Verdin, Georges. *Zza kulis herezji maryjawickiej–na podstawie własnych spostrzeżeń*. Płock: Drukarnia Towarzystwa Wydawniczego 'Dziennik Płocki', 1923.
Walicki, Andrzej. 'The Paris Lectures of Mickiewicz and Russian Slavophilism'. *The Slavonic and East European Review* 46 (1968): 155–175.
Walicki, Andrzej. 'Millenaryzm i mesjanizm religijny a romantyczny mesjanizm polski: zarys problematyki'. *Pamiętnik Literacki: Czasopismo kwartalne poświęcone historii i krytyce literatury polskiej* 62 (1971): 23–46.
Walicki, Andrzej. 'Mesjanistyczne koncepcje narodu i późniejsze losy tej tradycji'. *Idee i koncepcje narodu w polskiej myśli politycznej czasów porozbiorowych*. Edited by Janusz Goćkowski and Andrzej Walicki. Pp. 84–107. Warsaw: Państwowe Wydawnictwo Naukowe, 1977.
Walicki, Andrzej. 'Polish Romantic Messianism in Comparative Perspective'. *Slavic Studies* 22 (1978): 1–15.
Walicki, Andrzej. *Między filozofią, religią i polityką: Studia o myśli polskiej epoki romantyzmu*. Warsaw: Wyd. Państwowy Instytut Wydawniczy, 1983.
Wandycz, Piotr S. *The Lands of Partitioned Poland, 1795–1918*. London: University of Washington Press, 1974.
Warchoł, Edward *Starokatolicki Kościół Mariawitów w okresie II Rzeczypospolitej*. Sandomierz: Wyd. Diecezjalne, 1997.
Warchoł, Edward. *Proces wydzielania się Związku Mariawitów Nieustającej Adoracji Ubłagania z doktrynalnych i organizacyjnych ram Kościoła rzymskokatolickiego*. Radom: Wyd. Diecezjalne, 2006.
Warchoł, Edward. *Reakcja biskupa Jerzego Szembeka na formowanie się ideologii religijnej i kształtowanie się struktury organizacyjnej mariawitów*. Radom: Wyd. Diecezjalne, 2006.
Warchoł, Edward. *Wybrane zagadnienia z historii mariawityzmu*. Radom: Wyd. Diecezjalne, 2007.
Warchoł, Edward, ed. *Ważniejsze dokumenty na temat Mariawitów i Mariawityzmu (1903–1906)*. Radom: Wyd. Diecezjalne, 2009.
Warchoł, Edward. *Podobieństwa i różnice między Starokatolickim Kościołem Mariawitów i Polskim Narodowym Kościołem Katolickim od ich powstania do końca okresu międzywojennego*. Sandomierz: Wyd. Diecezjalne, 2012.
Warzeszak, Józef. 'Wartości religijno–patriotyczne w piśmiennictwie Sługi Bożego ks. Ignacego Kłopotowskiego (1866–1931)'. *Warszawskie Studia Teologiczne* 17 (2004): 253–265.
Waugh, Evelyn. *The Life of Right Reverend Ronald Knox*. London: Penguin Books, 2012.

Weima, Jeffrey A. D. and Stanley E. Porter. *An Annotated Bibliography of 1 and 2 Thessalonians*. Leiden, Netherlands: Brill Publishers, 1998.

Werner, Maria. *O. Honorat Koźmiński, Kapucyn 1829–1916*. Warsaw, Poznań: Wyd. Pallottinum, 1972.

Werth, Paul W. *Freedom of Conscience and the Redefinition of Confessional Boundaries in Imperial Russia, 1905–1914*. Washington: The National Council for Eurasian and East European Research, 2002.

Wessinger, Catherine. 'Millennialism in Cross-Cultural Perspective'. *The Oxford Handbook of Millennialism*. Pp. 3–24. Edited by Catherine Wessinger. Oxford: Oxford University Press, 2011.

Widengren, Geo. *Fenomenologia religii*. Translated by Joannna Białek. Krakow: NOMOS, 2008.

Wiebe, Philip H. *Visions of Jesus*. Oxford: Oxford University Press, 1997.

Własta. 'Odpowiedź ws. małżeństw mistycznych'. https://www.ekumenizm.pl/religia/inne/odpowiedz-ws-malzenstw-mistycznych/

Wilson, Bryan A. 'Millennialism in Comparative Perspective'. *Comparative Studies in Society and History* 6 (1963): 93–114. https://doi.org/10.1017/S0010417500002000

Włodarski, Szczepan. *Siedem Soborów*. Warszaw: IW Odrodzenie, 1968.

Wojciechowska, Kalina. 'Postać podobna Synowi Człowieczemu z kobiecym biustem przepasanym złotym pasem (por. Ap 1, 13) – teologiczne konsekwencje zróżnicowania terminów στῆθος oraz μᾶστοί w przekładzie Apokalipsy Arcybiskupa Jana Marii Michała Kowalskiego używanym w Kościołach Mariawitów w Polsce'. *Colloquia Theologica Ottoniana* 2 (2017): 227–245. https://doi.org/10.18276/cto.2017.2-13

Wojnicz, Andrzej. 'Istota Chrześcijaństwa w światopoglądzie Augusta Cieszkowskiego'. *PNS* 2 (1997): 4–6.

Wood, Philip. *The Chronicle of Seert: Christian Historical Imagination in Late Antique Iraq*. Oxford: Oxford University Press, 2013.

Wortley, John, ed. and trans. *The Anonymous Sayings of the Desert Fathers: A Select Edition and Complete English Translation*. Cambridge: Cambridge University Press, 2013.

Z Papieżem czy bez Papieża? Pytanie do odpowiedzi dla katolików i maryawitów. Warsaw: Druk 'Polaka-Katolika', 1911.

Zawadzki, W. H. 'Russia and the Reopening of the Polish Question, 1801–1814'. *The International History Review* 7 (1985): 19–44. https://doi.org/10.1080/07075332.1985.9640368

Zawada, Zenon. 'The Black Madonna'. https://web.archive.org/web/20080126124229/http://www.ukraine-observer.com/articles/217/814

Zeller, Benjamin E. 'The Fraternité Notre Dame: From Emergence in Fréchou to Sojourn in Chicago'. *Numen* 67 (2020): 191–225. https://doi.org/10.1163/15685276-12341573

Zieliński, Zygmunt. *Papiestwo i papieże dwóch ostatnich wieków*. Poznań: Wyd. Poznańskie, 2007.

Index of Names

(The index omits Jesus Christ, Mary (Theotokos), Feliksa Magdalena Maria Franciszka Kozłowska and Jan Maria Michał Kowalski)

A
Aaron 125, 147
Abraham, abba 159
Abraham of Clermont, abbot 75
Abraham, patriarch 138, 189
Adam 127, 144, 145, 148, 149, 158, 159, 191
Afanasiev, Nicholas 173
Alexander II of Russia 22, 24
Alighieri, Dante 128
Allison, Dale C. 34
Ambrose of Milan, bishop 115
Ambrose, priest 163
Amoun 139
Anselm of Canterbury 145
Anthony the Great 135
Aphrahat the Persian 187
Apollonius of Ephesus 107
Appolis, Emile 120
Arason, Jón 144
Athanasius of Alexandria 133, 173
Athenagoras of Athens 147
Atto of Vercelli 163
Augustine of Hippo 45, 93, 118, 134, 143, 145, 149, 196, 200

B
Babi, Marek M. Karol 18
Balter, Lucjan 96
Bandrowski J. 81
Barnabas 95, 170
Barsauma of Nisibis 140
Bartholomew 163
Basil of Ancyra, hieromartyr 140

Basil of Caesarea, bishop 36, 95, 186
Beauduin, Lambert 99
Behr, John 97
Benedict XVI 53
Bernard of Clairvaux 145
Boccaccio, Giovanni 154
Bojaxhiu, Agnes Gonxha (Mother Teresa) 7
Bolesław II the Bold (Boleslaw II) 135
Boleyn, Anne 84
Bołoczko, Antoni M. Serafin 152
Boniface VIII 79
Borniński, Piotr 57, 64, 72
Borromeo, Federico 66
Boullan, Joseph-Antoine 132
Bourlemont, Pica di 34
Bridget of Sweden 49
Brown, Antoinette Louisa 161
Bulgakov, Sergei 150
Bullivant, Stephen 89

C
Caesarius of Arles 75
Cain 113, 149
Callixtus I 90
Castissima (Emerald) 160
Catherine of Siena, mystic 35, 48, 124
Catherine II of Russia, empress 23
Cerdo 97
Cerinthus 153
Cerula 164
Chaadayev, Pyotr 27
Chiniquy, Charles 154
Cieszkowski, August 27, 29, 31, 32, 81, 128, 192, 194, 196, 197
Clare of Assisi 49, 123
Claudius 163
Clement of Alexandria, theologian 9, 83, 133, 137, 147, 151, 160, 162

Index of Names

Clement XI, pope 161
Cohn, Norman 43, 192
Colette of Corbie 48
Coltman, Constance 160
Coltri, Marzia A. 48
Connecte, Thomas 84
Crossley, James 33
Cyprian of Carthage 69, 172
Cyril, monk 98
Cyril of Alexandria, pope 92
Czaplicki 54
Czernohorski-Fehérváry, Juliusz M. Otto 49
Czerwiński, Czesław M. Maciej 67
Czychlarzowa, Maria (Mary of Prague) 104, 105, 106, 107

D

Daniel, abba 154
Daniel, prophet 47
Darczewska, Krystyna 27
David 145, 191
Davies, Eleanor, poet 127
Davies, Mark, bishop 189
Davies, Norman, author 23
Demmel, Josef 102
Didymus the Blind 134
Dimitrije 148
Diognetus 44
Dionysius of Alexandria 152, 153
Drozdov, Philaret 6
Dwojnych, Andrzej 17, 18

E

Ehrman, Bart 4, 90
Eli 71
Elijah 135
Elizabeth, mother of John the Baptist 34
Elizabeth I, queen 84
Emmelia of Caesarea 40
Ephrem the Syrian 95
Epiphanius of Salamis 159, 189
Eugene III 84
Eugenia of Rome 160
Eulalia of Barcelona 119
Eulogius 179
Euodia 162
Euphrosyne of Alexandria 160

Eustathius of Sebaste 172
Eve 144, 145, 149, 158, 159

F

Feldman, Klemens M. Filip 11, 100, 120, 130, 145, 148, 153, 161, 167, 168, 177, 179, 181, 182, 190
Felix of Cantalice 37
Ferrata, Domenico 58, 61
Ferrer, Vincent 75
Fichte, Johann G. 45
Fiore, Joachim de 28, 194
Firmilian 92
Flavian 124
Fortuna, Michał M. Grzegorz 100
Fourier, Jean Baptiste Joseph 28
Francis de Sales, bishop 48
Francis of Assisi, mystic 34, 37, 40, 43, 49, 61, 75, 76, 79, 80, 97, 114, 118, 123, 124, 141
Francis, pope 129

G

Gajkowski Jan 49
Galen 165
Garibaldi, Giuseppe 22
Gathercole, Simon 160
Gelasius I 163
Georgiyevsky, Eulogius 142
Giuliani, Veronica 36
Goczalska 74
Gołębiowski, Leon M. Andrzej, bishop 11, 53, 56, 57, 58, 59, 62, 70, 96, 100, 102, 103, 124, 185
Gołębiowski, Sławomir, author 16, 18, 96, 152, 153
Gołębiowski, Wacław M. Innocent, prime bishop 153
Gostyński, Roman M. Augustyn 68
Górecki, Artur 17
Graff, Agnieszka 49
Gregory of Nyssa, bishop 40, 92, 133
Gregory I, pope 97
Gregory IV, pope 92
Gregory VII, pope 70, 144
Gregory XIII, pope 61
Gregory XVI, pope 22, 28, 36
Grimston, Mary Ann de 48

Gromulski, Franciszek M. Alojzy 100
Gruszczyńska, Kazimiera 37
Gul, Gerardus 102
Guzman, Dominic 43

H
Harnack, Adolf 33
Hegesippus 139
Heijkamp, Johannes 47
Hempel, Jan 33
Hildegard of Bingen 167, 195
Hippolytus of Rome 90, 137, 147
Hitler, Adolf 136
Hodur, Franciszek 106
Hoene-Wroński, Józef Maria 27, 29, 196
Homer 135
Honorius I 92
Hosea 69, 138
Hus, Jan 84, 115

I
Ignatius of Antioch 89, 90, 95, 119, 126, 131, 136, 150, 191
Innocent III 84
Irenaeus of Lyon 95, 112, 132, 137, 144, 189
Isaac 138, 191
Isaiah 121
Iwaszkiewicz, Jarosław 88

J
Jacob, apostle 108
Jacob, patriarch 138
Jaczewski, Franciszek 56, 57, 71, 73
Jadwiga of Poland 98
James, apostle 92
James, brother of Jesus 92
James, William, philosopher 32, 33
Jaroszyński, Piotr 30
Jarzymowski, Henryk M. Fabian 78
Jenkins, Philip 89
Jerome 91, 95, 139, 144
Joan 164
Joanna de Chantal 48
John of Leiden, Anabaptist leader 155
John, apostle 35, 91, 92, 127, 139, 163, 185, 194

John Chrysostom, patriarch 92, 124, 149, 172
John the Faster, patriarch 139
John Paul II, pope 25, 40
John the Merciful, pope 131
John the Baptist, preacher 34, 135, 156, 189, 197
John, presbyter 153
Jonathan 145
Joseph 107, 149
Jozafata 41
Junia 162
Justin Martyr 47

K
Kahl, Czesław M. Polikarp 68
Katharina von Bora 139
Ker, Ian 145
Kirejew, Alexander 101
Klichowska, M. Honorata 58, 59, 147, 161
Kłopotowski, Ignacy M. Tomasz 53
Knox, Ronald 108
Komorowska, M. Rafaela 161
Konarski, Agrypin 23
Konopnicka, Maria 27
Kościuszko, Tadeusz 198
Kowalska, Faustina 52, 116
Kozik, Jean Marie 89
Kozłowska, Anna M. Hortulana 34, 36, 40
Kozłowski, Jakub 23, 34
Koźmiński, Honorat (Florentyn Wacław Jan Stefan Koźmiński) 25, 34, 37, 38, 41, 48, 50, 52, 54, 72, 78, 106, 122
Krakiewicz, Tomasz M. Gabriel 152
Krasiński, Zygmunt 13, 27, 29, 30, 31, 156, 197
Kraszewska, Wiktoria M. Celestyna 161, 167
Kraśkiewicz, Tomasz 78
Kubicka, M. Melania 161
Kwiek, Zenon M. Szymon 78, 80

L
Lactantius 200
Lamarine, Joséphine 72

Lamennais, Hugues Felicité Robert de 28
Lanfranc 145
Langogne, Pius de 59, 61, 71, 74
Lasocki 68
Lechicki, Czesław 45
Leo I, pope 124
Leo X, pope 61
Leo XIII, pope 3, 24, 45, 58, 69, 129, 130
Leta 164
Liberius 94
Linus 95
Lisiecki, Stanisław 157
Lossky, Vladimir 190
Lucia of Syracuse 157
Luther, Martin 6, 45, 139, 172, 202
Lutosławski, Wincenty 128

Ł

Łabanowska, Jakobina 52, 53
Łętocha, Rafał 17, 18
Łubieński, Bernard Alojzy 81

M

Macoch, Damazy 178
Macrina the Younger 40, 150
Maistre, Joseph de 27, 28
Malchus 139
Malczewska, Wanda 42
Mamai 140
Mames, Tomasz M. Daniel 9, 17, 18, 77, 190
Marcion 97
Mariamne 162
Mark the Evangelist 95
Marks, Edward M. Serafin 68, 152
Marx, Karl 22
Mary Magdalene, apostle to the apostles 163
Mary of Egypt, hermit 160
Mary, mother of John Mark 159
Marynowska, M. Cherubina 161
Mathew, Arnold 102
Mazur, Krzysztof 16, 18, 59
Melania 150
Meletius IV 99
Merezhkovsky, Dmitry 187

Merici, Angela 46
Methodius 98
Michelet, Jules 196
Mickiewicz, Adam 13, 27, 29, 30, 31, 44, 45, 91, 115, 128, 130, 132, 135, 152, 161, 168, 173, 174, 184, 185, 186, 194, 196, 197, 198
Męsicka, Matylda 142
Mikhail of Tver 135
Mikuliczówna, Agnieszka 160
Miriam 147
Modrzejewski, Jan M. Ignacy 152
Mogila, Peter 112
Molland, Einar 170
Montanus 40
Montfort, Louis-Marie Grignion de 101
Moriconi, Pietro di Bernardone dei 34
Moses 135, 147, 180, 188
Moue 131
Mswati III 155
Mucha, Wiktoria M. Dilekta 182
Muhammad 155
Mussolini, Benito 136

N

Nectarios of Aegina 93
Nepos 152
Newman, John Henry 124, 145
Nicholas of Cusa, bishop 91
Nicholas I of Russia, emperor 21, 22, 29
Nicholas II of Russia, emperor 26
Nicholas I, pope 8
Nicz, Jan 'Leopolita' 11
Niederwimmer, Kurt 138
Nietzsche, Friedrich 194
Nikephoros I 69, 115
Nitrophan 177
Nowakowska, M. Illuminata 109
Nowodworski, Michał 54, 55
Nowowiejski, Antoni Julian 40, 52, 53, 57, 64, 66, 67, 78, 109
Nykówna, M. Eufemia 161

O

Origen of Alexandria 8, 51, 133, 134, 137, 150, 185, 187
Ostrogski, Konstanty 110

P

Padre Pio 79
Pagani, Antoni 64, 74, 87
Palladius of Galatia 124
Paphnutius 144
Papias of Hierapolis 18
Pasek, Zbigniew 16
Paul, apostle 35, 46, 47, 66, 92, 95, 113, 118, 119, 121, 126, 138, 148, 162, 165, 170, 194
Paul of Samosata, bishop 140
Paul IV, pope 98
Paul V, pope 99
Pągowski, Józef M. Wawrzyniec, priest 68, 142, 152, 154
Pelczar, Józef Sebastian 105
Peppiatt, Lucy 165
Peter, apostle 35, 65, 79, 91, 92, 93, 94, 95, 113, 123, 138, 139, 143, 148, 194
Peter the Great of Russia, emperor 23
Peterkiewicz (Pietrkiewicz), Jerzy 18, 65, 132, 150, 187, 203
Petronilla 138
Petrykowski, Wincenty 55, 102
Philip 108, 138, 139, 163
Philotheus of Pskov 110
Phoebe 162
Photios the Great 6
Pietras, Henryk 170
Pigoń, Stanisław 161
Piłsudski, Józef 198
Piotrowska, M. Emma 161
Pius VII, pope 46
Pius IX, pope 22, 24, 44, 79
Pius X, pope 25, 59, 61, 62, 64, 66, 71, 72, 74, 77, 80, 82, 94, 145, 156
Pius XI, pope 120
Plato 95, 157
Polycarp of Smyrna 126, 150
Popiel, Wincenty Teofil 24, 56, 57, 58, 66, 67, 74, 82, 84
Poradowski, Józef M. Czesław 68
Portinari, Beatrice 128
Potamiaena 149
Prophet, Elizabeth Clare 48
Próchniewski, Roman M. Jakub 5, 11, 15, 34, 37, 53, 56, 59, 61, 62, 71, 74, 96, 100, 102, 103, 124, 130, 145, 147, 177, 185
Przyjemski, Kazimierz M. Jan 40, 51, 52, 53, 54, 55, 56, 70, 73, 96, 102, 106, 130
Przysiecki, Wacław M. Bartłomiej 11, 14, 40, 100, 109, 130, 135, 141, 161, 167, 177, 196
Pushkin, Alexander 29
Pydynkowski, Henryk 55

Q

Quesnel, Paschasius 161
Quinet, Edgar 196

R

Rachel 138
Radziwiłł, Michał Piotr 72
Rafaela 148
Ramet, Sabrina P. 23
Rebecca 138
Rembieliński, Roman 70
Rohling, August 156
Romenko, Tatiana 78
Rostawicka, M. Dilekta 161, 167
Rostworowski, Wawrzyniec M. Franciszek 67
Różyk, Wojciech 77
Rudnicki, Konrad M. Paweł 5, 8, 16, 18, 132, 134, 138, 141, 163, 164, 189
Rufinus 75
Ruszkiewicz, Kazimierz 55, 56, 66
Rutherford, Joseph Franklin 193
Rybak, Stanisław 16
Ryttel, Ludwik M. Alfons 73, 152

S

Sabatier, Paul 141
Safrai, Shmuel 155
Saint-Simon, Henri de 28
Saios 131
Sarah 138
Sarrazin, Gabriel 123
Sasinówna, M. Nadzieja 161
Savonarola, Girolamo 84
Scaramelli, Giovanni B. 45
Schelling, Fredrich W. J. 30, 45
Schram, Dominic 144

Septimius Severus 149
Seweryniak, Henryk 57, 64
Siedlecki, Stanisław M. T. 171
Sigismund II Augustus, king 98
Skarbek 35
Skarga, Piotr 35, 81
Skirmunt 84
Skolimowski, Paweł M. Dominik 63, 64, 96
Skrudlik, Mieczysław 154
Słowacki, Juliusz 13, 27, 29, 30, 31, 65, 91, 128, 130, 135, 152, 173, 192, 197, 198
Smith 160
Socrates of Constantinople 153
Solomon 191
Soule, Caroline 160
Spit, Nicholas 102
Spodarówna, M. Dezyderia 161
Stalin, Joseph 136
Stephen I 92
Steyaert, Denis Alphonse 61
St. John, Ambrose 124, 145
Strowski, Fortunat 196
Strumiłło, Felicjan M. Franciszek 48, 50
Suárez, Francisco 35
Swedenborg, Emanuel 45
Symon, Franciszek Albin 55, 64
Syntyche 162
Szembek, Jerzy Józef 49, 56, 57, 59, 61, 62, 67, 122, 145
Szulborski 54
Szulgowicz, Damiana M. Beatrycze 9, 18, 132
Szumska, Rozalia 38
Szymanowski, Feliks M. Mateusz, priest 100, 109
Szymanowski, Józef M. Stanisław, priest 68
Szymański, Piotr 36

T

Tamisier, Emile 44
Tatian the Syrian 144
Tempczyk, Katarzyna 9, 17, 135, 155
Teresa of Avila 48, 62
Tertullian 142, 147, 148, 153, 155

Thaumaturgus Gregory 165
Thecla 162
Thiel, Jakob van 102
Thomas Aquinas, theologian 189
Thompson, Augustine 141
Tobias 138
Torres, Francisco 164
Towiański, Andrzej 29, 30, 115, 119, 123, 125, 128, 130, 135, 152, 161, 169, 174, 184, 191, 196, 197, 198
Trafilska, Weronika 106, 107
Trentowski, Bronisław Ferdynand 196
Trypho the Jew 131
Tymieniecki, Wincenty 152

U

Uchański, Jakub 98
Ulrich 36
Urban VIII 48

V

Val, Rafael Merry del 59
Valentinian I 153
Valentinus 97
Vannutelli, Serafino 62, 63, 66
Venantius Fortunatus 137
Verdin, George 20
Victor 97
Vincent of Lerins 5
Vintras, Eugène 132
Vives y Tuto, José de Calasanz 59, 63

W

Walicki, Andrzej 26, 192, 197
Wandycz, Piotr 23
Warchoł, Edward 17, 40
Weber, Max 33
Weloński, Kazimierz 39, 41, 49, 52, 53, 54
White, Ellen G. 48
Wiechowicz, Bolesław M. Łukasz 53, 67
Wilson, Bryan A. 192
Wiłucka-Kowalska, Antonina M. Izabela 133, 147, 148, 149, 161, 167, 184, 185
Wnukowski, Apolinary 67, 70, 73, 82
Wnukówna, M. Miłość 161

Woińska, Hanna M. Rafaela 18
Wojciechowski, Józef M. Rafael 15, 16, 56, 80, 94, 125, 166
Wujek, Jakub (or Jakób) 10, 11
Wysłouch, Izydor Kajetan 25

Y
Young, Brigham 152

Z
Zaborek, Józef M. Polikarp 182
Zaczyński, Leopold Łukasz 37
Zaremba, Aleksander 52, 56
Zawisza Czarny 133
Zdzitowiecki, Stanisław 84
Zechariah 34
Zegadłowicz, Emil 155
Zipporah 147
Zonaras, Joannes 164

Ż
Żebrowski, Wacław 104, 105, 106, 107
Żeleński, Tadeusz Boy 135
Żmudzki, Roman M. Cyryl 152

www.ingramcontent.com/pod-product-compliance
Lightning Source LLC
Chambersburg PA
CBHW062013220426
43662CB00010B/1308